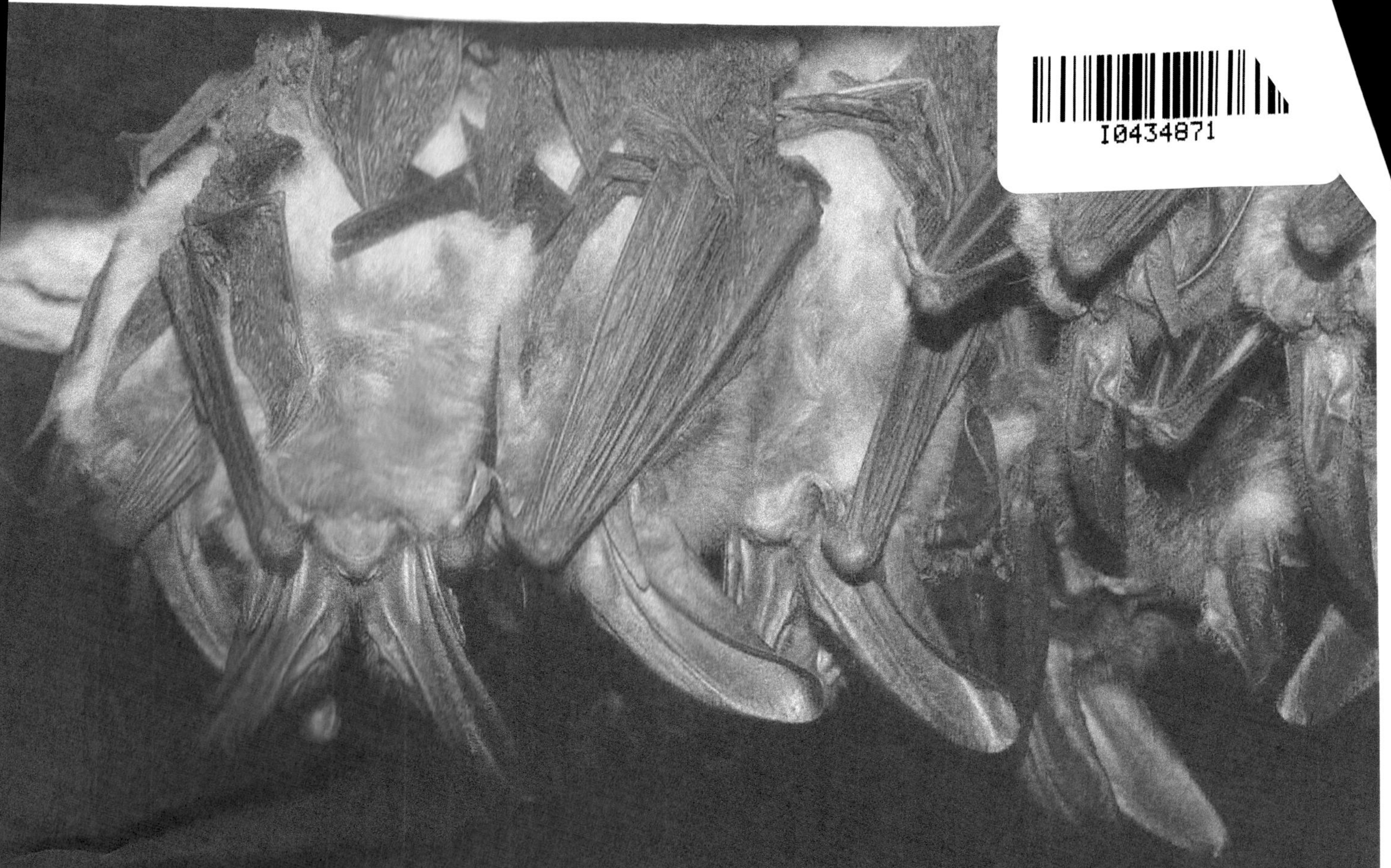

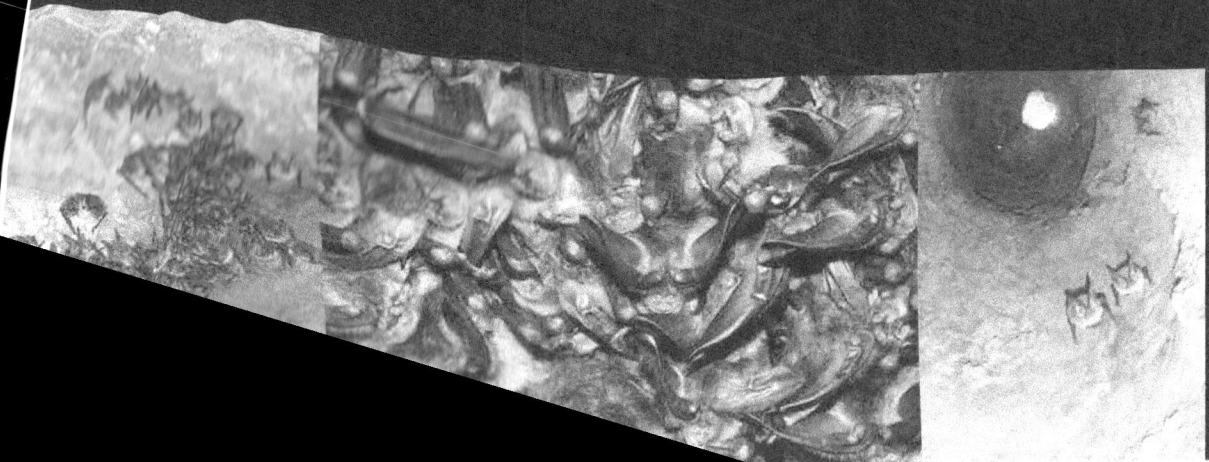

Conservation and Management of Eastern Big-eared Bats

A Symposium

Edited by Susan C. Loeb, Michael J. Lacki, and Darren A. Miller

U.S. Department of Agriculture

Forest Service

Southern Research Station

General Technical Report SRS-145

DISCLAIMER

December 2011
Southern Research Station
200 W.T. Weaver Blvd.
Asheville, NC 28804

Conservation and Management of Eastern Big-eared Bats: A Symposium

Athens, Georgia
March 9–10, 2010

Edited by:

Susan C. Loeb
U.S Department of Agriculture Forest Service
Southern Research Station

Michael J. Lacki
University of Kentucky

Darren A. Miller
Weyerhaeuser NR Company

Sponsored by:

Forest Service

Bat Conservation International

National Council for Air and Stream Improvement (NCASI)

Warnell School of Forestry and Natural Resources

Offield Family Foundation

CONTENTS

PREFACE

In February 2007, the inaugural meeting of the Rafinesque's Big-Eared Bat Working Group was held in Destin, FL. The goal of the working group was to provide a forum for communication on research, management, and conservation of Rafinesque's big-eared bats (*Corynorhinus rafinesquii*), a rare and sensitive species. There was consensus among participants at the meeting that much information remained to be acquired before effective management of these animals was possible. It was also evident from the presentations and discussion that a considerable amount of research had been conducted on the species, especially over the past several years, but much of the research has not been published or is not readily available. Thus, potentially valuable information remained in filing cabinets and desk drawers and not in the hands of the people who need it most—the biologists and managers of State, Federal, and private lands that harbor these bats, and the State and Federal Agencies responsible for their conservation. It was also agreed that a similar situation likely existed for the two other taxa of big-eared bats in the Eastern United States, the Virginia big-eared bat (*C. t. virginianus*) and the Ozark big-eared bat (*C. t. ingens*), which are federally listed as endangered. Thus, it was decided to hold a symposium to encourage researchers and biologists to present and publish new information on the biology, ecology, and status of eastern big-eared bats and to synthesize existing information. A further goal of this symposium was to stimulate discussion on future conservation, management, and research needs of these bats.

The symposium, held in Athens, GA, in March 2010, consisted of 7 invited presentations on general ecological topics, 15 contributed oral presentations and 3 poster presentations on more specific research results, and a panel discussion on future directions in research and management.

Authors were encouraged, but not required, to submit their contributions for publication in these proceedings. The symposium was sponsored by Bat Conservation International; the National Council for Air and Stream Improvement; the U.S. Forest Service, Savannah River; the Offield Family Foundation; the Southeastern Bat Diversity Network; and the University of Georgia, Warnell School of Forestry and Natural Resources. The planning committee was chaired by Steven B. Castleberry, University of Georgia. Other members of the planning committee were Mary Kay Clark, Moonlight Environmental Consulting; Susan C. Loeb, U.S. Forest Service, Southern Research Station; Darren A. Miller, Weyerhaeuser NR Company; and David A. Saugey, U.S. Forest Service, Ouachita National Forest.

The goal of these proceedings is to provide an easily accessible publication that can be used by biologists and managers as they draft management strategies and policy, and to further the understanding of the ecology of these species. The papers in this volume were subjected to the scientific peer-review process. Each manuscript was assigned to one of the three editors and reviewed by two professionals familiar with the organisms and topic. Comments and suggestions by the reviewers improved the quality of the manuscripts and we are grateful to the following professionals for their time and expertise: Michael Baker, Troy Best, Eric Britzke, Timothy Carter, Brian Carver, Steven Castleberry, Matthew Clement, Chris Comer, Barbara Douglas, Mark Ford, Shauna Ginger, Joe Johnson, Matina Kalcounis-Rüeppell, Jim Kennedy, Dennis Krusac, Paul Leberg, Chester Martin, Darren Miller, Joy O'Keefe, Richard Reynolds, Christopher Rice, Lynn Robbins, Blake Sasse, David Saugey, Austin Trousdale, Maarten Vonhof, John Whitaker, and Bently Wigley.

CONSERVATION AND MANAGEMENT OF EASTERN BIG-EARED BATS: AN INTRODUCTION

Susan C. Loeb, Research Ecologist, U.S. Department of Agriculture Forest Service, Southern Research Station, Clemson, SC 29634

Michael J. Lacki, Professor, University of Kentucky, Department of Forestry, Lexington, KY 40546

Darren A. Miller, Manager, Weyerhaeuser NR Company, Southern Environmental Research, Columbus, MS 39704

Abstract—Three taxa of big-eared bats (genus *Corynorhinus*) inhabit the Eastern United States. Rafinesque's big-eared bats (*C. rafinesquii*) are widely distributed from West Virginia to Texas whereas the Virginia big-eared bat (*C. t. virginianus*) and the Ozark big-eared bat (*C. t. ingens*) have limited ranges. Over the past 20 years, research on the biology, ecology, and conservation of bats throughout the world has increased, but research on big-eared bats of the Eastern United States has been less extensive. In evaluating the current state of knowledge, we reviewed the existing literature on big-eared bats that inhabit the Eastern United States and found 155 references, of which 101 were research notes, full articles, or review papers. In contrast, we found 239 references on the Indiana bat (*Myotis sodalis*), an endangered species with a similar geographic range size in the Eastern United States. Through our assessment of the literature on big-eared bats, we identified many gaps in our knowledge and understanding, including demography, population dynamics, social organization, hibernation and other aspects of physiological ecology, foraging behavior and diet, the effects of forest management, and the effects of conservation efforts. We also found that research on Virginia and Ozark big-eared bats has decreased in recent years while research on Rafinesque's big-eared bats has increased. Papers in these proceedings fill many of the knowledge gaps but much research is still needed to provide managers with the information they need to conserve these sensitive species.

INTRODUCTION

Big-eared bats (genus *Corynorhinus*) are some of the most striking and recognizable bats in the Eastern United States. They are distinguished from all other bats in the region by their large ears which are joined at the base, and by the enlarged glands between their eyes and nostrils (Whitaker and Hamilton 1998). Rafinesque's big-eared bats (*C. rafinesquii*) have a wide distribution that ranges from West Virginia to Florida in the east and southern Illinois to eastern Texas in the west (fig. 1), but they appear to be sparsely distributed within their range (Whitaker and Hamilton 1998). Conversely, Virginia (*C. townsendii virginianus*) and Ozark big-eared bats (*C. t. ingens*) have restricted distributions and are isolated from the rest of the Townsend's big-eared bat species complex (Hall 1981; fig. 1). All of the big-eared bats in the Eastern United States (hereafter in this paper these bats will be referred to as eastern big-eared bats) are species of special conservation concern. The Virginia and Ozark big-eared bats were listed as endangered in 1979 (U.S. Fish and Wildlife Service 1979) and Rafinesque's big-eared bats were Candidate 2 Species until 1996 when the U.S. Fish and Wildlife Service discontinued this list (U.S. Fish and Wildlife Service 1996).

Past and present threats to all these taxa include habitat loss, disturbance to hibernacula and maternity sites, contaminants, genetic isolation, and disease (Bayless and others 2011;

Piaggio and others 2009; Szymanski 2009; U.S. Fish and Wildlife Service 1995, 2008). Urbanization and development are projected to increase in the coming decades (Alig and others 2003, 2004) which will result in further habitat loss. Loss of forested and open areas will impact all taxa but could be particularly detrimental to Rafinesque's big-eared bats, which often use trees for roosting. Further, although unknown at this time, the effects of white-nose syndrome, a newly emerging disease that has killed large numbers of cave-hibernating bats in the Northeastern United States (Turner and Reeder 2009), could greatly impact Ozark and Virginia big-eared bats and cave-dwelling Rafinesque's big-eared bats.

Research on biology, ecology, and conservation of bats has increased greatly worldwide in the past two decades (Arnett 2003). In North America, much of this work has concentrated on forest-dwelling bats, and many studies have used acoustic detectors (Brigham 2007). Because big-eared bats are "whispering bats" and have low-intensity echolocation calls (Fenton 1982), they are rarely recorded by ultrasonic detectors deployed to assess composition of bat communities, their habitat associations, and their responses to forest management. Due to their rarity and high maneuverability, big-eared bats are often difficult to capture, which further limits our ability to conduct research. Therefore, our objective was to conduct an overview of the current body of published literature on eastern big-eared bats

Citation for proceedings: Loeb, Susan C.; Lacki, Michael J.; Miller, Darren A., eds. 2011. Conservation and management of eastern big-eared bats: a symposium. Gen. Tech. Rep. SRS-145. Asheville, NC: U.S. Department of Agriculture, Forest Service, Southern Research Station. 157 p.

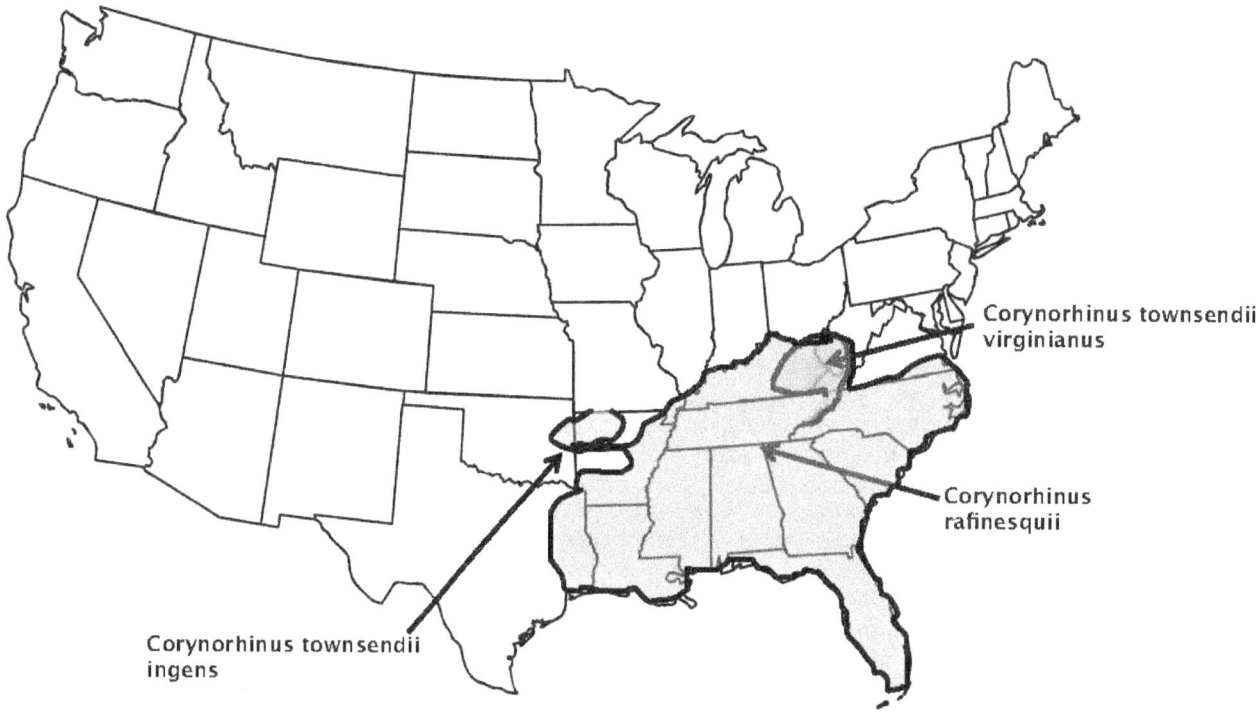

Figure 1—Distribution of Virginia big-eared bats (*Corynorhinus townsendii virginianus*), Ozark big-eared bats (*C. townsendii ingens*), and Rafinesque's big-eared bats (*C. rafinesquii*).

and present an analysis of the types of information available by taxa and topic. We then assessed areas that remain in greatest need of future research and introduce the papers of this symposium to illustrate how these papers fill some of the knowledge gaps.

REVIEW OF EXISTING LITERATURE

We searched the BIOSIS and Zoological Record databases using *Corynorhinus* and *Plecotus* as keywords for literature on eastern big-eared bats. We exported all papers and abstracts that pertained to eastern big-eared bats to a citation database (EndNote X3®, Thomson Reuters, New York, NY). Because BIOSIS and Zoological Records cover only 1969 to the present, we also examined the literature cited sections in the Mammalian Species accounts for Townsend's big-eared bats (Kunz and Martin 1982) and Rafinesque's big-eared bats (Jones 1977). We included those papers that pertained to eastern big-eared bats, were in English, and were accessible. We did not include theses and dissertations in the database because most have been published and our inclusion would duplicate the material. We classified each reference by species and whether the reference was an abstract, research note, full research article, or review paper. We also determined the

State or States in which the research was conducted. For comparison, we conducted a similar search of the Indiana bat (*Myotis sodalis*) literature in BIOSIS and the Zoological Record databases and the Mammalian Species account (Thomson 1982). We chose the Indiana bat for comparison because it also inhabits the Eastern United States, is an endangered species, and has a similar geographic range size to that of eastern big-eared bats.

We found 155 references on eastern big-eared bats. Of these references, 101 were research notes, full articles, or review papers (fig. 2). Although most of the 101 published papers on eastern big-eared bats were in abstracted databases, many of them are not easily accessible by managers. For example, many of the papers are in proceedings of State academies of science, are not available online, and may not even be available at most university libraries. In contrast, we found 239 references on Indiana bats; 141 of these references were research notes or full articles. These numbers do not include the 27 papers in the Indiana Bat symposium proceedings (Kurta and Kennedy 2002). Thus, even though the distribution of the Indiana bat is similar in size to that of eastern big-eared bats, considerably more research has been conducted on the ecology and management of Indiana bats than eastern big-eared bats.

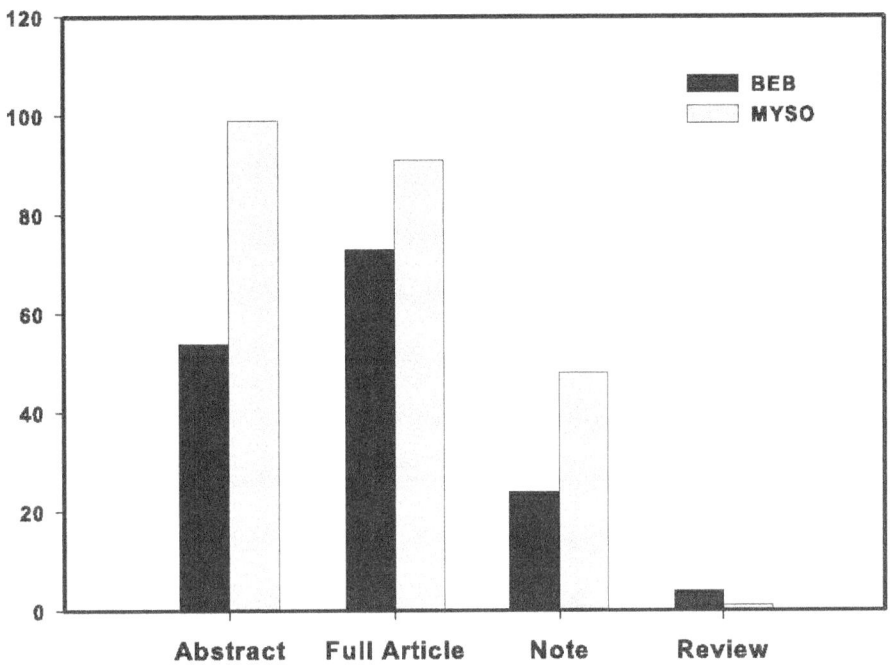

Figure 2—Number of abstracts, full articles, research notes, and review papers on eastern big-eared bats (BEB) and Indiana bats (MYSO) through 2009 and additional articles as cited in Mammalian Species accounts.

The larger body of literature on Indiana bats may be due to many factors. Although Indiana bats and Rafinesque's big-eared bats have similar geographic range sizes, Rafinesque's big-eared bats are not listed as an endangered species, and thus there has been less funding directed towards research and management of Rafinesque's big-eared bats. Indiana bats are often found in association with more common species such as little brown bats (*M. lucifugus*) and northern long-eared bats (*M. septentrionalis*) during summer and winter. Studies of hibernacula use often focus on multiple species, including Indiana bats, but big-eared bats are rarely represented in these studies (e.g., Brack 2007, Davis and Reite 1967, Gates and others 1984, Raesly and Gates 1987). In contrast to big-eared bats, Indiana bats can be detected acoustically and thus are often included in studies that rely on bat detectors (e.g., Ford and others 2005, Owen and others 2004, Schrimacher and others 2007, Yates and Muzika 2006). Because management of Indiana bat habitat is frequently in conflict with forest management and human development (e.g., Krusac and Mighton 2002, Whitaker and others 2004), considerable funding and research have been directed toward the Indiana bat in the past decade to provide the information necessary to mitigate these conflicts. Conversely, even though Virginia and Ozark big-eared bats are endangered, their year-round reliance on caves reduces potential conflicts with forest managers and other human enterprises other than caving (but see Miller and others 2011). Because big-eared bats cannot be reliably detected with ultrasonic detectors,

fewer studies on foraging and commuting habitat use of big-eared bats have been conducted because the data must be gained through more costly and labor-intensive techniques, such as radiotelemetry (e.g., Adam and others 1994, Clark and others 1993).

Far more abstracts, papers, and notes have been published on Rafinesque's big-eared bats than Virginia or Ozark big-eared bats (fig. 3). The greater number of publications on Rafinesque's big-eared bats is not surprising, given the larger geographic distribution and population sizes of these bats. A comparable number of studies have been conducted on Virginia and Ozark big-eared bats. Research on Rafinesque's big-eared bats has been relatively evenly distributed across the range, although Rafinesque's big-eared bats in some States have received little research. For example, limited research has been conducted on Rafinesque's big-eared bats in Alabama, Georgia, Tennessee, Virginia, and West Virginia, whereas several studies have been conducted in Arkansas, Louisiana, Kentucky, Mississippi, and Texas (fig. 4A). The number of references (abstracts and published papers) on Ozark big-eared bats is similar between Arkansas and Oklahoma, but there are approximately twice as many published papers on Ozark big-eared bats in Oklahoma than in Arkansas (fig. 4B). Most research on Virginia big-eared bats has been conducted in Kentucky, but several studies have also been conducted in West Virginia and Virginia (fig. 4C). There has been a considerable increase

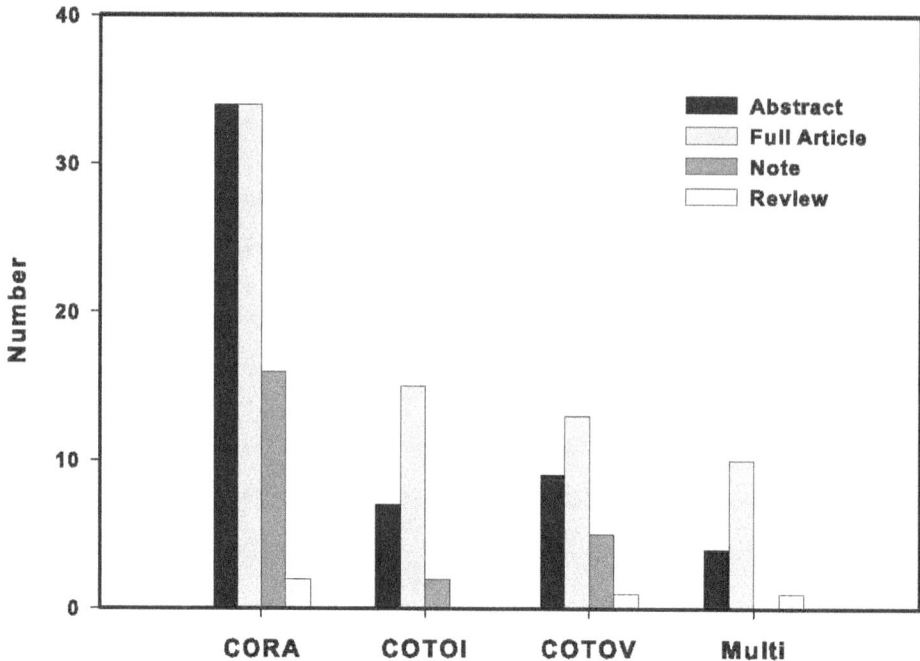

Figure 3—Number of abstracts, full articles, research notes, and review papers through 2009 on Rafinesque's big-eared bats (CORA), Ozark big-eared bats (COTOI), Virginia big-eared bats (COTOV), and ≥ two taxa (Multi).

in the number of studies on Rafinesque's big-eared bats over the past decade (fig. 5). In contrast, research on Ozark and Virginia big-eared bats peaked in the 1990s and has subsequently declined. The primary research emphasis areas for Rafinesque's big-eared bats have been roosting ecology and studies of distribution and status, whereas research on Ozark and Virginia big-eared bats has primarily focused on foraging habitat use and diet along with reports on distribution and status (fig. 6).

IDENTIFICATION OF KNOWLEDGE GAPS

The preceding examination of existing literature on eastern big-eared bats identifies several gaps in our knowledge base. One of the largest gaps concerns population ecology. There are no studies on demography, population dynamics, or social organization of any of the eastern big-eared bats, although recent studies of population genetics have shed some light on dispersal (Piaggio and others 2009). Estimating population sizes and demographic parameters such as reproductive success and survival is difficult for most bat species, but is easiest for those that use observable roosts, are colonial, and have relatively small colony sizes (e.g., < 1,000 individuals; Kunz and others 2009, O'Donnell 2009). Several demographic studies have recently been conducted on colonial species that are faithful to artificial roosts such as big brown bats (*Eptesicus fuscus*; Ellison and others 2007), little brown bats (Frick and others 2010), Yuma

bats (*M. yumanensis*; Frick and others 2007), and Leisler's bats (*Nyctalus leisleri*; Schorcht and others 2009). Because eastern big-eared bats form small colonies and are often in easily accessible roost sites, similar demographic studies may be achievable for big-eared bats as well.

Additional areas in need of research include studies of foraging habitat use and selection. Although several studies have been conducted on the foraging behavior and habitat use of Virginia and Ozark big-eared bats (e.g., Adam and others 1994, Burford and Lacki 1995, Clark and others 1993, Wethington and others 1996, Wilhide and others 1998), only three studies have been conducted on foraging habitat use by Rafinesque's big-eared bats (Hurst and Lacki 1999, Medlin and Risch 2008, Menzel and others 2001). Several studies have been conducted on food habits of each taxa, but relative to their large geographic range, fewer have been conducted on Rafinesque's big-eared bats. Further, no study has been conducted on prey availability for Rafinesque's big-eared bats, whereas several studies have investigated this aspect of the feeding ecology of Virginia and Ozark big-eared bats (Burford and others 1999, Dodd and others 2008, Leslie and Clark 2002).

Physiological aspects of big-eared bat ecology also have been ignored. We found no study that examined hibernation energetics or seasonal patterns of hibernation in eastern big-eared bats. While other aspects of physiology, such as the energetics of growth and reproduction, are important,

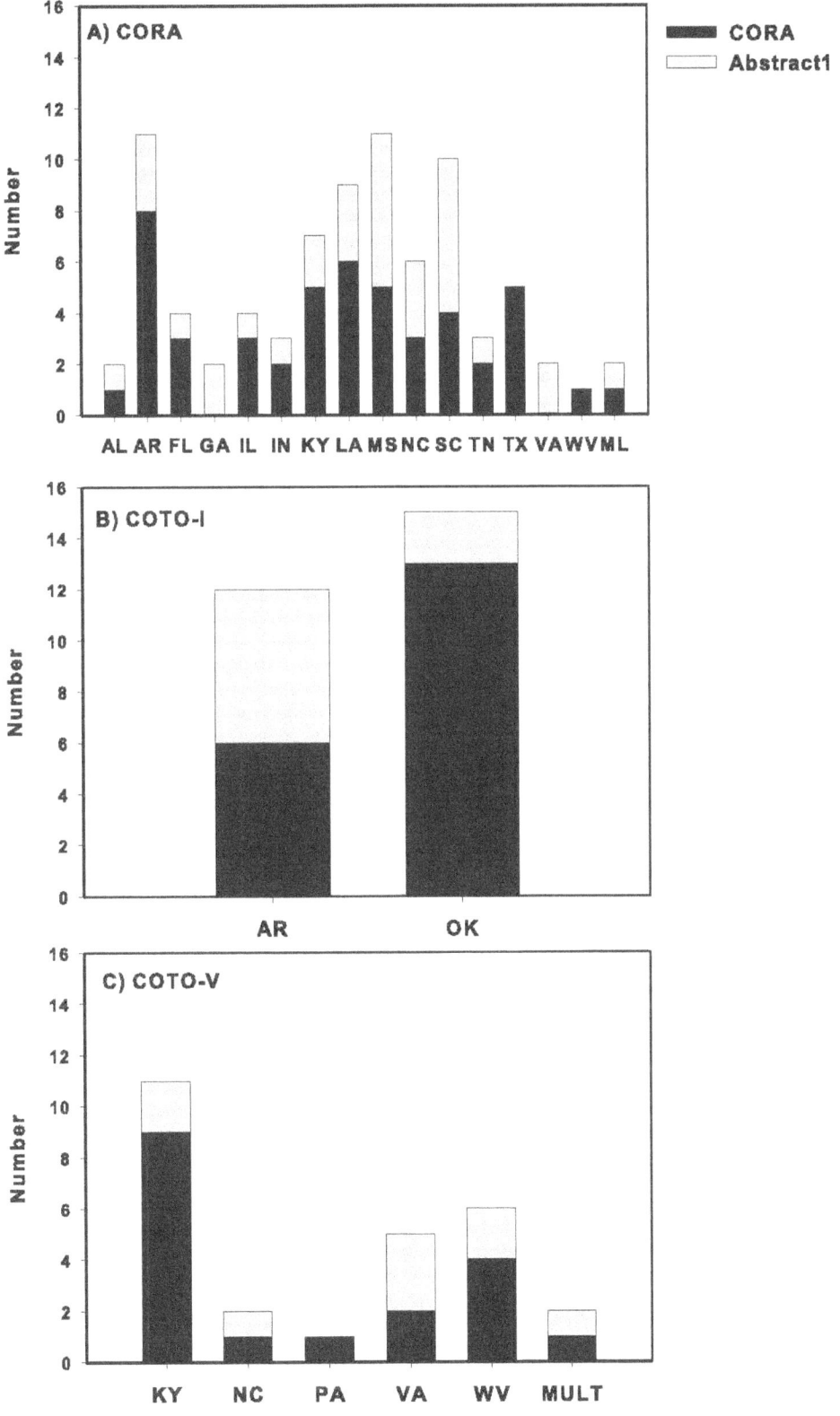

Figure 4—Number of abstracts and published papers by State through 2009 on (A) Rafinesque's big-eared bats (CORA), (B) Ozark big-eared bats (COTOI), and (C) Virginia big-eared bats (COTOV). (AL = Alabama, AR = Arkansas, FL = Florida, GA = Georgia, IL = Illinois, IN = Indiana, KY = Kentucky, LA = Louisiana, MS = Mississippi, NC = North Carolina, SC = South Carolina, TN = Tennessee, TX = Texas, VA = Virginia, WV = West Virginia, ML = Multi, OK = Oklahoma, PA = Pennsylvania.)

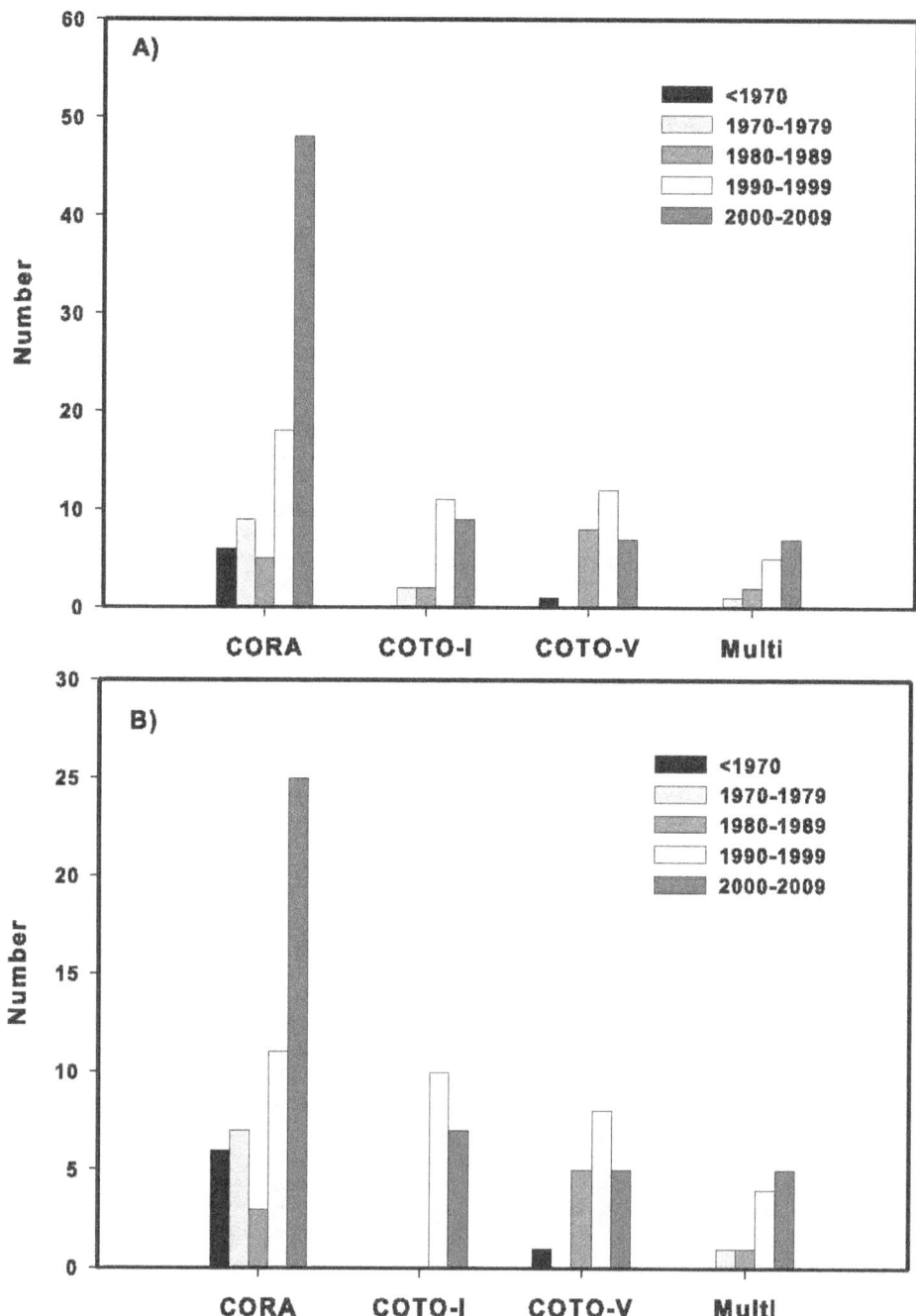

Figure 5—Number of papers published through 2009 by time period on Rafinesque's big-eared bats (CORA), Ozark big-eared bats (COTOI), Virginia big-eared bats (COTOV), and ≥ two taxa (Multi). (A) Abstracts and published papers and (B) published papers only.

understanding hibernation patterns of cave-roosting big-eared bats is particularly critical due to the advent of white-nose syndrome and its effects on bats during hibernation (Cryan and others 2010). Understanding hibernation energetics (e.g., fat storage, metabolic rates, arousal costs) will also allow biologists to predict effects of climate change and suitability of hibernacula under various climate scenarios (e.g., Humphries and others 2002). Further, we found few

studies that examined roost use or selection of caves or mines by big-eared bats. Thus, we know little about basic characteristics such as temperature, humidity, or structural characteristics that make some caves or mines suitable and others unsuitable for use during summer or winter.

Effects of management activities on eastern big-eared bats have also received limited attention. A few papers have been

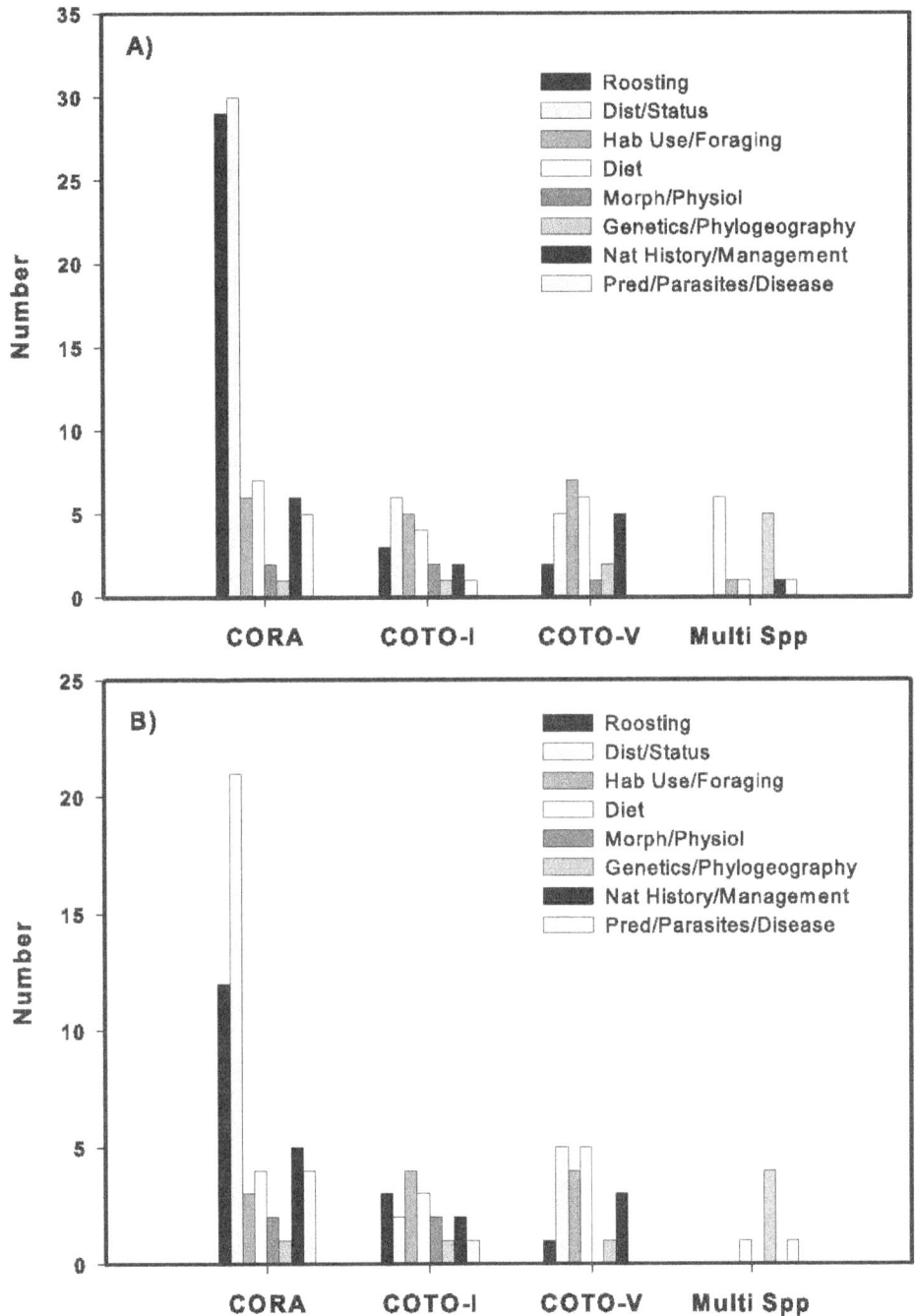

Figure 6—Number of papers published through 2009 by topic on Rafinesque's big-eared bats (CORA), Ozark big-eared bats (COTOI), Virginia big-eared bats (COTOV), and ≥ two taxa (Multi). (A) Abstracts and published papers and (B) published papers only.

published on cave gates for Virginia and Ozark big-eared bats (Martin and others 2000, White and Seginak 1987). Except for a study that examined effects of prescribed fire on Ozark big-eared bats (Caviness 2003), no empirical studies have tested effects of silvicultural practices (e.g., thinning, clearcut harvest, selective harvest, prescribed fire) for any of the species, although Adam and others (1994) suggested that logging may be detrimental to Virginia big-eared bats. Other management activities that could affect big-eared bats include wetlands management (e.g., alteration of water flow regimes), provisioning of artificial roosts, bridge maintenance and construction, and land use changes in surrounding landscapes. Although Clark (2003) outlined procedures for monitoring big-eared bats in bottomland hardwood forests, no study has tested the effectiveness of various survey and monitoring techniques for cave- or tree-roosting big-eared bats.

THIS VOLUME

In the previous section, we identified numerous gaps in our knowledge regarding ecology and management of eastern big-eared bats. Areas in need of research range from basic biology and ecology to methodology and management effects. In this section, we discuss how these information gaps are partially filled by papers in these proceedings.

The four succeeding papers summarize and synthesize existing knowledge on various aspects of big-eared bat ecology and conservation. These papers provide the first step in understanding the biology and ecology of these animals and are an entry into the published literature and reports for researchers, biologists, managers, and policymakers unfamiliar with big-eared bats. The first of these papers by Bayless and others provides an extensive overview of the status and distribution of eastern big-eared bats. Status and distribution data are essential for development of effective conservation strategies, and the authors provide a thorough summary of the historic and current distributions of all three taxa, estimates of current population numbers, and a discussion of population trends. Specific threats for each taxa are also discussed.

Roosts are one of the most critical resources for bats and understanding roost site use, selection, and fidelity are essential for effective conservation and management (Barclay and Kurta 2007, Kunz and Lumsden 2003). Roosting ecology is one of the most studied aspects of Rafinesque's big-eared bats (fig. 6), and in the next paper, Trousdale synthesizes this research. In addition to summarizing what is known about roost use and selection at various spatial scales, Trousdale also discusses roost fidelity and intraspecific and interspecific interactions of tree-roosting Rafinesque's big-eared bats.

There have been several food habit studies of eastern big-eared bats, yet we know little about the interactions between big-eared bats and their prey. Lacki and Dodd provide an extensive summary of the food habit studies of eastern big-eared bats and show that moths are the main component of the diet of all three taxa. The authors also show how these species have evolved a variety of morphological and behavioral adaptations that increase their success as moth predators. Lacki and Dodd also examine habitat use of big-eared bats in relation to habitat use of their moth prey.

The final synthesis paper provides a context for future conservation and management of eastern big-eared bats. In addition to reviewing past conservation efforts, Miller and others examine current forest conditions in the South and how changes in forest conditions may impact big-eared bats. They also discuss challenges faced by managers of big-eared bats, identify research that is needed to provide the necessary information for effective management, and suggest some important management actions to conserve these animals.

The final nine papers of the proceedings provide new data on ecology and conservation of eastern big-eared bats. One of the first obstacles to managing big-eared bats is lack of information on the status and distribution of these species. Although Bayless and others provide a general overview of the status of big-eared bats across their range, specific information on status and distribution of big-eared bats is needed for effective management at the local level. Martin and others provide a detailed update on the status and distribution of Rafinesque's big-eared bats in Mississippi, while Stihler reviews the status of Virginia big-eared bats based on 27 years of cave monitoring in West Virginia and documents an overall increase in the number of Virginia big-eared bats in West Virginia. Genetic tools can also be used to help understand the status of eastern big-eared bats; such tools include taxonomic status, genetic "health" such as inbreeding depression, and effective population size. Piaggio and others provide evidence to suggest that the previously named subspecies of Rafinesque's big-eared bats are probably not valid, although there are two major clades within the species. They also analyzed mitochondrial and microsatellite DNA of Rafinesque's big-eared bats from five roosts in Arkansas to determine genetic diversity, connectivity, and effective population size and illustrate the conservation consequences of these genetic data. Because of the dispersed nature of Rafinesque's big-eared bats, much of the information on their status and distribution is unreliable (Bayless and other 2011). Gaining this information will require new tools and techniques for inventorying and monitoring this species, especially those that rely on trees for roosting. Clement and Castleberry tested three techniques for inventorying Rafinesque's big-eared bats in Coastal Plain forests and compare their cost-effectiveness.

Other than studies of hibernation, most bat research has been conducted during the summer reproductive period, and little is known about the ecology of bats during spring, fall, and winter (Weller and others 2009). Two papers address this gap for Rafinesque's big-eared bats. Sasse and others describe winter roosting ecology of Rafinesque's big-eared bats in Arkansas, and Loeb and Zarnoch examine year-round roost use by Rafinesque's big-eared bats in the Coastal Plain of South Carolina. Although Rafinesque's big-eared bat summer roost use in bottomland hardwood forests has received considerable study (Trousdale 2011), there is still much to be learned about the roosting ecology of this species and how it varies across the range. Summer roost characteristics of Rafinesque's big-eared bats are described for two geographic areas that have received little attention. Roby and others describe roost characteristics of Rafinesque's big-eared bats in the Coastal Plain of North Carolina, and Johnson and

Lacki describe summer roost characteristics of Rafinesque's big-eared bats in floodplain forests of Kentucky.

Information on big-eared bat foraging habitat is critical for managing landscapes surrounding roosts. As discussed previously, use of radiotelemetry is essential for obtaining data on foraging habitat use of big-eared bats and few data are available, particularly for Rafinesque's big-eared bats. The paper by Johnson and Lacki, who address foraging behavior of Rafinesque's big-eared bats in western Kentucky, helps to fill this gap, while Stihler provides further data on habitat use of Virginia big-eared bats in West Virginia.

CONCLUSIONS

Basic information on biology and management of big-eared bats in the Eastern United States is available but many gaps remain in our understanding of big-eared bat ecology and management. Papers in these proceedings fill some of the knowledge gaps but also point out many areas where our knowledge and understanding are lacking. While much of the needed information has direct application for conservation and management, we also lack basic ecological data. Although it is important to focus on immediate management needs, it is also essential to anticipate future threats and amass a body of knowledge and understanding that will permit managers to deal with these future threats. In addition to focusing on the basic life requisites of big-eared bats (e.g., roosting and foraging ecology), research also must target an understanding of the entire ecological context in which these animals exist, including interactions with conspecifics, other bat species, insect communities, predators and parasites, and other organisms in the ecosystems they inhabit (e.g., the fauna and flora that inhabit the caves, mines, and hollow trees in which these animals roost). This is a difficult task in research on any species, but perhaps more so in research on the particularly cryptic eastern big-eared bat species. We hope that current and future technology, coupled with interest from stakeholders, will provide the necessary resources to address issues relative to long-term conservation of these unique bat species.

LITERATURE CITED

Adam, M.D.; Lacki, M.J.; Barnes, T.G. 1994. Foraging areas and habitat use of the Virginia big-eared bat in Kentucky. Journal of Wildlife Management. 58: 462-469.

Alig, R.J.; Kline, J.D.; Lichtenstein, M. 2004. Urbanization on the US landscape: looking ahead in the 21st century. Landscape and Urban Planning. 69: 219-234.

Alig, R.J.; Platinga, A.J.; Ahn, S. [and others]. 2003. Land use changes involving forestry in the United States: 1952 to 1997,

with projections to 2050. Gen. Tech. Rep. PNW-587. Portland, OR: U.S. Department of Agriculture Forest Service, Pacific Northwest Research Station. 92 p.

Arnett, E.B. 2003. Advancing science and partnerships for the conservation of bats and their habitats. Wildlife Society Bulletin. 31: 2-5.

Barclay, R.M.R.; Kurta, A. 2007. Ecology and behavior of bats roosting in tree cavities and under bark. In: Lacki, M.J.; Hayes, J.P.; Kurta, A., eds. Bats in forests: conservation and management. Baltimore, MD: Johns Hopkins University Press: 17-59.

Bayless, M.L.; Clark, M.K., Stark, R.C. [and others]. 2011. Distribution and status of eastern big-eared bats (*Corynorhinus* spp.). In: Loeb, S.C.; Lacki, M.J.; Miller, D.A., eds. Conservation and management of eastern big-eared bats: a symposium. Gen. Tech. Rep. SRS-145. Asheville, NC: U.S. Department of Agriculture Forest Service, Southern Research Station: 13-25.

Brack, V., Jr. 2007. Temperatures and locations used by hibernating bats, including *Myotis sodalis* (Indiana bat), in a limestone mine: implications for conservation and management. Environmental Management. 40: 739-746.

Brigham, R.M. 2007. Bats in forests: what we know and what we need to learn. In: Lacki, M.J.; Hayes, J.P.; Kurta, A., eds. Bats in forests: conservation and management. Baltimore, MD: Johns Hopkins University Press: 1-15.

Burford, L.S.; Lacki, M.J. 1995. Habitat use by *Corynorhinus townsendii virginianus* in the Daniel Boone National Forest. American Midland Naturalist. 134: 340-345.

Burford, L.S.; Lacki, M.J.; Covell, C.V., Jr. 1999. Occurrence of moths among habitats in a mixed mesophytic forest: implications for management of forest bats. Forest Science. 45: 323-332.

Caviness, M. 2003. Effects of prescribed fire on cave environment and bat inhabitants. Bat Research News. 44: 130.

Clark, B.S.; Leslie, D.M., Jr.; Carter, T.S. 1993. Foraging activity of adult female Ozark big-eared bats (*Plecotus townsendii ingens*) in summer. Journal of Mammalogy. 74: 422-427.

Clark, M.K. 2003. Survey and monitoring of rare bats in bottomland hardwood forests. In: O'Shea, T.J.; Bogan, M.A., eds. Monitoring trends in bat populations of the United States and territories: problems and prospects. Inf. and Tech. Rep. USGS/BRD/ITR-2003-003. Springfield, VA: U.S. Geological Survey, Biological Resources Division: 79-90.

Cryan, P.M.; Meteyer, C.U.; Boyles, J.G.; Blehert, D.S. 2010. Wing pathology of white-nose syndrome in bats suggests life-threatening disruption of physiology. BMC Biology. 8(135): 1-8.

Davis, W.H.; Reite, O.B. 1967. Responses of bats from temperate regions to changes in ambient temperature. Biological Bulletin. 132: 320-328.

Dodd, L.E.; Lacki, M.J.; Rieske, L.K. 2008. Variation in moth occurrence and implications for foraging habitat of Ozark big-eared bats. Forest Ecology and Management. 255: 3866-3872.

Ellison, L.E.; O'Shea, T.J.; Neubaum, D.J. [and others]. 2007. A comparison of conventional capture versus PIT reader techniques for estimating survival and capture probabilities of big brown bats (*Eptesicus fuscus*). Acta Chiropterologica. 9: 149-160.

Fenton, M.B. 1982. Echolocation, insect hearing, and feeding ecology of insectivorous bats. In: Kunz, T.H., ed. Ecology of bats. New York: Plenum Press: 261-285.

Ford, W.M.; Menzel, M.A.; Rodrigue, J.L. [and others]. 2005. Relating bat species presence to simple habitat measures in a central Appalachian forest. Biological Conservation. 126: 528-539.

Frick, W.F.; Rainey, W.E.; Pierson, E.D. 2007. Potential effects of environmental contamination on Yuma myotis demography and population growth. Ecological Applications. 17: 1213-1222.

Frick, W.F.; Reynolds, D.S.; Kunz, T.H. 2010. Influence of climate and reproductive timing on demography of little brown myotis *Myotis lucifugus*. Journal of Animal Ecology. 79: 128-136.

Gates, J.E.; Feldhamer, G.A.; Griffith, L.A. [and others]. 1984. Status of cave-dwelling bats in Maryland: importance of marginal habitats. Wildlife Society Bulletin. 12: 162-169.

Hall, E.R. 1981. The mammals of North America, 2d ed. New York: John Wiley and Sons. 600 p.

Humphries, M.M.; Thomas, D.W.; Speakman, J.R. 2002. Climate-mediated energetic constraints on the distribution of hibernating mammals. Nature. 418: 313-316.

Hurst, T.E.; Lacki, M.J. 1999. Roost selection, population size and habitat use by a colony of Rafinesque's big-eared bats (*Corynorhinus rafinesquii*). American Midland Naturalist. 142: 363-371.

Jones, C. 1977. *Plecotus rafinesquii*. Mammalian Species. 69: 1-4.

Krusac, D.L.; Mighton, S.R. 2002. Conservation of the Indiana bat in national forests: where we have been and where we should be going. In: Kurta, A.; Kennedy, J., eds. The Indiana bat: biology and management of an endangered species. Austin, TX: Bat Conservation International: 55-65.

Kunz, T.H.; Betke, M.; Hristov, N.I.; Vonhof, M.J. 2009. Methods for assessing colony size, population size, and relative abundance of bats. In: Kunz, T.H.; Parsons, S., eds. Ecological and behavioral methods for the study of bats. 2d ed. Baltimore, MD: Johns Hopkins University Press: 133-157.

Kunz, T.H.; Lumsden, L.F. 2003. Ecology of cavity and foliage roosting bats. In: Kunz, T.H.; Fenton, M.B., eds. Bat ecology. Chicago: The University of Chicago Press: 3-89.

Kunz, T.H.; Martin, R.A. 1982. *Plecotus townsendii*. Mammalian Species. 175: 1-6.

Kurta, A.; Kennedy, J., eds. 2002. The Indiana bat: biology and management of an endangered species. Austin, TX: Bat Conservation International. 253 p.

Leslie, D.M.; Clark, B.S. 2002. Feeding habits of the endangered Ozark big-eared bat (*Corynorhinus townsendii ingens*) relative to prey abundance. Acta Chiropterologica. 4: 173-182.

Martin, K.W.; Puckette, W.L.; Hensley, S.L.; Leslie, D.M., Jr. 2000. Internal cave gating as a means of protecting cave-dwelling bat populations in eastern Oklahoma. Proceedings of the Oklahoma Academy of Science. 80: 133-137.

Medlin, R.E., Jr.; Risch, T.S. 2008. Habitat associations of bottomland bats, with focus on Rafinesque's big-eared bat and southeastern myotis. American Midland Naturalist. 160: 400-412.

Menzel, M.A.; Menzel, J.M.; Ford, W.M. [and others]. 2001. Home range and habitat use of male Rafinesque's big-eared bats (*Corynorhinus rafinesquii*). American Midland Naturalist. 145: 402-408.

Miller, D.A.; Sasse, D.B.; Reynolds, R. [and others]. 2011. Conservation and management of eastern big-eared bats (*Corynorhinus* spp.). In: Loeb, S.C.; Lacki, M.J.; Miller, D.A., eds. Conservation and management of eastern big-eared bats: a symposium. Gen. Tech. Rep. SRS-145. Asheville, NC: U.S. Department of Agriculture Forest Service, Southern Research Station: 53-61.

O'Donnell, C.F.J. 2009. Population dynamics and survivorship in bats. In: Kunz, T.H.; Parsons, S., eds. Ecological and behavioral methods for the study of bats. 2d ed. Baltimore, MD: Johns Hopkins University Press: 158-176.

Owen, S.F.; Menzel, M.A.; Edwards, J.W. [and others]. 2004. Bat activity in harvested and intact forest stands in the Allegheny Mountains. Northern Journal of Applied Forestry. 21: 154-159.

Piaggio, A.J.; Navo, K.W.; Stihler, C.W. 2009. Intraspecific comparison of population structure, genetic diversity, and dispersal among three subspecies of Townsend's big-eared bats, *Corynorhinus townsendii*, *C. t. pallescens*, and the endangered *C. t. virginianus*. Conservation Genetics. 10: 143-159.

Raesly, R.L.; Gates, J.E. 1987. Winter habitat selection by north temperate cave bats. American Midland Naturalist. 118: 15-31.

Schirmacher, M.R.; Castleberry, S.B.; Ford, W.M. [and others]. 2007. Habitat associations of bats in south-central West Virginia.

Proceedings of the Annual Conference Southeastern Association of Fish and Wildlife Agencies. 61: 46-52.

Schorcht, W.; Bontadina, F.; Schaub, M. 2009. Variation of adult survival drives population dynamics in a migrating forest bat. Journal of Animal Ecology. 78: 1182-1190.

Szymanski, J.A.; Runge, M.C.; Parkin, M.J. [and others]. 2009. White-nose syndrome management: report on structured decision making initiative. Fort Snelling, MN: U.S. Department of the Interior, U.S. Fish and Wildlife Service. 51 p.

Thomson, C.E. 1982. *Myotis sodalis*. Mammalian Species. 163: 1-5.

Trousdale, A.W. 2011. Ecology of tree-roosting Rafinesque's big-eared bats in the Eastern United States. In: Loeb, S.C.; Lacki, M.J.; Miller, D.A., eds. Conservation and management of eastern big-eared bats: a symposium. Gen. Tech. Rep. SRS-145. Asheville, NC: U.S. Department of Agriculture, Forest Service, Southern Research Station: 27-38.

Turner, G.G.; Reeder, D.M. 2009. Update of white nose syndrome in bats, September 2009. Bat Research News. 50: 47-53.

U.S. Fish and Wildlife Service. 1979. 50 CFR Part 17. Endangered and threatened wildlife and plants: listing of Virginia and Ozark big-eared bats as endangered species, and critical habitat determination. [Washington, DC]: U.S. National Archives and Records Administration. Federal Register. 44(232): 69,206-69,208.

U.S. Fish and Wildlife Service. 1995. Ozark big-eared bat (*Plecotus townsendii ingens* [Handley]) revised recovery plan. Tulsa, OK: U.S. Fish and Wildlife Service. 112 p.

U.S. Fish and Wildlife Service. 1996. 50 CFR Part 17. Endangered and threatened wildlife and plants; notice of final decision identification of candidates for listing as endangered or threatened. [Washington, DC]: U.S. National Archives and Records Administration. Federal Register. 61: 64,481-64,485.

U.S. Fish and Wildlife Service. 2008. Virginia big-eared bat (*Corynorhinus townsendii virginianus*). 5-year review: summary and evaluation. Elkins, WV. 21 p.

Weller, T.J.; Cryan, P.M.; O'Shea, T.J. 2009. Broadening the focus of bat conservation and research in the USA for the 21st century. Endangered Species Research. 8: 129-145.

Wethington, T.A.; Leslie, D.M., Jr.; Gregory, M.S.; Wethington, M.K. 1996. Prehibernation habitat use and foraging activity by endangered Ozark big-eared bats (*Plecotus townsendii ingens*). American Midland Naturalist. 135: 218-230.

Whitaker, J.O., Jr.; Hamilton, W.J., Jr. 1998. Mammals of the Eastern United States. Ithaca, NY: Cornell University Press. 583 p.

Whitaker, J.O., Jr.; Sparks, D.W.; Brack, V., Jr. 2004. Bats of the Indianapolis International Airport area, 1991-2001. Proceedings of the Indiana Academy of Science. 113: 151-161.

White, D.H.; Seginak, J.T. 1987. Cave gate designs for use in protecting endangered bats. Wildlife Society Bulletin. 15: 445-449.

Wilhide, J.D.; McDaniel, V.R.; Harvey, M.J.; White, D.R. 1998. Telemetric observations of foraging Ozark big-eared bats in Arkansas. Journal of the Arkansas Academy of Science. 52: 113-116.

Yates, M.D.; Muzika, R.M. 2006. Effect of forest structure and fragmentation on site occupancy of bat species in Missouri Ozark forests. Journal of Wildlife Management. 70: 1238-1248.

DISTRIBUTION AND STATUS OF EASTERN BIG-EARED BATS
(*CORYNORHINUS* SPP.)

Mylea L. Bayless, Conservation Biologist, Bat Conservation International, Austin, TX 78716

Mary Kay Clark, Biologist, Moonlight Environmental Consulting, Raleigh, NC 27614

Richard C. Stark, Fish and Wildlife Biologist, U.S. Fish and Wildlife Service,
Oklahoma Ecological Services Field Office, Tulsa, OK 74129

Barbara S. Douglas, Senior Endangered Species Biologist, U.S. Fish and Wildlife Service,
West Virginia Field Office, Elkins, WV 26241

Shauna M. Ginger, Wildlife Biologist, U.S. Fish and Wildlife Service, Mississippi Field Office,
Jackson, MS 39213

Abstract—Recent information describing distribution and status of Rafinesque's big-eared bat (*Corynorhinus rafinesquii*) and Townsend's big-eared bat (*C. townsendii*) in the Eastern United States is currently scattered among the scientific and gray literature. Therefore, our objective was to collate available information to better enable managers and researchers to use known distribution and population data relative to conservation for these species. The two eastern subspecies of *C. townsendii* [Ozark big-eared bat (*C. t. ingens*) and Virginia big-eared bat (*C. t. virginianus*)] have been listed as federally endangered since 1979, and recent 5-year reviews recommend retaining their endangered status because recovery criteria have not been met. These species remain vulnerable due to existence of only small, widely separated remnant populations. Surveys to locate additional sites for these endangered taxa are warranted, although locating new colonies is unlikely to change their status. Rafinesque's big-eared bat is listed as a species of concern throughout its range although exact status remains undetermined largely due to challenges of assessing population trends for this species. Historical loss of mature, bottomland hardwood forests, assumed to represent a loss of natural roosting structure, suggests population declines. Recent research has improved distributional data for this species, including recognition of a distributional gap in the Piedmont region separating Coastal Plain and karst populations. Improved methods for population estimation are needed, although the means of establishing a baseline for monitoring population trends over time remains unclear. In parts of the range where Rafinesque's big-eared bat primarily uses tree cavities, it may be possible to use structure-based monitoring to provide an index of abundance in a given area. More traditional methods of monitoring population size in caves and mines may be usable in areas where significant hibernation and maternity colonies occupy these structures. Consistent monitoring requires funding that is often lacking for this species. While distribution and abundance are reasonably well documented for the two subspecies of *C. townsendii*, additional work to fill-in distribution gaps and assess population status is needed for *C. rafinesquii*. In the interim, conservation of natural and manmade roosts appears to be a critical need.

INTRODUCTION

Bats of the genus *Corynorhinus* are among the most distinctive in North America, easily recognizable by large glandular masses on their muzzle and enormous ears which extend about one-third of the total body length of the bat. The genus appears throughout the Southeastern and Western United States, southwestern Canada, and northern and central Mexico (Jones 1977, Kunz and Martin 1982). *Corynorhinus* species are gregarious, typically roosting in caves, mines, hollow trees, buildings, and under bridges (Jones 1977, Kunz and Martin 1982, Miller and others 2011, Trousdale 2011). Their exotic appearance has historically made them targets of both collection and intensive observation (U.S. Fish and Wildlife Service 1984).

There are three *Corynorhinus* species, two of which occur in the Eastern United States: Rafinesque's big-eared bat (*C. rafinesquii*) and Townsend's big-eared bat (*C. townsendii*). Both Eastern United States species are considered to be relatively uncommon and are vulnerable due to their apparent low tolerance to disturbance, habit of roosting near cave entrances (increases potential for disturbance), low population numbers, disjunct populations, and roost loss (Hahn 1908, Handley 1959, Harvey and others 1999, Hurst and Lacki 1999, Mohr 1933, Miller and others 2011, Piaggio and others 2011).

Eastern populations of Townsend's big-eared bat are limited to small ranges occupied by two endangered subspecies: Ozark big-eared bat (*C. t. ingens*) and Virginia big-eared bat (*C. t. virginianus*) as described by Handley (1959) in a revision of the genera *Euderma* and *Plecotus* (*Corynorhinus* was formerly *Plecotus*). Although Rafinesque's big-eared bats are more widely distributed, their range is not well documented. The distribution map published in Handley's 1959 revision became the baseline map for future publications on the U.S. big-eared bats, and later maps for the eastern taxa (e.g., Barbour and Davis 1969, Whitaker and Hamilton 1998) show little change from the original

Citation for proceedings: Loeb, Susan C.; Lacki, Michael J.; Miller, Darren A., eds. 2011. Conservation and management of eastern big-eared bats: a symposium. Gen. Tech. Rep. SRS-145. Asheville, NC: U.S. Department of Agriculture, Forest Service, Southern Research Station. 157 p.

map, with the singular change being that the more recent maps include the few findings of new sites for the Ozark and Virginia big-eared bats (U.S. Fish and Wildlife Service 2008a, 2008b).

The endangered status determination of the two Townsend's big-eared bat taxa was based on the small population sizes and disjunct populations (U.S. Fish and Wildlife Service 2008a, 2008b). Both taxa were among the first to be listed under the Endangered Species Act (1979). However, the status of Rafinesque's big-eared bat has always been in question with many authors over time suggesting that it is rare. For example, Barbour and Davis (1969) state that is not well known and "It is nowhere abundant, but is readily available for study at many localities." Thirty years later, Harvey and others (1999) stated similarly that this species is one of the least known of all bats in the Eastern United States and that it is uncommon throughout its range.

Previous investigations of Ozark and Virginia big-eared bats were initiated by researchers per requirements of the Endangered Species Act and continue to yield new information on population trends for those taxa (U.S. Fish and Wildlife Service 2008a, 2008b). Additionally, in the past 10 to 15 years, there has been a rise in the number of investigations on Rafinesque's big-eared bat (e.g., this symposium; Bennett and others 2008, Hurst and Lacki 1999, Lacki 2000, Trousdale and Beckett 2004). The result should be that for all the eastern *Corynorhinus* there is more data for conservation and management planning. However, much of the current distribution and status information for the eastern *Corynorhinus*, in particular for Rafinesque's big-eared bat, is found in unpublished literature (e.g., Clark 1999, Clark and DeTour 1995, Clark and Williams 1993, Harvey 1999, Horner and Maxey 2007; see also Martin and others 2011) and is not readily available. As such, land managers, conservationists, and others have difficulty finding basic information that can assist them with much needed investigations. To that end, our objectives were: (1) to provide a more current distribution map for eastern *Corynorhinus*; (2) summarize what is known about distribution, status, and population trends; and (3) identify gaps and areas where future work on eastern *Corynorhinus* can better guide investigations of the distribution, status, and population trends of these species.

METHODS

We reviewed published and unpublished literature on status and distribution of eastern *Corynorhinus* taxa and consulted experts on these species for additional information. Material presented for both the Ozark big-eared bat and the Virginia big-eared bat was primarily derived from U.S. Fish and Wildlife Service reports including recovery plans, 5-year

reviews, and unpublished monitoring data (U.S. Fish and Wildlife Service 1984, 1995, 2008a, 2008b). Much of the Rafinesque's big-eared bat distribution and status data were obtained through a partnership begun in 2008 to create a conservation strategy for Rafinesque's big-eared bat and the southeastern bat (*Myotis austroriparius*). To derive the most current information on distribution for these two species, a 2-year data-gathering period was established in which data were compiled from State natural heritage agencies and other sources. Additionally, local experts were involved in two multiday workshops (Raleigh, NC, September 24–25, 2008; Nashville, TN, March 31 to April 1, 2009) to gather expert opinion. This multipartner conservation project will result in a white-paper working strategy (currently being drafted by Bayless and others) through cooperative agreements with Bat Conservation International (Bat Conservation International, P.O. Box 162603, Austin, TX 78716). The data-gathering effort was supported in part by the National Fish and Wildlife Foundation (Protecting America's Bats—III project no. 2008-0094-000; Bayless and Clark 2009).

DISTRIBUTION

Ozark Big-Eared Bat

The Ozark big-eared bat is endemic to the Ozark Highlands and Boston Mountains ecoregions (Omernik 1987) where it occurs in oak-hickory (*Quercus* spp.-*Carya* spp.) hardwood forests (Clark 1991, Leslie and Clark 2002, U.S. Fish and Wildlife Service 1995). At the time of listing, the Ozark big-eared bat was known from only a few caves in northwestern Arkansas, southwestern Missouri, and northeastern Oklahoma. Since listing, additional caves used by maternity colonies in the summer and as hibernacula have been discovered in Oklahoma and Arkansas (Miller and others 2011, U.S. Fish and Wildlife Service 2008a). However, the bats have abandoned other caves including all known sites in Missouri and are, therefore, considered extirpated from that State (U.S. Fish and Wildlife Service 2008a; but see Elliot and others 1999). Consequently, the current range of the Ozark big-eared bat is limited to northeastern Oklahoma and northwestern and northcentral Arkansas.

In Oklahoma, Ozark big-eared bats currently are known to occur in Adair, Cherokee, and Sequoyah Counties. They were historically known from two caves in Delaware County, but have not been observed there recently. Twelve caves considered essential (defined in the recovery plan as caves that are necessary for the bat's continued existence because they are used as maternity sites and/or hibernacula; U.S. Fish and Wildlife Service 1995) for the continued existence of the Ozark big-eared bat occur in Oklahoma. In Arkansas, the Ozark big-eared bat is known to occur in Crawford, Marion, Searcy, Washington, and Franklin Counties. Seven essential caves occur in Arkansas. In addition to known sites, this species may potentially occur in additional Arkansas counties (Baxter, Benton, Boone, Carroll, Logan, Newton, Johnson, Madison, and Pope) based on evidence of probable use (neatly clipped moth wings and guano characteristic of this species feeding behavior), proximity to known range, and presence of suitable roosting and foraging habitat (U.S. Fish and Wildlife Service 2008a). Recent surveys have documented possible evidence of this species in Stone and Barry Counties in Missouri (Elliott and others 1999).

Virginia Big-Eared Bat

Virginia big-eared bats roost in a wide range of caves, rock shelters, and other karst features year round and are typically located in karst regions dominated by oak-hickory or beech-maple-hemlock (*Fagus* spp.-*Acer* spp.-*Tsuga* spp.) associations (Barbour and Davis 1969, Lacki and others 1993). At the time of listing (1979), the Virginia big-eared bat was documented from Jackson, Lee, Powell, and Rowan Counties, KY; Tazewell County, VA; and Pendleton, Grant, Randolph, Hardy, Tucker, and Preston Counties, WV (U.S. Fish and Wildlife Service 1984).[1] Currently, the population is documented from four States: Kentucky, North Carolina, Virginia, and West Virginia (fig. 1). Virginia big-eared bats are known to have significant active colony sites in Lee County, KY; Avery County, NC; Tazewell and Highland Counties, VA; and Pendleton, Grant, Tucker, and Fayette Counties, WV, with occasional or low-level use of sites in West Virginia (Hardy and Randolph Counties), Virginia (Bath, Bland, Highland, Rockingham, and Shenandoah Counties) and Kentucky (Bath, Estill, Jackson, Menifee, Morgan, Powell, Rockcastle, Rowan, and Wolfe Counties) (U.S. Fish and Wildlife Service 2008b, see footnote 1).

A review of several theories regarding the break in distribution of Townsend's big-eared bats and emergence of the Virginia subspecies was discussed in the recovery plan (U.S. Fish and Wildlife Service 1984: appendix 2). Recent phylogenetic investigations (Piaggio and others 2009b) have found divergence from Handley's (1959) original description. The apparent loss of connectivity among populations within this range has resulted in four genetically unique populations that should be considered distinct evolutionary units: Pendleton and Grant Counties, WV, and Highland County, VA; Fayette County, WV; Tazewell County, VA; and Lee, Estill, and Jackson Counties, KY (Piaggio and others 2009b).

[1] Personal communication. 2010. Traci Hemberger, Wildlife Biologist, Kentucky Department of Fish and Wildlife Resources, #1 Sportsman's Lane, Frankfort, KY 40601. Personal communication. 2010. Rick Reynolds, Wildlife Biologist, Virginia Department of Game and Inland Fisheries, 4010 West Broad Street, Richmond, VA 23230. Personal communication. 2010. Craig Stihler, Wildlife Biologist, West Virginia Division of Natural Resources, 324 Fourth Avenue, South Charleston, WV 25303.

Rafinesque's Big-Eared Bat

Rafinesque's big-eared bats are found sporadically throughout much of the Southeastern United States. Historically, populations occurred from eastern Texas to southern Missouri in the western part of its range, north to southern Illinois, Indiana, and Ohio, eastward to West Virginia and Virginia, then south along the coast through central Florida (Harvey and others 1999, Jones 1977). Harvey and Saugey (2001) defined the species' distribution as including portions of all Southern States, except northwestern Arkansas and northern Virginia. Although they continue to be widespread in the Eastern United States, and are still found throughout most of their historic range, they are now apparently absent from Ohio, Indiana, and eastern Illinois (fig. 1). The reasons for their absence along the northern edge of the range are unclear.

Most authors illustrate distribution of Rafinesque's big-eared bat as continuous across the Southeastern United States (e.g., Whitaker and Hamilton 1998), but careful plotting of records indicates that this bat has a somewhat sporadic distribution (fig. 1; Bayless and Clark 2009). Absence of records from the Piedmont region (fig. 1) of the Southern States suggest that the bats may not be found there, although this could be an artifact of sampling as most studies have been conducted in mountain (Hurst and Lacki 1999, Lacki and LaDeur 2001) and Coastal Plain regions (e.g., Carver and Ashley 2008, Clark 1990, Gooding and Langford 2004, Mirowsky and others 2004; also see Trousdale and 2011 for a summary). Further surveys may provide additional information to clarify this apparent gap in distribution. For example, systematic surveys of bridges in South Carolina documented most roosts (94.7 percent) in the upper and lower Coastal Plains of that State, but did identify 5.3 percent of roosts in the Piedmont (Bennett and others 2008).

Rafinesque's big-eared bat has demonstrated preferences for specific features (e.g., Carver and Ashley 2008, Gooding and Langford 2004, Hurst and Lacki 1999, Trousdale 2011) that do not occur evenly across the landscape, which may account for its sporadic distribution. Mountain regions contain karst features such as rock shelters and caves that are used for hibernation and maternity sites. Barbour and Davis (1969) described this species as a bat of the southeastern forests and subsequent field work has demonstrated a strong affiliation for both age class (Carver and Ashley 2008, Gooding and Langford 2004, Trousdale and Beckett 2005) and tree species that hollow readily (Stevenson 2008). Coastal Plain forests of the Eastern United States include mature forests that are preferred by this species (Trousdale 2011). In particular, mature cypress-gum swamp forests (*Taxodium* spp-*Nyssa* spp.) have been found to provide both roosting and foraging habitat (Clark 2003, Gooding and Langford 2004, Trousdale

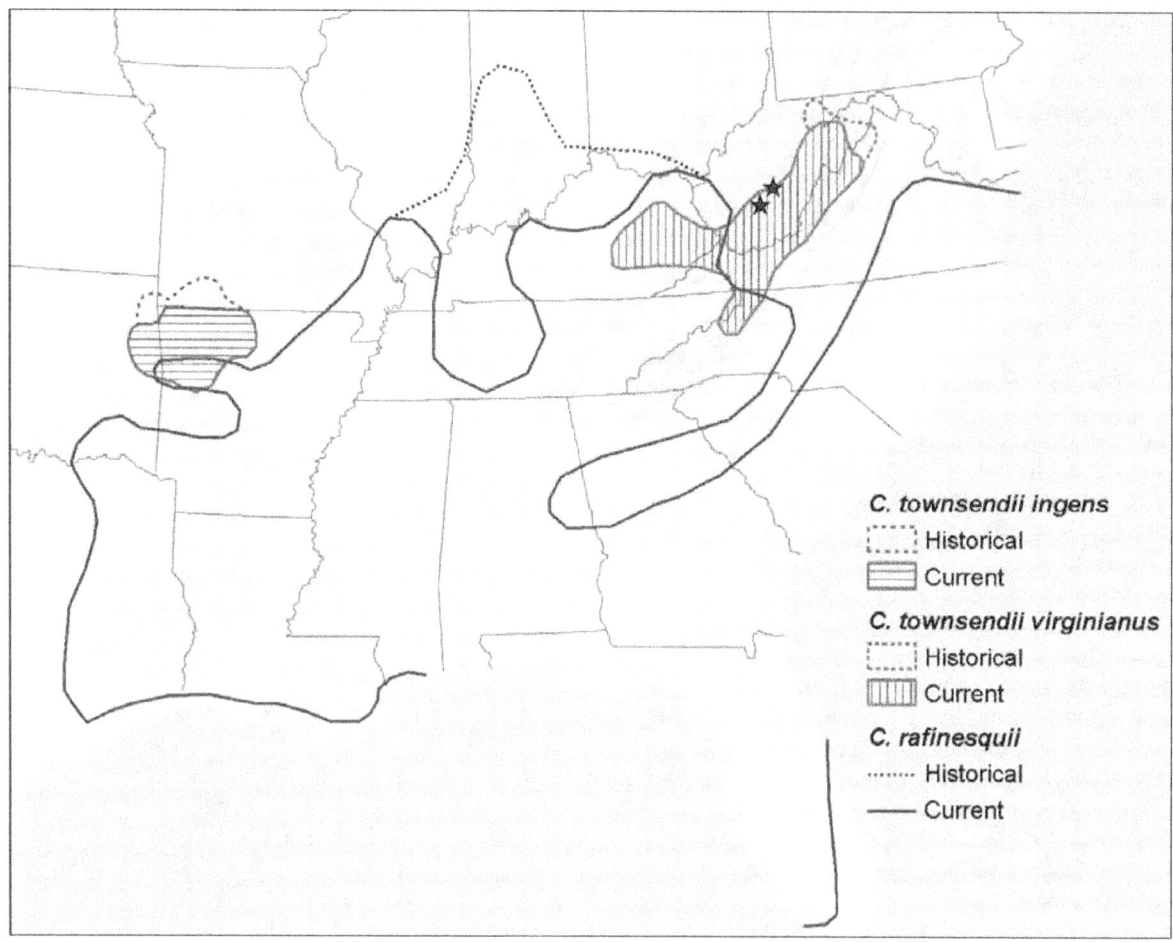

Figure 1—Geographic range of *Corynorhinus rafinesquii*, *C. townsendii ingens*, and *C. townsendii virginianus* in the Eastern United States. Black stars indicate occurrence records outside the contiguous range of *C. rafinesquii*.

2011). This bottomland forest type is restricted to certain hydrologic conditions where it develops adjacent to slow-moving river systems (Conner and others 1981, Faulkner and others 2009). In surveys conducted in high-quality bottomland tracts in North Carolina (Roanoke River bottomlands) and South Carolina (Francis Beidler Forest), Rafinesque's big-eared bats were captured more frequently than other species (Clark 1999, Clark and Black 1997). Menzel and others (2001) have also radio tracked male Rafinesque's big-eared bat foraging over young pine (*Pinus* spp.) forests where the roost site was in a building near bottomland forest. Although many of the records used for creating the updated distribution map for Rafinesque's big-eared bat (fig. 1; Bayless and Clark 1990) were based on the recent studies in bottomland hardwood forests, Rafinesque's big-eared bat is known to use a variety of manmade roost sites that occur in other forest types (Martin and others 2011). Therefore, more roosting and foraging studies are needed in other forest types to clarify habitat relationships for this species.

POPULATION DATA

Ozark Big-Eared Bat

At time of listing, the entire population of Ozark big-eared bats was estimated to consist of about 100 to 200 individuals (U.S. Fish and Wildlife Service 1984). Since listing, Ozark big-eared bat populations at essential hibernacula and maternity sites have been monitored using minimal census techniques at each essential site to obtain estimates on colony size and population trends (Harvey and others 2006, Puckette 2009). Monitoring data have revealed a disparity between summer and winter population estimates with numbers of Ozark big-eared bats estimated from summer maternity counts being larger than those found during winter hibernacula counts. For example, during the last year in which a representative count of both Ozark big-eared bat hibernacula and maternity sites occurred (2003), 701 bats were counted at hibernacula while maternity counts resulted in an estimate of about 1,600 bats (U.S. Fish and Wildlife Service 2008a). This indicates there are likely major hibernacula that have not yet been located. Population estimates and trends are, therefore, based on maternity colony counts. The population is estimated to currently consist of about 1,600 to 1,800 individual bats with about 400 to 600 in Arkansas and 1,200 to 1,400 in Oklahoma.[2] Recent population trend analyses were recently published for all known essential sites, and pooled. Results indicate an increasing population trend for seven colonies and a declining trend for three colonies, while the count data for four colonies were too variable to detect any trend (Graening and others 2011).

Virginia Big-Eared Bat

When the recovery plan was drafted, the known population of Virginia big-eared bats within maternity colonies was approximately 3,600 and the known hibernating population was approximately 2,585 (U.S. Fish and Wildlife Service 2008b). Since listing, all States within the range of the Virginia big-eared bat have implemented a periodic monitoring program at both hibernacula and maternity sites, but a standardized survey protocol has not been formalized (U.S. Fish and Wildlife Service 2008b). Estimates derived during 2009 hibernacula surveys approximate the Virginia big-eared bat population at 15,000 individuals; approximately 12,000 of these bats hibernate in West Virginia (U.S. Fish and Wildlife Service 2009). Summer estimates at rangewide maternity colonies the same year accounted for 8,400 individuals.[3] Thirteen caves support hibernating colonies of ≥ 20 Virginia big-eared bats, and only 8 of these contain over 100 hibernating individuals. Maternity sites are limited to 17 caves and 6 other caves support summer bachelor colonies with ≥ 20 individuals. The U.S. Fish and Wildlife Service determined in their 5-year review that although there have been fluctuations and population declines within individual caves, the rangewide population within both hibernacula and maternity colonies has increased since the time of listing (U.S. Fish and Wildlife Service 2008b). They further note that the documented range of the species has expanded with discovery of additional occupied caves, including one significant hibernaculum in Avery County, NC (Clark and Lee 1987).

Rafinesque's Big-Eared Bat

A minimum of 1,138 known roost sites for Rafinesque's big-eared bats were recorded during a data compilation effort in 2008 and 2009 spanning a time period from 1864 to 2009 (Bayless and Clark 2009). Some detailed data exist for the largest populations of bats in karst areas, but limited survey data are available for the remaining colonies which occur throughout the Southeastern United States in groups typically ranging from 1 to 50 individuals throughout the year, with several larger maternity colonies numbering around 100 adults (Bayless and Clark 2009). The largest colonies of Rafinesque's big-eared bats have been documented in Kentucky, North Carolina, and Tennessee where roughly 4,100 hibernate in 10 significant hibernacula in the Appalachian Mountains and central plateaus. Recent hibernation surveys for these 10 sites reported the following colony size estimates: 2 abandoned mines in Great Smoky Mountains National Park, NC (1,294 bats[4]); 2 sandstone rock shelters in Daniel Boone National Forest, KY (607 bats[5]); 4 caves in Mammoth Cave National Park (1,345 bats[6]); and 2 privately owned caves in Kentucky and Tennessee (935 bats[7]). Mammoth Cave National Park has documented 13 maternity colonies which contain roughly 700 to 800 Rafinesque's big-eared bats (see footnote 6). Burghardt (2003) reported that one maternity chamber at the Eagle Creek Copper Mine in the Great Smoky Mountains National Park, NC, undoubtedly hosted many more bats at one time than known to inhabit the site, as attested by numerous guano piles up to 0.6 m in height.

Information on population trends is generally lacking for Rafinesque's big-eared bat for a number of reasons. First, methods of acquiring population trend data for Ozark and Virginia big-eared bats do not apply to Rafinesque's big-eared bat over most of its range. Most data used for colonial bat population monitoring are obtained at cave and mine roosts where significant numbers of bats are predictably roosting for the hibernation or maternity season. A few cave and mine roosts with significant colonies have been regularly monitored in Kentucky, Tennessee, and North Carolina, but for the most part no regular monitoring is in place for

[2] Personal communication. 2010. Richard C. Stark, Fish and Wildlife Biologist, U.S. Fish and Wildlife Service, Oklahoma Ecological Services Field Office, 9014 East 21st Street, Tulsa, OK 74129.

[3] Personal communication. 2010. Barbara S. Douglas, Senior Endangered Species Biologist, U.S. Fish and Wildlife Service, West Virginia Field Office, 694 Beverly Pike, Elkins, WV 26241.

[4] Personal communication. 2010. Dan Nolfi, Biological Science Technician, Resource Management and Science, Great Smoky Mountains National Park, 107 Park Headquarters Road, Gatlinburg, TN 37738.

[5] Personal communication. 2010. Brooke Slack, Bat Ecologist, Kentucky Department of Fish and Wildlife Resources, #1 Sportsman's Lane, Frankfort, KY 40601.

[6] Personal communication. 2010. Steven C. Thomas, National Park Service Monitoring Program Leader, Cumberland Piedmont Network, P.O. Box 8, Mammoth Cave, KY 42259.

[7] Personal communication. 2010. Jim Kennedy, Conservation Specialist, Bat Conservation International, P.O. Box 162603, Austin, TX 78716; Personal communication. 2010. Dan Nolfi, Resource Management and Science, Great Smoky Mountains National Park, 107 Park Headquarters Road, Gatlinburg, TN 37738.

Rafinesque's big-eared bats. Agencies generally prioritize listed species, thus financial and other resources are often lacking for baseline survey and monitoring activities for non-federally protected species.

Second, much of the range of Rafinesque's big-eared bat is devoid of karst features; in these areas bats roost in tree hollows and manmade structures (Bennett and others 2008, Mirowsky and others 2004, Trousdale 2011). These sites present special challenges for monitoring. In bottomland hardwood forests, Rafinesque's big-eared bats often switch roost trees (Carver and Ashley 2008, Clark 2003, Gooding and Langford 2004, Rice 2009, Stevenson 2008) making it difficult to know which tree to monitor. Lastly, due to cavity configuration and other logistics associated with tree roosts, it is difficult to observe and count bats entering and exiting these types of roosts, particularly during winter months (Rice 2009). Additionally, mark-recapture models for estimating populations are not generally used for bats due to the low recapture rates of banded bats (O'Shea and Bogan 2003).

STATUS

Ozark Big-Eared Bat

Although the Townsend's big-eared bat has been listed as a species of least concern (LC) by the World Conservation Union's 2004 IUCN Red List of Threatened Species (International Union for Conservation 2010), the Ozark subspecies is ranked as a critically imperiled subspecies by NatureServe (2008) and is either extirpated or critically imperiled in every State where it occurs (tables 1 and 2). The Ozark big-eared bat was federally listed as endangered

on November 30, 1979, due to its small population size, reduced and limited distribution, and vulnerability to human disturbance (U.S. Fish and Wildlife Service 1984). The original U.S. Fish and Wildlife Service recovery plan was approved in 1984 and included both federally listed subspecies of *Corynorhinus townsendii* (Ozark big-eared bat and Virginia big-eared bat). In 1995, a revised recovery plan was developed to update the information and recovery tasks specifically for Ozark big-eared bats. In this plan, both downlisting (to threatened status) and delisting criteria were outlined (U.S. Fish and Wildlife Service 1995). Habitat loss, disturbance, predation, and pollutants are among the identified threats in the recovery plan (U.S. Fish and Wildlife Service 2008b). Although significant recovery accomplishments have occurred over the 32 years since listing, vulnerability of Ozark big-eared bats to extinction remains high due to the same factors that justified its designation. During the recent 5-year review on the current status of the Ozark big-eared bat, the U.S. Fish and Wildlife Service (2008a) determined that neither the downlisting nor delisting criteria identified in the current recovery plan (U.S. Fish and Wildlife Service 1995) had been met, and that the Federal endangered status of the species was still valid because significant threats to this species persist. For example, although additional essential caves have been discovered and protected since the time of listing, not all known caves have been afforded some form of protection, e.g., a cave gate/grill, signs, fee-title purchase, conservation easement. In addition to the threats that justified the original listing designation, vandalism, human population growth, climate change, and white-nose syndrome have been identified as factors that may impact the future status of Ozark big-eared bat populations (Bogan 2003, Leslie and Clark 2002, Wethington and others 1996; see footnote 2).

Table 1—State-level natural heritage rankings for eastern *Corynorhinus* are listed for the 18 Eastern States in which one or more *Corynorhinus* taxa occur[a]

Corynorhinus taxa	AL	AR	FL	GA	IL	IN	KY	LA	MS	MO	NC	OH	OK	SC	TN	TX	VA	WV
C. townsendii ingens	—	S1	—	—	—	—	—	—	—	SX	—	—	S1	—	—	—	—	—
C. townsendii virginianus	—	—	—	—	—	—	S1	—	—	—	S1	—	—	—	—	—	S1	S2
C. rafinesquii	S2	S3	S2	S3?	S1	SH	S3	S3/S4	S2	SU	S3	SH	S1	S2?	S3	S3	S2	S1

— = not applicable.

AL = Alabama; AR = Arkansas; FL = Florida; GA = Georgia; IL = Illinois; IN = Indiana; KY = Kentucky; LA = Louisiana; MS = Mississippi; MO = Missouri; NC = North Carolina; OH = Ohio; OK = Oklahoma; SC = South Carolina; TN = Tennessee; TX = Texas; VA = Virginia; WV = West Virginia.

[a] The conservation status of a species or ecosystem is designated by a number from 1 to 5, preceded by a letter reflecting the appropriate geographic scale of the assessment (S = subnational). The numbers have the following meaning: 1 = critically imperiled; 2 = imperiled; 3 = vulnerable; 4 = apparently secure; 5 = secure; X = presumed extinct or extirpated; H = possibly extinct or extirpated; U = unrankable; ? = inexact numeric rank.

Source: NatureServe (2008).

Table 2—Designations from Comprehensive Wildlife Conservation Strategies prepared by State wildlife agencies are shown for eastern *Corynorhinus* that occur in 18 Eastern States; designation terminology is not consistent among States, making it difficult to compare status between States[a]

State	C. townsendii ingens	C. townsendii virginianus	C. rafinesquii
Alabama	—	—	Species of greatest conservation need; highest conservation concern; P1
Arkansas	Species of greatest conservation need; critically imperiled; S1; endangered	—	Species of greatest conservation need; imperiled; S2
Florida	—	—	Species of greatest conservation need
Georgia	—	—	Species of greatest conservation need; high priority species; rare
Illinois	—	—	Species of greatest conservation need; endangered
Indiana	—	—	Species of greatest conservation need; special concern
Kentucky	—	Species of greatest conservation need; critically imperiled/stable; S1; endangered	Species of greatest conservation need; vulnerable/stable; S3
Louisiana	—	—	Not listed
Mississippi	—	—	Species of greatest conservation need; needs timely conservation action; tier 2
Missouri	Extirpated/endangered	—	Not listed
North Carolina	—	Priority wildlife species; endangered	Priority wildlife species; threatened
Ohio	—	—	Species of greatest conservation need; species of concern
Oklahoma	Species of greatest conservation need; tier 1; endangered	—	Species of greatest conservation need; tier 2; special concern
South Carolina	—	—	Priority species; high; endangered
Tennessee	—	Species of greatest conservation need; potentially occurring; SP	Species of greatest conservation need; rare and uncommon; S3; special concern (deemed in need of management)
Texas	—	—	Priority species; threatened
Virginia	—	Species of greatest conservation need; tier 2; endangered	Species of greatest conservation need; tier 1; endangered
West Virginia	—	Species of greatest conservation need; S2; endangered	Species of greatest conservation need; S1

— = not applicable.

[a] The conservation status of a species or ecosystem is designated by a number from 1 to 5, preceded by a letter reflecting the appropriate geographic scale of the assessment (S = subnational). The numbers have the following meaning: 1 = critically imperiled; 2 = imperiled; 3 = vulnerable; 5 = secure; X = presumed extinct or extirpated; H = possibly extinct or extirpated; U = unrankable; ? = inexact numeric rank.

Source: Alabama Department of Conservation and Natural Resources (2005); Anderson (2006); D.J. Case & Associates (2005); Florida Fish and Wildlife Conservation Commission (2005); Georgia Department of Natural Resources (2005); Illinois Department of Natural Resources (2005); Kentucky's Comprehensive Wildlife Conservation Strategy (2010); Lester and others (2005); Mississippi Museum of Natural Science (2005); Missouri Department of Conservation (2005); North Carolina Wildlife Resources Commission (2005); Ohio Department of Natural Resources, Division of Wildlife (2005); Oklahoma Department of Wildlife Conservation (2005); South Carolina Department of Natural Resources (2005); Tennessee Wildlife Resources Agency (2005); Texas Parks and Wildlife Department (2005); Virginia Department of Game and Inland Fisheries (2005); West Virginia Division of Natural Resources (2006).

Virginia Big-Eared Bat

The Virginia big-eared bat is ranked as an imperiled subspecies by NatureServe (2008) and are either critically imperiled or imperiled in every State where they occur (tables 1 and 2). Virginia big-eared bats have been listed as a federally endangered species and managed as such by the U.S. Fish and Wildlife Service since 1979 (U.S. Fish and Wildlife Service 1984). As noted above, the original U.S. Fish and Wildlife Service recovery plan was approved in 1984 and included both federally listed subspecies of *Corynorhinus townsendii* (Virginia big-eared bat and Ozark big-eared bat). Virginia big-eared bats were originally listed as federally endangered due to small population size, limited distribution, and vulnerability to human disturbance (U.S. Fish and Wildlife Service 1984). Habitat loss, disturbance, predation, and pollutants are among the identified threats in the recovery plan (U.S. Fish and Wildlife Service 2008b). The U.S. Fish and Wildlife Service in its 1984 recovery plan outlined criteria for downlisting to threatened status, which they believed could be achieved through long-term roost site protection, subsequent stable or increasing populations over a 5-year period, protection of foraging areas, and establishing a monitoring program.

According to the 5-year review, the recovery plan is in need of revision to address current species information, including genetics, distribution, and emerging threats (U.S. Fish and Wildlife Service 2008b). Although the recovery potential for the Virginia big-eared bat is relatively high, at this time three of the four approved recovery criteria have not been met. Thus, the U.S. Fish and Wildlife Service currently recommends retaining endangered listing status because gains made in cave protection and population increases do not sufficiently offset continuing and emerging threats to the species (U.S. Fish and Wildlife Service 2008b). Mortality from wind turbines, white-nose syndrome, predation, vandalism, and natural changes in cave conditions pose potential emerging threats to Virginia big-eared bats in addition to those that were originally listed (U.S. Fish and Wildlife Service 2008b).

Rafinesque's Big-Eared Bat

Although they are widely distributed over much of the Southeastern United States, Rafinesque's big-eared bats have never been considered common (Barbour and Davis 1969, Harvey 1999, Whitaker and Hamilton 1998). Globally, Rafinesque's big-eared bats are listed as a species of LC by the World Conservation Union's IUCN Red List of Threatened Species (Arroyo-Cabrales and Castaneda 2008), but are ranked as a vulnerable species by NatureServe (2008). NatureServe (2008) does not provide consistent State ranks (table 1) and no rangewide statistics on trends are available, but four States (Georgia, West Virginia, South

Carolina, and Tennessee) have reported population declines based on sound documentation. Populations in Indiana and Ohio probably have been extirpated (Arroyo-Cabrales and Castaneda 2008). Four other States (Alabama, Arkansas, Illinois, and North Carolina) reported suspected declines (Arroyo-Cabrales and Castaneda 2008).

Rafinesque's big-eared bats are identified on State priority species lists within the State wildlife action plans of every State within their range, except Louisiana and Missouri (table 2) and considered a species of special concern by U.S. Fish and Wildlife Service (2010). The U.S. Forest Service Southern Region designates them as sensitive species (U.S. Department of Agriculture Forest Service 2009). Because this species is known or suspected to be declining in more than half (10 out of 18) of the States within its range, the U.S. Fish and Wildlife Service is currently conducting a rangewide review of the species (Arroyo-Cabrales and Castaneda 2008).[8]

DISCUSSION

Baseline data on distribution and status of Ozark and Virginia big-eared bat populations were established in the years following Federal listing. Subsequent work to locate new colonies has resulted in discovery of a limited number of additional sites. Although it is unlikely that many new sites will be found, field investigations for new locations are warranted. For example, in 2002, Virginia big-eared bats were found using abandoned mine portals in Fayette County, WV, within the National Park Service's New River Gorge National River (Johnson and others 2003). This was a new locality and the first documented occurrence of Virginia big-eared bats using this habitat type (Johnson and others 2003). Importantly, genetic analyses indicate that this population is genetically distinct (Johnson and others 2003, Piaggio and others 2009b).

Because these endangered taxa have high-site fidelity and low tolerance to disturbance, protection of each known cave roost has contributed significantly to recovery of individual bat colonies (U.S. Fish and Wildlife Service 2008a). The Federal "endangered" status provides regulatory protection for the Ozark and Virginia big-eared bats and facilitates the application of resources (personnel and money) toward their recovery. Because these populations are small and disjunct, vulnerability of these taxa to catastrophic events, e.g., white-nose syndrome, is high. These factors also contribute to problems that may occur due to reduced gene flow among populations. Research on phylogeny of the Townsend's big-eared bat subspecies in the Eastern United States and effects

---

[8] Personal communication. 2010. Mike Armstrong, U.S. Fish and Wildlife Biologist, U.S. Fish and Wildlife Service, 330 W. Broadway, Frankfort, KY 40601.

of isolation are likely to provide some of the most relevant management information to maintain viable populations in the future (Piaggio and others 2011).

For Rafinesque's big-eared bat, there is a wealth of new data on distribution and other aspects of its natural history, although much of it is not yet in the published literature (Bayless and Clark 2009, Rice 2009, Stevenson 2008). Recent investigations have focused on bottomland hardwood forests of the Coastal Plain regions (Trousdale 2011). Even so, many gaps in our knowledge of this species' distribution remain for both this region and more interior parts of the range. For example, there are few records of winter hibernacula in the Coastal Plain regions of the Eastern United States and few summer records in interior regions. An absence of this species in the Piedmont of coastal States appears when records are individually plotted, but it is not clear whether this is an artifact of sampling. More field work to accurately delineate the distribution is needed.

Because Rafinesque's big-eared bats are more widespread than the other eastern big-eared bats and use a much broader range of roosts (structurally, seasonally, and geographically), baseline inventory and monitoring is more challenging. The status of this species remains unclear. Roosting habits and unknown aspects of demography confound efforts to devise a reliable means of assessing their status. Estimating abundance of bats, necessary for establishing baselines and for documenting change in population size, typically relies on complete enumeration (Kunz and Parsons 2009). Counting methods for bats roosting in caves and mines have been established and have been used in some cases for Rafinesque's big-eared bats (see footnote 6). However, for the more widely dispersed populations occurring in forested areas, a method of estimating populations needs to be established. Given that Rafinesque's big-eared bats have preferences for certain tree species [e.g., *Nyssa* spp. and bald cypress (*T. distichum*)] and structural types of tree roosts (extensive hollows in large diameter trees), it may be possible to develop structure-based monitoring (Clark 2003, Kunz and Parsons 2009). For example, tracking abundance, characteristics, and distribution of mature cypress-gum swamp forest could provide an index to abundance in that habitat type.

Mature bottomland hardwood forest has experienced significant declines in the past (Miller and others 2011) and loss of this forest type continues in some areas. Loss of mature stands of bottomland forests, especially those containing cypress-gum communities, likely decreases number of roosts available for Rafinesque's big-eared bat which may have a detrimental effect on population numbers. Monitoring of mature bottomland hardwood forest may provide information about potential for Rafinesque's

big-eared bat distribution and data that can assist with population status assessments. Using Forest Inventory and Analysis (FIA) data derived by the U.S. Forest Service may be one approach for beginning to understand distribution of potential roosting areas (Miller and others 2011), but care should be taken with pooled FIA data as they may not capture the local impacts of forest growth and loss trends. North Carolina, for example, lost 5.5 percent of its forests between 1990 and 2002. However, at the county level, some counties lost between 25 and 35 percent of their forests in that time period (Brown 2004). Additionally, colonies of Rafinesque's big-eared bats that roost and forage in forested wetlands may be significantly affected by small-scale forest loss because this species does not move far from roosts for foraging or overwintering (Clark 2003, Clark and Black 1977, Rice 2009).

Although Rafinesque's big-eared bat populations are not as isolated as Ozark and Virginia big-eared bats, there appears to be potential for reduced gene flow, indicating a need for more research on phylogenetics of Rafinesque's big-eared bats (Piaggio and others 2011). Remnants of mature bottomlands that are not connected by forested corridors may create an isolating effect similar to the disjunct populations with Townsend's big-eared bat in the Eastern United States. Additionally, the gap in the Piedmont region may isolate interior populations from those in the Coastal Plain. This work is now possible due to recently developed microsatellite markers for Rafinesque's big-eared bat (Piaggio and others 2009a) which provide variability for estimation of population connectivity, demographic parameters, and genetic diversity. This information will be necessary for future status determinations.

ACKNOWLEDGMENTS

We thank those who contributed data to update range and distribution information for Rafinesque's big-eared bats. Many records were provided by participants working on a conservation strategy for this species at two workshops in 2008 and 2009. Partial funding was provided by the National Fish and Wildlife Foundation (Protecting America's Bats—III project no. 2008-0094-000), the Offield Family Foundation, and the Beneficia Foundation. Two anonymous referees and T. Bayless provided valuable comments on an earlier draft.

LITERATURE CITED

Alabama Department of Conservation and Natural Resources, Wildlife and Freshwater Fisheries Division. 2005. Conserving Alabama's wildlife: a comprehensive strategy. Montgomery, AL. 322 p.

Anderson, J.E., ed. 2006. Arkansas wildlife action plan. Little Rock, AR: Arkansas Game and Fish Commission. 2,028 p.

Arroyo-Cabrales, J.; Ticul Alvarez Castaneda, S. 2008. *Corynorhinus rafinesquii*. In: IUCN. IUCN red list of threatened species. Version 2009.2. http://www.iucnredlist.org. [Date accessed: February 27, 2010].

Barbour, R.W.; Davis, W.J. 1969. Bats of America. Lexington, KY: The University Press of Kentucky. 286 p.

Bayless, M.L.; Clark, M.K. 2009. A conservation strategy for Rafinesque's big-eared bats and southeastern myotis [Abstract]. In: Proceedings of the Annual Conference of Southeastern Association of Fish and Wildlife Agencies. 63: 219.

Bennett, F.M.; Loeb, S.C.; Bunch, M.S.; Bowerman,W.W. 2008. Use and selection of bridges by Rafinesque's big-eared bats. American Midland Naturalist. 160: 386-399.

Bogan, M.A. 2003. Potential effects of global change on bats. http://geochange.er.usgs.gov/sw/impacts/biology/bats/. [Date accessed: June 30, 2009].

Brown, M.J. 2004. Forest statistics for North Carolina, 2002. Resour. Bull. SRS-88. Asheville, NC: U.S. Department of Agriculture Forest Service, Southern Research Station. 86 p.

Burghardt, J.E. 2003. Bat-compatible closures of abandoned underground mines in the National Park System. In: Proceedings of the 2003 arid southwest lands habitat restoration conference. http://www.dmg.gov/resto-pres/sessions.html. [Date accessed: February 27, 2010].

Carver, B.D.; Ashley, N. 2008. Roost tree use by sympatric Rafinesque's big-eared bats (*Corynorhinus rafinesquii*) and southeastern myotis (*Myotis austroriparius*). American Midland Naturalist. 160: 364-373.

Clark, B.S. 1991. Activity patterns, habitat use, and prey selection by the Ozark big-eared bat (*Plecotus townsendii ingens*). Stillwater, OK: Oklahoma State University. 80 p. Ph.D. dissertation.

Clark, M.K. 1990. Roosting ecology of the eastern big-eared bat, *Plecotus rafinesquii*, in North Carolina. Raleigh, NC: North Carolina State University. 111 p. M.S. thesis.

Clark, M.K. 1999. Results of a bat survey in the Lower Roanoke River Basin. Raleigh, NC: North Carolina Natural Heritage Program, North Carolina Natural Heritage Trust Fund. 36 p.

Clark, M.K. 2003. Survey and monitoring of rare bats in bottomland hardwood forests. In: O'Shea, T.J.; Bogan, M.A., eds. Monitoring trends in bat populations of the United States and territories: problems and prospects. Inf. and Tech. Rep. USGS/BED/TTR-2003-0003. U.S. Department of the Interior, U.S. Geological Survey, Biological Resources Discipline: 79-90. Available from: National Technical Information Service, 5285 Port Royal Road, Springfield, VA 22161 (call toll free 1-800-553-6847), or the Defense Technical Information Center, 8725 Kingman Rd., Suite 0944, Fort Belvoir, VA 22060-6218.

Clark, M.K.; Black, E.H. 1997. Radio-tracking of *Corynorhinus rafinesquii* and *Myotis austroriparius* in South Carolina. Bat Research News. 38: 17-30.

Clark, M.K.; DeTour, D.F. 1995. Survey for Rafinesque's big-eared bat, *Plecotus rafinesquii*, in Florida. [Place of publication unknown]: Nongame Wildlife Program of the Florida Game and Freshwater Fish Commission. [Number of pages unknown].

Clark, M.K.; Lee, D.S. 1987. Big-eared bat, *Plecotus townsendii*, in western North Carolina. Brimleyana. 13: 137-140.

Clark, M.K.; Williams, S.B. 1993. Results of a survey for the eastern big-eared bat (*Plecotus rafinesquii macrotis*) in southeastern Virginia. [Place of publication unknown]: Virginia Department of Game and Inland Fisheries. [Number of pages unknown].

Conner, W.H.; Gosselink, J.G.; Parrando, R.T. 1981. Comparison of the vegetation of three Louisiana swamp sites with different flooding regimes. American Journal of Botany. 68: 320-331.

D.J. Case & Associates. 2005. Indiana comprehensive wildlife strategy. http://www.djcase.com/projects/indiana-comprehensive-wildlife-conservation-strategy. [Date accessed: April 22, 2011].

Elliott, W.R.; Lister, K.B.; Shiver, M.A. 1999. A survey for Ozark big-eared bats (*Corynorhinus townsendii ingens*) and a cave crayfish (*Cambarus aculabrum*) in southern Missouri. Jefferson City, MO: Missouri Department of Conservation. 29 p.

Faulkner, S.P.; Bhattarai, P.; Allen, Y. [and others]. 2009. Identifying baldcypress-water tupelo regeneration classes in forested wetlands of the Atchafalaya Basin, Louisiana. Wetlands. 29(3): 809-817.

Florida Fish and Wildlife Conservation Commission. 2005. Florida's wildlife legacy initiative. Florida's comprehensive wildlife conservation strategy. Tallahassee, FL: Florida Fish and Wildlife Conservation Commission. 540 p.

Georgia Department of Natural Resources. 2005. A comprehensive wildlife conservation strategy for Georgia. Social Circle, GA: Georgia Department of Natural Resources, Wildlife Resources Division. 202 p.

Gooding, G.; Langford, J.R. 2004. Characteristics of tree roosts of Rafinesque's big-eared bat and southeastern bat in northeastern Louisiana. Southwestern Naturalist. 49(1): 61-67.

Graening, G.O.; Harvey, M.J.; Puckette, W.L. [and others]. 2011. Conservation status of the endangered Ozark big-eared bat (*Corynorhinus townsendii ingens*)—a 34-year assessment. Publications of the Oklahoma Biological Survey. 11: 1-16.

Hahn, W.L. 1908. Some habits and sensory adaptations of cave-inhabiting bats. Woods Hole, MA: Biological Bulletin of the Marine Biological Laboratory. 15: 135-193.

Handley, C.O., Jr. 1959. A revision of American bats of the genera *Euderma* and *Plecotus*. Proceedings of the U.S. National Museum. 110: 95-246.

Harvey, M. 1999. Endangered bats of Arkansas: distribution, status and ecology (1998-99). [Place of publication unknown]: Arkansas Game and Fish Commission. [Number of pages unknown].

Harvey, M.J.; Altenbach, J.S.; Best, T.L. 1999. Bats of the United States. Little Rock, AR: Arkansas Game and Fish Commission. 64 p.

Harvey, M.J.; Redman, R.K.; Chaney, C.S. 2006. Endangered bats of Arkansas: distribution, status, and ecology (2005-2006). Project W-56-R. [Place of publication unknown]: Arkansas Game and Fish Commission. [Number of pages unknown].

Harvey, M.J.; Saugey, D.A. 2001. Bats. In: Dickson, J.G., ed. Wildlife of southern forests: habitat and management. Blaine, WA: Hancock House Publishers, Ltd.: 359-371.

Horner, P.A.; Maxey, R.W. 2007. East Texas rare bat survey. Austin, TX: Texas Parks and Wildlife. [Number of pages unknown].

Hurst, T.E.; Lacki, M.J. 1999. Roost selection, population size and habitat use by a colony of Rafinesque's big-eared bats (*Corynorhinus rafinesquii*). American Midland Naturalist. 142(2): 363-371.

Illinois Department of Natural Resources. 2005. Illinois' wildlife action plan. Version 1.0. Springfield, IL: Illinois Department of Natural Resources. 353 p.

International Union for Conservation of Nature. 2010. IUCN red list of threatened species. Version 2010.3. http://www.iucnredlist.org. [Date accessed: September 2].

Johnson, J.B.; Wood, P.B.; Edwards, J.W. 2003. Survey of abandoned mine portals for bats at the New River Gorge National River and Gauley River National Recreation Area, West Virginia. [Place of publication unkown]: National Park Service, New River Gorge National River. 97 p.

Jones, C. 1977. *Plecotus rafinesquii*. Mammalian Species. 69: 1-4.

Kentucky's Comprehensive Wildlife Conservation Strategy. 2010. Kentucky's comprehensive wildlife conservation strategy. Frankfort, KY: Kentucky Department of Fish and Wildlife Resources. http://fw.ky.gov/kfwis/stwg/. [Date accessed: September 17].

Kunz, T.H.; Martin, R.A. 1982. *Plecotus townsendii*. Mammalian Species. 175: 1-6.

Kunz, T.H.; Parsons, S., eds. 2009. Ecological and behavioral methods for the study of bats. 2d ed. Baltimore, MD: Johns Hopkins University Press. 901 p.

Lacki, M.J. 2000. Effect of trail users at a maternity roost of Rafinesque's big-eared bats. Journal of Cave and Karst Studies. 62(3): 163-168.

Lacki, M.J.; Adam, M.D.; Shoemaker, L.G. 1993. Characteristics of feeding roosts of Virginia big-eared bats in Daniel Boone National Forest. Journal of Wildlife Management. 57: 539-543.

Lacki, M.J.; LaDeur, K.M. 2001. Seasonal use of lepidopteran prey by Rafinesque's big-eared bats (*Corynorhinus rafinesquii*). American Midland Naturalist. 145: 213-217.

Leslie, D.M.; Clark, B.S. 2002. Feeding habits of the endangered Ozark big-eared bat (*Corynorhinus townsendii ingens*) relative to prey abundance. Acta Chiropterologia. 4(2): 173-182.

Lester, G.D.; Sorensen, S.G.; Faulkner, P.L. [and others]. 2005. Louisiana comprehensive wildlife conservation strategy. Baton Rouge, LA: Louisiana Department of Wildlife and Fisheries. 455 p.

Martin, C.O.; McCartney, A.S.; Richardson, D. [and others]. 2011. Rafinesque's big-eared bats (*Corynorhinus rafinesquii*) in Mississippi: distribution, current status, and conservation needs. In: Loeb, S.C.; Lacki, M.J.; Miller, D.A., eds. Conservation and management of eastern big-eared bats: a symposium. Gen. Tech. Rep. SRS-145. Asheville, NC: U.S. Department of Agriculture Forest Service, Southern Research Station: 63-73.

Menzel, M.A.; Menzel, J.M.; Ford, W.M. [and others]. 2001. Home range and habitat use of male Rafinesque's big-eared bats (*Corynorhinus rafinesquii*). American Midland Naturalist. 145: 402-408.

Miller, D.A.; Castleberry, S.B.; Stihler, C.W. [and others]. 2011. Conservation and management of eastern big-eared bats (*Corynorhinus* spp.). In: Loeb, S.C.; Lacki, M.J.; Miller, D.A., eds. Conservation and management of eastern big-eared bats: a symposium. Gen. Tech. Rep. SRS-145. Asheville, NC: U.S. Department of Agriculture Forest Service, Southern Research Station: 53-61.

Mirowsky, K.M.; Horner, P.R.; Maxey, R.W.; Smith, S.A. 2004. Distributional records and roosts of southeastern myotis and Rafinesque's big-eared bats in eastern Texas. The Southwestern Naturalist. 72(2): 294-298.

Mississippi Museum of Natural Science. 2005. Mississippi's comprehensive wildlife conservation strategy. Jackson, MS: Mississippi Department of Wildlife, Fisheries and Parks, Mississippi Museum of Natural Science. 329 p.

Missouri Department of Conservation. 2005. Missouri's comprehensive wildlife conservation strategy. Jefferson City, MO: Missouri Department of Conservation. 24 p.

Mohr, C.E. 1933. Observations on the young of cave-dwelling bats. Journal of Mammalogy. 14: 49-53.

NatureServe. 2008. NatureServe explorer: an online encyclopedia of life [Web application]. Version 7.1. http://services.natureserve. org. [Date accessed: February 26, 2010].

North Carolina Wildlife Resources Commission. 2005. North Carolina wildlife action plan. Raleigh, NC: North Carolina Wildlife Resources Commission. 498 p.

Ohio Department of Natural Resources—Division of Wildlife. 2005. Ohio comprehensive wildlife conservation strategy. Columbus, OH: Ohio Department of Natural Resources. 980 p.

Oklahoma Department of Wildlife Conservation. 2005. Oklahoma comprehensive wildlife conservation strategy: planning for the future for Oklahoma's wildlife. Oklahoma City: Oklahoma Department of Wildlife Conservation. 439 p.

Omernik, J.M. 1987. Ecoregions of the conterminous United States. Rev. 1: 7,500,000. Annals of the Association of American Geographers. 77(1): 118-125.

O'Shea, T.J.; Bogan, M.A. 2003. Monitoring trends in bat populations of the United States and territories: problems and prospectus. Inf. and Tech. Rep. USGS/BED/TTR-2003-0003. U.S. Department of the Interior, U.S. Geological Survey, Biological Resources Discipline: 79-90. Available from: National Technical Information Service, 5285 Port Royal Road, Springfield, VA 22161 (call toll free 1-800-553-6847), or the Defense Technical Information Center, 8725 Kingman Rd., Suite 0944, Fort Belvoir, VA 22060-6218.

Piaggio, A.J.; Figuero, J.A.; Perkins, S.L. 2009a. Development and characterization of 15 polymorphic microsatellite loci isolated from Rafinesque's big-eared bat, *Corynorhinus rafinesquii*. Molecular Ecology Resources. 9: 1191-1193.

Piaggio, A.J.; Navo, K.W.; Stihler, C.W. 2009b. Intraspecific comparison of population structure, genetic diversity, and dispersal among three subspecies of Townsend's big-eared bats, *Corynorhinus townsendii townsendii*, *C. t. pallescens*, and the endangered *C. t. virginianus*. Conservation Genetics. 10: 143-159.

Piaggio, A.J.; Saugey, D.A.; Sasse, D.B. 2011. Phylogenetic and population genetic assessment of Rafinesque's big-eared bat (*Corynorhinus rafinesquii*). In: Loeb, S.C.; Lacki, M.J.; Miller, D.A., eds. Conservation and management of eastern big-eared bats: a symposium. Gen. Tech. Rep. SRS-145. Asheville, NC: U.S. Department of Agriculture Forest Service, Southern Research Station: 85-99.

Puckette, W.L. 2009. Cave search and monitoring annual report (October 1, 2007–September 30, 2008). [Place of publication unknown]: U.S. Fish and Wildlife Service, Oklahoma Ecological Service Field Office. [Not paged].

Rice, C.L. 2009. Roosting ecology of *Corynorhinus rafinesquii* (Rafinesque's big-eared bat) and *Myotis austroriparius* (southeastern myotis) in tree cavities found in a northeastern

Louisiana bottomland hardwood forest streambed. Monroe, LA: University of Louisiana. 124 p. M.S. thesis.

South Carolina Department of Natural Resources. 2005. South Carolina comprehensive wildlife conservation strategy. Columbia, SC: South Carolina Department of Natural Resources. 848 p.

Stevenson, C.L. 2008. Availability and seasonal use of diurnal roosts by Rafinesque's big-eared bat and southeastern myotis in bottomland hardwoods of Mississippi. Starkville, MS: Mississippi State University. 109 p. M.S. thesis.

Tennessee Wildlife Resources Agency. 2005. Tennessee's comprehensive wildlife conservation strategy. Nashville, TN: Tennessee Wildlife Resources Agency. 217 p.

Texas Parks and Wildlife Department. 2005. Texas comprehensive wildlife conservation strategy, 2005-2010. Austin, TX: Texas Parks and Wildlife Department. 1,131 p.

Trousdale, A.W. 2011. Ecology of tree-roosting Rafinesque's big-eared bats in the Eastern United States. In: Loeb, S.C.; Lacki, M.J.; Miller, D.A., eds. Conservation and management of eastern big-eared bats: a symposium. Gen. Tech. Rep. SRS-145. Asheville, NC: U.S. Department of Agriculture Forest Service, Southern Research Station: 27-38.

Trousdale, A.W.; Beckett, D.C. 2004. Seasonal use of bridges by Rafinesque's big-eared bat, *Corynorhinus rafinesquii*, in southern Mississippi. Southeastern Naturalist. 3: 103-112.

Trousdale, A.W.; Beckett, D.C. 2005. Characteristics of tree roosts of Rafinesque's big-eared bat (*Corynorhinus rafinesquii*) in southeastern Mississippi. American Midland Naturalist. 154: 442-449.

U.S. Department of Agriculture Forest Service. 2009. Eastern regional forester's sensitive species list. http://www.fs.fed.us/r9/wildlife/tes/. [Date accessed: September 17, 2010].

U.S. Fish and Wildlife Service. 1984. A recovery plan for the Ozark big-eared bat and Virginia big-eared bat. Fort Snelling, MN: U.S. Fish and Wildlife Service. 119 p.

U.S. Fish and Wildlife Service. 1995. Ozark big-eared bat (*Plecotus townsendii ingens* [Handley]) revised recovery plan. Tulsa, OK: U.S. Fish and Wildlife Service. 51p.

U.S. Fish and Wildlife Service. 2008a. Ozark big-eared bat (*Corynorhinus townsendii ingens*) 5-year review: summary and evaluation. Tulsa, OK: U.S. Fish and Wildlife Service. 40 p.

U.S. Fish and Wildlife Service. 2008b. Virginia big-eared bat (*Corynorhinus townsendii virginianus*): 5-year review: summary and evaluation. Elkins, WV: U.S. Fish and Wildlife Service. 20 p.

U.S. Fish and Wildlife Service. 2009. Virginia big-eared bat (*Corynorhinus townsendii virginianus*) plan for controlled holding, propagation, and reintroduction. Elkins, WV: U.S. Fish and Wildlife Service. 24 p.

U.S. Fish and Wildlife Service. 2010. Species profile: Rafinesque's big-eared bat (*Plecotus rafinesquii*). http://ecos.fws.gov/speciesProfile/profile/speciesProfile.action?spcode=A0AI#status. [Date accessed: September 15].

Virginia Department of Game and Inland Fisheries. 2005. Virginia's comprehensive wildlife conservation strategy. Richmond, VA: Virginia Department of Game and Inland Fisheries. 712 p.

West Virginia Division of Natural Resources. 2006. It's about habitat . . . (WV wildlife conservation action plan). Elkins, WV: West Virginia Division of Natural Resources, Wildlife Resources Section. 965 p.

Wethington, T.A.; Leslie, D.M.; Gregory, M.S.; Wethington, M.K. 1996. Prehibernation habitat use and foraging activity by endangered Ozark big-eared bats (*Plecotus townsendii ingens*). American Midland Naturalist. 135: 218-230.

Whitaker, J.O.; Hamilton, W.J., Jr. 1998. Mammals of the Eastern United States. Ithaca, NY: Cornell University Press. 583 p.

ECOLOGY OF TREE-ROOSTING RAFINESQUE'S BIG-EARED BATS IN THE EASTERN UNITED STATES

Austin W. Trousdale, Assistant Professor of Biology, Lander University, Department of Biology, Greenwood, SC 29649

Abstract—Tree-roosting big-eared bats in the Eastern United States are represented solely by Rafinesque's big-eared bat (*Corynorhinus rafinesquii*). Studies of tree-roosting *C. rafinesquii* have been largely descriptive rather than manipulative, and habitat selection of this species beyond the scale of the roost tree is poorly understood. Regardless, general trends in the roosting ecology of this species are evident. *C. rafinesquii* roosts primarily in hollows of live trees in bottomland hardwood forest, especially tupelos, e.g., *Nyssa aquatica* and *N. sylvatica*. Dimensions, type, access, and thermal characteristics are factors in cavity selection. In selecting tall trees (mean = 21.5 m) of large diameter (mean = 110 cm), *C. rafinesquii* conforms to broad trends in roosting preferences of North American forest-dwelling bats. Roost trees are often clumped in distribution, enabling bats to travel short distances (usually < 1 km) among day roosts. *C. rafinesquii* exhibits low daily fidelity to tree roosts yet remains faithful to tree roosts over years. Overlap in species of trees used for roosting exists between *C. rafinesquii* and syntopic southeastern myotis (*Myotis austroriparius*), but differences in tree size and position of individuals within cavities may minimize interspecific competition. The interaction of roost abundance and quality with local population dynamics warrants further attention, as does the importance of internal microclimate to the value of roosts. Incorporating the needs of tree-roosting big-eared bats in reforestation strategies remains an important conservation measure in bottomland hardwood forests in the Eastern United States.

INTRODUCTION

Tree-roosting big-eared bats (genus *Corynorhinus*) in the Eastern United States are represented exclusively by Rafinesque's big-eared bat (*C. rafinesquii*). Although Fellers and Pierson (2002) documented Townsend's big-eared bat (*C. townsendii*) roosting in tree hollows in Western North America, populations of eastern subspecies (*C. t. ingens* and *C. t. virginianus*) roost exclusively in caves and abandoned mines (Kunz and Martin 1982, Whitaker and Hamilton 1998). The distribution of *C. rafinesquii* includes Southeastern and South Central North America (Barbour and Davis 1969), and use of hollow trees of various species as roosts by *C. rafinesquii* has been reported for populations across its range (table 1). Tree roosts are especially important to *C. rafinesquii* in the Mississippi Alluvial Valley and Gulf Coastal Plain where caves are scarce (Clark 2003). This bat also roosts in anthropogenic structures (Clark 1990; England and others 1990; Ferrara and Leberg 2005a, 2005b; Hoffmeister and Goodpaster 1963; Lance and others 2001) and in some areas moves among artificial structures and trees (Lance and others 2001, Trousdale and Beckett 2005, Trousdale and others 2008).

Roosts are essential to all bats, and characteristics of these roost types have driven morphological, physiological, and behavioral adaptations in bats (Kunz and Lumsden 2003). Likewise, constraints in availability of roosts at local scales, and the vulnerability of bats while using these structures, may adversely affect bat populations (O'Shea and Bogan 2003). Descriptions of roosts, and an understanding of their spatio-temporal use by bats, are important for design and implementation of effective conservation strategies (Sherwin

and others 2005). Bats that use cavities and crevices of trees require forests to meet their ecological demands, because tree-roosting bats move among roosts to varying extents, both among and within species, and because roosts are dynamic in quality and quantity (Barclay and Kurta 2007). Kalcounis-Rüeppell and others (2005) quantitatively summarized patterns in characteristics of trees used by cavity- and crevice-roosting bats in North America. These authors established a "profile" of roost trees as being relatively tall with large diameter at breast height (d.b.h.) and located within comparatively open stands of high snag density and close proximity to water relative to randomly available trees.

Here I summarize the current state of knowledge of the behavior of tree-roosting *C. rafinesquii* in the Eastern United States. I discuss the extent to which *C. rafinesquii* conforms to the generalizations of Kalcounis-Rüeppell and others (2005), and review the dimensions and thermal characteristics of cavity roosts reported. In addition to roost selection, I explore behavioral patterns, such as roost switching and sociality, of tree-roosting populations of this species. My synthesis of these diverse but interrelated topics identifies broad generalizations that hopefully enhance the formulation and implementation of conservation strategies for *C. rafinesquii* in the Eastern United States.

ROOST SELECTION

The proximate goal of resource selection by an individual organism is to satisfy an immediate need, while the ultimate goal is to maximize fitness. Hence, the decision of where

Citation for proceedings: Loeb, Susan C.; Lacki, Michael J.; Miller, Darren A., eds. 2011. Conservation and management of eastern big-eared bats: a symposium. Gen. Tech. Rep. SRS-145. Asheville, NC: U.S. Department of Agriculture, Forest Service, Southern Research Station. 157 p.

Table 1—Tree species used as day roosts by *Corynorhinus rafinesquii* by geographic location in the Eastern United States; all reported roosting sites were in tree cavities

Tree species		Location
Scientific name	Common name	
Carya glabra	Pignut hickory	Mississippi[a]
C. ovata	Shagbark hickory	Mississippi[a]
Fagus grandifolia	American beech	Kentucky[b], Mississippi[a], Texas[c]
Liquidambar styraciflua	Sweetgum	Mississippi[a], South Carolina[d]
Magnolia grandiflora	Southern magnolia	Mississippi[e]
Nyssa aquatica	Water tupelo	Arkansas[f], Louisiana[g,h], Mississippi[e]
N. sylvatica	Black tupelo	Louisiana[i], Mississippi[a]
Platanus occidentalis	American sycamore	Mississippi[a]
Populus deltoides	Eastern cottonwood	Mississippi[a]
Quercus alba	White oak	Mississippi[a]
Q. lyrata	Overcup oak	Mississippi[a]
Q. michauxii	Swamp chestnut oak	Mississippi[a]
Q. nigra	Water oak	Mississippi[a]
Q. pagoda	Cherrybark oak	Mississippi[a]
Q. phellos	Willow oak	Mississippi[a]
Taxodium distichum	Bald cypress	Georgia[k], Louisiana[h], Mississippi[a], South Carolina[d]

[a] Stevenson (2008).

[b] Hurst and Lacki (1999).

[c] Mirowsky and others (2004).

[d] Lucas (2009).

[e] Trousdale and Beckett (2005).

[f] Cochran (1999).

[g] Gooding and Langford (2004).

[h] Rice (2009).

[i] Carver and Ashley (2008).

[j] Lance and others (2001).

[k] Clement and Castleberry (2008).

to roost should reflect the physiological and ecological requirements of bats (Barclay and Kurta 2007). These may differ within an individual, e.g., by season, and among individuals, e.g., pregnancy versus lactation. Unfortunately, authors have often pooled data among bat species and demographic categories in an effort to increase statistical power, potentially obscuring important distinctions (Miller and others 2003). Further, knowledge of the tree-roosting ecology of *C. rafinesquii* has been derived from observational rather than manipulative studies. Consequently, demonstrated roost selection has more often been inferential rather than experimental. Lastly, habitat selection of tree-roosting bats is hierarchical (Perry and others 2008); however, most studies of *C. rafinesquii* have worked at small spatial scales, i.e., the roost tree and habitat immediately surrounding it. Thus, we are still a long way from a comprehensive view of the tree-roosting ecology of *C. rafinesquii*.

Species and Condition of Roost Trees

Roosts of *C. rafinesquii* in trees have been located by opportunistic searches of tree hollows and other structures and by radio tracking individuals following their capture on the wing or at other roosts. Studies have largely been conducted in bottomland hardwood forests (BLHs) within and adjacent to river floodplains. Although the species is by no means restricted to these systems (Hurst and Lacki 1999, Menzel and others 2001), BLHs contain the tree species that dependably form cavities in which bats may roost (Stevenson 2008). Past land use may continue to influence tree roost selection by *C. rafinesquii*; individual trees currently used by the species might have been spared from logging due to their relative inaccessibility. Association of *C. rafinesquii* with water tupelo (*Nyssa aquatica*) and black tupelo (*N. sylvatica*) has been well documented (table 1). *Nyssa* is capable of producing extensive hollows due to erosion of the heartwood (Burns and Honkala 1990). Roosts have also been reported from other cavity-forming BLH trees that provide entrances either at the base or in branch scars higher on the stem (table 1). Based on this diversity, *C. rafinesquii* more likely discriminates among individual trees by physical characteristics rather than species (Stevenson 2008), a generalization that can be extended to forest-roosting bats inhabiting different ecosystems (Barclay and Kurta 2007, Vonhof and Barclay 1996).

C. rafinesquii roosts are located within live trees more frequently than snags (Carver and Ashley 2008, Lucas 2009, Mirowsky and others 2004, Stevenson 2008, Trousdale and Beckett 2005). A proximal advantage of selecting a cavity in a live tree instead of a snag may be enhanced thermoregulation facilitated by a more stable microclimate. In forested systems outside the distribution of *C. rafinesquii*, live trees better retain heat at night than do snags (Coombs and others 2010, Paclik and Weidinger 2007), although cavities in live trees appear to heat more slowly than ones in snags (Kalcounis and Brigham 1998). Cavity-denning endotherms may benefit from the relative thermal stability conferred by the intact, water-containing woody tissue of a live tree (McComb and Noble 1981), and it follows that the comparatively thick bark of a live stem may enable its hollow to better retain heat (Sedgeley and O'Donnell 1999). The ultimate benefit to *C. rafinesquii* of preferentially roosting in live trees may be formation and maintenance of "roost networks" that facilitate information transfer (Rhodes 2007, Rhodes and others 2006). This outcome is perhaps better facilitated when structures remain intact and available to the local population for generations (Barclay and Kurta 2007).

Dimensions of Roost Trees

Authors typically comment on the large size of roost trees used by *C. rafinesquii* (table 2). Aside from possessing sizeable cavities and accessible entrances, the most important characteristic of trees appears to be that they possess relatively large d.b.h. Average d.b.h. of roost trees reported from studies across the species' distribution was 110 cm

($n = 7$; see table 2). When compared to random trees, tree roosts of *C. rafinesquii* had greater d.b.h. in western Tennessee (Carver and Ashley 2008) and in Congaree Swamp, SC (Lucas 2009). In Louisiana, tree diameter and internal height of the cavity of tree roosts were significantly, positively related (Rice 2009). Average height of roost trees reported from studies across the species' distribution was 21 m ($n = 5$; see table 2). Trees containing maternity roosts were significantly taller than random trees in BLHs (Lucas 2009). Although tree height may simply reflect age, in some cases the advantage to an individual bat in locating the tree at the stand and landscape scale likely increases with height (Britzke and others 2003, Campbell and others 1996, Vonhof and Barclay 1996). A taller stem may also enable the individual bat to roost at sufficient height to benefit from increased solar exposure on the stem and by extension, a warmer roost microclimate, although this relationship has been much better documented in crevice and bark roosts (Kurta and others 1993) than for roosts in hollows. Considering that hollow trees occupied by *C. rafinesquii* have greater cavity volumes than unoccupied hollow trees (Clement and Castleberry 2008), a preference for taller trees may highlight the importance of a spacious cavity (Gellman and Zielinski 1996, Lucas 2009, Stevenson 2008).

Cavity Type, Dimensions, and Orientation

C. rafinesquii is known to roost in tree cavities accessible via triangular basal entrances (fig. 1). Use of this roost type by *C. rafinesquii* is predominant in BLHs in Louisiana (Gooding and Langford 2004), northern Mississippi (Stevenson 2008), the Francis Beidler Forest in South Carolina (Clark 2003), western Tennessee (Carver and Ashley 2008), and eastern Texas (Mirowsky and others 2004). However, *C. rafinesquii* also makes use of trunk hollows (Trousdale and Beckett 2005) or cavities accessible via a single or multiple openings higher on the stem. The terms "upper bole cavities" (Lucas 2009) and "chimneys" (Rice 2009) have also been used to describe these roosts. Trunk hollows made up nearly all tree roosts of *C. rafinesquii* found in a mixed hardwood-pine system in southern Mississippi (Trousdale and Beckett 2005) and a considerable portion of roosts found in Congaree Swamp (Lucas 2009). The configuration of trunk hollows may promote a more favorable microclimate for entering and maintaining torpor when food is scarce, considering that cold air entering a trunk hollow would sink whereas warm air entering a basal cavity would rise (Rice 2009). Trunk hollows are probably less likely than basal cavities to be inundated by winter flooding, a predictable occurrence in BLHs (Clark 2003, Gooding and Langford 2004), and seasonally high water coincides with absence of *C. rafinesquii* from basal cavities in Louisiana (Rice 2009). If trunk hollows were also less accessible to predators of *C. rafinesquii* than basal openings (Cochran 1999), allowing bats to enter deep torpor more safely (Lausen and Barclay

Table 2—Means (SE), unless noted otherwise, of characteristics of tree roosts of *Corynorhinus rafinesquii* in the Eastern United States

Author (date)	Tree height	D.b.h.	Cavities	Height of cavity roost[a]	Width of cavity entrance	Interior height of cavity
n	*m*	*cm*	*no.*	--------------------*cm*--------------------		*m*
Carver and Ashley (2008) 24	26 (1.3)	124 (7.5)	1.6 (0.1)	120 (15.3)	40 (5.2)	9 (0.7)
Clark (1990) 1			1	170	70	5
Cochran (1999) 3	11 (1.9)[b]	155 (26.8)	1			
Gooding and Langford (2004) 44	25 (0.6)	120 (3.5)	1.7 (0.1)	132 (10)	48 (4)	6 (0.3)
Lance and others (2001) 4		{59, 103}				
Lucas (2009) 43	27 (1.3)	107 (4.7)				
Rice (2009) 26		82 (25.4)[b]		104 (54.5)	46 (40.3)	6 (2.8)
Stevenson (2008) 49		100 (5.4)		70 (9.4)	40 (4.5)	6 (0.5)
Trousdale and Beckett (2005) 14	18 (10.7)[b]	79 (18.9)	1.1 (0.4)			

D.b.h. = diameter at breast height.

[a] Largest entrance if multiple cavities.

[b] SD reported by author.

2006), these cavities would be particularly valuable winter roosts. Supporting data are lacking for this hypothesis.

It remains unclear whether minimum dimensions of cavity entrance, height, and width must be met for *C. rafinesquii* to use potential roost trees. Cochran (1999) noted use of two water tupelos by *C. rafinesquii* that each contained a central cavity accessible only via a knothole opening ≤ 8 cm across. Some cavity-roosting bats, e.g., the New Zealand long-tailed bat (*Chalinolobus tuberculatus*), Leisler's bat or the lesser noctule (*Nyctalus leisleri*), and the noctule bat (*N. noctula*), prefer spaces with smaller entrances, perhaps to reduce susceptibility to predation or convective heat loss (Ruczyński 2006, Sedgeley 2001). Internal cavity height averaged 6.4 m across studies (*n* = 5; see table 2). Stevenson (2008) found that this variable was greater by > 300 cm for tree roosts than for cavities from which *C. rafinesquii* was not documented. *C. rafinesquii* appears to use a fission-fusion behavioral strategy (see below) that may compensate for occasional limitations in cavity volume that prevent all members of a colony from roosting concurrently.

Orientation of a cavity opening is a predictor of roost use by some tree-roosting bats, e.g., big brown bats (*Eptesicus fuscus*) (Kalcounis and Brigham 1998), but this variable apparently does not influence occupancy by *C. rafinesquii*. For *C. rafinesquii*, aspect did not differ from random in Louisiana (Gooding and Langford 2004), and a wide range of values for orientation were reported in Mississippi (Trousdale and Beckett 2005). In western Tennessee, *C. rafinesquii* roosts tend toward a north-northeasterly direction, but orientation of these cavities does not differ from that of available tree hollows (Carver and Ashley 2008).

Location of the roost cavity in relation to forest structure is potentially relevant to its use by bats. Cavities used by maternity colonies of *Nyctalus* and *C. tuberculatus* are located further from nearby trees or other vegetation and placed higher off the ground than are unused cavities (Ruczyński 2006, Sedgeley and O'Donnell 1999). A cavity situated in a relatively uncluttered environment would seem to be particularly important to *C. rafinesquii*, as other plecotine bats are known to find potential roosts using

Figure 1—A roost tree of *Corynorhinus rafinesquii* accessed through a basal entrance. (Photo by Brian D. Carver)

echolocation while hovering at close distance from the stem surface (Ruczyński and others 2009). Nevertheless, canopy closure at tree roosts of *C. rafinesquii* is high (> 90 percent) in southeastern Mississippi, although proximity to streambeds may reduce clutter surrounding cavity entrances (Trousdale and Beckett 2005).

Thermal Characteristics of Roosts

Over much of its distribution, *C. rafinesquii* is resident year round within its home range (Jones 1977, Mirowsky and others 2004, Rice 2009, Stevenson 2008, Trousdale 2008), yet roosting ecology of the species has traditionally been studied during warmer seasons (but see Rice 2009) and the temperature requirements of the species inside tree roosts are only beginning to be understood [see Hurst and Lacki (1999) for discussion of temperature relations of *C. rafinesquii* in a cave roost]. As endotherms that possess a large surface area to volume ratio, bats are susceptible to a high rate of heat loss (Speakman and Thomas 2003). For insectivorous bats living in the temperate zone this problem is compounded by the seasonal scarcity of prey. *C. rafinesquii* uses daily torpor to reduce its energy expenditure, especially during cool weather, and enters hibernation during extended periods of unfavorable conditions (Hoffmeister and Goodpaster 1963, Jones 1977, Pearson 1962). Success of this strategy depends on an individual roosting at a temperature just low enough to reduce energetic requirements and within a space effectively insulated to minimize fluctuations in temperature that could trigger periodic arousals (Neuwiler 2000).

Data on temperatures inside *C. rafinesquii* roosts have been collected from relatively little of the species' distribution. However, *C. rafinesquii* generally favors roosts with microclimates that are stable over the short term. Changes in air temperature apparently prompt *C. rafinesquii* to alter roosting locations within and among caves and anthropogenic structures (Hurst and Lacki 1999, Jones and Suttkus 1975). In North Carolina, daily spring temperatures fluctuate more in abandoned buildings than in *C. rafinesquii* roost tree cavities (Clark 1990). Rice (2009) performed the most comprehensive study of thermal relations of tree-roosting *C. rafinesquii* to date. He compared internal temperatures of *Nyssa* among individual trees grouped by cavity opening type: trunk, basal, or both and found that temperatures within all cavity types were generally milder than ambient conditions regardless of season. During summer, mean cavity temperature (approximately 22 °C) did not differ by tree configuration, nor did *C. rafinesquii* select any particular cavity type. However, on occasions when the previous night's temperature did not exceed 17 °C, individuals largely restricted tree use to roosts with trunk hollows only. During winter, temperatures in trunk hollows were more stable than those of basal cavities and cavities with both basal and chimney openings. Within these trunk hollows, *C. rafinesquii* seasonally adjusts its relative roosting height, occupying the bottom half of the cavity in late summer and roosting near the top during winter. Such movement is consistent with the prediction that each individual selects the height in the chamber where microclimate is most favorable (fig. 2), assuming that temperatures are stratified within the cavity (Rice 2009).

Thermal characteristics of a tree cavity or crevice appear to play an important role in resource selection by insectivorous bats that roost in these structures (Barclay and Kurta 2007, Crampton and Barclay 1998, Kalcounis and Brigham 1998, Kerth and others 2000, Sedgeley 2001). Microclimates of vacant roosts of *C. tuberculatus*, situated in knotholes, possess higher minimum temperatures than do available, presumably unused cavities. These sites also sustain their

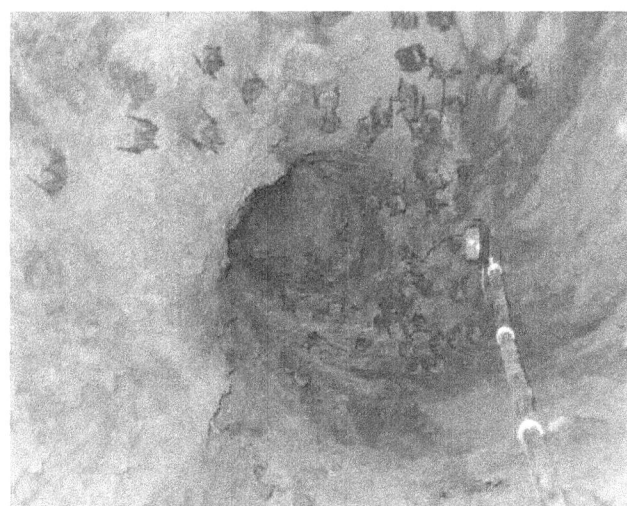

Figure 2—View of a maternity colony of *Corynorhinus rafinesquii* with bats roosting at varying heights inside the cavity of a tree roost. (Photo by Christopher L. Rice)

maximum temperatures and humidity for a significantly longer time than cavities of both comparable and dissimilar configurations (Sedgeley 2001). Bat pups are born naked; as neonates their ability to thermoregulate is poor (Kunz 1987). When adult females leave the roost to forage, pups are dependent upon heat retained within the roosting structure to remain warm (Ruczyński 2006, Sedgeley 2001). A thicker stem wall should promote a more stable internal microclimate (Sedgeley and O'Donnell 1999); this variable is positively correlated with tree d.b.h. of *C. rafinesquii* roosts in Mississippi (Stevenson 2008). An optimal roost for a social species like *C. rafinesquii* should also provide space sufficient to contain the group size at which thermoregulatory benefits materialize; future research efforts are needed to elucidate this relationship. *C. rafinesquii* forms large aggregations when roosting in anthropogenic structures during cold weather (Hoffmeister and Goodpaster 1963) and some tree-roosting populations conform to this pattern. For example, Stevenson (2008) reported a very large group (> 200 individuals) roosting within a tree cavity in winter in Mississippi.

The geographic distribution of *C. rafinesquii* includes areas that experiences very warm, humid summers. Heat stress could, therefore, become a problem during the day and may influence roost selection by individuals and colonies during this time of year. Relief from heat may help explain why this bat often roosts underneath concrete bridges in summer, even when tree cavities are located nearby (Trousdale and others 2008). Roosting flush with the concrete wall of a compartment enables an individual to contact a surface considerably cooler than ambient daytime temperatures (Ferrara and Leberg 2005a). This pattern has not been demonstrated using summer temperature data from tree roosts of *C. rafinesquii*. However, avoidance of heat stress may influence *E. fuscus* in Saskatchewan, Canada, to roost in live-tree cavities that are cooler than afternoon ambient temperatures and cooler in the mornings than cavities in snags (Kalcounis and Brigham 1998).

Distribution of Tree Roosts

Authors have noted that tree roosts of *C. rafinesquii* tend to be located in close proximity to one another (Carver and Ashley 2008, Clark 2003, Gooding and Langford 2004, Trousdale and Beckett 2005). However, mean distance to nearest cavity tree is greater for tree roosts than nonused trees in Mississippi (Stevenson 2008), implying a more uniform dispersion pattern. In contrast, Lucas (2009) identified a clustered dispersion pattern in Congaree Swamp. Roost distribution across the landscape is likely affected by a combination of hydrology and soil chemistry that shape floodplain plant communities (Mitsch and Gosselink 2007), and characteristics of the biology of cavity-forming trees tolerant of these conditions (Burns and Honkala

1990). Past land use, e.g., timber extraction, that shapes current vegetation is also influential in determining the distribution of tree roosts (Gooding and Langford 2004). Patches of forest with a high density of potential roosts may be characterized by even-aged stands of older trees (Clark 2003), and inhabiting these areas is likely advantageous to *C. rafinesquii*. Given that *C. rafinesquii* has a low wing loading and aspect ratio (Jones and Suttkus 1971, Norberg and Rayner 1987), the flight of this species is highly maneuverable but also energetically expensive (Norberg and Rayner 1987). Therefore, individuals would be expected to travel conservative distances when foraging or commuting (Entwistle and others 1996, Lacki and Dodd 2011). For example, in a population that uses both trees and bridges as day roosts, individuals moved among sequential tree roosts at an average of approximately 360 m (Trousdale and Beckett 2005), comparable to 234 m moved in BLHs in Louisiana (Rice 2009). Furthermore, roosts of solitary males and females in maternity colonies are concentrated in areas averaging < 3 ha, based on minimum convex polygons surrounding point locations of trees used by *C. rafinesquii* in Congaree National Park (Lucas 2009).

Selection at Stand and Landscape Scales

Species composition of stands seems to more consistently influence roost selection of *C. rafinesquii* than does stand structure. The dominant vegetation within these stands generally corroborates the notion that *C. rafinesquii* depends on BLHs or, at least, a substantial hardwood component within the forest types used for roosting. In a mixed pine-hardwood system, 10 of 14 *C. rafinesquii* roosts were in stands characterized by the U.S. Forest Service as bottomland hardwood, with the remainder in loblolly pine (*Pinus taeda*) or laurel oak (*Quercus laurifolia*)-willow oak (*Q. phellos*) stands (Trousdale and others 2008). In old-growth BLHs, > 76 percent of roosts were located in a bald cypress (*Taxodium distichum*)-water tupelo-Carolina ash (*Fraxinus caroliniana*) association, with separate complexes of sweetgum (*Liquidambar styraciflua*), hackberry (*Celtis laevigata*), and beech (*Fagus grandifolia*) also represented (Lucas 2009). A Louisiana stand containing 44 roosts used over a 3-month span was almost entirely comprised of water tupelo (Gooding and Langford 2004).

The relative importance of basal area and canopy closure in determining suitability of stands for roost locations of *C. rafinesquii* is somewhat ambiguous. Gooding and Langford's (2004) study area supported a mean basal area of 72.3 m^2/ha, while that of Stevenson (2008) was 21.8 m^2/ha. Plots containing tree roosts of *C. rafinesquii* have a higher basal area (120.5 m^2/ha) than do random plots (71.3 m^2/ha) in Congaree National Park (Lucas 2009). Conversely, neither basal area nor canopy closure differs between stands containing roosts and random trees in Mississippi, where canopy closure exceeds 90 percent (Stevenson 2008). Although *C. rafinesquii* follows the general trend of roosting in stands with a high density of potential roosts (i.e., snags, Kalcounis-Rüeppell and others 2005), its preferences apparently do not include open canopies surrounding roosts.

Stand- and landscape-level characteristics seem to be less important than those of individual roost trees for *C. rafinesquii* (Lucas 2009, Stevenson 2008). In Mississippi, distance to the nearest hollow tree is the only landscape variable that predicts cavity use by *C. rafinesquii*, as tree roosts are located farther away from these structures than nonroost trees (Stevenson 2008). In Lucas' (2009) analysis, multivariate models that included landscape variables poorly explained roost selection in this species. However, maternity colonies roost in trees significantly farther from edge habitat than random trees, suggesting that interior forest is more optimal for cavity formation or associated with less predation pressure (Lucas 2009). Selection of roost trees away from edge habitats to reduce predation pressure has been purported for foliage-roosting red bats (*Lasiurus borealis*) (Hutchinson and Lacki 2000).

ROOST FIDELITY AND SOCIAL BEHAVIOR

During warm weather, *C. rafinesquii* shows limited day-to-day fidelity to tree roosts but strong fidelity to the patch of forest enclosing these roosts within and across years (Clark 2003, Gooding and Langford 2004, Lucas 2009, Stevenson 2008, Trousdale and Beckett 2005). In this sense, roost fidelity for the species is scale-dependent and resembles behavior of other bats, e.g., big brown bat (Willis and others 2003), Indiana bat (*Myotis sodalist*) (Kurta and Murray 2002), and tri-colored bat (*Perimyotis subflavus*) (Veilleux and Veilleux 2004). The lower daily fidelity that *C. rafinesquii* shows to tree roosts compared to anthropogenic roosts may be due to these bats seeking optimal microclimates relative to ambient temperatures and the individual's physiological demands (Kerth and others 2000, Rice 2009). Alternatively, if roosts in buildings or under bridges possess a more stable, agreeable microclimate than do tree cavities, or are subject to relaxed parasitism or predation pressures, such circumstances may remove incentives to switch more frequently. Lewis (1995) argued that relative densities of roosts within the landscape or their differences in degree of permanence could lead bats to adjust roost fidelity accordingly; *C. rafinesquii* met this prediction where roosts varied in these attributes over the landscape (Trousdale and others 2008). Proximity to adequate foraging habitat surrounding a cave also likely contributes to fidelity of *C. rafinesquii* to a cave in Kentucky (Hurst and Lacki 1999). In contrast, where multiple roosts are concentrated within the same forest patch, recurrent roost switching by *C. rafinesquii* and other insectivorous bats involves distances

that are likely insufficient to reflect shifts in food supply, thus, having little impact on an individual's daily energy budget (Barclay and Kurta 2007).

The low roost fidelity of *C. rafinesquii* to trees and the tendency of female individuals to roost communally during the reproductive season have important consequences for the species' behavior. Fenton (2003) argued that a colony is more than simply an aggregation of individuals that cooccupy a roost at a given time, but rather a discrete social unit. Groups of *C. rafinesquii* that cohabit tree cavities appear to be colonies that exhibit fission-fusion social behavior (Kerth and König 1999). Marked individuals associate together among multiple roosts in southeastern Mississippi (Trousdale and Beckett 2005), and several other investigations (Gooding and Langford 2004, Lucas 2009, Rice 2009) noted variable group size within and among roosts based on daytime cavity surveys or exit counts. Fluidity in composition may be an adaptation, used in combination with recurrent roost switching, to maintain group cohesion despite differences in size of cavities among trees (Willis and Brigham 2004, Willis and others 2006). In proximal terms, the mobility that such loosely cohesive group living offers might benefit the individual by decreasing parasite loads and lessening the length of time before odors accumulate within a roost, potentially attracting predators guided by olfaction (Lewis 1995). Regular movement among tree cavities may also familiarize the individual with locations of alternate roosts (Kurta and others 2002). In this context, behavior of individuals which habitually roost apart from a colony, e.g., adult males, would be less subject to these factors and, predictably, should switch roosts less often (Rice 2009, Trousdale 2008). Data from Congaree National Park indicate that solitary-roosting *C. rafinesquii* show higher fidelity to roosts than bats from maternity colonies (Lucas 2009).

RELATIONSHIP WITH *MYOTIS AUSTRORIPARIUS*

In the Coastal Plain and the Mississippi Alluvial Valley, *C. rafinesquii* is syntopic with southeastern myotis (*M. austroriparius*), another rare bat dependent on hollow trees in BLHs for roosting (Barbour and Davis 1969, Clark 2003, Gooding and Langford 2004). Southeastern myotis and *C. rafinesquii* cohabit tree hollows throughout most of the year in Louisiana (Rice 2009) and Mississippi (Stevenson 2008), and share anthropogenic roosts during winter in Texas (Mirowsky and others 2004). However, resource partitioning between the two species with respect to roosts likely occurs (table 3). In western Tennessee, tree diameter is greater for roosts of *C. rafinesquii* than those trees used only by southeastern myotis, and the particular trees that the two species share are among the largest

Table 3—Grand means of tree roost characteristics of *Corynorhinus rafinesquii* and *Myotis austroriparius* in the Eastern United States

Bat species	Tree height	D.b.h.	Cavities	Height of cavity roost[a]	Width of cavity entrance	Interior height of cavity
	m	*cm*	*no.*	------------------------cm------------------------		*m*
CORA	21	110	1.3	119	49	6
MYAU	26[b]	93[c]	1.3[d]	103[e]	39[f]	7[g]

D.b.h. = diameter at breast height; CORA = *Corynorhinus rafinesquii*; MYAU = *Myotis austroriparius*.

[a] Largest entrance if multiple cavities.

[b] *n* = 2. Carver and Ashley (2008), Gooding and Langford (2004).

[c] *n* = 5. Carver and Ashley (2008), Gooding and Langford (2004), Hofmann and others (1999), Rice (2009), Stevenson (2008).

[d] *n* = 3. Carver and Ashley (2008), Gooding and Langford (2004), Hofmann and others (1999).

[e] *n* = 5. Carver and Ashley (2008), Gooding and Langford (2004), Hofmann and others (1999), Rice (2009), Stevenson (2008).

[f] *n* = 5. Carver and Ashley (2008), Gooding and Langford (2004), Hofmann and others (1999), Rice (2009), Stevenson (2008).

[g] *n* = 4. Carver and Ashley (2008), Hofmann and others (1999), Rice (2009), Stevenson (2008).

used by southeastern myotis, but among the smallest used by *C. rafinesquii* (Carver and Ashley 2008). Stevenson (2008) noted a similar partitioning of tree roosts, with southeastern myotis preferring smaller trees (d.b.h. = 40 to 70 cm) than *C. rafinesquii* as solitary roosts, whereas overall, *C. rafinesquii* more frequently roosting in the largest cavity-bearing trees (≥ 100 cm d.b.h.) in the study area. Overall, *C. rafinesquii* select trees ≥ 80 cm in d.b.h., whereas southeastern myotis use trees at random with regard to species and size (Stevenson 2008). In some cases, the two species may discriminate between tree roosts based on number and type of cavities present. *C. rafinesquii* tree roosts average 1.58 entrances compared to 1.0 opening in roosts of southeastern myotis (Carver and Ashley 2008). In Louisiana, southeastern myotis roost in hollow trees with basal openings exclusively, while *C. rafinesquii* roost in trees with basal and trunk hollows (Rice 2009).

Further evidence of niche separation between *C. rafinesquii* and southeastern myotis comes from observations of their roosting habits and behavior. Although the two species both use particular trees during summer in western Tennessee, they do so on different occasions (Carver and Ashley 2008). In Mississippi, maternity colonies of *C. rafinesquii* and southeastern myotis segregated, occupying different individual trees (Stevenson 2008). Investigators have noted that groups of *C. rafinesquii* tend to roost along the sides of the chamber and easily awaken, but southeastern myotis generally cluster at the "ceiling" and typically appear less disturbed by cavity inspections (Carver and Ashley 2008, Stevenson 2008), although Rice (2009) noted that larger aggregations of day-roosting southeastern myotis

are often awake (evident by their noise) even prior to observation. Differences in dispersion of individuals inside cavity chambers suggest each species' own microclimatic preferences within roosts (Rice 2009).

IMPLICATIONS FOR CONSERVATION AND MANAGEMENT

The effects of timber extraction on roost selection by *C. rafinesquii* have not been examined. Although selective logging could be used to avoid particular cavity-containing trees, exposure of roosts to increased solar radiation would likely occur due to thinning of the canopy (Carver and Ashley 2008). This change is potentially important considering that basal area in stands surrounding tree roosts may be high (Gooding and Langford 2004, Lucas 2009), as is canopy closure (Gooding and Langford 2004, Trousdale and Beckett 2005). Opening up the canopy and midstory, whether by mechanical thinning or by fire (in upland areas), could alter the microclimate within cavities of relict trees, as well as encourage the growth of understory vegetation surrounding the entrance to cavities (Carver and Ashley 2008).

In locations where BLHs remain largely intact, I encourage managers interested in conserving habitat of *C. rafinesquii* to promote survival and recruitment of large (≥ 50-cm d.b.h.) trees, especially water tupelo and black tupelo. American beech, sweetgum, American sycamore (*Platanus occidentalis*), and bald cypress are species of trees that should also receive priority due to their propensity to form cavities (Stevenson 2008). Where BLHs have been removed and reforestation is an option, I recommend that managers propagate these trees. In floodplains, restoration of a hydrologic regime with pulses of inundation to seasonally promote hydric/hypoxic soil conditions should especially favor tupelo and bald cypress trees over less-desirable species. Within a matrix of commercial timber lands, streamside management zones or buffer strips adjacent to wetland habitats could help fulfill this purpose. As reforestation proceeds, deployment of artificial structures that mimic natural cavities in configuration and dimensions might aid in nurturing local populations of *C. rafinesquii* until suitable trees develop natural cavities for roosting.

CONCLUSIONS

C. rafinesquii roosts in hollow trees possessing cavities accessible either by basal entrances or upper bole openings. Like other forest-dwelling bats, *C. rafinesquii* seems to prefer tall, live trees with large diameters often situated in areas with higher densities of potential tree roosts. In contrast to trees occupied by other cavity-roosting bat species of North America (Kalcounis-Rüppell and others 2005), those of *C. rafinesquii* are surrounded by closed canopies. The apparent fission-fusion behavior of colonies, coupled with low daily fidelity shown by individuals and colonies to tree roosts highlights the importance of stands surrounding cavity trees. Opportunity to enhance thermoregulation may lead *C. rafinesquii* to seek different tree roosts at different times of the year and may possibly explain movements by individuals in the short term. Based on my review of the literature, conservation of tree-roosting *C. rafinesquii* populations is not likely to succeed by merely protecting single-roosting structures. Instead, managers will benefit by identifying, retaining, and understanding the relationships among patches of roosting habitat, consistent with the blueprint for successful conservation of diverse tree-roosting bats that depend on forests (Brigham 2007).

Effective survey techniques to assess and monitor abundance of *C. rafinesquii* in BLHs and upland mixed pine-hardwood systems continue to be developed (Clark 2003, Clement and Castleberry 2011). Research should be directed toward investigating the interaction of roost density and quality with the local abundance of bats. For example, the efficacy of artificial roosts to adequately compensate for diminished supply of natural structures should be evaluated. The extent to which the internal microclimate of a tree cavity determines its value as a roost should be measured during the reproductive season and winter hibernation period, and applied to both solitary individuals and colonies. As fragmentation of remaining forests continues, and managed lands are expected to provide multiple uses on decreasing available acreage, roost selection at larger spatial scales should be explored.

LITERATURE CITED

Barbour, R.W.; Davis, W.H. 1969. Bats of America. Lexington, KY: University of Kentucky Press. 286 p.

Barclay, R.M.R.; Kurta, A. 2007. Ecology and behavior of bats roosting in tree cavities and under bark. In: Lacki, M.J.; Hayes, J.P.; Kurta, A., eds. Bats in forests: conservation and management. Baltimore, MD: Johns Hopkins University Press: 17-59.

Brigham, R.M. 2007. Bats in forests: what we know and what we need to learn. In: Lacki, M.J.; Hayes, J.P.; Kurta, A., eds. Bats in forests: conservation and management. Baltimore, MD: Johns Hopkins University Press: 1-15.

Britzke, E.R.; Harvey, M.J.; Loeb, S.C. 2003. Indiana bat, *Myotis sodalis*, roosts in the Southern United States. Southeastern Naturalist. 2: 235-242.

Burns, R.M.; Honkala, B.H., eds. 1990. Silvics of North America. Washington, DC: U.S. Department of Agriculture Forest Service. 654 p. 2 vols.

Campbell, L.A.; Hallett, J.G.; O'Connell, M.A. 1996. Conservation of bats in managed forests: use of roosts by *Lasionycteris noctivagans*. Journal of Mammalogy. 77: 976-984.

Carver, B.D.; Ashley, N. 2008. Roost tree use by sympatric Rafinesque's big-eared bats (*Corynorhinus rafinesquii*) and southeastern myotis (*Myotis austroriparius*). American Midland Naturalist. 160: 364-373.

Clark, M.K. 1990. Roosting ecology of the eastern big-eared bat, *Plecotus rafinesquii*, in North Carolina. Raleigh, NC: North Carolina State University. 112 p. M.S. thesis.

Clark, M.K. 2003. Survey and monitoring of rare bats in bottomland hardwood forests. In: O'Shea, T.J.; Bogan, M.A., eds. Monitoring trends in bat populations of the United States and territories: problems and prospects. Inf. and Tech. Rep. USGS/BRD/ITR-2003-003. Reston, VA: U.S. Geological Survey, Biological Resources Discipline: 1-274.

Clement, M.J.; Castleberry, S.E. 2008. Distribution and habitat relationships of Rafinesque's big-eared bat in the Coastal Plain of Georgia [Abstract]. In: Eighteenth colloquium on the conservation of mammals in the Southeastern United States. http://warnell.forestry.uga.edu/Big_Eared_Bats/documents/abstract_example.pdf. [Date accessed: April 26, 2011].

Clement, M.J.; Castleberry, S.E. 2011. Comparison of survey methods for Rafinesque's big-eared bats. In: Loeb, S.C.; Lacki, M.J.; Miller, D.A., eds. Conservation and management of eastern big-eared bats: a symposium. Gen. Tech. Rep. SRS-145. Asheville, NC: U.S. Department of Agriculture Forest Service, Southern Research Station: 147-158.

Cochran, S.M. 1999. Roosting and habitat use by Rafinesque's big-eared bat and other species in a bottomland hardwood forest ecosystem. Jonesboro, AR: Arkansas State University. 50 p. M.S. thesis.

Coombs, A.B.; Bowman, J.; Garroway, C.J. 2010. Thermal properties of tree cavities during winter in a northern hardwood forest. Journal of Wildlife Management. 74: 1875-1881.

Crampton, L.H.; Barclay, R.M.R. 1998. Selection of roosting and foraging habitat by bats in different-aged aspen mixed wood stands. Conservation Biology. 12: 1347-1358.

England, D.R.; Saugey, D.A.; McDaniel, V.R. [and others]. 1990. Observations on the life history of Rafinesque's big-eared bat, *Plecotus rafinesquii*, in southern Arkansas [Abstract]. Bat Research News. 30: 62-63.

Entwistle, A.C.; Racey, P.A.; Speakman, J.R. 1996. Habitat exploitation by a gleaning bat, *Plecotus auritus*. Philosophical Transactions: Biological Sciences. 351: 921-931.

Fellers, G.M.; Pierson, E.D. 2002. Habitat use and foraging behavior of Townsend's big-eared bat (*Corynorhinus townsendii*) in coastal California. Journal of Mammalogy. 83: 167-177.

Fenton, M.B. 2003. Science and the conservation of bats: where to next? Wildlife Society Bulletin. 31: 6-15.

Ferrara, F.J.; Leberg, P.L. 2005a. Characteristics of positions selected by day-roosting bats under bridges in Louisiana. Journal of Mammalogy. 86: 729-735.

Ferrara, F.J.; Leberg, P.L. 2005b. Influence of investigator disturbance and temporal variation on surveys of bats roosting under bridges. Wildlife Society Bulletin. 33: 1113-1122.

Gellman, S.T.; Zielinski, W.J. 1996. Use by bats of old-growth redwood hollows on the north coast of California. Journal of Mammalogy. 77: 255-265.

Gooding, G.; Langford, J.R. 2004. Characteristics of tree roosts of Rafinesque's big-eared bat and southeastern bat in northeastern Louisiana. Southwestern Naturalist. 49: 61-67.

Hoffmeister, D.F.; Goodpaster, W.W. 1963. Observations on a colony of big-eared bats, *Plecotus rafinesquii*. Transactions of the Illinois Academy of Science. 55: 87-89.

Hofmann, J.E.; Gardner, J.E.; Krejca, J.K.; Garner, J.D. 1999. Summer records and a maternity roost of the southeastern myotis (*Myotis austroriparius*) in Illinois. Transactions of the Illinois State Academy of Science. 92: 95-107.

Hurst, T.E.; Lacki, M.J. 1999. Roost selection, population size, and habitat use by a colony of Rafinesque's big-eared bats (*Corynorhinus rafinesquii*). American Midland Naturalist. 142: 363-371.

Hutchinson, J.T.; Lacki, M.J. 2000. Selection of day roosts by red bats in mixed mesophytic forests. Journal of Wildlife Management. 64: 87-94.

Jones, C. 1977. *Plecotus rafinesquii*. Mammalian Species. 69: 1-4.

Jones, C.; Suttkus, R.D. 1971. Wing loading in *Plecotus rafinesquii*. Journal of Mammalogy. 52: 458-460.

Jones, C.; Suttkus, R.D. 1975. Notes on the natural history of *Plecotus rafinesquii*. Occasional Papers of the Museum of Natural History. Baton Rouge, LA: Louisiana State University. 47: 1-14.

Kalcounis, M.C.; Brigham, R.M. 1998. Secondary use of aspen cavities by tree-roosting big brown bats. Journal of Wildlife Management. 62: 603-611.

Kalcounis-Rüeppell, M.C.; Psyllakis, J.M.; Brigham, R.M. 2005. Tree roost selection by bats: an empirical synthesis using meta-analysis. Journal of Wildlife Management. 33: 1123-1132.

Kerth, G.; König, B. 1999. Fission, fusion, and nonrandom associations in female Bechstein's bats (*Myotis bechsteinii*). Behaviour. 136: 1187-1202.

Kerth, G.; Weissmann, K.; König, B. 2000. Day roost selection in female Bechstein's bats (*Myotis bechsteinii*): a field experiment to determine the influence of roost temperature. Oecologia. 126: 1-9.

Kunz, T.H. 1987. Post-natal growth and energetics of suckling bats. In: Fenton, M.B.; Racey, P.; Rayner, J.V.M., eds. Recent advances in the study of bats. Cambridge, UK: Cambridge University Press: 395-420.

Kunz, T.H.; Lumsden, L.F. 2003. Ecology of cavity and foliage roosting bats. In: Kunz, T.H.; Fenton, M.B., eds. Bat ecology. Chicago: University of Chicago Press: 3-89.

Kunz, T.H.; Martin, R.A. 1982. *Plecotus townsendii*. Mammalian Species. 175: 1-6.

Kurta, A.; Kath, J.; Smith, E.L. [and others]. 1993. A maternity roost of the endangered Indiana bat (*Myotis sodalis*) in an unshaded, hollow, sycamore tree (*Platanus occidentalis*). American Midland Naturalist. 130: 405-407.

Kurta, A.; Murray, S.W. 2002. Philopatry and migration of banded Indiana bats (*Myotis sodalis*) and effects of radio transmitters. Journal of Mammalogy. 83: 585-589.

Kurta, A.; Murray, S.W.; Miller, D.H. 2002. Roost selection and movements across the summer landscape. In: Kurta, A.; Kennedy, J., eds. The Indiana bat: biology and management of an endangered species. Austin, TX: Bat Conservation International, Inc.: 118-129.

Lacki, M.J.; Dodd, L.E. 2011. Diet and foraging behavior of *Corynorhinus* in Eastern North America. In: Loeb, S.C.; Lacki, M.J.; Miller, D.A., eds. Conservation and management of eastern big-eared bats: a symposium. Gen. Tech. Rep. SRS-145. Asheville, NC: U.S. Department of Agriculture Forest Service, Southern Research Station: 39-52.

Lance, R.F.; Hardcastle, B.T.; Talley, A.; Leberg, P.L. 2001. Day-roost selection by Rafinesque's big-eared bat (*Corynorhinus rafinesquii*) in Louisiana forests. Journal of Mammalogy. 82: 166-172.

Lausen, C.L.; Barclay, R.M.R. 2006. Benefits of living in a building: big brown bats (*Eptesicus fuscus*) in rocks versus buildings. Journal of Mammalogy. 87: 362-370.

Lewis, S.E. 1995. Roost fidelity of bats: a review. Journal of Mammalogy. 76: 481-496.

Lucas, J.S. 2009. Roost selection by Rafinesque's big-eared bats (*Corynorhinus rafinesquii*) in Congaree National Park—a multiscale approach. Clemson, SC: Clemson University. 48 p. M.S. thesis.

McComb, W.C.; Noble, R.E. 1981. Microclimates of nest boxes and natural cavities in bottomland hardwoods. Journal of Wildlife Management. 45: 284-289.

Menzel, M.A.; Menzel, J.M.; Ford, W.M. [and others]. 2001. Home range and habitat use of male Rafinesque's big-eared bats (*Corynorhinus rafinesquii*). American Midland Naturalist. 145: 402-408.

Miller, D.A.; Arnett, E.B.; Lacki, M.J. 2003. Habitat management for forest-roosting bats of North America: a critical review of habitat studies. Wildlife Society Bulletin. 31: 30-44.

Mirowsky, K.; Horner, P.A.; Maxey, R.W.; Smith, S.A. 2004. Distributional records and roosts of southeastern myotis and Rafinesque's big-eared bat in eastern Texas. Southwestern Naturalist. 49: 294-298.

Mitsch, W.J.; Gosselink, J.G. 2007. Wetlands. 4th ed. Hoboken, NJ: John Wiley. 600 p.

Neuweiler, G. 2000. The biology of bats. New York: Oxford University Press. 310 p.

Norberg, U.M.; Rayner, J.M.V. 1987. Ecological morphology and flight in bats (Mammalia: Chiroptera): wing adaptations, flight performance, foraging strategy and echolocation. Philosophical Transactions of the Royal Society of London, Series B, Biological Sciences. 316: 335-427.

O'Shea, T.J.; Bogan, M.A. 2003. Introduction. In: O'Shea, T.J.; Bogan, M.A., eds. Monitoring trends in bat populations of the United States and territories: problems and prospects. Inf. and Tech. Rep. USGS/BRD/ITR-2003-003. Reston, VA: U.S. Geological Survey, Biological Resources Discipline: 1-274. Available from: National Technical Information Service, 5285 Port Royal Road, Springfield, VA 22161 (call toll free 1-800-553-6847), or the Defense Technical Information Center, 8725 Kingman Rd., Suite 0944, Fort Belvoir, VA 22060-6218.

Paclik, M.; Weidinger, K. 2007. Microclimate of tree cavities during winter nights—implications for roost site selection in birds. International Journal of Biometeorology. 51: 287-293.

Pearson, E.W. 1962. Bats hibernating in silica mines in southern Illinois. Journal of Mammalogy. 43: 27-33.

Perry, R.W.; Thill, R.E.; Leslie, D.E., Jr. 2008. Scale-dependent effects of landscape structure and composition on diurnal roost selection of forest bats. Journal of Wildlife Management. 72: 913-925.

Rhodes, M. 2007. Roost fidelity and fission-fusion dynamics of white-striped free-tailed bats *Tadarida australis*. Journal of Mammalogy. 88: 1252-1260.

Rhodes, M.; Wardell-Johnson, G.W.; Rhodes, M.P.; Raymond, B. 2006. Applying network analysis to the conservation of habitat trees in urban environments: a case study from Brisbane, Australia. Conservation Biology. 20: 861-870.

Rice, C.L. 2009. Roosting ecology of *Corynorhinus rafinesquii* (Rafinesque's big-eared bat) and *Myotis austroriparius* (southeastern myotis) in tree cavities found in a northeastern Louisiana bottomland hardwood forest streambed. Monroe, LA: The University of Louisiana at Monroe. 117 p. M.S. thesis.

Ruczyński, I. 2006. Influence of temperature on maternity roost selection by noctule bats (*Nyctalus noctula*) and Leisler's bats (*N. leisleri*) in Białowieża Primeval Forest, Poland. Canadian Journal of Zoology. 84: 900-907.

Ruczyński, I.; Kalko, E.K.V.; Siemers, B.M. 2009. Calls in the forest: a comparative approach to how bats find tree cavities. Ethology. 115: 167-177.

Sedgeley, J.A. 2001. Quality of cavity microclimate as a factor influencing selection of maternity roosts by a tree-dwelling bat, *Chalinolobus tuberculatus*, in New Zealand. Journal of Applied Ecology. 38: 425-438.

Sedgeley, J.A.; O'Donnell, C.F.J. 1999. Factors influencing the selection of roost cavities by a temperate rainforest bat (Vespertilionidae: *Chalinolobus tuberculatus*) in New Zealand. Journal of Zoology, London. 249: 437-446.

Sherwin, R.E.; Gannon, W.L.; Altenbach, J.S. 2005. Managing complex systems simply: understanding inherent variation in the use of roosts by Townsend's big-eared bat. Wildlife Society Bulletin. 31: 62-72.

Speakman, J.R.; Thomas, D.W. 2003. Physiological ecology and energetics of bats. In: Kunz, T.H.; Fenton, M.B., eds. Bat ecology. Chicago: University of Chicago Press: 430-490.

Stevenson, C.L. 2008. Availability and seasonal use of diurnal roosts by Rafinesque's big-eared bat and southeastern myotis in bottomland hardwoods of Mississippi. Mississippi State, MS: Mississippi State University. 109 p. M.S. thesis.

Trousdale, A.W. 2008. Roosting ecology of Rafinesque's big-eared bat (*Corynorhinus rafinesquii*) in southeastern Mississippi. Hattiesburg, MS: University of Southern Mississippi. 107 p. Ph.D. dissertation.

Trousdale, A.W.; Beckett, D.C. 2005. Characteristics of tree roosts of Rafinesque's big-eared bats (*Corynorhinus rafinesquii*) in southeastern Mississippi. American Midland Naturalist. 154: 442-449.

Trousdale, A.W.; Beckett, D.C.; Hammond, S.L. 2008. Short-term roost fidelity of Rafinesque's big-eared bat (*Corynorhinus rafinesquii*) varies with habitat. Journal of Mammalogy. 89: 477-484.

Veilleux, J.P.; Veilleux, S.L. 2004. Intra-annual and interannual fidelity to summer roost areas by female eastern pipistrelles, *Pipistrellus subflavus*. American Midland Naturalist. 152: 196-200.

Vonhof, M.J.; Barclay, R.M.R. 1996. Roost-site selection and roosting ecology of forest-dwelling bats in southern British Columbia. Canadian Journal of Zoology. 74: 1797-1805.

Whitaker, J.O., Jr.; Hamilton, W.J. 1998. Mammals of the Eastern United States. 3rd ed. Ithaca, NY: Comstock Publishing Associates. 583 p.

Willis, C.K.R.; Brigham, R.M. 2004. Roost switching, roost sharing, and social cohesion: forest-dwelling big brown bats, *Eptesicus fuscus*, conform to the fission-fusion model. Animal Behaviour. 68: 495-505.

Willis, C.K.R.; Kolar, K.A.; Kolar, A.L. [and others]. 2003. Medium- and long-term reuse of trembling aspen cavities as roosts by big brown bats (*Eptesicus fuscus*). Acta Chiropterologica. 5: 85-90.

Willis, C.K.R.; Voss, C.M.; Brigham, R.M. 2006. Roost selection by forest-living female big brown bats (*Eptesicus fuscus*). Journal of Mammalogy. 87: 345-350.

DIET AND FORAGING BEHAVIOR OF *CORYNORHINUS* IN EASTERN NORTH AMERICA

Michael J. Lacki, Professor, University of Kentucky, Department of Forestry, Lexington, KY 40546

Luke E. Dodd, Post-Doctoral Scholar, University of Kentucky, Department of Forestry, Lexington, KY 40546

Abstract—Big-eared bats of the genus *Corynorhinus* occupy a specialized feeding niche due to their possession of enlarged and elongated ears and their use of low-intensity echolocation calls. These adaptations, along with passive listening to locate moving prey, allow *Corynorhinus* to effectively use both gleaning and aerial hawking foraging strategies in specializing on the capture of moths. A total of 114 species/genera and 11 families of moths are recorded in the diet of eastern *Corynorhinus*, along with 11 other orders of insects. Lepidopteran prey comprises > 80 percent volume of the diet of all *Corynorhinus* species. Noctuidae are the most commonly eaten moths at > 39 percent for eastern *Corynorhinus*, with Geometridae, Notodontidae, Sphingidae, and Arctiidae comprising > 10 percent of the culled wings found beneath feeding perches of at least one *Corynorhinus* species. Average maximum wingspan size for all species eaten is 47.0 mm ± 1.3 (SE), and eastern *Corynorhinus* differentially select by size from among available moth prey within the Geometridae, Noctuidae, Sphingidae, Arctiidae, and Saturniidae. Average foraging area size appears to be greater for Rafinesque's big-eared bats (*C. rafinesquii*) (137.4 ha) than for Ozark big-eared bats (*C. townsendii ingens*) (71.5 ha) and average maximum flight distances are shorter for eastern *Corynorhinus* (1 to 6.3 km) than western big-eared bats (*C. t. pallescens*) (14.7 km), which occupy pine forests throughout much of Western United States. Edges at the forest-clearing interface and both forested and riparian corridors are habitats consistently selected by *Corynorhinus* when foraging. Nevertheless, edge habitats are avoided and riparian habitats preferred by most families of moths eaten by eastern *Corynorhinus*, suggesting selection of foraging habitats by *Corynorhinus* is predicated on both structural configuration of the habitat, i.e., availability of vertical and horizontal surface area for gleaning, and the local abundance of preferred moths. The majority (> 71 percent) of moth species eaten by eastern *Corynorhinus* depend entirely on woody plant hosts for their larval development. Nineteen species (16.7 percent) of moths eaten by eastern *Corynorhinus* are pests in the larval stage, thus, these bats may serve as natural controls of pest species in areas where they occur. Long-term conservation of eastern *Corynorhinus* will require managing forested habitat in ways that promote local woody plant diversity, sustaining indirectly the diversity of moth species in landscapes where these bats feed.

INTRODUCTION

North American big-eared bats of the genus *Corynorhinus* are one of five genera that comprise the plecotine group or "long-eared bats" (Koopman and Jones 1970) within the family Vespertilionidae. *Corynorhinus* occupy a specialized feeding niche as lepidopteran specialists (Hurst and Lacki 1997, Lacki and others 2007, Ross 1967), which is facilitated by possession of enlarged and elongated pinnae or ears (Handley 1959); their use of low intensity echolocation calls (Griffin 1958, Grinnell 1963, Obrist and others 1993); and their ability to use passive listening to locate stationary prey (Fenton 1984). These adaptations along with their occurrence in North America, where the number of species of bats that glean is fewer than in other regions of the northern temperate zone (Swift 1998), allow *Corynorhinus* to effectively use both gleaning and aerial hawking foraging strategies in the successful capture of moths (Fenton 1990, Kunz and Martin 1982). Nevertheless, recent studies have added greatly to our understanding of foraging behavior, habitat use, and diet of eastern *Corynorhinus*. In this paper we: (1) overview morphological adaptations associated with foraging in eastern *Corynorhinus*, (2) evaluate data from dietary studies, (3) describe activity patterns as they relate to foraging, (4) review studies that address foraging habitat use and aboveground movement, and (5) discuss the implications of these findings with respect to conservation needs of these bats. Where appropriate, data for Western North American species of *Corynorhinus* are compared, along with findings from studies on other plecotine bats.

MORPHOLOGY AND GLEANING

Plecotine bats, including all bats of the genus *Corynorhinus*, possess a suite of morphological adaptations that facilitate foraging tactics which involve slow-maneuverable flight, where prey can be captured in air or from the surface of objects. The long ears or pinnae are part of an auditory system that is highly sensitive to low-frequency sound, including frequencies below those used in echolocation (Swift 1998). Coles and others (1989) demonstrated that the large pinnae in the brown long-eared bat (*Plecotus auritus*) produce acoustic gains up to 20 dB at frequencies between 8 and 20 kHz. This enhanced sensitivity at low frequencies likely aids in detection of prey moving on substrate surfaces, but also permits *Corynorhinus* species to use low-frequency calls (ca. 20 kHz) of low intensity during echolocation

Citation for proceedings: Loeb, Susan C.; Lacki, Michael J.; Miller, Darren A., eds. 2011. Conservation and management of eastern big-eared bats: a symposium. Gen. Tech. Rep. SRS-145. Asheville, NC: U.S. Department of Agriculture, Forest Service, Southern Research Station. 157 p.

(Grinnell 1963, Kunz and Martin 1982). Plecotine bats, including *Corynorhinus*, also possess enlarged nostrils which are believed to be used in the production of ultrasonic sounds (Howard 1995, Swift 1998). Long ears impart constraints due to the drag produced in flight that results in higher energetic costs (Norberg 1976) especially as flight speeds increase (Rayner 1987). Thus, use of low-frequency sounds during echolocation combined with a slow agile flight, allow *Corynorhinus* to effectively use their enlarged pinnae in locating and capturing prey resting on substrate surfaces, while minimizing energetic costs due to drag.

Corynorhinus possess wingspans and wing areas that result in relatively low wing loadings [Townsend's big-eared bat (*C. townsendii*): 0.052 to 0.087 gr/cm^2, Farney and Fleharty (1969); Rafinesque's big-eared bat (*C. rafinesquii*): 0.057 to 0.077 gr/cm^2, Jones and Suttkus (1971)]. Low wing loadings aid in maneuverability in flight, and in the use of hover-gleaning to catch prey from surfaces (Norberg and Rayner 1987). Wing loadings are higher for newly volant young, due to smaller wing areas (Jones and Suttkus 1971), and this likely hinders flight capability in young bats until the wings are fully developed; around 25 days after birth in brown long-eared bats (De Fanis and Jones 1995).

Swift (1998) has detailed the advantages of gleaning as a foraging strategy. Gleaning bats are not dependent on having insect prey actively flying during foraging bouts, thus, gleaning bats can feed later in the night and at cooler temperatures than bats which rely solely on aerial hawking to capture prey. Barclay (1991) demonstrated that gleaning bats were able to reproduce successfully in cooler climates when aerial-hawking bats did not; he attributed this pattern to the ability of gleaning bats to forage successfully on more nights and for a longer period of the season than aerial-hawking bats. Gleaning also permits larger prey, including moths, to be captured and consumed as they do not have to be handled or carried in flight (Swift 1998). Lacki and others (2007), however, have suggested that even among gleaners there appear to be upper limits to the size of prey captured and eaten. Moths at rest are especially vulnerable to gleaning bats because species that are capable of detecting and reacting to bat calls have few options for escape when at rest (Werner 1981). Existing data indicate that moths have yet to develop adequate defenses against gleaning bats (Swift 1998), and because of this gleaning bats have been labeled "predatory cheaters" in the evolution of bat-moth interactions (Faure and others 1993).

SPECIALIZATION ON LEPIDOPTERA

Lepidopteran prey comprise > 80 percent volume of the diet of all *Corynorhinus* (table 1), consistent with the suggestion that *Corynorhinus* bats are "foraging specialists" (Lacki and

others 2007). Data indicate these bats also feed on 11 other orders of insects, including some at > 10 percent frequency in the diet such as Coeloptera, Diptera, Homoptera, and Blattodea. It is likely that these groups are captured opportunistically. Spiders (Araneae) are a prey group used as an indicator of gleaning in insectivorous bats (Whitaker 2004). In *Corynorhinus*, spiders have only been found in the diet of Virginia big-eared bats (*C. t. virginianus*) and only at ≤ 0.02 percent volume (Sample and Whitmore 1993), further evidence that *Corynorhinus* bats are lepidopteran specialists. Based upon combined data for percent volume and percent frequency, it appears that Townsend's big-eared bat, western big-eared bat (*C. t. pallescens*), and the Virginia big-eared bat eat moths more exclusively than do Rafinesque's big-eared bat and the Ozark big-eared bat (*C. t. ingens*). The diet of the Mexican big-eared bat (*C. t. mexicanus*) has yet to be studied (Tumlison 1992).

Other members of the plecotine group (*Plecotus*) do not exhibit the same degree of specialization for moths observed in *Corynorhinus* (Swift 1998). For example, Lepidoptera are < 41 percent frequency of the diet of brown long-eared bats in Scotland (Swift and Racey 1983), Sweden (Rydell 1989), and Ireland (Shiel and others 1991). Populations of the grey long-eared bat (*P. austriacus*) in Czech Republic eat lepidopterans at only 72 percent frequency of the diet (Bauerova 1982). Swift (1998) hypothesized that the degree of specialization for moths observed in *Corynorhinus*, not seen in other plecotine species, is a direct result of a lower density of gleaning species in North America relative to other temperate zone regions, leading to reduced interspecific competition for the gleaning foraging niche among North American bats.

Early studies of the diet of *Corynorhinus* based their findings on bats captured or collected during flight, resulting in limited data due to difficulty of capture and the tendency for these bats to possess empty stomachs (Ross 1967, Whitaker and others 1977). Ross (1967) concluded from the limited samples obtained that western *Corynorhinus* ate mostly moths and emphasized microlepidopterans (wingspan = 3 to 10 mm) in their diet. Subsequent studies demonstrated that eastern *Corynorhinus* use feeding roosts, i.e., sites where bats perch to eat their prey and discard inedible parts such as wings or elytra, especially along cliffs and canyon walls (Lacki and LaDeur 2001, Lacki and others 1993). Surveys at feeding roosts of eastern *Corynorhinus* have demonstrated consumption of 114 species/genera and 11 families of moths by these bats (appendix). Most species of moths recorded in the diet of these bats are macrolepidopterans, with an average wingspan of 47.0 mm ± 1.3 (SE); much larger than the 6-mm average proposed by Ross (1967) for western big-eared bats. However, microlepidopterans have also been recovered beneath feeding roosts of eastern *Corynorhinus* including Lasiocampidae, Lymantriidae, Megalopygidae, Pyralidae, and Thyatiridae.

Table 1—Average percent volume and percent frequency of insect orders in the diet of *Corynorhinus*

Order	*C. rafinesquii* % v	*C. rafinesquii* % f	*C. t. virginianus* % v	*C. t. virginianus* % f	*C. t. ingens* % v	*C. t. ingens* % f	*C. townsendii*[a] % v	*C. townsendii*[a] % f
Lepidoptera	80.4	89.2	96.4	99.3	85.2	66.5	99.7	96.0
Coleoptera	2.6	41.8	1.8	35.2	3.4	18.9	—	2.6
Diptera	16.6	38.4	1.0	13.6	3.7	6.5	—	1.3
Hymenoptera	tr[b]	3.8	0.9	6.2	1.5	1.3	—	1.3
Neuroptera	—	—	tr	0.4	0.1	0.8	—	1.3
Orthoptera	—	—	—	1.4	—	0.1	—	1.3
Homoptera	0.2	14.0	0.1	—	1.7	2.2	—	—
Hemiptera	tr	5.8	tr	0.6	—	—	0.3	3.4
Trichoptera	tr	1.4	—	—	0.3	1.0	—	—
Odonata	—	—	—	—	—	0.2	—	—
Plecoptera	—	—	tr	—	—	—	—	—
Blattodea	—	—	—	—	—	13.4	—	—

% v = percent volume; % f = percent frequency; — = not found in samples.

[a] Includes data for *C. t. townsendii* and *C. t. pallescens*.

[b] Trace amounts.

Source: Bauer (1992), Dalton and others (1986), Dodd and Lacki (2007), Ellis (1993), Hurst and Lacki (1997), Leslie and Clark (2002), Ross (1967), Sample and Whitmore (1993), Whitaker and others (1977).

Noctuidae are the most commonly eaten moths at > 39 percent of culled wings recovered for all eastern *Corynorhinus*, with Geometridae, Notodontidae, Sphingidae, and Arctiidae comprising > 10 percent of the culled wings found beneath feeding perches of at least one eastern *Corynorhinus* species (table 2). More species of Noctuidae ($n = 62$) have been recorded in the diet of eastern *Corynorhinus* than any other moth family, followed by Geometridae ($n = 23$), Notodontidae ($n = 10$), and Arctiidae ($n = 6$, appendix). This is consistent with data for other plecotine species, e.g., *Plecotus*, demonstrating the importance of noctuid moths in the diet relative to other moth families (Robinson 1990, Thompson 1982, Walhovd and Hoegh-Guildberg 1984).

We compared average wingspan size for all species of moths eaten by eastern *Corynorhinus* to values presented in Covell (1984) for species of moths available in Eastern North America. We generated grand means for wingspan size for individual families of moths (table 3), and tested these values against the averages for species eaten in these families using *t*-tests for single population means (Daniel 1974). Within families of moths, eastern *Corynorhinus* bats differentially select by size from among available moth prey. Among families of larger sized moths, Sphingidae (88.5-mm wingspan; $t = 5.93$, df = 4, $P < 0.01$) and Saturniidae (98.2 mm; $t = 3.8$, df = 1, $P < 0.1$), eastern

Corynorhinus bats choose species that are smaller than average in size (table 3). Conversely, among families of smaller sized moths, such as Geometridae (31.6 mm; $t = 4.65$, df = 22, $P < 0.01$), Noctuidae (41.0 mm; $t = 2.53$, df = 61, $P < 0.01$), and Arctiidae (40.6 mm; $t = 2.84$, df = 5, $P < 0.05$), eastern *Corynorhinus* bats select species that are larger in size (table 3). Although sample sizes are small, data for microlepidopterans eaten by eastern *Corynorhinus* also indicate a preference for species larger than average in size (appendix). Results for Notodontidae were not significant ($t = 0.97$, df = 9, $P > 0.1$), suggesting moths of this family are taken by size in proportion to their availability (table 3).

The importance of size, i.e., wingspan, in the selection of moth prey by eastern *Corynorhinus* has been suggested in several studies (Burford and Lacki 1998, Hurst and Lacki 1997, Lacki and LaDeur 2001). Lacki and LaDeur (2001) demonstrated that overall wingspan size of moth prey of Rafinesque's big-eared bat varied little throughout spring, summer, and autumn regardless of the mix of species eaten. Burford and Lacki (1998) were the first to suggest that *Corynorhinus* bats differentially select among moths by size within families, although their conclusion that smaller than average species of Noctuidae are eaten was not supported by our analyses (table 3). Nevertheless, average wingspan size of moth prey appears similar for all eastern *Corynorhinus*

Table 2—Relative abundance and number of species of families of moths eaten by eastern *Corynorhinus*

Moth family	C. rafinesquii		C. t. virginianus		C. t. ingens	
	Total	Species	Total	Species	Total	Species
	%	n	%	n	%	n
Arctiidae	12.1	3	3.8	3	4.8	3
Geometridae	24.2	8	20.2	14	15.9	9
Lasiocampidae	—		—		1.6	1
Megalopygidae	3.0	1	—		—	
Lymantriidae	—		1.3	1	—	
Noctuidae	39.4	11	54.4	43	54.0	27
Notodontidae	9.1	1	11.4	6	11.1	6
Pyralidae	—		—		3.2	2
Saturniidae	—		—		3.2	2
Sphingidae	12.1	3	7.6	5	6.3	2
Thyatiridae	—		1.3	1	—	

— = not found in samples.

Source: Burford and Lacki (1998), Dalton and others (1989), Dodd and Lacki (2007), Hurst and Lacki (1997), Lacki and LaDeur (2001), Sample and Whitmore (1993).

Table 3—Average wingspans for families of moths in Eastern North America compared with average wingspans of families of moths eaten by eastern *Corynorhinus*

Moth family	Available species		Moth species eaten		
	Wingspan (mm)		Wingspan (mm)		
	Mean	SE	Mean	SE	P-value
Arctiidae	40.6	1.6	61.8	7.5	< 0.05
Geometridae	31.6	0.6	41.7	2.2	< 0.01
Noctuidae	41.0	0.7	45.3	1.7	< 0.01
Notodontidae	46.8	1.3	49.1	2.4	NS
Saturniidae	98.2	7.7	73.5	6.5	< 0.1
Sphingidae	88.5	3.6	68.4	3.4	< 0.01

SE = standard error; NS = [not sampled].

Source: Burford and Lacki (1998), Covell (1984), Dalton and others (1989), Dodd and Lacki (2007), Hurst and Lacki (1997), Lacki and LaDeur (2001), Sample and Whitmore (1993).

[Ozark big-eared bat = 48.0 mm (Dodd and Lacki 2007), Rafinesque's big-eared bat = 45.4 mm (Hurst and Lacki 1997), Virginia big-eared bat = 47.0 mm (Burford and Lacki 1998)], suggesting that upper and lower limits to prey size may be governed by the ability of these bats to optimally capture and handle individual moths (Lacki and others 2007). Evidence presented here suggests that the average wingspan size for moth prey has an approximate range of 40 to 65 mm, with overall wingspan size of moths eaten ranging from 14 to 178 mm.

ACTIVITY AND FORAGING BEHAVIOR

Corynorhinus bats are late flyers, emerging from roosts after dark to feed (Barbour and Davis 1969). Typically, they circle inside roosts for up to 30 minutes before sunset (Clark and others 1993), often "light sampling" or briefly emerging and reentering during this preemergence phase. Bats then begin exiting roosts approximately 26 to 60 minutes after dark (Clark and others 1993, 2002; Dobkin and others 1995). Emergence of Ozark big-eared bats is not impeded by light to moderate rainfall (Clark and others 2002). *Corynorhinus* exhibit a bimodal pattern of activity in spring and early summer (Cockrum and Cross 1964, Pierson and others 1991) that shifts to a trimodal pattern during lactation (Clark and others 1993, Lacki and others 1994). During postlactation, the frequency of foraging bouts declines and bats do not reenter roosts until sunrise in late summer and early autumn (Clark and others 1993, Lacki and others 1994). Level of flight activity in Virginia big-eared bats is negatively associated with moon phase and wind speed, and directly related to percent relative humidity (Adam and others 1994b); the authors postulate that these bats reduce activity at low humidity to avoid extreme vapor pressure deficits and subsequent dehydration due to water loss.

Flight behavior in *Corynorhinus* has been observed directly using light tagging (Caire and others 1984, Clark 1991, Dalton and others 1989, Fellers and Pierson 2002), or inferred indirectly due to the composition of the diet (Ellis 1993), or behavior of radiotagged bats (Adam and others 1994a, Clark and others 1993, Hurst and Lacki 1999). *Corynorhinus* has been observed foraging along the perimeter of tree canopies (Dalton and others 1989, Fellers and Pierson 2002, Hurst and Lacki 1999), the edges of forests (Clark and others 1993, Dalton and others 1989, Fellers and Pierson 2002), traveling in and out of riparian corridors (Caire and others 1984, Fellers and Pierson 2002),

and along cliffs and canyon walls (Adam and others 1994a, Caire and others 1984). These behaviors are consistent with bats that glean insects from the surface of objects and, thus, rely on the structural configuration of the habitat, i.e., availability of vertical and horizontal surface area, when capturing prey. These bats are also known to fly close to ground level, especially over the vegetation of open fields and agricultural areas (Clark 1991, Dalton and others 1989); this behavior is believed to be the explanation for the presence of male tabanid flies in the diet of Rafinesque's big-eared bat (Ellis 1993). When flying over open areas, Virginia big-eared bats exhibit horizontal sweeps of up to 6 m, with vertical flights approximately 0.6 to 1.0 m above the surface of vegetation (Dalton and others 1989). This behavior is often interrupted with deeper vertical drops of 2 to 30 m as bats shift back and forth between the surface of clearings and the edge of forest canopies (Dalton and others 1989, Fellers and Pierson 2002).

FORAGING AREAS

Average size of foraging areas of *Corynorhinus* reported in the literature range from 10 to 262.8 ha (table 4), suggesting that there likely is substantial variation in the amount of area used for foraging among seasons and sex and reproductive condition of individual bats. Average foraging area size appears to be greatest for Rafinesque's big-eared bat (137.4 ha) and least for Ozark big-eared bat (71.5 ha). Length of maximum flight distance does not appear to be linked to size of foraging areas among species; however, average maximum flight distances are shorter for eastern (1 to 6.3 km) than western big-eared bats (14.7 km), which are widespread

Table 4—Average size and ranges of foraging areas and maximum flight distances of *Corynorhinus*

Species	Foraging area size[a]	Maximum flight distance
	ha	*km*
C. rafinesquii	137.4 (93.1–165)	1.1 (1–1.2)
C. t. virginianus	113.1 (24.6–262.8)	6.3 (3.6–8.4)
C. t. ingens	71.5 (10–156.9)	3.2 (0.8–5.5)
C. t. pallescens	—	14.7 (8–24)
C. t. townsendii	—	2.25 (1.3–3.2)

— = no data.

[a] Methods for calculating foraging areas varied among sources and include 100 and 95 percent polygons, calculated using kernel estimators or minimum convex polygons.

Source: Adam and others (1994a), Clark and others (1993), Dobkin and others (1995), England and Saugey (1998), Fellers and Pierson (2002), Hurst and Lacki (1999), Menzel and others (2001), Saugey (2000), Stihler (unpublished data), and Wethington and others (1996).

throughout coniferous forests in Western United States. The longer flight distances of western big-eared bats appear to be associated with their occupation of drier forests (Dobkin and others 1995, Pierson and others 1999), where xeric conditions likely result in sporadic sources of water and less frequent and predictable patches of prey. This is supported by behavior of Townsend's big-eared bats inhabiting wet coastal forests in California, where maximum flight distances were similar to those of eastern *Corynorhinus* species and did not exceed 3.2 km (Fellers and Pierson 2002).

Size of foraging areas of *Corynorhinus* appears surprisingly consistent across hardwood forests, mixed (forest/ agriculture) habitats, or pine forests (ca. 97.5 ha), although data for bats inhabiting pine forests are limited due to the lack of information on western subspecies of *Corynorhinus* (table 5). Nevertheless, maximum flight distances are greater for *Corynorhinus* in pine forests than hardwood forests or mixed habitats due to the extreme values reported for western big-eared bats (Dobkin and others 1995). It is generally accepted that other plecotine bats, particularly *Plecotus* species, forage close to their roosts (Swift 1998), with maximum flight distances of 1.1 km (Swift and Racey 1983) and 3.3 km (Fuhrmann and Seitz 1992). These values are comparable in length to those of *Corynorhinus* in Eastern North America.

Behavioral differences in foraging between the sexes is less clear for *Corynorhinus* because few studies have tracked both males and females simultaneously, and most studies that have tagged both sexes have tagged far fewer males than females (Adam and others 1994a, Dobkin and others 1995, Fellers and Pierson 2002, Wethington and others 1996). Available data indicate that females travel further distances than males in Townsend's and western big-eared bats (Dobkin and others 1995, Fellers and Pierson 2002),

with the opposite observed for Virginia big-eared bats (Adam and others 1994a). Results for Ozark big-eared bats are inconclusive, as length of flight distances were reported to be greater for males (Wilhide and others 1998), while no difference was observed between the sexes by Wethington and others (1996). Flight distances of reproductively active female Ozark big-eared bats increased from lactation to postlactation, with individual Ozark big-eared bats using up to four foraging sites during 10-day tracking periods (Clark and others 1993). Flight distances of female Ozark big-eared bats declined in length during the prehibernation phase in late autumn (Wethington and others 1996). There appears to be no difference in length of flight distances or size of foraging areas between male and female Rafinesque's big-eared bats, although published data are limited (Hurst and Lacki 1999, Menzel and others 2001). Size of foraging areas also was not different between male and female Ozark big-eared bats (Wethington and others 1996) and Virginia big-eared bats (Adam and others 1994a), respectively.

HABITAT USE

Considerable variation exists in use of foraging habitat among *Corynorhinus* (table 6). Much of the variation is attributable to differences in habitat associations, i.e., what habitats are actually available to the bats in the region where they occur. For example, Virginia big-eared bats and Ozark big-eared bats occur in upland hardwoods, especially those in proximity to cliffs and rocky bluffs (Adam and others 1994a, Clark and others 1993). Nevertheless, their use of mature versus successional forested habitats varies across locations (table 6). In turn, western big-eared bats and Townsend's big-eared bats are largely found in pine forests. Rafinesque's big-eared bats appear to be a forest habitat generalist relative to the other *Corynorhinus* species, as these bats inhabit upland

Table 5—Average size and ranges of foraging areas and maximum flight distances of *Corynorhinus* by forested habitat

Forested habitat	Foraging area size[a]	Maximum flight distance
	ha	*km*
Upland hardwoods	95.4 (10–262.8)	3.0 (0.5–8.4)
Mixed (upland hardwoods/agriculture)	104.1 (65.5–156.9)	4.3 (2–7)
Pine	93.1 (—)	9.7 (1.3–24)

— = no data.

[a] Methods for calculating foraging areas varied among sources and include 100 and 95 percent polygons, calculated using kernel estimators or minimum convex polygons.

Source: Adam and others (1994a), Clark and others (1993), Dobkin and others (1995), England and Saugey (1998), Fellers and Pierson (2002), Hurst and Lacki (1999), Menzel and others (2001), Saugey (2000), Stihler (unpublished data), Wethington and others (1996).

Table 6—Habitats preferred, used at random, and avoided by _Corynorhinus_

Species	Habitats								
	MUHW	SUHW	BHW	MPINE	SPINE	OPEN	CORR	EDGE	AQUATIC
C. rafinesquii	P, R	R	A	A	P	R	P, A	—	R, A
C. t. virginianus	P, A	A	—	—	—	P, A	P, A	P	—
C. t. ingens	P, A	—	—	—	—	R	P	P, R	—
C. t. pallescens	—	—	—	P	A	P	P	P	—
C. t. townsendii	—	—	—	—	—	A	P	P	—

— = no data; MUHW = mature upland hardwood; SUHW = successional upland hardwood; BHW = bottomland hardwood; MPINE = mature pine; SPINE = successional pine; OPEN = open (old fields, croplands, etc.); CORR = corridor (forested and riverine corridors); EDGE = edge (forest/field, scrub or clearcut interface); AQUATIC = aquatic (open water); P = preferred; R = random; A = avoided.

Source: Adam and others (1994a), Burford and Lacki (1995), Caire and others (1984), Clark and others (1993), Dalton and others (1989), Dobkin and others (1995), Fellers and Pierson (2002), Hurst and Lacki (1999), Leslie and Clark (2002), Medlin and Risch (2008), Menzel and others (2001), Wethington and others (1996), Wilhide and others (1998).

hardwoods, pine forests, and bottomland hardwood forests. Presently, only one study exists on use of foraging habitats by Rafinesque's big-eared bats in bottomland forests (Medlin and Risch 2008). Data for plecotine bats demonstrate the importance of flyways, i.e., linear landscape elements, during flight, including fence lines, streambanks, and railway lines (Swift 1998). Swift (1998) hypothesized that flyways are used as navigational cues and for avoidance of aerial predators, and it is likely these same explanations apply to _Corynorhinus_. Flyways are used repeatedly throughout summer, with flight speeds often exceeding those used in foraging flight (Barataud 1990, Howard 1995).

Habitat affinities of families of moths eaten by _Corynorhinus_ demonstrate variability between studies and geographic locations (table 7). Burford and others (1999) captured the majority of moths in mature timber and found several families avoid clearings or open habitats, including Limacodidae, Geometridae, Notodontidae, and Arctiidae.

Dodd and others (2008) found many families were positively associated with riparian and upland forest, with forested edges, sapling stands, and pastures typically avoided or used at random. The avoidance of forested edges and open areas, combined with the preference for riparian habitats by moth families commonly eaten by _Corynorhinus_, suggests an intriguing interplay between moths and _Corynorhinus_. An overriding pattern is a preference by _Corynorhinus_ for abrupt changes in vertical structure, such as along forested and riparian corridors and forest/edge interfaces (table 6). The vertical surfaces possibly help _Corynorhinus_ in capturing stationary moth prey. Regardless, because most of these same habitats are avoided by families of moths eaten by _Corynorhinus_ (table 7), we suggest these data further support the idea that use of foraging habitats by _Corynorhinus_ is predicated on structural configuration of the habitat, i.e., availability of vertical and horizontal surface area for gleaning, as much as on the local abundance of preferred moth prey.

Table 7—Habitats preferred, used at random, and avoided by families of moths eaten by _Corynorhinus_

Family	Habitats				
	Sawtimber	Poletimber	Open areas[a]	Forested edge	Riparian
Arctiidae	P	P	A	A	P
Geometridae	P, A	P, R	R, A	A	P
Noctuidae	R, A	R	R	A	P
Notodontidae	P, R	P, R	A	A	R

P = preferred; R = random; A = avoided.

[a] Includes old fields and clearcuts.

Source: Burford and others (1999), Dodd and others (2008).

CONCLUSIONS

The foraging behavior of eastern *Corynorhinus* is inextricably linked to their life history strategy which emphasizes moths in the diet (Lacki and others 2007). This specialization is accompanied by morphological and behavioral adaptations that allow these bats to preferentially capture and eat moths, using both gleaning and aerial hawking strategies, while foraging in habitats with substrate conditions conducive to a gleaning foraging behavior (Fenton 1984, Griffin 1958, Grinnell 1963, Handley 1959, Obrist and others 1993). Regardless of where or how eastern *Corynorhinus* bats locate food, the majority (> 71 percent) of moth species eaten depends entirely on woody plant hosts for their larval development (appendix). Sustaining landscapes with sufficient acreage in forest, while providing for corridors and other forest/edge interfaces, will be important in the long-term conservation of eastern *Corynorhinus* (Burford and others 1999, Dodd and others 2008). What constitutes "sufficient" acreage of forested habitat, however, remains to be determined. Lepidopteran diversity appears to be resilient to moderate levels of timber harvesting in temperate zone forests, but requires a diversity and abundance of local plant species (Summerville and Crist 2002, 2003). Therefore, management of habitats for *Corynorhinus* should promote woody plant diversity to help ensure the prey base needed to sustain these bats (Burford and others 1999, Dodd and others 2008). Big-eared bats are usually not abundant numerically and are not likely to be a major factor in regulating insect populations. Regardless, 19 species (16.7 percent of total) of moths known to be eaten by eastern *Corynorhinus* are pests in the larval stage, so these bats do serve as one of several natural controls of insect pests. Further, because they specialize on moth prey, their ability to affect the numbers of lepidopteran pest species in an area may be underappreciated and warrants further study. We suggest that long-term conservation of eastern *Corynorhinus* will require managing forest habitat in ways that promote local woody plant diversity to help sustain moth diversity.

ACKNOWLEDGMENTS

The lead author is grateful to the sponsors who contributed and supported his research program on *Corynorhinus* over the past 20 years including the U.S. Forest Service, U.S. Fish and Wildlife Service, Kentucky Department of Fish and Wildlife Resources, Arkansas Game and Fish Commission, East Kentucky Power, Natural Bridge State Park, and Kentucky State Nature Preserves Commission. The authors thank D. Saugey for providing unpublished data on *Corynorhinus*. Support for preparation of this manuscript was provided by the University of Kentucky, College of Agriculture. We thank the anonymous reviewers for their thoughtful comments and suggestions. This is a project of the Kentucky Agricultural Experiment Station (KAES No. 09-09-080) and is published with the approval of the director.

LITERATURE CITED

Adam, M.D.; Lacki, M.J.; Barnes, T.G. 1994a. Foraging areas and habitat use of the Virginia big-eared bat in Kentucky. Journal of Wildlife Management. 58: 462-469.

Adam, M.D.; Lacki, M.J.; Shoemaker, L.G. 1994b. Influence of environmental conditions on flight activity of *Plecotus townsendii virginianus* (Chiroptera: Vespertilionidae). Brimleyana. 21: 77-85.

Barataud, M. 1990. Eléments sur le comportement alimentaire des Oreillards brun et gris, *Plecotus auritus* (Linnaeus, 1758) et *Plecotus austriacus* (Fischer, 1829). Le Rhinolophe. 7: 3-10. In French.

Barbour, R.W.; Davis, W.H. 1969. Bats of America. Lexington, KY: University Press of Kentucky. 286 p.

Barclay, R.M.R. 1991. Population structure of temperate zone insectivorous bats in relation to foraging behaviour and energy demand. Journal of Animal Ecology. 60: 165-178.

Bauer, E.D. 1992. The summer food habits of a bachelor colony of Virginia big-eared bats in eastern Kentucky with observations on associated feeding shelters. Richmond, KY: Eastern Kentucky University. 79 p. M.A. thesis.

Bauerova, Z. 1982. Contribution to the trophic ecology of the grey long-eared bat, *Plecotus austriacus*. Folia Zoologica. 31: 113-122.

Burford, L.S.; Lacki, M.J. 1995. Habitat use by *Corynorhinus townsendii virginianus* in the Daniel Boone National Forest. American Midland Naturalist. 134: 340-345.

Burford, L.S.; Lacki, M.J. 1998. Moths consumed by *Corynorhinus townsendii virginianus* in eastern Kentucky. American Midland Naturalist. 139: 141-146.

Burford, L.S.; Lacki, M.J.; Covell, C.V., Jr. 1999. Occurrence of moths among habitats in a mixed mesophytic forest: implications for management of forest bats. Forest Science. 45: 323-332.

Caire, W.; Smith, J.F.; McGuire, S.; Royce, M.A. 1984. Early foraging behavior of insectivorous bats in western Oklahoma. Journal of Mammalogy. 65: 319-324.

Clark, B.S.; Clark, B.K.; Leslie, D.M., Jr. 2002. Seasonal variation in activity patterns of the endangered Ozark big-eared bat (*Corynorhinus townsendii ingens*). Journal of Mammalogy. 83: 590-598.

Clark, B.S.; Leslie, D.M., Jr.; Carter, T.S. 1993. Foraging activity of adult female Ozark big-eared bats (*Plecotus townsendii ingens*) in summer. Journal of Mammalogy. 74: 422-427.

Clark, M.K. 1991. Foraging ecology of Rafinesque's big-eared bat, *Plecotus rafinesquii*, in North Carolina. Bat Research News. 33: 68.

Cockrum, E.L.; Cross, S.P. 1964. Time of bat activity over water holes. Journal of Mammalogy. 45: 635-636.

Coles, R.B.; Guppy, A.; Anderson, M.E.; Schlegel, P. 1989. Frequency sensitivity and directional hearing in the gleaning bat *Plecotus auritus* (Linnaeus 1758). Journal of Comparative Physiology A. 165: 269-280.

Covell, C.V., Jr. 1984. A field guide to the moths of Eastern North America. Boston: Houghton Mifflin Co. 496 p.

Dalton, V.; Brack, V.W., Jr.; Williams, C. 1989. Foraging ecology of the Virginia big-eared bat. Richmond, VA: Virginia Division of Game; progress report; contract EW-2-1 III III-A: 32-46.

Dalton, V.M.; Brack, V., Jr.; McTeer, P.M. 1986. Food habits of the big-eared bat, *Plecotus townsendii virginianus*, in Virginia. Virginia Journal of Science. 37: 248-254.

Daniel, W.W. 1974. Biostatistics: a foundation for analysis in the health sciences. New York: John Wiley. 448 p.

De Fanis, E.; Jones, G. 1995. Post-natal growth, mother-infant interactions and development of vocalizations in the vespertilionid bat *Plecotus auritus*. Journal of Zoology London. 235: 85-97.

Dobkin, D.S.; Gettinger, R.D.; Gerdes, M.G. 1995. Springtime movements, roost use, and foraging activity of Townsend's big-eared bat (*Plecotus townsendii*) in central Oregon. Great Basin Naturalist. 55: 315-321.

Dodd, L.E.; Lacki, M.J. 2007. Prey consumed by *Corynorhinus townsendii ingens* in the Ozark Mountain region. Acta Chiropterologica. 9: 451-461.

Dodd, L.E.; Lacki, M.J.; Rieske, L.K. 2008. Variation in moth occurrence and implications for foraging habitat of Ozark big-eared bats. Forest Ecology and Management. 255: 3866-3872.

Ellis, S.E. 1993. Tabanidae as dietary items of Rafinesque's big-eared bat: implications for its foraging behavior. Entomological News. 104: 118-122.

England, D.R.; Saugey, D.A. 1998. Radiotelemetry study of Rafinesque's big-eared bat (*Corynorhinus rafinesquii*) in southern Arkansas. Little Rock, AR: Arkansas Game and Fish Commission; completion report. 21 p.

Farney, J.; Fleharty, E.D. 1969. Aspect ratio, loading, wing span, and membrane areas of bats. Journal of Mammalogy. 50: 362-367.

Faure, P.A.; Fullard, J.H.; Dawson, J.W. 1993. The gleaning attacks of the northern long-eared bat, *Myotis septentrionalis*, are relatively inaudible to moths. Journal of Experimental Biology. 178: 173-189.

Fellers, G.M.; Pierson, E.D. 2002. Habitat use and foraging behavior of Townsend's big-eared bat (*Corynorhinus townsendii*) in coastal California. Journal of Mammalogy. 83: 167-177.

Fenton, M.B. 1984. Echolocation: implications for the ecology and evolution of bats. Quarterly Review of Biology. 59: 33-53.

Fenton, M.B. 1990. The foraging behaviour and ecology of animal-eating bats. Canadian Journal of Zoology. 68: 411-422.

Fuhrmann, M.; Seitz, A. 1992. Nocturnal activity of the brown long-eared bat (*Plecotus auritus* L. 1758): data from radiotracking in the Lenneberg Forest near Mainz (Germany). In: Priede, I.G.; Swift, S.M., eds. Wildlife telemetry. Remote monitoring and tracking of animals. Chichester, UK: Ellis Horwood: 538-548.

Griffin, D.R. 1958. Listening in the dark. New Haven, CT: Yale University Press. 413 p.

Grinnell, A.D. 1963. The neurophysiology of audition in bats: intensity and frequency parameters. Journal of Physiology. 167: 38-66.

Handley, C.O., Jr. 1959. A revision of American bats of the genera *Euderma* and *Plecotus*. Proceedings of the U.S. National Museum. 110: 95-246.

Howard, R.W. 1995. Auritus: a natural history of the brown long-eared bat. York, UK: William Sessions. 154 p.

Hurst, T.E.; Lacki, M.J. 1997. Food habits of Rafinesque's big-eared bat in southeastern Kentucky. Journal of Mammalogy. 78: 525-528.

Hurst, T.E.; Lacki, M.J. 1999. Roost selection, population size and habitat use by a colony of Rafinesque's big-eared bats (*Corynorhinus rafinesquii*). American Midland Naturalist. 142: 363-371.

Jones, C.; Suttkus, R.D. 1971. Wing loading in *Plecotus rafinesquii*. Journal of Mammalogy. 52: 458-460.

Koopman, K.F.; Jones, J.K. 1970. Classification of bats. In: Slaughter, B.H.; Walton, D.W., eds. About bats: a Chiropteran symposium. Dallas: Southern Methodist University Press: 22-28.

Kunz, T.H.; Martin, R.A. 1982. *Plecotus townsendii*. Mammalian Species. 175: 1-6.

Lacki, M.J.; Adam, M.D.; Shoemaker, L.G. 1993. Characteristics of feeding roosts of Virginia big-eared bats in Daniel Boone National Forest. Journal of Wildlife Management. 57: 539-543.

Lacki, M.J.; Adam, M.D.; Shoemaker, L.G. 1994. Observations on seasonal cycle, population patterns and roost selection in summer colonies of *Plecotus townsendii virginianus* in Kentucky. American Midland Naturalist. 131: 34-42.

Lacki, M.J.; Amelon, S.K.; Baker, M.D. 2007. Foraging ecology of bats in forests. In: Lacki, M.J.; Hayes, J.P.; Kurta, A., eds. Bats in forests: conservation and management. Baltimore, MD: Johns Hopkins University Press: 83-127.

Lacki, M.J.; LaDeur, K.M. 2001. Seasonal use of lepidopteran prey by Rafinesque's big-eared bats (*Corynorhinus rafinesquii*). American Midland Naturalist. 145: 213-217.

Leslie, D.M., Jr.; Clark, B.S. 2002. Feeding habits of the endangered Ozark big-eared bat (*Corynorhinus townsendii ingens*) relative to prey abundance. Acta Chiropterologica. 4: 173-182.

Medlin, R.E., Jr.; Risch, T.S. 2008. Habitat associations of bottomland bats, with focus on Rafinesque's big-eared bat and southeastern myotis. American Midland Naturalist. 160: 400-412.

Menzel, M.A.; Menzel, J.M.; Ford, W.M. [and others]. 2001. Home range and habitat use of male Rafinesque's big-eared bats (*Corynorhinus rafinesquii*). American Midland Naturalist. 145: 402-408.

Norberg, U.M. 1976. Aerodynamics, kinematics and energetics of horizontal flapping flight in the long-eared bat *Plecotus auritus*. Journal of Experimental Biology. 65: 179-212.

Norberg, U.M.; Rayner, J.M.V. 1987. Ecological morphology and flight in bats (Mammalia: Chiroptera): wing adaptations, flight performance, foraging strategy and echolocation. Philosophical Transactions of the Royal Society of London B. 316: 335-427.

Obrist, M.K.; Fenton, M.B.; Eger, J.L.; Schlegel, P.A. 1993. What ears do for bats: a comparative study of pinna sound pressure transformation in Chiroptera. Journal of Experimental Biology. 180: 119-152.

Pierson, E.D.; Rainey, W.E.; Koontz, D.M. 1991. Bats and mines: experimental mitigation for Townsend's big-eared bat at the McLaughlin mine in California. In: Proceedings of the Thorne Ecological Institute: issues and technology in the management of impacted wildlife. Snowmass, CO: [Thorne Ecological Institute]: 31-42.

Pierson, E.D.; Wackenhut, M.C.; Altenbach, J.S. [and others]. 1999. Species conservation assessment and strategy for the Townsend's big-eared bat (*Corynorhinus townsendii townsendii* and *Corynorhinus townsendii pallescens*). Boise, ID: Idaho Department of Fish and Game, Idaho Conservation Effort. 52 p.

Rayner, J.M.V. 1987. The mechanics of flapping flight in bats. In: Fenton, M.B.; Racey, P.A.; Rayner, J.M.V., eds. Recent advances in the study of bats. Cambridge, UK: Cambridge University Press: 23-42.

Robinson, M.F. 1990. Prey selection by the brown long-eared bat (*Plecotus auritus*). Myotis. 28: 5-18.

Ross, A. 1967. Ecological aspects of the food habits of insectivorous bats. Western Foundation of Vertebrate Zoology. 1(4): 205-263.

Rydell, J. 1989. Food habits of northern (*Eptesicus nilssoni*) and brown-long eared (*Plecotus auritus*) bats in Sweden. Holarctic Ecology. 12: 16-20.

Sample, B.E.; Whitmore, R.C. 1993. Food habits of the endangered Virginia big-eared bat in West Virginia. Journal of Mammalogy. 74: 428-435.

Saugey, D.A. 2000. Radiotelemetry study of Rafinesque's big-eared bat (*Corynorhinus rafinesquii*) in southern Arkansas. Little Rock, AR: Arkansas Game and Fish Commission; completion report. 97 p.

Shiel, C.B.; McAney, C.M.; Fairley, J.S. 1991. Analysis of the diet of Natterer's bat *Myotis nattereri* and the common long-eared bat *Plecotus auritus* in the west of Ireland. Journal of Zoology (London). 223: 299-305.

Summerville, K.S.; Crist, T.O. 2002. Effects of timber harvest on forest lepidoptera: community, guild, and species responses. Ecological Applications. 12: 820-835.

Summerville, K.S.; Crist, T.O. 2003. Determinants of lepidopteran community composition and species diversity in eastern deciduous forests: roles of season, eco-region, and patch size. Oikos. 100: 134-148.

Swift, S.M. 1998. Long-eared bats. Cambridge, UK: Cambridge University Press. 182 p.

Swift, S.M.; Racey, P.A. 1983. Resource partitioning in two species of vespertilionid bats (Chiroptera) occupying the same roost. Journal of Zoology (London). 200: 249-259.

Thompson, M.J.A. 1982. A common long-eared bat *Plecotus auritus*: moth predator-prey relationship. Naturalist. 107: 87-97.

Tumlison, R. 1992. *Plecotus mexicanus*. Mammalian Species. 401: 1-3.

Walhovd, H.; Hoegh-Guildberg, O. 1984. On the feeding habits of the common long-eared bat, *Plecotus auritus*. Flora og Fauna. 90: 115-118.

Werner, T.K. 1981. Responses of nonflying moths to ultrasound: the threat of gleaning bats. Canadian Journal of Zoology. 59: 525-529.

Wethington, T.A.; Leslie, D.M., Jr.; Gregory, M.S.; Wethington, M.K. 1996. Prehibernation habitat use and foraging activity by endangered Ozark big-eared bats (*Plecotus townsendii ingens*). American Midland Naturalist. 135: 218-230.

Wilhide, J.D.; McDaniel, V.R.; Harvey, M.J.; White, D.R. 1998. Telemetric observations of foraging Ozark big-eared bats in Arkansas. Journal of the Arkansas Academy of Science. 52: 113-116.

Whitaker, J.O., Jr. 2004. Prey selection in a temperate zone insectivorous bat community. Journal of Mammalogy. 85: 460-469.

Whitaker, J.O., Jr.; Maser, C.; Keller, L.E. 1977. Food habits of bats of western Oregon. Northwest Science. 51: 46-55.

Appendix—List of moth species eaten by *Corynorhinus* in Eastern North America

Family/species	CR	CTV	CTI	Larval habitat	Wingspan[a]
					mm
Arctiidae					
Apantesis sp.			x	Field	42
Ecpantheria scribonia	x		x	Field/For	91
Estigmene acrea[b]		x		Field	68
Grammia virgo		x		Field	70
Halysidota tessellaris	x	x	x	For	45
Haploa sp.	x			For	55
Geometridae					
Anticlea multiferata			x	Field	25
Campaea perlata	x	x		For	51
Dichorda iridaria			x	Field	30
Ectropis crepuscularia		x		For	37
Epimecis hortaria	x	x	x	For	55
Euchlaena amoenaria		x		Unknown	49
E. irraria	x			For	48
E. pectinaria		x	x	For	46
E. tigrinaria		x		For	41
Eusarca confusaria		x		Field	41
Eutrapela clemataria	x	x		For	56
Hydria prunivorata			x	For	35
Hypagyrtis unipunctata			x	For	47
Itame pustularia[b]		x		For	27
Melanolophia canadaria		x		For	36
Nacophora quernaria	x			For	56
Patalene olyzonaria			x	For	21
Plagodis fervidaria		x		For	31
Probole nyssaria	x		x	For	35
Prochoerodes transversata[b]	x			For	50
Selenia kentaria		x	x	For	52
Tetracis cachexiata	x	x		For	50
Xanthotype urticaria		x		Field/For	40
Lasiocampidae					
Malacosoma americanum[b]			x	For	44
Lymantriidae					
Dasychira basiflava		x		For	54

continued

Appendix—List of moth species eaten by *Corynorhinus* in Eastern North America (continued)

Family/species	CR	CTV	CTI	Larval habitat	Wingspan[e]
					mm
Megalopygidae					
Lagoa crispata	x			For	40
Noctuidae					
Abagrotis alternata[b]	x	x	x	For	42
Acronicta americana		x	x	For	65
A. innotata	x			For	40
A. lobeliae			x	For	60
A. radcliffei	x			For	38
A. spinigera		x		For	48
Agrotis ipsilon[b]		x	x	Field	51
Allagrapha aerea	x			Field	42
Allotria elonympha			x	For	45
Amphipyra pyramidoides		x	x	For	52
Argyrogrammia basigera			x	Unknown	33
Autographa biloba		x		Field	40
Caenurgina erechtea[b]		x		Field	42
Callopistria cordata			x	For	28
Catocala epione		x		For	65
C. ilia			x	For	82
C. neogama		x		For	85
C. paleogama		x		For	70
C. vidua		x		For	85
Chaetaglaea sericea	x			For	45
Chytonix palliatricula		x		Field	33
Cosmia calami		x		For	34
Crocigrapha normani		x		For	40
Euparthenos nubilis		x	x	For	70
Euplexia benesimilis		x		Field	36
Eupsilia sp.			x	Field/For	40
Euxoa bostoniensis[b]		x		Field	45
E. immixta		x		Unknown	40
Heliothis zea[b]			x	Field	45
Hypsoropha hormos		x		For	34
H. monilis			x	For	42
Lacinipolia renigera[b]		x	x	Field	30
Leucania multilinea		x		Field	50

continued

Appendix—List of moth species eaten by *Corynorhinus* in Eastern North America (continued)

Family/species	CR	CTV	CTI	Larval habitat	Wingspan[a]
					mm
Lithophane antennata[b]		x		For	42
L. hemina		x		For	38
Metalectra discalis		x		Unknown	29
Metaxaglaea semitaria		x		For	54
Oligia modica		x		Unknown	32
Orthodes cynica			x	Field	34
Orthosia alurina		x		For	40
O. hibisci[b]		x		For	42
O. rubescens		x		For	40
Paectes pygmaea			x	For	23
Panopoda carneicosta			x	For	46
P. rufimargo	x	x	x	For	46
Panthea furcilla			x	For	50
Parallelia bistriaris[b]	x	x		For	43
Peridroma saucia[b]		x		Field	52
Platysenta sutor			x	Field	38
Polia latex	x			For	51
P. purpurissata		x		For	55
Protolampra brunneicollis			x	Field	43
Pseudaletia unipuncta[b]	x	x	x	Field	47
Pseudorthodes vecors			x	Field	35
Renia fraternalis			x	For	25
Scolecocampa liburna	x		x	For	43
Scoliopteryx libatrix	x			For	45
Spaelotis clandestina[b]		x		Field/For	43
Xestia dolosa[b]		x		Field	46
Zale bethunei		x		For	40
Z. lunata			x	For	55
Zanclognatha sp.			x	For	35
Notodontidae					
Datana angusii			x	For	48
Heterocampa guttivitta		x		For	45
H. umbrata		x		For	62
Lochmaeus bilineata			x	For	40
L. manteo[b]		x	x	For	50
Nadata gibbosa	x	x	x	For	59

continued

Appendix—List of moth species eaten by *Corynorhinus* in Eastern North America (continued)

Family/species	CR	CTV	CTI	Larval habitat	Wingspan[a]
					mm
Notodontidae (continued)					
Nerice bidentata			x	For	40
Peridea angulosa		x		For	55
Schizura sp.		x		For	47
Symmerista albifrons			x	For	45
Pyralidae					
Blepharomastix ranalis			x	Field	20
Pantographa limata[b]			x	For	37
Saturniidae					
Automeris io			x	For	80
Sphingicampa bicolor			x	For	67
Sphingidae					
Darapsa myron	x	x	x	For	65
D. pholus	x	x		For	75
Deidamia inscripta	x	x		For	70
Laothoe juglandis		x	x	For	75
Lapara coniferarum		x		For	57
Thyatiridae					
Euthyatira pudens		x		For	46

CR = *Corynorhinus rafinesquii*; CTV = *C. townsendii virginianus*; CTI = *C. t. ingens*.

[a] Source: Covell (1984).

[b] Denotes pest species in the larval stage.

CONSERVATION AND MANAGEMENT OF EASTERN BIG-EARED BATS (*CORYNORHINUS* SPP.)

Darren A. Miller, Southern Environmental Research Manager, Southern Timberlands Technology, Weyerhaeuser NR Company, P.O. Box 2288, Columbus, MS 39704

Craig W. Stihler, Wildlife Biologist, West Virginia Division of Natural Resources, P.O. Box 67, Elkins, WV 26241

D. Blake Sasse, Nongame Mammal Program Coordinator, Arkansas Game and Fish Commission, 213A Highway 89 South, Mayflower, AR 72106

Rick Reynolds, Wildlife Biologist, Virginia Department of Game and Inland Fisheries, 4010 West Broad Street, Richmond, VA 23230

Paul Van Deusen, Principal Research Scientist, National Council for Air and Stream Improvement, 600 Suffolk Street, Lowell, MA 01854

Steven B. Castleberry, Professor, University of Georgia, Daniel B. Warnell School of Forestry and Natural Resources, Athens, GA 30602

Abstract—There are two species of big-eared bats in the Eastern United States, Rafinesque's big-eared bat (RBEB) (*Corynorhinus rafinesquii*) and Townsend's big-eared bat (*C. townsendii*). The two eastern subspecies of *C. townsendii* [Ozark big-eared bat (OBEB) (*C. t. ingens*) and Virginia big-eared bat (VBEB) (*C. t. virginianus*)] are listed as federally endangered and *C. rafinesquii* is both a Federal species of concern and State-listed in many States where it occurs. These bats occur across a broad geographic area encompassing different ecoregions and forest associations. Current primary threats for RBEBs include habitat loss, primarily due to urbanization, and loss of natural and manmade roosts. Current primary threats for OBEBs and VBEBs include small population sizes, limited cave/karst areas, wind energy development, and potential reduction of food resources/foraging areas. White-nose syndrome (WNS) is a potential threat to all three big-eared bats but most immediately concerns OBEB and VBEB populations. Conservation actions for OBEBs and VBEBs include protection of caves, e.g., reduction of disturbance, developing responses to WNS, and identifying new summer caves and hibernacula. For RBEBs, habitat conservation, protection of caves, provisioning of artificial roosts, and protection of existing manmade roosts appear key. A large amount of potential RBEB habitat occurs on private lands and bat conservation efforts need to involve private landowners, who own 87 percent of forested lands in the Southeastern United States. A lack of research is a conservation need as, in many cases, critical data are lacking for making informed management decisions.

INTRODUCTION

Two species of big-eared bats [*Corynorhinus* (formerly *Plecotus*) spp.] occur in the Eastern United States: Rafinesque's big-eared bat (*C. rafinesquii*; RBEB) and Townsend's big-eared bat (*C. townsendii*) (Whitaker and Hamilton 1998). There are two recognized subspecies of Townsend's big-eared bats in the region—the Ozark big-eared bat (*C. t. ingens*; OBEB) (Sealander and Heidt 1990) and the Virginia big-eared bat (*C. t. virginianus*; VBEB) (Whitaker and Hamilton 1998). Both Townsend's subspecies have restricted ranges with the OBEBs occurring only in northwestern and northcentral Arkansas; southwest Missouri [but not observed there since 1971 (U.S. Fish and Wildlife Service 2008a), but see Elliott and others 1999]; and eastern Oklahoma (Sealander and Heidt 1990) and the VBEBs only occurring in five disjunct areas (two in West Virginia and one each in Virginia, North Carolina, and Kentucky) (U.S. Fish and Wildlife Service 2008b). Both OBEBs and VBEBs were listed as federally endangered by the U.S. Fish and Wildlife Service in 1979 (Federal Register 44(232): 69206-69208) due to restricted ranges; dependence on few caves; overutilization, e.g., intentional killing and scientific study/collection; and inadequacy of existing regulations. Additionally, recent genetic evidence suggests that the disjunct VBEB populations should be considered evolutionary significant units (ESUs; Piaggio and others 2009, U.S. Fish and Wildlife Service 2008b).

Rafinesque's big-eared bat has a broader distribution than either eastern Townsend's subspecies, occurring across the Southeastern United States, bordered to the north by Kentucky and West Virginia, southeastern Missouri and southeast Virginia, as far south as most of Florida, and west into eastern Texas (Bayless and others 2011, Whitaker and Hamilton 1998). However, even with this broad distribution, this species is designated as a species of concern by the U.S. Fish and Wildlife Service [http://ecos.fws.gov/speciesProfile/profile/speciesProfile.action?spcode=A0AI#status (Date accessed: January 25, 2010)] and has some type of listing status in almost every State in which it occurs (Bayless and others 2011). The primary reason for status as species of

Citation for proceedings: Loeb, Susan C.; Lacki, Michael J.; Miller, Darren A., eds. 2011. Conservation and management of eastern big-eared bats: a symposium. Gen. Tech. Rep. SRS-145. Asheville, NC: U.S. Department of Agriculture, Forest Service, Southern Research Station. 157 p.

conservation concern is perceived population declines and loss of habitat (Arroyo-Cabrales and Castenada 2008).

Given the conservation needs of these species, it is imperative to understand current and potential conservation actions that may be used to help conserve these species. Additionally, emerging threats, such as white-nose syndrome (WNS), will require an understanding of conservation issues so these needs can be considered as new challenges arise. To date, however, we are unaware of any efforts to collectively discuss conservation challenges and solutions for eastern big-eared bats. Therefore, our objectives were to (1) examine the current threats facing these three taxa, (2) review past and current efforts to conserve these species, and (3) identify research needs relative to management and conservation of these species.

CONCERNS AND THREATS

Changes in Forest Cover and Structure

Although VBEBs and OBEBs appear to be habitat generalists relative to foraging (Dalton and others 1989, Stihler 2011a, Wethington and others 1996) and are strongly affiliated with karst and other rock features used for roosting and hibernation, bats are obviously impacted by trends in forest cover, which also may be an indicator of ecosystem health. Additionally, RBEBs are strongly associated with bottomland hardwood forests throughout the Coastal Plain (Clark 1990, Gooding and Langford 2004, Lance and others 2001, Mirowsky and others 2004, Trousdale and Beckett 2005) and to other forest types in karst areas (e.g., Hurst and Lacki 1999) where this species roosts in caves. Within Coastal Plain populations of RBEBs, forest trends are particularly important because habitat loss and adequacy (type and abundance) of roost sites are the greatest perceived threats for this species (Arroyo-Cabrales and Castaneda 2008). Finally, it is important to understand the projected landscape context within the geographic range of these species to help frame conservation needs.

Overall, area of forest land remained relatively stable in the Southeastern United States during the early 1900s to 2007 (Smith and others 2009) with upland hardwoods increasing in acreage between 1953 and 1999 (Wear and Greis 2002). Although the area of bottomland hardwood forests in the Southeastern United States declined over 80 percent since pre-European settlement primarily due to conversion to agriculture (Wear and Greis 2002), during 1970 to 1992 area of this forest type remained essentially stable (Wear and Greis 2002). Restoration of former bottomland hardwood forests through afforestation, particularly in the lower Mississippi Alluvial Valley, has been a focus among private landowners

and Federal Agencies.[1] However, effects of widespread deforestation, extensive drainage, and channelization make ecological restoration of these systems difficult.

The largest threat to future forest cover in the Southeastern United States is urbanization (National Commission on Science for Sustainable Forestry 2005, Smith and others 2009, Wear and Greis 2002). Between 1992 and 2040, an estimated 12.5 million ha of forest land in the region could be lost to urbanization (Wear and Greis 2002). In spite of this threat, Wear and Greis (2002) projected that gains in forest cover will be made primarily through conversion of agricultural lands to forests (4 million ha between 1992 and 2020 and an additional 6 million ha afforested between 2020 and 2040). Areas of largest potential gain in forest cover appear to be in the lower Gulf Coastal Plain, including large areas of Arkansas, Mississippi, and Louisiana with no projected net loss in total forest cover and current annual forest growth exceeding removals by 70 percent (Smith and others 2009). However, trends within forest types are expected to vary. Although Wear and Greis (2002) predicted acreage of planted pine (*Pinus* spp.) to increase between 1995 and 2040, more recent analyses, based on market conditions, suggest acreage of plantations (22 percent of all forests are of planted origin; Smith and others 2009) may remain relatively unchanged (National Commission on Science for Sustainable Forestry 2005, Smith and others 2009). Regardless, slight declines in acreage of natural pine, mixed oak-pine, upland hardwoods, and bottomland hardwoods are expected during 1995 to 2040 (Wear and Greis 2002).

Although only slight declines in acreage of bottomland hardwood forests are projected through 2040, structure of these forests may not currently be suitable for RBEBs, which appear to require specific, older aged portions of bottomland hardwood forests for roosting (Whitaker and Hamilton 1998). Within the bottomland forest type, most roosts occur in large [> 50 cm diameter at breast height (d.b.h.)] water tupelo (*Nyssa aquatica*), with other tree species, such as bald cypress (*Taxodium distichum*), red maple (*Acer rubrum*), and oaks (*Quercus* spp.) comprising a small percentage of roosts (Gooding and Langford 2004, Lance and others 2001, Trousdale and Beckett 2005). Although RBEBs routinely roost in manmade structures such as bridges and culverts (Bennett and others 2008, Lance and others 2001, Trousdale and Beckett 2004); abandoned buildings (Clark 1990, England and others 1990, Menzel and others 2001, Mirowsky and others 2004); and artificial roost structures,[2]

---

[1] Personal communication. 2010. Kevin Nelms, Wildlife Biologist, National Resource Conservation Service, 517 Brentwood Avenue, Greenwood, MS 38930.

[2] Personal communication. 2010. Mylea Bayless, Biologist, Bat Conservation International, 500 N. Capital of Texas Highway, Building 1, Suite 200, Austin, TX 78746.

use of these structures varies seasonally (Loeb and Zarnoch 2011, Trousdale and Beckett 2004) and may indicate natural roost sites are critically important even in areas with abundant manmade roost sites.

To provide an initial assessment of potential availability of RBEB roosting habitat, we used U.S. Forest Service Forest Inventory and Analysis (FIA) data [http://fia.fs.fed. us/. (Date accessed: March 11, 2010)] to estimate area of potential, natural RBEB roosting habitat within the Coastal Plain. Our search criterion was presence of water tupelo > 50 cm d.b.h. We calculated area by forest ownership category for the nine Southeastern States that contain the most bottomland hardwood forest (table 1). Our analysis indicates there are 308 000 ha of forest containing water tupelo > 50 cm d.b.h. with most (29 percent) occurring in Louisiana (table 1). Most (72 percent) of the potential roosting habitat occurred on privately owned land. These results should be considered preliminary, with ground truthing and further investigation required to more precisely quantify area of potential roosting habitat, suitability of these areas, and if they are currently occupied by RBEBs. Additionally, this search did not include presence of other species of potential roost trees. However, we suggest FIA data may be another resource to estimate and monitor trends in habitat availability for big-eared bats.

Associated with urbanization is an increase in human population, which is of particular concern for OBEBs as much of the area inhabited by this species has experienced rapid population growth in the last few decades. During 1990 to 2000, human population increased by 14, 25, 39, and 59 percent in the four counties of eastern Oklahoma and northwestern Arkansas where most OBEB sites are concentrated (U.S. Fish and Wildlife Service 2008a). Increased development is also a concern within foraging areas for VBEBs (U.S. Fish and Wildlife Service 2008b). This development potentially reduces availability of foraging areas and may increase potential for human intrusion into caves used by these species. Additionally, Stein and others (2010) identified areas within the Southeastern United States that are at greatest risk of future housing development; many of the "medium change" to "high change" areas are currently occupied by big-eared bats.

Small Population Size and Limited Habitat Features

The small populations of VBEBs in each core population area (Piaggio and others 2009) and of OBEBs (U.S. Fish and Wildlife Service 2008a), coupled with limited dispersal distances (e.g., Weyandt and others 2005), makes both subspecies susceptible to extirpation and possible

Table 1—Area of potential Rafinesque's big-eared bat roosting habitat in the Coastal Plain of nine States in the Southeastern United States by ownership type; potential habitat was defined as stands containing stands of water tupelo (*Nyssa aquatica*) trees > 50 cm d.b.h.[a]

| State | Land ownership | | | | |
	U.S. Forest Service	Other Federal	State/local	Private	Total
	------------------------------thousands of ha------------------------------				
Alabama			4.9	16.5	21.4
Arkansas		2.4	2.8	23.5	28.7
Florida	6.1	2.4	33.6	14.2	56.3
Georgia			2.4	21.5	23.9
Louisiana		4.9	4.9	80.6	90.4
Mississippi		7.3		12.6	19.9
North Carolina		4.0		30.8	34.8
South Carolina	2.4	2.4	2.4	16.6	23.8
Texas		2.4		7.3	9.7
Total	8.5	25.8	51.0	223.6	308.9

[a] Data based on U.S. Forest Service Forest Inventory and Analysis plots, 2010.

extinction. Related to small populations are the very limited numbers of known hibernacula and maternity and bachelor sites (U.S. Fish and Wildlife Service 2008a, 2008b). Within the core area with the largest number of VBEBs, over 95 percent of known hibernating VBEBs are concentrated in just three caves (Stihler 2011b). The combination of low vagility, geographic isolation of ESUs for VBEBs, and a reproductive output of only one pup per year (Kunz and Martin 1982) raises concern regarding maintenance of genetic diversity and long-term persistence of these subspecies. Additionally, the low number of known caves used by these subspecies leads to potential for stochastic events, e.g., vandalism, flooding, contaminants, disturbance, to have a catastrophic impact on populations (U.S. Fish and Wildlife Service 2008b). Although RBEBs are more widespread, they may also be suffering from reduced genetic diversity and gene flow among populations due to relatively recent isolating mechanisms (i.e., habitat loss; Piaggio and others 2011).

The key habitat components that underlie protection and management of big-eared bats in karst areas are caves which are used throughout the year as hibernacula, maternity and bachelor caves, and swarming sites (Barbour and Davis 1969). In particular, the limited number of sites available and used by OBEBs and VBEBs make these habitat components critical for conservation of this species. While core areas for VBEBs are predominately rural and somewhat isolated, potential impacts to habitat features include lack of sufficient protection for caves and the area immediately surrounding caves, adjoining rural development, and other potential site disturbances (e.g., limestone quarrying, oil drilling activities; U.S. Fish and Wildlife Service 2008a, 2008b).

White-Nose Syndrome

The discovery of WNS in the Northeastern United States and associated high-mortality rates in cave-dwelling bats, and the rapid spread of WNS southward through Pennsylvania, West Virginia, Virginia, and westward to Oklahoma has raised concerns for all species of cave-dwelling bats in affected States (Blehert and others 2009). WNS has not been documented in VBEBs. A recent visit (February 2010) to Hellhole Cave in West Virginia, which houses the largest single winter concentration of VBEBs, revealed no VBEB deaths and no live VBEBs exhibiting signs of WNS even though a large number of dead and living little brown bats (*Myotis lucifugus*) and tri-colored bats (*Perimyotis subflavus*) showed signs of WNS. However, it is too early to determine if WNS will affect big-eared bat populations.

Wind Energy Development

Wind energy development is a potential threat for all of the eastern big-eared bats (Arnett and others 2007),

but this threat is probably most relevant for OBEB and VBEB populations. Even though there are no documented occurrences of big-eared bat deaths at wind turbine sites in the United States, there is a record of a plecotine bat (*Plecotus austriacus*) being killed at a wind turbine site in Germany (Dürr and Bach 2004), and placement of wind facilities near or adjacent to maternity sites and hibernacula may impact these populations (U.S. Fish and Wildlife Service 2008b). Currently, there are proposed wind facilities near known big-eared bat sites in Arkansas, Virginia, and West Virginia. The proposed wind facility in Virginia is within 8.5 km of a known maternity site and within 21 km of the only hibernaculum in the Tazewell County, VA, core area. Although inactive at this time, another proposed facility in West Virginia is within 8.3 km of six VBEB hibernacula and two maternity colonies and within 16.7 km of the largest known hibernaculum for this bat. If these sites are developed, then two of the five VBEB ESUs, including the largest known population, may be potentially impacted by wind energy development.

Food Resources

Although moths, the primary prey of big-eared bats (Dalton and others 1986, Dodd and Lacki 2007, Ross 1967, Whitaker and others 1977), do not appear to negatively respond to forest management practices (Lacki and Dodd 2011), research has documented reduced moth abundance and diversity in pastures and cleared areas compared to forested sites (Burford and others 1999, Dodd and others 2008). However, VBEBs in West Virginia forage over hay fields and old fields although they seldom forage over grazed pastures (Stihler 2011a). These seemingly contradictory results may be explained by different vegetation structure in different types of cleared areas, which affect invertebrate abundance (e.g., Hermann and others 1998) and landscape or regional differences between study areas. Regardless, for VBEBs, it appears that some amount of open areas, with appropriate vegetation structure, may be important. These open areas could be lost due to natural succession, lack of management, and/or development. In portions of the range of VBEBs, gypsy moth (*Lymantria dispar*) infestations and gypsy moth control methods, especially nonselective treatments, could impact local forest moth populations. Impacts to local moth populations through pesticides, habitat conversion, or degradation may affect foraging distance and prey selection for these species.

CURRENT CONSERVATION AND MANAGEMENT ACTIONS

Ozark Big-Eared Bats

Conservation of OBEBs has primarily focused on acquiring caves, protecting caves, and addressing WNS. Of the

19 known essential OBEB sites (caves that are used as hibernacula and/or maternity sites that are essential to continued existence of OBEBs; U.S. Fish and Wildlife Service 1995), 9 are in public ownership or management, 1 is managed by the National Speleological Society, and 1 is managed by The Nature Conservancy. One notable aspect of OBEB conservation is the formation of the Ozark Plateau National Wildlife Refuge specifically created to protect endangered bats. This refuge was established in 1986 as the Oklahoma Bat Caves National Wildlife Refuge and redesignated with its current name in 1995. Its 1517 ha contain three essential OBEB caves that have been protected by purchase, conservation easement, and cooperative agreements managed by the U.S. Fish and Wildlife Service. The potential acquisition boundary for the refuge in eastern Oklahoma was increased to 6073 ha in 2005 (U.S. Fish and Wildlife Service 2008a). All of the essential caves (one hibernacula and two maternity colony caves) associated with the northcentral Arkansas population of OBEBs have been purchased by the Arkansas Natural Heritage Commission or are managed by The Nature Conservancy. One essential maternity colony is owned by the U.S. Forest Service, and a complex of essential hibernacula is found within Devil's Den State Park, owned by the Arkansas Department of Parks and Tourism (U.S. Fish and Wildlife Service 2008a).

Four essential OBEB maternity caves, two hibernacula, and one other cave site have been protected with bat gates (Martin and others 2000, U.S. Fish and Wildlife Service 2008a). In Oklahoma, 11 nonessential sites have been gated and 1 fenced.[3] Two essential sites in Arkansas have closure signs, one of which is also fitted with an alarm system. Upon sensing light within the cave's dark zone, an alarm is triggered and transmitted to the agency which can then dispatch law enforcement personnel to the site (Harvey 1996, U.S. Fish and Wildlife Service 2008a).

With the recent discovery in Missouri and Oklahoma of *Geomyces destructans*, the fungus associated with WNS, this pathogen is a possible threat for OBEBs. There have been discussions regarding potential establishment of captive OBEB colonies as was attempted for VBEBs (see below).

Virginia Big-Eared Bats

Conservation actions for management of VBEBs have largely focused on WNS, protecting caves, and reducing disturbance to bats while they are in caves. The unexpected presence of WNS in the Pendleton County ESU triggered an emergency response by the U.S. Fish and Wildlife Service to consider captive holding and propagation as a management tool to preserve the species. In consultation with State agencies,

the U.S. Fish and Wildlife Service captured and transported 40 VBEBs from Pendleton County, WV, to the Smithsonian Conservation Biology Institute near Front Royal, VA, to examine feasibility of maintaining VBEBs in captivity. This effort was mostly a failure due to mortality of captive bats.

As of 2008, 7 of 13 "major" (> 200 bats) maternity colonies have long-term protection (U.S. Fish and Wildlife Service 2008b). Evidence suggests reduction of disturbance has led to increased population numbers at protected caves (U.S. Fish and Wildlife Service 2008b). In the early 1980s, many sites were gated using round-bar gates. All of these have subsequently been regated using more bat-friendly and more secure angle-iron gates. Also, the Monongahela National Forest's management plan addresses activities within 61 m of VBEB cave entrances and buildings near caves that may serve as night roosts or roosts for small numbers of male VBEBs (U.S. Department of Agriculture Forest Service 2006). The Daniel Boone National Forest management plan has direction to maintain mature forest cover 30 m above and 60 m below cliffline communities and provide a 0.4-km buffer around all maternity, bachelor, and hibernation sites for all *Corynorhinus* species (U.S. Department of Agriculture Forest Service 2004). Prohibited activities within buffers include construction of roads, trails, wildlife openings, cutting of overstory vegetation, prescribed burning, and pesticide application. In addition to site protection, management efforts have focused on identifying additional sites that support summer or winter populations. For example, in Tazewell County, VA, the number of breeding females is lower than expected based on the winter numbers and, assuming a 1:1 sex ratio, suggests additional undiscovered maternity sites. Unlike bat populations in Virginia, the number of bats in West Virginia hibernacula is lower than expected based on summer numbers and, assuming a 1:1 sex ratio, suggests there are additional undiscovered hibernation sites.

Rafinesque's Big-Eared Bat

Because of the wide distribution and relatively large populations of RBEBs (as compared to OBEBs and VBEBs), it is difficult to summarize specific conservation efforts. However, it appears that besides the obvious need for continued conservation and management of bottomland hardwood forests, current management activities for RBEBs most often involve identification and protection of roost sites. This includes manmade roosting structures, e.g., cisterns, buildings, etc.; natural tree roosts; caves; and creation of artificial roost structures. For example, the Arkansas Game and Fish Commission signed management agreements with two private landowners and Deltic Timber Corporation to manage five wells used by RBEBs as winter hibernacula and placed steel covers over the wells that allow bat access but alleviate human safety concerns. To date, the most successful

---

[3] Personal communication. 2009. Steve Hensley, Biologist, Ozark Plateau National Wildlife Refuge, Route 1, Box 18A, Vian, OK 74962.

artificial roost structures appear to be cinder block towers (Bayless 2006). There are also research projects underway or recently completed to identify natural roosts for RBEBs (e.g., Rice 2009, Stevenson 2008, Trousdale and Beckett 2005) and examine microclimate characteristics of artificial and natural RBEB roosts to aid in development of effective artificial roosts and conservation of natural roost structures (Bayless 2006, Rice 2009). Measures to conserve cave roosts for RBEBs are similar to those for OBEBs and VBEBs, which include reducing disturbance and documenting additional cave roosts.

CONSERVATION NEEDS

For all three big-eared bat taxa, there is a strong need for research to better understand basic ecology and examine effectiveness of conservation actions (Loeb and others 2011). However, the most pressing need for conservation of OBEBs, VBEBs, and cave and mine roosting RBEBs at this time is addressing WNS. Although establishment of a captive colony may be a critical step (see above), there is much to be learned about husbandry protocols and propagation of insectivorous bats, especially big-eared bats, in captivity. Detailed genetic information is needed to insure the captive population reflects the genetic diversity of the wild population, and this information is being gathered. There is also a need to develop an effective treatment for WNS which can be applied in the field and which will not harm the bats or other cave life. Based on comparisons of the number of bats observed in summer and winter, it appears very likely there are additional unknown summer colony roosts and hibernacula for VBEBs that should be located and protected (U.S. Fish and Wildlife Service 2008b). Efforts to understand effects of wind energy facilities on VBEBs and ways to mitigate these effects are also needed. Wind energy projects should not be sited in areas where there is a high risk to VBEBs [http://www.fws.gov/habitatconservation/Service%20Interim%20Guidelines.pdf. (Date accessed: March 8, 2010)], and effective strategies for minimizing bat kills (e.g., Arnett and others 2007) should be developed, implemented, and evaluated at sites where VBEBs are not present before wind facilities are considered in areas where VBEBs are likely to occur.

For OBEBs, much progress has been made in the discovery of occupied caves, but continued searches for new caves are warranted, particularly in the vicinity of essential caves that have not been paired with caves used by that population in the opposite season (U.S. Fish and Wildlife Service 2008a). For example, the Devil's Den complex in western Arkansas has one of the largest winter populations in the State, but it is not known where these bats spend the summer. Finding such

sites can be difficult as OBEBs use caves that range from a small crevice to caves > 14.5 km in length (U.S. Fish and Wildlife Service 2008a).

Integration of RBEB habitat needs with easement programs on private lands, such as the Natural Resources Conservation Service (NRCS) Wetland's Reserve Program (WRP) [http://www.nrcs.usda.gov/PROGRAMS/wrp/. (Date accessed: February 25, 2010)], may be an opportunity to ensure habitat needs for this species in the Coastal Plain. Similar to the Conservation Reserve Program (CRP), WRP uses economic incentives to encourage private landowners to restore natural wetland systems to former agricultural lands. This includes tree plantings, restoration of natural hydrology, and/or natural regeneration. The potential impact of this program is substantial. Throughout the Southeastern United States, five States (Arkansas, Florida, Louisiana, Missouri, and Mississippi) have > 40 000 ha in WRP easements; three States (North Carolina, South Carolina, and Tennessee) have > 12 000 ha of easements; and two States (Georgia and Kentucky) have > 6000 ha of WRP easements (see footnote 1). In Mississippi, there are currently 68 623 ha under WRP contract with 52 672 ha restored to bottomland hardwoods (see footnote 1). Species planted in hardwood restoration are usually site-dependent but include a wide variety of oak species and potential roost tress for RBEBs, such as bald cypress, sweetgum (*Liquidambar styraciflua*), and tupelo gum (Clark 1990, Rice 2009, Stevenson 2008).

Forest ownership patterns are important to understand to direct conservation efforts. In 1999, private, nonindustrial landowners owned 69 percent of southern forest land, followed by forest industry (20 percent), national forest (6 percent), and other public ownership (5 percent). Later assessments verify approximately 87 percent of forest land in the South is privately owned [www.fia.fs.fed.us/program-features/rpa/. (Date accessed: March 4, 2010)]. The U.S. Fish and Wildlife Service (2008a) has acknowledged the need to work with private landowners to conserve foraging areas for OBEBs.

This need also exists for VBEBs as they may move up to approximately 11 km from maternity caves to foraging sites (Stihler 2011a). As noted previously, many opportunities exist for managing RBEBs on private land. However, a challenge for big-eared bat conservation on private land is a continuing shift in forest ownership patterns with parcelization of large blocks of private forest land leading to a larger number of owners of smaller parcels of land (Smith and other 2009, Wigley and others 2007). This is exacerbated by fragmentation due to urbanization (Mehmood and Zhang 2001) and the reduced ability to manage forests on landscapes with increasing human populations (Wear and others 1999). Additionally, many new industrial forest landowners are investment firms, e.g., timberland investment management organizations, with land management objectives that may not include long-term ownership and management of forested lands (Block and Sample 2001, Ravenel and others 2002, Stein and others 2010, Wigley and others 2007). This may make future conservation actions on these landscapes more challenging as innovative approaches will be needed to develop cohesive management plans for many species, including big-eared bats, across a greater diversity and number of forest owners with divergent management objectives. Potential approaches to improving conservation for species on private lands include partnerships among conservation organizations to work with private landowners toward common goals and to encourage multispecies management. A recent agreement between Bat Conservation International and the National Wild Turkey Federation highlights such an opportunity. Another approach is to ensure big-eared bats are considered as part of broader plans to conserve biodiversity (Wigley and others 2007). Additionally, conservation organizations and agencies providing input regarding habitat needs of big-eared bats in conservation easement programs, whether within public or private agencies, may be another way to engage private landowners in effective conservation.

Finally, as noted in this volume (Loeb and others 2011) and by others (e.g., Miller and others 2003), there is a need to allocate resources for bat research, particularly big-eared bats. In many cases, basic ecological information is lacking which hampers efforts to develop management recommendations for these bats. In particular, there is a general lack of understanding of foraging requirements for RBEBs, with only limited data available to date (e.g., Menzel and others 2001). Also, much of the current research on RBEBs has focused on identification of roost tree characteristics without a full understanding of whether roost sites are limiting and how other factors, e.g., landscape composition, habitat/cavity availability, location/type of foraging areas, may affect roost site selection. Information on importance of artificial versus natural roosts relative to long-term survival of RBEB populations is also needed. Because Coastal Plain populations of RBEBs are more dispersed and difficult to locate, more data are needed regarding methods to estimate and monitor population abundance, distribution, and response to various land management and conservation options on public and private lands. For VBEBs and OBEBs, and RBEBs in karst areas, information needs include factors influencing selection of caves and location of new maternity caves and hibernacula. Critical research needs for all three big-eared bats include movements and foraging area characteristics, basic population parameters (survival, fecundity, dispersal), susceptibility and potential mortality from WNS, and potential impacts of wind energy development.

LITERATURE CITED

Arnett, E.B.; Inkley, D.B; Johnson, D.H. [and others]. 2007. Impacts of wind energy facilities on wildlife and wildlife habitat. Technical Review 07-2. Bethesda, MD: The Wildlife Society. 49 p.

Arroyo-Cabrales, J.; Ticul Alvarez Castaneda, S. 2008. *Corynorhinus rafinesquii*. In: 2008 IUCN red list of threatened species. http://www.iucnredlist.org/details/17600. [Date accessed: August 27, 2010].

Barbour, R.W.; Davis, W.H. 1969. Bats of America. Lexington, KY: University of Kentucky Press. 286 p.

Bayless, M.L. 2006. Designing homes for forest bats. Bats. 26: 9-11.

Bayless, M.L.; Clark, M.K.; Stark, R.C. [and others]. 2011. Distribution and status of eastern big-eared bats (*Corynorhinus* spp.). In: Loeb, S.C.; Lacki, M.J.; Miller, D.A., eds. Conservation and management of eastern big-eared bats: a symposium. Gen. Tech. Rep. SRS-145. Asheville, NC: U.S. Department of Agriculture Forest Service, Southern Research Station: 13-25.

Bennett, F.M.; Loeb, S.C.; Bunch, M.S.; Bowerman, W.W. 2008. Use and selection of bridges as day roosts by Rafinesque's big-eared bats. American Midland Naturalist. 160(2): 386-399.

Blehert, D.S.; Hicks, A.C.; Behr, M. [and others]. 2009. Bat white-nose syndrome: an emerging fungal pathogen? Science. 323: 227.

Block, N.E.; Sample, V.A. 2001. Industrial timberland divestitures and investments: opportunities and challenges in forestland conservation. Washington, DC: Pinchot Institute for Conservation. 50 p.

Burford, L.S.; Lacki, M.J.; Covell, C.V., Jr. 1999. Occurrence of moths among habitats in a mixed mesophytic forest: implications for management of forest bats. Forest Science. 45(3): 323-332.

Clark, M.K. 1990. Roosting ecology of the eastern big-eared bat, *Plecotus rafinesquii*. Raleigh, NC: North Carolina State University. 111 p. M.S. thesis.

Dalton, V.M.; Brack, V., Jr.; McTeer, P.M. 1986. Food habits of the big-eared bat, *Plecotus townsendii virginianus*, in Virginia. Virginia Journal of Science. 37(4): 248-254.

Dalton, V.M.; Brack, V.W., Jr.; Williams, C. 1989. Foraging ecology of the Virginia big-eared bat; performance report. Richmond, VA: Virginia Department of Game and Inland Fisheries: 32-46.

Dodd, L.E.; Lacki, M.J. 2007. Prey consumed by *Corynorhinus townsendii ingens* in the Ozark Mountain region. Acta Chiropterologica. 9(2): 451-461.

Dodd, L.E.; Lacki, M.J.; Rieske, L.K. 2008. Variation in moth occurrence and implications for foraging habitat of Ozark big-eared bats. Forest Ecology and Management. 255: 3866-3872.

Dürr, T.; Bach, L. 2004. Bat deaths at wind turbines—a review of current knowledge, and of the information available in the database for Germany. Bremer Beiträge für Naturkunde und Naturschutz. 7: 253-264.

England, D.R.; Saugey, D.A.; McDaniel, V.R.; Speight, S.M. 1990. Observations on the life history of Rafinesque's big-eared bat, *Plecotus rafinesquii*, in southern Arkansas [Abstract]. Bat Research News. 30: 62-63.

Elliott, W.R.; Lister, K.B.; Shiver, M.A. 1999. A survey for Ozark big-eared bats *Corynorhinus townsendii ingens* and a cave crayfish *Cambarus aculabrum* in southern Missouri. 29 p. Unpublished report. On file with: Missouri Department of Conservation, 1907 Hillcrest Drive, Columbia, MO 65201.

Gooding, G.; Langford, J.R. 2004. Characteristics of tree roosts of Rafinesque's big-eared bat and southeastern bat in northeastern Louisiana. Southwestern Naturalist. 49(1): 61-67.

Harvey, M.J. 1996. Status and management of endangered bats in Arkansas. Proceedings of the Southeastern Association of Fish and Wildlife Agencies. 50: 246-253.

Hermann, S.M.; Hook, T.V.; Flowers, R.W. [and others]. 1998. Fire and biodiversity: studies of vegetation and arthropods. Transactions of the North American Wildlife and Natural Resources Conference. 63: 384-401.

Hurst, T.E.; Lacki, M.J. 1999. Roost selection, population size and habitat use by a colony of Rafinesque's big-eared bats (*Corynorhinus rafinesquii*). The American Midland Naturalist. 142(2): 363-371.

Kunz, T.H.; Martin, R.A. 1982. *Plecotus townsendii*. Mammalian Species. 175: 1-6.

Lacki, M.J.; Dodd, L.E. 2011. Diet and foraging behavior of *Corynorhinus* in Eastern North America. In: Loeb, S.C.; Lacki, M.J.; Miller, D.A., eds. Conservation and management of eastern big-eared bats: a symposium. Gen. Tech. Rep. SRS-145. Asheville, NC: U.S. Department of Agriculture Forest Service, Southern Research Station: 39-52.

Lance, R.F.; Hardcastle, B.T.; Talley, A.; Leberg, P.L. 2001. Day-roost selection by Rafinesque's big-eared bats (*Corynorhinus rafinesquii*) in Louisiana forests. Journal of Mammalogy. 82(1): 166-172.

Loeb, S.B.; Lacki, M.J.; Miller, D.A. 2011. Conservation and management of eastern big-eared bats: an introduction. In: Loeb, S.C.; Lacki, M.J.; Miller, D.A., eds. Conservation and management of eastern big-eared bats: a symposium. Gen. Tech. Rep. SRS-145. Asheville, NC: U.S. Department of Agriculture Forest Service, Southern Research Station: 1-11.

Loeb, S.B.; Zarnoch, S.J. 2011. Seasonal and multiannual roost use by Rafinesque's big-eared bats in the Coastal Plain of South Carolina. In: Loeb, S.C.; Lacki, M.J.; Miller, D.A., eds. Conservation and management of eastern big-eared bats: a symposium. Gen. Tech. Rep. SRS-145. Asheville, NC: U.S. Department of Agriculture Forest Service, Southern Research Station: 111-120.

Martin, K.W.; Puckette, W.L.; Hensley, S.L.; Leslie, D.M., Jr. 2000. Internal cave gating as a means of protecting cave-dwelling bat populations in eastern Oklahoma. Proceedings of the Oklahoma Academy of Sciences. 80: 133-137.

Mehmood, S.R.; Zhang, D. 2001. Forest parcelization in the United States: a study of contributing factors. Journal of Forestry. 99(4): 30-34.

Menzel, M.A.; Menzel, J.M.; Ford, W.M. [and others]. 2001. Home range and habitat use of male Rafinesque's big-eared bats (*Corynorhinus rafinesquii*). American Midland Naturalist. 145(2): 402-408.

Miller, D.A.; Arnett, E.B.; Lacki, M.J. 2003. Habitat management for forest-roosting bats of North America: a critical review of habitat studies. Wildlife Society Bulletin. 31(1): 30-44.

Mirowsky, K.M.; Horner, P.A.; Maxev, R.W.; Smith, S.A. 2004. Distributional records and roosts of southeastern myotis and Rafinesque's big-eared bat in eastern Texas. Southwestern Naturalist. 49(2): 294-298.

National Commission on Science for Sustainable Forestry. 2005. Global markets forum summary report, May 4, 2005. NCSSF Proj. C9. Washington, DC. 20 p.

Piaggio, A.J.; Navo, K.W.; Stihler, C.W. 2009. Intraspecific comparison of population structure, genetic diversity, and dispersal among three subspecies of Townsend's big-eared bats, *Corynorhinus townsendii townsendii*, *C. t. pallescens*, and the endangered *C. t. virginianus*. Conservation Genetics. 10(1): 143-159.

Piaggio, A.J.; Saugey, D.A.; Sasse, D.B. 2011. Phylogenetic and population genetic assessment of Rafinesque's big-eared bat (*Corynorhinus rafinesquii*). In: Loeb, S.C.; Lacki, M.J.; Miller, D.A., eds. Conservation and management of eastern big-eared bats: a symposium. Gen. Tech. Rep. SRS-145. Asheville, NC: U.S. Department of Agriculture Forest Service, Southern Research Station: 85-99.

Ravenel, R.; Tyrrell, M.; Mendelsohn, R. 2002. Institutional timberland investment: a summary of a forum exploring changing ownership patterns and the implications for conservation and environmental values. New Haven, CT: Yale University, Global Institute of Sustainable Forestry, School of Forestry and Environmental Studies. Yale Forest Forum Review. 5(2). 30 p.

Rice, C.L. 2009. Roosting ecology of *Corynorhinus rafinesquii* (Rafinesque's big-eared bat) and *Myotis austroriparius* (southeastern myotis) in tree cavities found in a northeastern Louisiana bottomland hardwood forest streambed. Monroe, LA: University of Louisiana at Monroe. 124 p. M.S. thesis.

Ross, A. 1967. Ecological aspects of the food habits of insectivorous bats. Proceedings of the Western Foundation of Vertebrate Zoology. 1: 205-265.

Sealander, J.A.; Heidt, G.A. 2002. Arkansas mammals. Fayetteville, AR: University of Arkansas Press. 308 p.

Smith, W.B.; Miles, P.D.; Perry, C.H.; Pugh, S.A. 2009. Forest resources of the United States, 2007. Gen. Tech. Rep. WO-78. Washington, DC: U.S. Department of Agriculture Forest Service. 336 p.

Stein, S.M.; McRoberts, R.E.; Nelson, M.D. [and others]. 2010. Private forest habitat for at-risk species: where is it and where might it be changing? Journal of Forestry. 108(2): 61-70.

Stevenson, C.L. 2008. Availability and seasonal use of diurnal roosts by Rafinesque's big-eared bat and southeastern myotis in bottomland hardwoods of Mississippi. Starkville, MS: Mississippi State University. 109 p. M.S. thesis.

Stihler, C.W. 2011a. Radiotelemetry studies of female Virginia big-eared bats (*Corynorhinus townsendii virginianus*) in Pendleton County, West Virginia. In: Loeb, S.C.; Lacki, M.J.; Miller, D.A., eds. Conservation and management of eastern big-eared bats: a symposium. Gen. Tech. Rep. SRS-145. Asheville, NC: U.S. Department of Agriculture Forest Service, Southern Research Station: 139–146.

Stihler, C.W. 2011b. Status of the Virginia big-eared bat (*Corynorhinus townsendii virginianus*) in West Virginia: twenty-seven years of monitoring cave roosts. In: Loeb, S.C.; Lacki, M.J.; Miller, D.A., eds. Conservation and management of eastern big-eared bats: a symposium. Gen. Tech. Rep. SRS-145. Asheville, NC: U.S. Department of Agriculture Forest Service, Southern Research Station: 75-84.

Trousdale, A.W.; Beckett, D.C. 2004. Seasonal use of bridges by Rafinesque's big-eared bat, *Corynorhinus rafinesquii*, in southern Mississippi. Southeastern Naturalist. 3(1): 103-112.

Trousdale, A.W.; Beckett, D.C. 2005. Characteristics of tree roosts of Rafinesque's big-eared bat (*Corynorhinus rafinesquii*) in southeastern Mississippi. American Midland Naturalist. 154(2): 442-449.

U.S. Department of Agriculture Forest Service. 2004. Land and resources management plan for the Daniel Boone National Forest. 286 p. http://www.fs.fed.us/r8/boone/documents/ planning/revplan/forest_plan/plan_whole_doc.pdf. [Date accessed: August 27, 2010].

U.S. Department of Agriculture Forest Service. 2006. Land resource management plan for the Monongahela National Forest. 246 p. http://www.fs.usda.gov/Internet/FSE_DOCUMENTS/ fsm9_011359.pdf. [Date accessed: August 27, 2010].

U.S. Fish and Wildlife Service. 1995. Ozark big-eared bat (*Plecotus townsendii ingens* [Handley]) revised recovery plan. Tulsa, OK. 51 p. http://ecos.fws.gov/docs/recovery_plan/950328b.pdf. [Date accessed: August 27, 2010].

U.S. Fish and Wildlife Service. 2008a. Ozark big-eared bat (*Corynorhinus townsendii ingens*) 5-year review: summary and evaluation. Tulsa, OK. 40 p.

U.S. Fish and Wildlife Service. 2008b. Virginia big-eared bat (*Corynorhinus townsendii virginianus*) 5-year review: summary and evaluation. Elkins, WV. 21 p.

Wear, D.N.; Greis, J.G. 2002. The Southern Forest Resource Assessment: summary report. Gen. Tech. Rep. SRS-54. Asheville, NC: U.S. Department of Agriculture Forest Service, Southern Research Station. 104 p.

Wear, D.N.; Liu, R.; Foreman, J.M.; Sheffield, R.M. 1999. The effects of population growth on timber management and inventories in Virginia. Forest Ecology and Management. 118: 107-115.

Wethington, T.A.; Leslie, D.M., Jr.; Gregory, M.S.; Wethington, M.K. 1996. Prehibernation habitat use and foraging activity by endangered Ozark big-eared bats (*Corynorhinus townsendii ingens*). American Midland Naturalist. 135(2): 218-230.

Weyandt, S.E.; Van Den Bussche, R.A.; Hamilton, M.J.; Leslie, D.M., Jr. 2005. Unraveling the effects of sex and dispersal: Ozark big-eared bat (*Corynorhinus townsendii ingens*) conservation genetics. Journal of Mammalogy. 86(6): 1136-1143.

Whitaker, J.O, Jr.; Hamilton, W.J., Jr. 1998. Mammals of the Eastern United States. 3d ed. Ithaca, NY: Cornell University Press. 583 p.

Whitaker, J.O., Jr.; Maser, C.; Keller, L.E. 1977. Food habits of bats of western Oregon. Northwest Science. 51(1): 46-55.

Wigley, T.B.; Miller, D.A.; Yarrow, G.K. 2007. Planning for bats on forest industry lands in North America. In: Lacki, M.J.; Hayes, J.P.; Kurta, A., eds. Bats in forests: conservation and management. Baltimore, MD: John Hopkins University Press: 293-318.

RAFINESQUE'S BIG-EARED BAT (*CORYNORHINUS RAFINESQUII*) IN MISSISSIPPI: DISTRIBUTION, CURRENT STATUS, AND CONSERVATION NEEDS

Chester O. Martin, Research Emeritus, U.S. Army Engineer Research & Development Center, Environmental Laboratory, Vicksburg, MS 39180

Alison S. McCartney, Natural Resource Specialist, U.S. Bureau of Land Management, Jackson, MS 39206

David Richardson, Wildlife Biologist, U.S. Fish and Wildlife Service, Noxubee National Wildlife Refuge, Brookeville, MS 39739

Austin W. Trousdale, Assistant Professor, Lander University, Department of Biology, Greenwood, SC 29649

Monica S. Wolters, Student, Mississippi College, Education Department, Clinton, MS 39206

Abstract—Rafinesque's big-eared bat (*Corynorhinus rafinesquii*) is a "Species of Greatest Conservation Need" in Mississippi that is potentially negatively affected by habitat changes resulting from natural and anthropogenic events. Historical records and recent investigations indicate that the species is widespread in Mississippi, but surveys and monitoring sufficient to ascertain status of its populations have been limited in spatial and temporal scope. To date, big-eared bats have been documented in 27 counties. The species is typically associated with mature bottomland hardwood forests but also occurs in upland mixed woodlands, and several maternity roosts have been found in abandoned houses in upland pine (*Pinus* spp.) forests. Most studies in Mississippi have yielded data on current distribution and extent that artificial structures serve as maternity roosts. There is a need to further investigate use of natural roosts using radiotelemetry in certain forest types, e.g., bottomlands within the floodplain of large rivers and mixed woodlands of the Loess Hills. Studies of winter roosts and foraging habitat also are needed to gain a more complete understanding of ecology of the species. Management should include identification and protection of natural and artificial roosts, location and protection of wells and cisterns that potentially serve as winter roosts, selective management for appropriate cavity-producing trees, and improved coordination and cooperation among government agencies and private landowners.

INTRODUCTION

Rafinesque's big-eared bat (*Corynorhinus rafinesquii*) occurs throughout the Southeastern United States but is considered uncommon over most of its range, including Mississippi (Harvey and others 1999). The species is State-listed as endangered, threatened, or of special concern in all States where it occurs, and it is listed as a "Species of Greatest Conservation Need" in Mississippi (Mississippi Museum of Natural Science 2005). Prior to the early 1990s, Rafinesque's big-eared bats had been reported only from scattered localities from 12 counties in Mississippi, but recent surveys throughout portions of the State have documented their occurrence in 15 additional counties (fig. 1). Although several recent big-eared bat studies conducted in Mississippi have been published in professional journals (e.g., Trousdale and Beckett 2002, 2004, 2005; Trousdale and others 2008), results of most field studies are currently available only in unpublished theses (Sherman 2004, Stevenson 2008, Wilf 2004) and agency reports (e.g., Martin and others 2007, 2008; McCartney 2007). Thus, we identified a need to examine recent published and unpublished studies and consolidate information on this species for Mississippi. This was necessary to provide researchers and managers the most up-to-date information for assessing species status and making management decisions. Herein, we describe distribution of known populations, status of roost sites and maternity colonies, management practices implemented to conserve the species and provide roosting habitat, and conservation needs for Rafinesque's big-eared bats in Mississippi.

DISTRIBUTION AND STATUS

Historical records of Rafinesque's big-eared bats in Mississippi indicated that the species was uncommon in the State. Big-eared bats catalogued in the Mississippi Museum of Natural Science (MMNS) Natural Heritage Database during 1894 to 1941 consisted of specimens collected in Hinds, Pearl River, Rankin, Simpson, Washington, Wayne, and Yazoo Counties (fig. 1). No additional specimens were deposited in the museum until 1990. Wolfe (1971) stated that although not common, big-eared bats were distributed throughout the State and had been reported from buildings, caves (usually near the entrance), and hollow bald cypress (*Taxodium distichum*) trees. At that time populations were known to occur in eight counties, five of which were

Citation for proceedings: Loeb, Susan C.; Lacki, Michael J.; Miller, Darren A., eds. 2011. Conservation and management of eastern big-eared bats: a symposium. Gen. Tech. Rep. SRS-145. Asheville, NC: U.S. Department of Agriculture, Forest Service, Southern Research Station. 157 p.

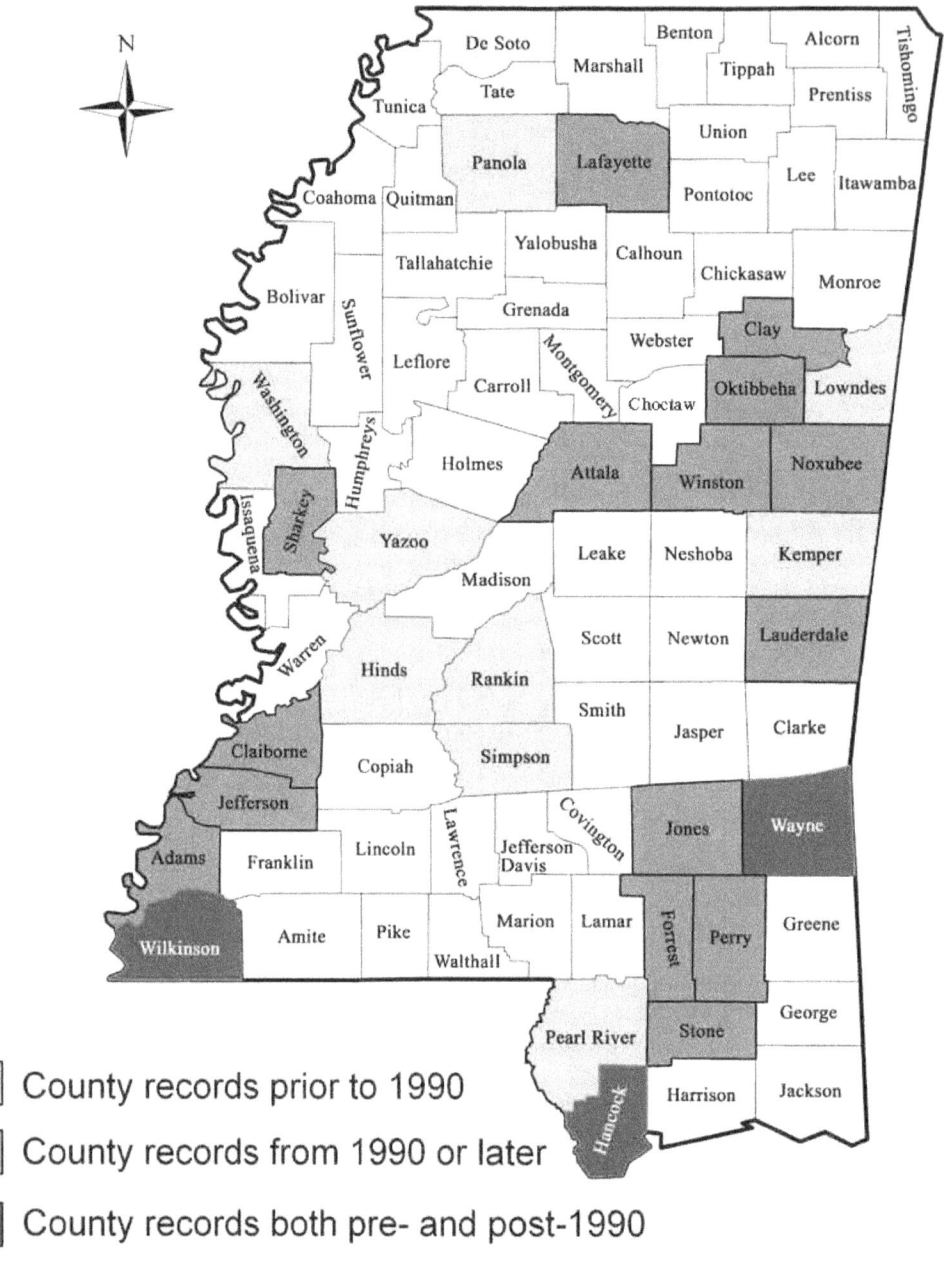

Figure 1—Known distribution of Rafinesque's big-eared bat based on early museum and literature records (pre-1990) and recent surveys (1998 to 2009).

☐ County records prior to 1990

▨ County records from 1990 or later

■ County records both pre- and post-1990

represented by specimens in the MMNS and three of which were reported in the literature. These included counties in the northeastern (Oktibbeha and Lowndes), northern (Panola), westcentral (Yazoo and Rankin), southwestern (Wilkinson), and southern (Wayne, Pearl River, and Hancock) parts of the State. Kennedy and others (1974) listed records from the following nine counties, all of which were derived from the literature: Hancock, Kemper, Lowndes, Panola, Pearl River, Rankin, Wayne, Wilkinson, and Yazoo. Jones and Carter (1989) stated that the species was statewide in occurrence, with the subspecies *C. r. rafinesquii* along the northern

edge of the State and *C. r. macrotis* throughout the rest of Mississippi. Specimens catalogued in the MMNS during 1990 to 2001 were collected in Clay, Hancock, Perry, and Wayne Counties.

Recent studies have revealed Rafinesque's big-eared bats in several additional areas in Mississippi. Trousdale and Beckett (2002, 2004) conducted surveys in southern Mississippi and located colonies beneath bridges in five counties (Jones, Perry, Stone, Wayne, and Wilkinson). Most bridges surveyed were within or near the DeSoto or Bienville National

Forests (NF). Terrain consisted of a mosaic of habitat types including upland and lowland mixed hardwood-pine (*Pinus* spp.) forest, upland mesic hardwood forest, bottomland hardwoods, and bald cypress/tupelo (*Nyssa* spp.) swamps. Other locations in southern Mississippi include several sites on Camp Shelby Army National Guard Training Site, now referred to as the Camp Shelby Joint Forces Training Center (JFTC) in Forrest and Perry Counties. Sites on Camp Shelby where big-eared bats were captured with mist nets primarily were narrow riparian corridors adjacent to pine-hardwood forests (Martin and others 2007).

Several studies also have documented occurrence in western and southwestern counties. Wilf (2004) captured a single male in a mist net on Delta NF in Sharkey County. Sherman (2004) examined maternity colonies roosting in abandoned houses on St. Catherine Creek National Wildlife Refuge (NWR) in Adams County. One of the colonies was reported to contain 60 individuals in 1990 (Sherman 2004). St. Catherine Creek NWR consisted of a mixture of bottomland hardwoods, upland mixed hardwoods, and open water areas managed primarily for waterfowl. Big-eared bats also have been documented using bridges as roosts at crossings along tributaries of Bayou Pierre in Claiborne County. One of the bridges supports a maternity colony of about 30 individuals (Wolters and Martin 2000, 2011); the surrounding area was primarily recently harvested hardwood forest. In August 2009, a large population consisting of about 150 individuals was located in an abandoned building in Jefferson County.[1] This represents the largest known maternity colony of Rafinesque's big-eared bats in Mississippi.

Limited surveys for big-eared bats have been conducted in northcentral and eastern counties, except for studies of roosting habitat in bottomland hardwood areas on the Noxubee NWR (Richardson 2007, Stevenson 2008). Several colonies have been located in hollow bald cypress and American sycamore (*Platanus occidentalis*) trees on this refuge in Oktibbeha, Winston, and Noxubee Counties. An abandoned house in Clay County has served as a maternity roost since 1988. A maternity colony recently discovered in an abandoned seismograph building in Lafayette County in northcentral Mississippi was reported to contain 85 to 100 individuals during summer 2008.[2] We confirmed that this structure contained about 70 hibernating Rafinesque's big-eared bats on March 3, 2009. Big-eared bats were documented from Lauderdale County in eastern Mississippi when five individuals were observed roosting in an elongated airstrip culvert on Naval Air Station (NAS) Meridian on

October 11, 2000 (Martin and others 2005). Finally, one specimen was captured during a mist net survey conducted by the Mississippi Bat Working Group (MBWG) in Attala County in July 2007.

ROOST SITES

Rafinesque's big-eared bats roost in natural sites and a variety of humanmade structures throughout their range (Bennett and others 2008, Clark 1990, Gooding and Langford 2004, Jones 1977, Lance and others 2001, Trousdale and Beckett 2004, Trousdale and others 2008). Although Wolfe (1971) indicated that big-eared bats were known from sites near openings of caves in Mississippi, use of caves in Mississippi has not been documented during more recent surveys. McCartney (2007) surveyed 22 caves in Mississippi (primarily on private property) in 11 counties during 2005 to 2007 and found no evidence of big-eared bats. Trousdale and Beckett (2002) surveyed five of these caves and three additional caves in two counties and likewise did not observe big-eared bats.

In Mississippi, big-eared bats have been documented using a variety of roosts including tree cavities, bridges, culverts, wells, cisterns, abandoned structures, and specially designed artificial roosts. They were observed in 18 hollow trees and 3 abandoned buildings on Noxubee NWR (Stevenson 2008); 14 trees, 16 bridges, and 3 abandoned houses on DeSoto NF (Trousdale and Beckett 2005, Trousdale and others 2008); 6 additional bridge sites, an abandoned house, and a well in southwestern Mississippi (Claiborne and Jefferson Counties); 5 abandoned buildings on St. Catherine Creek NWR (Sherman 2004); an abandoned house, an old well, and a bald cypress tree on the Delta NF in western Mississippi (Wilf 2004); old bunkers and the digester tank of an abandoned water treatment plant on Camp Shelby JFTC in southern Mississippi (Martin and others 2007); and cinder block artificial roosts on St. Catherine Creek NWR (McCartney 2007) and DeSoto NF.[3] Big-eared bats once were observed roosting in elongated airstrip culverts in eastern Mississippi (Martin and others 2005).

Studies of natural roosts of big-eared bats in Mississippi have only been conducted on DeSoto NF (Trousdale and Beckett 2005) and Noxubee NWR (Richardson 2007, Stevenson 2008). Trees used as roosts on DeSoto NF were hollow tupelo and southern magnolia (*Magnolia grandiflora*), most of which were alive, relatively large (mean d.b.h. = 79.4 cm), and possessed openings to cavities located well above the base of the tree. Roosts were in 14 trees, all of which were within bottomland hardwood or loblolly pine

---

[1] Personal communication. 2009. Lann M. Wilf, Deer Program Biologist, Mississippi Department of Wildlife, Fisheries and Parks, 30095 Peacely Ferry Road, Aberdeen, MS 39730.

[2] Personal communication. 2009. Edmund Keiser, Professor (retired). University of Mississippi, Biology Department, 211 Saint Andrews Circle, Oxford, MS 38655.

[3] Personal communication. 2010. Stephanie Steele, Wildlife Biologist, U.S. Forest Service, Chickasawhay Ranger District, 968 Highway 15 South, Laurel, MS 39443.

(*P. taeda*)-hardwood stands. Stevenson (2008) documented relative abundance of cavities in trees and their use by big-eared bats within bottomland hardwood forests. Large hollow trees (mean d.b.h. = 100 cm) were used most often as roosts, but some bats used cavities in trees as small as 41 cm d.b.h. Rafinesque's big-eared bats most often selected roosts in cavities of bald cypress, black tupelo (*N. sylvatica*), American sycamore, pignut hickory (*Carya glabra*), and two oak (*Quercus* spp.) species—swamp chestnut oak (*Q. michauxii*) and water oak (*Q. nigra*). Other species that provided roost sites were sweetgum (*Liquidambar styraciflua*), American beech (*Fagus grandifolia*), overcup oak (*Q. lyrata*), shagbark hickory (*C. ovata*), cherrybark oak (*P. pagoda*), eastern cottonwood (*Populus deltoides*), willow oak (*Q. phellos*), and white oak (*Q. alba*) (Stevenson 2008).

Maternity Roosts

Most investigations of Rafinesque's big-eared bat roost sites in Mississippi have focused on maternity roosts (herein defined as a roost site occupied by multiple females and where birthing apparently has taken place) in artificial structures (table 1). However, few studies of maternity colonies in natural roosts have been conducted and these data should be viewed only as estimates. Maternity roosts in tree cavities have only been documented on DeSoto NF (Trousdale and Beckett 2005, Trousdale and others 2008) and Noxubee NWR (Stevenson 2008). Seven tupelo and southern magnolia trees on DeSoto NF were used by multiple individuals and considered to be maternity roosts (Trousdale and Beckett 2005). Stevenson (2008) located maternity roosts in four relict bald cypress

Table 1—County and status of recently surveyed maternity roosts of Rafinesque's big-eared bats in Mississippi[a]

Location	Type of roost	Bats	Date of last survey	Source
		no.		
Adams County	3 artificial roosts[b]	70	July 2007	McCartney (2007)
Claiborne County	Concrete bridge	30+	June 2009	Wolters (unpub. data)
Clay County	Abandoned house	75–90	2008	Richardson (unpub. data)
George County	1 concrete bridge	11	July 2001	Trousdale (2008)
Jefferson County	Abandoned stone building	150	Aug 2009	Wilf (pers. commun.)
Jones County (West locality[c])	2 concrete bridges	30+	July 2005	Trousdale (2008)
Lafayette County	Abandoned stone building	85–100	June 2008	Keiser (pers. commun.)
Perry County (Benndale[c])	3 concrete bridges	30	July 2004	Trousdale (2008)
Perry County (Cypress Creek[c])	1 concrete bridge	4	July 2004	Trousdale (unpub. data)
Perry County (Leaf River WMA[c])	2 concrete bridges	8	July 2004	Trousdale (2008)
Wayne County (East locality[c])	2 concrete bridges	6	May 2005	Trousdale (2008)
Wayne County (North locality[c])	2 concrete bridges	12	June 2004	Trousdale (2008)
Wayne County (Hollis Creek[c])	2 concrete bridges	10	July 2005	Trousdale (2008)
Wayne County (Thompson Creek[c])	2 concrete bridges	6	June 2004	Trousdale (2008)
DeSoto National Forest	14 tree roosts	33	Aug 2004	Trousdale (pers. commun.)
Noxubee National Wildlife Refuge	4 tree roosts	160	2007	Stevenson (pers. commun.)

WMA = Wildlife Management Area.

Numbers of bats associated with bridges represent values recorded on the most recent survey when bats were present; most bridges were surveyed multiple times over at least a 3-year period and numbers were quite variable.

[a] Number of bats includes adult females and young at highest count made during the latest survey.

[b] Previously in abandoned house.

[c] Locality [see Trousdale (2008) for description].

Figure 2—Concrete girder bridge in Claiborne County, MS, used as a maternity roost by > 30 Rafinesque's big-eared bats in 2009. (Photo by Monica Wolters)

trees (d.b.h. > 127.0 cm) with top openings on Noxubee NWR. The maximum number of bats in the 4 trees combined was estimated at 160, with 50 bats being the largest number estimated in a single roost at one time.[4]

Trousdale and Beckett (2002) surveyed 99 bridges in southern Mississippi and identified 6 bridges in 5 counties inhabited by big-eared bats. Repeated visits to these sites and other locations revealed that 36 bridges located on or near DeSoto NF were used at least once during 2002 to 2004, with 1 to 25 bats observed (Trousdale and Beckett 2004). All bridges used by bats were made of concrete and had rectangular compartments or girders on the underside. Additionally, Trousdale (2008) radio tracked big-eared bats to 25 roost structures in his study area. Besides the previously noted tree roosts, 11 were humanmade (8 bridges, 2 abandoned houses, and 1 empty oil storage tank). Maternity roosts were documented beneath 20 bridges, in 1 house, and in an oil tank (Trousdale and Beckett 2004). Populations roosting in bridges also have been documented in westcentral Mississippi. A maternity roost with 32 big-eared bats was discovered in April 2000 beneath a bridge over a tributary of Bayou Pierre in Claiborne County about 1 km from the Mississippi River (Wolters and Martin 2000, 2011). The bridge was a concrete girder structure with multiple compartments on each side

(fig. 2). Surveys of this bridge, four other bridges, and an abandoned house with an adjacent well were conducted during 2000 to 2009.[5] The maternity colony has fluctuated considerably since first observed (32 bats in 2000), with an estimate of 20 in 2001 to 30 in 2009. The other bridges surveyed did not support maternity colonies but commonly were used as day roosts by individual or small numbers of bats. Surveys on Camp Shelby JFTC in southcentral Mississippi documented big-eared bats roosting in seven cement structures, including observation point bunkers, an abandoned building, the digester tank of an old wastewater treatment plant, and two bridges. The bridges on Camp Shelby supported about 11 and 25 bats in 1999 (Trousdale and Beckett 2002). The digester tank historically supported a maternity population of 45 big-eared bats, but recent surveys have documented only a few individuals using the structure (Martin and others 2007). Small maternity colonies presently occur beneath two concrete bridges on secondary roads on the installation. Surveys of bridges in other regions of Mississippi have revealed little use by big-eared bats. No bats were roosting beneath 42 bridges examined on Noxubee NWR and vicinity in 2007 to 2008 (Stevenson 2008), 24 bridges on Theodore Roosevelt NWR in 2008, and 15 bridges in southeastern Mississippi along the Pascagoula River Basin in 2009 (McCartney 2010).

[4] Personal communication. 2010. Candice Stevenson, Refuge Operations Specialist, U.S. Fish and Wildlife Service, Merritt Island National Wildlife Refuge, P.O. Box 2683, Titusville, FL 32781.

[5] Personal observation. M. Wolters and C.O. Martin.

Figure 3—Abandoned house on St. Catherine Creek National Wildlife Refuge that historically served as a maternity roost for 40 to 60 Rafinesque's big-eared bats. (Photo by Alison McCartney)

Sherman (2004) examined artificial roosts used by Rafinesque's big-eared bats on St. Catherine Creek NWR and vicinity in southwestern Mississippi. Big-eared bats were observed using seven abandoned buildings, three of which were confirmed maternity colonies. Three of the sites were in bottomland hardwood swamp forest, two in upland mixed hardwood forest, and one in upland mixed hardwood-pine forest (McCartney 2007). The primary structure was a multilevel abandoned house that was historically a maternity roost containing 40 to 60 bats (fig. 3). This population declined substantially in the 1990s as the building deteriorated. The house contained 50 individuals in May 2002 (McCartney 2007). However, concrete culvert towers designed to mimic hollow trees were later installed on the refuge, and 70 big-eared bats were observed using the roosts in July 2007 (fig. 4). We observed another large maternity colony in 2008 in an abandoned house on private property in Clay County with numbers of bats ranging from 75 to 90. The MBWG attempted unsuccessfully to obtain permission to adopt the house and make minor structural improvements to ensure protection of the roost in 2007, but the request was declined by the property owner. The large colonies in abandoned buildings in Lafayette and Jefferson Counties likely represent maternity roosts but data on these sites are incomplete. We visited the Jefferson County site on May 21, 2010 and counted 147 big-eared bats in what appeared to be a maternity colony (fig. 5). However, no pups were present at that time and we were not able to return later to verify it as a maternity roost.

Figure 4—Concrete culvert tower roost installed on St. Catherine Creek National Wildlife Refuge. Seventy big-eared bats were observed using three of the structures in July 2007. (Photo by Alison McCartney)

Figure 5—Abandoned building in Jefferson County, MS, recently discovered as a roost site for > 150 Rafinesque's big-eared bats. (Photo by Chester Martin)

Winter Roosts

Winter roosts of big-eared bats in Mississippi are relatively unknown. Searches on Noxubee NWR revealed only a few large, old bald cypress trees that were used as winter roosts (Stevenson 2008). We observed about 200 wintering big-eared bats in a tree on Noxubee NWR in 2009. Several bridges checked by Trousdale (2008) on DeSoto NF were used as roosts by bats in torpor during winter. Big-eared bats hibernate in cisterns and wells in the northern part of their range (Harvey and Saugey 2001, Harvey and others 1999), but only limited surveys of these structures have been conducted in Mississippi. We observed clusters of 12 to 25 individuals during November through January 2001 to 2004 in a dilapidated well adjacent to an abandoned house in Claiborne County. We also observed big-eared bats during winter in a partially covered well in Winston County. Big-eared bats were not observed in any of 10 cisterns surveyed in southwestern Mississippi (McCartney 2007, Sherman 2004). However, big-eared bats have been documented from cisterns in other States (Harvey and Saugey 2001) and potentially occur in these structures in Mississippi. Single individuals were observed occasionally during winter in houses on St. Catherine Creek NWR in 2002 to 2003, and one big-eared bat was in a culvert on private land adjacent to the refuge in February 2003 (Sherman 2004). As previously noted, Rafinesque's big-eared bats have been observed hibernating in an abandoned concrete structure in northcentral Mississippi (fig. 6).

MANAGEMENT

Most management efforts for Rafinesque's big-eared bats in Mississippi have focused on provision and improvement of artificial roosts. In 2002, an alternative bat house with a shed design was constructed by personnel of St. Catherine Creek NWR near the original known primary roost site.

Figure 6—Cluster of Rafinesque's big-eared bats hibernating in a concrete structure in northcentral Mississippi. (Photo by Barry Moss)

This structure was not accepted by the bats as a roost site, so three additional roosts constructed of triple-stacked circular concrete culvert blocks were erected near the site in 2004. All three of the roosts have been occupied by big-eared bats and two appear to have served as alternative maternity roosts (McCartney 2007). Artificial roosts installed on DeSoto NF include 4 cinder block structures, 4 tall wooden roosts, and 18 plastic culvert roosts. To date, only solitary occurrences of big-eared bats have been observed in the cinder block roosts, and none have been observed in the wooden or plastic roosts. However, most of the structures have not been checked consistently since their construction (see footnote 3). Also, the U.S. Army Corps of Engineers at Sardis Lake project office has developed plans to construct a cinder block tower roost near the abandoned seismograph building in Lafayette County. The building is showing signs of decay and the proposed structure is intended to provide an alternate roost site for big-eared bats. The U.S. Fish and Wildlife Service is experimenting with a variety of designs on Noxubee NWR. A structure recently installed on the refuge consists of a 9.1-m tall by 76.2-cm diameter steel culvert with a wooden top and a 76.2- by 122-cm opening at the bottom, which is used during spring and autumn by 1 to 12 big-eared bats.

Although bridge roosting populations have been documented in several regions of Mississippi, few attempts have been made to protect these sites except on some Federal lands. The two bridges occupied by big-eared bats on Camp Shelby JFTC have been identified as protected sites, and one of the bridges recently was rebuilt using the "Choctaw style," a modification of the concrete girder T-beam design. Additionally, the U.S. Forest Service has developed specifications for replacement of bridges on secondary roads within the National Forests in Mississippi. The U.S. Forest Service and Mississippi Department of Transportation (MDOT) currently are collaborating on replacement guidelines for bridges using bat-friendly designs in southern Mississippi.

The U.S. Fish and Wildlife Service, in collaboration with Mississippi State University, has conducted studies of roosting habitat of big-eared bats and management needs in bottomland hardwood forests on Noxubee NWR (Stevenson 2008). About 650 randomly selected hollow trees were inspected during the study; it was determined that American beech and sweetgum have a high tendency to produce cavities, whereas this is not the case for oaks (Richardson 2007, Stevenson 2008). This research was used to provide recommendations for reforestation and silviculture that can be incorporated into land management practices for conserving big-eared bats and their habitat. Richardson (2007) also reported an experiment for increasing use of hollow trees without openings by cutting portals to allow access by bats to these chambers; this technique potentially provides an opportunity to increase naturally occurring roost

sites where suitable trees are rare or when entrances are too small for big-eared bats.

An important aspect of big-eared bat management in Mississippi has been development of outreach programs. The MBWG was formed in 2001 with the primary goal of promoting conservation of bats in the State through research, habitat management, and education. MBWG includes an ad hoc committee on education and outreach, and members routinely make presentations to local groups and civic organizations. Information on big-eared bat conservation and management is generally included in these presentations. Additionally, updates on big-eared bat research and management efforts are included in presentations at the MBWG annual meeting and professional conferences.

CONSERVATION NEEDS

A major threat to populations of Rafinesque's big-eared bats in Mississippi is loss of habitat, especially mature forest stands used for roosting. The documented association of big-eared bats with mature bottomland forest (Clark 1990, Cochran 1999, Gooding and Langford 2004, Lance and others 2001, Rice 2009) suggests that declines of this forest type have negatively affected the species. Historical records indicate that in the Mississippi Alluvial Valley (MAV) approximately 78 percent of forested wetlands (mostly bottomland hardwoods) had been converted to other land uses by the mid-1970s (MacDonald and others 1979), and bottomland hardwoods along the lower Mississippi River were being cleared for agriculture in tracts as large as 12,000 ha during the 1980s (Gosselink and Lee 1989). By the mid-1980s, the MAV forested landscape had been reduced to a highly fragmented 20 percent of its historical extent (Haynes 2004, Wilson and others 2007). Currently, about 19 percent of Mississippi's forest land is composed of bottomland hardwoods, and forested area in the Mississippi Delta has increased by 12 percent since 1994 (King and others 2006, Oswalt and others 2009). Additionally recent Natural Resource Conservation Service (NRCS) data shows that, under the Wetland Reserve Program (WRP), there are 68,623 ha of land under WRP contract in Mississippi, including 52,672 ha restored to bottomland hardwoods (Miller and others 2011). However, forests containing large-diameter trees suitable as Rafinesque's big-eared bat roost sites likely will not be available for decades since Rafinesque's big-eared bats appear to prefer to roost in large (> 50 cm d.b.h.) trees within bottomland hardwood forests (Stevenson 2008, Trousdale 2011). Significant populations of big-eared bats also have been documented from upland mixed forests, and males have been found foraging in sapling-stage pines (Menzel and others 2001). It is worthwhile to note that three of the four largest known roost sites in Mississippi are located in abandoned buildings in upland pine forests. Thus, other forest types may also be important, and further work is needed to fully understand habitat needs for this species.

Conservation of natural roosts is critical for conservation efforts to be effective. Hollow, large-diameter trees often are rare on the landscape due to management practices and natural events, e.g., tornadoes and hurricanes. For example, 14 percent of live trees in Mississippi's southern forest survey unit experienced wind-related damage during Hurricane Katrina in 2005 (Oswalt and others 2009). These included mature hardwood trees blown down on DeSoto NF and Camp Shelby, some of which had been documented previously as roosts. Therefore, known and potential roost trees should be protected, and forest management prescriptions should ensure a future supply of large trees, especially in lowland areas near water (fig. 7). Efforts should consider retention of bald cypress, water tupelo, blackgum, sweetgum, American beech, southern magnolia, and American sycamore which have the propensity to develop cavities used by big-eared bats.

Additional surveys are needed to locate natural roosts and roosts in artificial structures. Although extensive studies have been conducted on national forests (DeSoto and Delta), national wildlife refuges (St. Catherine Creek, Noxubee, and Theodore Roosevelt), U.S. Department of Defense installations (Camp Shelby, Camp McCain, NAS Meridian), one national park (Vicksburg National Military Park), and several State wildlife management areas in the Pascagoula River Basin, many areas of the State have never been surveyed. Also, traditional surveys have not proven suitable for determining roost habitat by big-eared bats, and few studies, except those conducted on DeSoto NF (Trousdale and Beckett 2004, 2005; Trousdale and others 2008), have attempted to locate roosts using radiotelemetry. There is also a need to conduct studies of foraging habitat in different areas of the State. Further, an apparent continuum of populations along the Loess Hills corridor in western Mississippi needs to be more extensively surveyed. Little information is available on ecology of Rafinesque's big-eared bats in winter, except for the study by Rice (2009) in bottomland hardwoods of northeastern Louisiana. Similar studies need to be conducted in Mississippi to provide information useful to identify forest management practices that benefit big-eared bats.

Management should include identification and protection of natural and artificial roosts. Roost switching has been well documented in Rafinesque's big-eared bats (Gooding and Langford 2004, Lance and others 2001, Trousdale and Beckett 2005), and populations use a combination of natural and artificial roost sites. Trousdale and others

Figure 7—Forest management prescriptions in Mississippi should ensure a future supply of large trees that have the propensity to develop cavities used by Rafinesque's big-eared bats. Preferred species include bald cypress, water tupelo, blackgum, American beech, southern magnolia, sweetgum, and American sycamore. (Photo by Candice Stevenson)

(2008) also demonstrated that roost fidelity of a population of big-eared bats in southeastern Mississippi varied with habitat type and recommended that conservation and roost monitoring programs include this flexibility with regard to potential movements among roosts within relatively short periods. Lance and others (2001) determined that amount of mature forest surrounding a bridge was a primary factor in determining occupancy by big-eared bats. Use of bridges may also be associated with tendency of the species to switch roosts frequently with bridges, abandoned buildings, and hollow trees serving as alternate roosts (Trousdale and Beckett 2004). Roosting in bridges may also result from limited availability of natural roosts. Bridges commonly were used by big-eared bats on the DeSoto NF where suitable roost trees were deficient (Trousdale and Beckett 2005) and in an area dominated by recently harvested forest stands along Bayou Pierre and its tributaries in westcentral Mississippi (Wolters and Martin 2000, 2011). Conversely, big-eared bats were never observed using bridges in more naturally forested areas with extensive stands of mature hardwoods in Noxubee NWR, Theodore Roosevelt NWR, and at sites along the Pascagoula River.

The largest maternity colonies documented in Mississippi occur in abandoned structures on private lands. These sites degrade through time and ultimately become unsuitable as roosting habitat. Wooden structures especially are subject to degradation and collapse, and remote buildings often are vandalized. A worthwhile effort would be to obtain permission to protect and stabilize important roost sites. However, landowners may be suspicious of actions that in their view cede control over their property to government agencies or conservation organizations, as was the case with the house in Clay County. Nevertheless, more effective interaction is needed among conservation organizations and private landowners regarding protection and management of bat habitat, especially as most (78 percent) Mississippi timberlands are privately owned (Oswalt and others 2009) and given that Miller and others (2011) calculated that there currently are approximately 19,900 ha of potential big-eared bat roosting habitat in Mississippi, with most potential suitable habitat (12,600 ha) on private land. There needs to be greater involvement with organizations such as Bat Conservation International when developing projects to protect roosts. Additionally, there needs to be more effective coordination with State offices and MDOT regarding protection of bridge roosting sites and use of bat-friendly designs when new bridges are constructed. Finally, both Federal and State agencies should acknowledge the need to protect and manage Rafinesque's big-eared bats by providing funding for research and habitat management. Conservation of the species ultimately will be tied to landscape-level management of forests.

ACKNOWLEDGMENTS

We thank the following agencies and organizations for providing logistical support for studies of Rafinesque's big-eared bat in Mississippi: Mississippi Museum of Natural Science, U.S. Fish and Wildlife Service, U.S. Army Engineer Research and Development Center (ERDC), U.S. Forest Service, U.S. Army National Guard Bureau, U.S. Naval Station Meridian, University of Southern Mississippi (USM), Mississippi State University (MSU), Jackson State University, Mississippi College, and Weyerhaeuser Company. D. Beckett (USM) provided direction for studies conducted in southern Mississippi. Field support was provided by M. McCartney (Mississippi Department of Environmental Quality, Jackson, MS); M.C. Like (3D Environmental, Longview, TX); and R.F. Lance, B. Sabol, P. Bailey, and K. Richards (ERDC). M. Bayless (Bat Conservation International) assisted with surveys and provided guidelines for artificial structures. An early version of the manuscript was reviewed by M.W. Ford and E.R. Britzke (ERDC).

LITERATURE CITED

Bennett, F.M.; Loeb, S.C.; Bunch, M.S.; Bowerman, W.W. 2008. Use and selection of bridges as day roosts by Rafinesque's big-eared bats. American Midland Naturalist. 160: 386-399.

Clark, M.K. 1990. Roosting ecology of the eastern big-eared bat, *Plecotus rafinesquii*, in North Carolina. Raleigh, NC: North Carolina State University. 110 p. M.S. thesis.

Cochran, S.M. 1999. Roosting and habitat use by Rafinesque's big-eared bat and other species in a bottomland hardwood ecosystem. Jonesboro, AR: Arkansas State University. 50 p. M.S. thesis.

Gooding, G.; Langford, J.R. 2004. Characteristics of tree roosts of Rafinesque's big-eared bats and southeastern bat in northeastern Louisiana. Southwestern Naturalist. 49: 61-67.

Gosselink, J.G.; Lee, L.C. 1989. Cumulative impact assessment in bottomland hardwood forests. Wetlands. 9: 89-174.

Harvey, M.J.; Altenbach, J.S.; Best, T.L. 1999. Bats of the United States. Little Rock, AR: Arkansas Game and Fish Commission. 64 p.

Harvey, M.J.; Saugey, D.A. 2001. Bats. In: Dickson, J.G., ed. Wildlife of southern forests: habitat and management. Blaine, WA: Hancock House Publishers: 359-371.

Haynes, R.J. 2004. The development of bottomland forest restoration in the lower Mississippi Alluvial Valley. Ecological Restoration. 22: 170-182.

Jones, C. 1977. *Plecotus rafinesquii*. Mammalian Species. 69: 1-4.

Jones, C.; Carter, C.H. 1989. Annotated checklist of the recent mammals of Mississippi. Occas. Pap. [Lubbock, TX]: Museum of Texas Tech University. 128: 1-9.

Kennedy, M.L.; Randolf, K.N.; Best, T.L. 1974. A review of Mississippi mammals. Portales, NM: Eastern New Mexico University, Studies in Natural Science. 2: 1-36.

King, S.L.; Twedt, D.J.; Wilson, R.R. 2006. The role of the Wetland Reserve Program in conservation efforts in the Mississippi Alluvial Valley. Wildlife Society Bulletin. 34: 914-920.

Lance, R.F.; Hardcastle, B.T.; Talley, A.; Leberg, P.L. 2001. Day-roost selection by Rafinesque's big-eared bats (*Corynorhinus rafinesquii*) in Louisiana forests. Journal of Mammalogy. 82: 166-172.

MacDonald, P.O.; Frazer, W.E.; Clauser, J.K. 1979. Documentation, chronology, and future projection of bottomland hardwood habitat loss in the lower Mississippi Alluvial Plain. Vicksburg, MS: U.S. Department of the Interior, Fish and Wildlife Service. 133 p. Vol. I.

Martin, C.O.; Lance, R.F.; Bucciantini, C.H. 2005. Collisions with aircraft and use of culverts under runways by bats at U.S. Naval Air Station Meridian, Meridian, Mississippi. Bat Research News. 46: 51-54.

Martin, C.O.; Lance, R.F.; Lee, A.A.; McCartney, A.S. 2007. A survey of the bat fauna and habitat management considerations for the Mississippi Army National Guard: Camp Shelby and Camp McCain. Jackson, MS: Mississippi Army National Guard; final report. Final report prepared for HQ, Mississippi Army National Guard, Jackson, MS, by the Environmental Laboratory, U.S. Army Engineer Research and Development Center, Vicksburg, MS. 140 p.

Martin, C.O.; Lance, R.F.; McCartney, A.S. 2008. The bat fauna of Naval Air Station Meridian, Meridian, MS: species occurrence, habitat use, and management recommendations. Meridian, MS: Environmental Department, U.S. Naval Air Station; final report. Final report prepared for Environmental Department, U.S. Naval Air Station Meridian, Meridian, MS, by the Environmental Laboratory, U.S. Army Engineer Research and Development Center, Vicksburg, MS. 184 p.

McCartney, A.S. 2007. Distribution and abundance of Rafinesque's big-eared bat (*Corynorhinus rafinesquii*) and southeastern myotis (*Myotis austroriparius*) in Mississippi. Jackson, MS: U.S. Fish and Wildlife Service; final report. 66 p.

McCartney, A.S. 2010. Bat surveys in the Pascagoula River Basin in Jackson, George, Stone, Perry, and Harrison Counties, Mississippi, January–December, 2009. Jackson, MS: Mississippi Department of Wildlife, Fisheries, and Parks; final report. 30 p.

Menzel, M.A.; Menzel, J.M.; Ford, W.M. [and others]. 2001. Home range and habitat use of male Rafinesque's big-eared bats (*Corynorhinus rafinesquii*). American Midland Naturalist. 145: 402-408.

Miller, D.A.; Stihler, C.W.; Sasse, D.B. [and others]. 2011. Conservation and management of eastern big-eared bats (*Corynorhinus* spp.). In: Loeb, S.C.; Lacki, M.J.; Miller, D.A., eds. Conservation and management of eastern big-eared bats: a symposium. Gen. Tech. Rep. SRS-145. Asheville, NC: U.S. Department of Agriculture Forest Service, Southern Research Station: 53-61.

Mississippi Museum of Natural Science. 2005. Mississippi's comprehensive wildlife conservation strategy. Jackson, MS: Mississippi Department of Wildlife, Fisheries and Parks.

Oswalt, S.N.; Johnson, T.G.; Coulston, J.W.; Oswalt, C.M. 2009. Mississippi's forests, 2006. Resour. Bull. SRS-147. Asheville, NC: U.S. Department of Agriculture Forest Service, Southern Research Station. 78 p.

Rice, C.L. 2009. Roosting ecology of *Corynorhinus rafinesquii* (Rafinesque's big-eared bat) and *Myotis austroriparius* (southeastern myotis) in tree cavities found in a northeastern Louisiana bottomland hardwood forest streambed. Monroe, LA: University of Louisiana at Monroe. 117 p. M.S. thesis.

Richardson, D. 2007. Helping nature provide hollow trees for bats. Bats. 24 (4): 6-8.

Sherman, A.R. 2004. *Corynorhinus rafinesquii* and *Myotis austroriparius* artificial roost characteristics in southwestern Mississippi. Jackson, MS: Jackson State University. 105 p. M.S. thesis.

Stevenson, C.L. 2008. Availability and seasonal use of diurnal roosts by Rafinesque's big-eared bat and southeastern myotis in bottomland hardwoods of Mississippi. Starkville, MS: Mississippi State University. 109 p. M.S. thesis.

Trousdale, A.W. 2008. Roosting ecology of Rafinesque's big-eared bat, *Corynorhinus rafinesquii*, in southeastern Mississippi. Hattiesburg, MS: The University of Southern Mississippi. 107 p. Ph.D. dissertation.

Trousdale, A.W. 2011. Ecology of tree-roosting Rafinesque's big-eared bats in the Eastern United States. In: Loeb, S.C.; Lacki, M.J.; Miller, D.A., eds. Conservation and management of eastern big-eared bats: a symposium. Gen. Tech. Rep. SRS-145. Asheville, NC: U.S. Department of Agriculture Forest Service, Southern Research Station: 27-38.

Trousdale, A.W.; Beckett, D.C. 2002. Bats (Mammalia: Chiroptera) recorded from mist-net and bridge surveys in southern Mississippi. Journal of the Mississippi Academy of Science. 47: 183-188.

Trousdale, A.W.; Beckett, D.C. 2004. Seasonal use of bridges by Rafinesque's big-eared bat, *Corynorhinus rafinesquii*, in southern Mississippi. Southeastern Naturalist. 3: 103-112.

Trousdale, A.W.; Beckett, D.C. 2005. Characteristics of tree roosts of Rafinesque's big-eared bat (*Corynorhinus rafinesquii*) in southeastern Mississippi. American Midland Naturalist. 154: 442-449.

Trousdale, A.W.; Beckett, D.C.; Hammond, S.L. 2008. Short-term roost fidelity of Rafinesque's big-eared bat (*Corynorhinus rafinesquii*) varies with habitat. Journal of Mammalogy. 89: 477-484.

Wilf, L.M. 2004. The species composition and habitat use by bat populations in Delta National Forest, Mississippi. Jonesboro, AR: Arkansas State University. 84 p. M.S. thesis.

Wilson, R.; Ribbeck, K.; King, S.; Twedt, D., eds. 2007. Restoration, management, and monitoring of forest resources in the Mississippi Alluvial Valley: recommendations for enhancing wildlife habitat. Vicksburg, MS: LMVJV Forest Resources Conservation Working Group, Lower Mississippi Valley Joint Venture Office. 88 p.

Wolfe, J.L. 1971. Mississippi land mammals. Jackson, MS: Mississippi Museum of Natural Science. 44 p.

Wolters, M.S.; Martin, C.O. 2000. A maternity colony of partially hairless bridge-roosting Rafinesque's big-eared bats in west-central Mississippi [Abstract]. Bat Research News. 42: 150.

Wolters, M.S.; Martin, C.O. 2011. Observations of parturition in Rafinesque's big-eared bats (*Corynorhinus rafinesquii*) beneath a concrete bridge. Southeastern Naturalist. 10: 178-180.

STATUS OF THE VIRGINIA BIG-EARED BAT (*CORYNORHINUS TOWNSENDII VIRGINIANUS*) IN WEST VIRGINIA: TWENTY-SEVEN YEARS OF MONITORING CAVE ROOSTS

Craig W. Stihler, Wildlife Biologist, West Virginia Division of Natural Resources, Elkins, WV 26241

Abstract—Maternity colonies and hibernacula of federally endangered Virginia big-eared bats (*Corynorhinus townsendii virginianus*) in West Virginia have been monitored annually since 1983 during June and biennially during winter to examine population trends after these sites were closed to human traffic when bats were present. Seven maternity colonies contained 3,073 bats in 1983 and 5,487 bats in 2009, an increase of 77 percent. These 7 colonies, with 3 additional maternity colonies discovered since 1983, bring the number of known bats to 7,245 during summer 2009 with mean colony size of 725 bats (range 235 to 1,298 bats). Twenty-five or more hibernating *C. t. virginianus* have been documented in 8 West Virginia caves with the largest known hibernating concentration of this subspecies in Hellhole (10,025 bats in winter 2010). In winter 1988 to 1989, the State's 3 largest hibernacula contained 5,170 *C. t. virginianus* (96 percent of observed bats). In 2009, these caves contained 11,559 individuals (124 percent increase) with the total number of hibernating bats estimated at 12,059. By early 2010, white-nose syndrome (WNS) was documented in five caves used by *C. t. virginianus* in Pendleton County including Hellhole. To date, no affected big-eared bats have been observed, but WNS could potentially decimate this population which has been increasing as a result of cave protection.

INTRODUCTION

Although both the common and scientific names of this bat have changed numerous times over the past decades, the Virginia big-eared bat (*Corynorhinus townsendii virginianus*), the easternmost subspecies of Townsend's big-eared bat, has long been recognized as a component of the cave fauna of West Virginia (fig. 1). These bats use caves year round and, during the active period, forage in both open areas and forests surrounding their roosts (Stihler 2011). Reese (1934) noted occurrence of this bat in two caves in Pendleton County and one cave in Randolph County. The holotype for this subspecies was collected in Schoolhouse Cave, Pendleton County, on November 12, 1939 (U.S. National Museum 269163). Kellogg (1937) noted occurrence of *C. t. virginianus* in Preston County, although no locations for the Preston County records were given. Wilson (1946) reported collection of two specimens from a cave in Hardy County in October 1944, and Frum (1947) reported specimens collected from a Grant County cave. Wilson (1948) and Kellogg (1937) noted that this species should be widespread in West Virginia although neither cited records to support these claims. In his review of the genera *Euderma* and *Plecotus*, Handley (1959) noted unpublished records from Frum of *C. t. virginianus* in a cave in Tucker County. He also noted that this bat had a "limited and apparently discontinuous distribution . . . within the bounds of the Appalachian Highlands" and was not known from the "well explored" karst regions in Pocahontas, Greenbrier, and Monroe Counties.

While these early reports rarely mention information regarding number of bats present when the caves were visited, by the late 1960s there was concern that populations were declining.

Barbour and Davis (1969) wrote, "In West Virginia the species is still rather abundant in certain caves. . . . The bats seem to be abandoning more caves each year, apparently as a result of ever increasing human disturbance as spelunking becomes more popular. The species is destined to perish in the eastern United States, unless the caves it uses receive protection."

In an October 15, 1976, letter addressed to Lynn Greenwalt, Director, U.S. Fish and Wildlife Service (USFWS), John S. Hall and Michael J. Harvey petitioned the USFWS to list two subspecies of *C. townsendii*, *C. t. virginianus*, and *C. t. ingens* as federally endangered. They noted in their cover letter that "It was the unanimous opinion of the Southeastern Section of the Wildlife Society… that these two bat subspecies should be considered endangered." For *C. t. virginianus*, the petition focused on the population in West Virginia, which included most of these bats, and where Hall had conducted surveys documenting population declines. The population was estimated at 2,500 to 3,000 individuals with an additional "few hundred individuals" in Kentucky and Virginia. The petition notes that the range of the subspecies did not appear to have been reduced, but number of bats was declining throughout its range. These declines appeared to be due to increased disturbance of bats in caves as a result of increasing spelunking activities. Three examples of recent population declines were provided for maternity colonies in Pendleton County, WV. The population in Hoffman School Cave declined from approximately 1,000 bats in 1962 to 450 individuals in 1975. During the same time period, the colony in Sinnett Cave declined from 250 to 20 bats and the population in Cave Mountain Cave declined from 1,000 to 800 bats. The petition noted that these bats were more dispersed in the winter, although subsequent data proved this not to be the case. One other factor considered in the petition

Citation for proceedings: Loeb, Susan C.; Lacki, Michael J.; Miller, Darren A., eds. 2011. Conservation and management of eastern big-eared bats: a symposium. Gen. Tech. Rep. SRS-145. Asheville, NC: U.S. Department of Agriculture, Forest Service, Southern Research Station. 157 p.

Figure 1—Location of West Virginia counties with records of *Corynorhinus townsendii virginianus*.

was presence of a limestone quarry only a few hundred yards from one significant *C. t. virginianus* cave, Hellhole.

In December 1977, the "Proposed endangered listing and critical habitat determination for the Virginia and Ozark big-eared bats" (Ozark big-eared bat = *C. t. ingens*) was published in the Federal Register (42 FR 61290 61292). In the proposal, six caves were proposed as critical habitat for *C. t. virginianus*. Five of these were in West Virginia: four caves were in Pendleton County [Cave Mountain Cave (maternity colony and minor winter use), Hellhole (hibernaculum and bachelor colony), Hoffman School Cave (maternity colony and minor winter use), and Sinnett Cave (maternity colony and minor winter use)]; and Cave Hollow/Arbogast Cave system was in Tucker County (maternity colony and hibernaculum). The final rule was published in November 1979 (44 FR 69206 69208) and, effective December 31, 1979, both subspecies were listed as endangered, and five caves in West Virginia were listed as critical habitat for *C. t. virginianus*. The sixth cave, located in Kentucky, was not listed because the landowner was already protecting the site and did not want to draw attention to it by publishing it in the Federal Register.

The recovery plan for the two big-eared bat subspecies was completed in May 1984 (U.S. Fish and Wildlife Service 1984). At that time, there were 10 caves known to be used by *C. t. virginianus* colonies in West Virginia, all of which were used as summer colonies, and 6 of which were used by hibernating bats. By the time the recovery plan was written, 5 of these 10 caves had been gated or fenced to reduce disturbance. Based on surveys conducted in 1981 and 1982, the recovery plan estimated the number of *C. t. virginianus* in maternity colonies in West Virginia to be approximately 3,450 individuals.

In recent years, surveys conducted at entrances of abandoned coal mines in the New River Gorge National River, Fayette County, by National Park Service personnel and their contractors during the late summer and fall swarming period have captured small numbers (usually less than five bats per portal per night) of *C. t. virginianus* using several mine portals (Varner 2008). No large colonies have been discovered in this area. The relationship of these bats to other populations is unclear, although this population appears to be genetically distinct and most closely related to the Tazewell County, VA, population (Piaggio and others 2009). The West Virginia Division of Natural Resources (WVDNR) has not received reports of *C. t. virginianus* captured at mine portals in other areas of the State. Because few data are available for the Fayette County population, this paper will focus on the more studied *C. t. virginianus* population in the Pendleton County area, the largest known concentration of this subspecies, and will examine population trends and effectiveness of cave protection activities.

METHODS

Because *C. t. virginianus* use caves during summer and winter, population trends can be examined at both maternity colonies and hibernacula. Maternity colony counts were conducted by tallying bats as they emerged from the caves in the evening; winter counts required entering caves to enumerate hibernating bats. Annual monitoring of *C. t. virginianus* in maternity colonies in West Virginia began in 1983 using the protocol of Bagley and Jacobs (1985). This method used infrared lights (mining lights fitted with infrared gel filters) to illuminate the cave entrance and night-vision scopes to watch and tally bats as they emerged in the evening to feed. As new technologies and information have become available, the methodology has evolved but still remains much like the original protocol. USFWS biologists provided technical advice and a loan of equipment during the first 5 years of monitoring; the WVDNR conducted the counts after that period.

As suggested by Bagley and Jacobs (1985), surveys were conducted in June before bats give birth when the entire colony usually emerges from the cave early in the night to forage. Once lactation begins, portions of the colony may be in the cave throughout the night as bats come and go to nurse their young.[1] Based on cave monitoring and radiotelemetry data collected by WVDNR personnel, the survey period was refined so that surveys were usually conducted between June 1 and June 20, with the surveys completed by June 15, when feasible. Because females in Cave Mountain Cave were documented to give birth earlier than the other colonies (e.g., young were observed on June 13, 1994,[2]), this cave was one of the first surveyed each summer beginning in 1995. Counts were conducted on warm nights (≥ 12 °C) when precipitation was not anticipated. If it rained during a count, the count was repeated on a later date. In addition, if any count was ≥ 10 percent lower than the previous year's count, the emergence was recounted later in the season to determine if the population was actually lower or if not all bats emerged during the first count.

Most emergence counts were conducted outside the cave at the entrance, but at two caves with large entrances (the Arbogast entrance of the Cave Hollow/Arbogast Cave system and Schoolhouse Cave) a more accurate count could be obtained by conducting the count a short distance into the cave at a location where the cave passage was more constricted. At both sites, this could be done without disturbing the colony which roosted farther back in the cave. Multiple entrances for the same cave were surveyed simultaneously. Equipment (see

below) was turned on, and observation of the cave entrance began shortly before the bats were expected to emerge from the cave (approximately 20^h55^m EDT in June). Emergences usually lasted 70 to 90 minutes.

Since 1983, night-vision scopes and a variety of lights fitted with infrared filters have been used to conduct emergence counts. Beginning in 2005, camcorders with night-vision capabilities (Sony® DCR-TRV38, Sony Corporation, Tokyo, Japan) were also used. Because these camcorders do not amplify available light, a brighter light source was needed, and high-intensity LED infrared lights (Wildlife Engineering, Tucson, AZ) were employed.

Caves with summer colonies of *C. t. virginianus* often contained a few (≤ 10) bats of other species during the summer (*Myotis* spp. and *Perimyotis subflavus*) which emerged in the evening. Because *C. t. virginianus* echolocation calls are lower in frequency and much quieter than those of other bats using the caves, since counts began in 1983, ultrasonic "bat detectors" were used to distinguish non-big-eared bats. When a non-big-eared bat emerged, a strong echolocation call was picked up if the detector was set at 50 to 55 kHz and pointed toward the cave entrance; a faint call or no call at all was heard when a big-eared bat emerged. Bat size and flight pattern also aided in distinguishing non-big-eared bats.

Prior to use of camcorders, all counts were done "live" with an observer watching bats exit the cave and recording observations on a microcassette recorder with a time mark recorded at 5-minute intervals. At the end of each emergence, the tape, with a recording such as "five bats out, five bats out, one bat in, two bats out, time . . ." was replayed, and numbers of bats were tallied for each 5-minute period. If the emergence had been videotaped, the tape was reviewed if there were any 5-minute time blocks where the observer felt the observations needed to be verified. Since 2005, emergences at four of the maternity colonies caves with large entrances and a large number of bats (Arbogast entrance of Cave Hollow/Arbogast Cave system, north entrance of Cliff Cave, and Mystic and Schoolhouse Caves) were recorded and counted later by two observers; one person counted only bats exiting, and the other counted only bats going back into the cave.

Hibernacula surveys were generally conducted in January or February in odd-numbered years between 1983 and 2010, although the Cave Hollow/Arbogast Cave system was sometimes surveyed during the last 2 weeks of December because access could be difficult later in the season due to snow and ice. Small crews (two to four people) entered the caves and conducted the surveys as quickly as possible. Because Hellhole is a large and complex cave with several areas within the cave where large numbers of bats hibernate, multiple crews were sometimes used, and each examined a different portion of the cave. Surveyors tallied and recorded number of *C. t. virginianus* in each cluster. Large clusters

[1] West Virginia Division of Natural Resources, unpublished data.
[2] West Virginia Division of Natural Resources, unpublished data.

(approximately 100 bats or more) were counted by 2 surveyors and the average of the 2 counts recorded. In three instances, a large cluster was photographed and enumerated later.

C. t. virginianus using Elkhorn Mountain Cave were monitored by WVDNR biologists summer through fall 1996 and spring through early summer 1997. Mist netting was used to capture bats to obtain information on sex and reproductive condition, and night-vision counts were conducted to obtain population estimates.

RESULTS

Distribution

Surveys conducted since 1983 documented presence of *C. t. virginianus* in all counties with historic records except Preston County. Maternity colonies and hibernacula containing more than 25 individuals were located in Grant, Pendleton, and Tucker Counties.

Summer Colonies

Maternity colonies—Although there have been population declines at certain caves over the 27-year monitoring period, the overall trend has been that of a population increase after human disturbance at these caves was curtailed (table 1). Number of bats at the 7 maternity colonies examined since 1983 increased 77 percent with 3,073 individuals observed in 1983 and 5,420 bats observed in 2009 (table 1). Three additional maternity colonies were discovered in Pendleton County after 1983: Lambert Cave in 1984, Cliff Cave in 1992, and Mill Run Cave in 1993. In June 1993, the first year all 10 maternity colonies were examined, these caves held 5,487 bats. In June 2009, these 10 caves contained 7,245 individuals. During this same period, number of bats in the "new" colonies increased 18 percent, from 1,540 to 1,816 bats (table 1). Therefore, the current estimated number of *C. t. virginianus* in maternity colonies in West Virginia is 7,245 in 10 colonies in 3 counties (Grant County, 1 colony; Pendleton County, 8 colonies; and Tucker County, 1 colony; table 1). This represents an increase of 4,172 individuals since 1983, including 1,816 bats in colonies discovered after 1983. In June 2009, colony sizes ranged from 235 to 1,298 bats with a mean colony size of 725 bats.

In spite of these increases, four examples illustrate potential site-specific problems. First, Cave Hollow/Arbogast Cave system, the only *C. t. virginianus* maternity colony cave on the west side of the Allegheny Front, had 1,137 bats in 1988 representing the largest maternity colony in the State at that time. The cave was protected by 3-m chain-link fences around the several entrances of the cave system. However, vandals were able to get past the fence, enter the cave, and build a fire inside the cave near where the largest portion of the maternity

colony roosted. In 1989, only 286 bats were present. In August 1996, the cave entrances were gated with angle iron gates. Since 1988, there has been no further vandalism at the site. Twenty years after the vandalism and population decline, the colony in this cave has rebounded to only 75 percent of the 1988 level (fig. 2). This emphasizes how slow recovery can be following significant population declines and importance of protecting cave roosts. In 2009, 57 percent of the *C. t. virginianus* in maternity colonies in West Virginia were at sites protected with angle iron gates, although all known maternity colony sites were closed to human traffic during the summer.

The second example is Lambert Cave which was impacted by changing habitat structure at the cave entrance. There were 132 bats in the colony in June 1994, before the cave was gated (angle iron gate) in October 1994. Following gating, number of bats remained fairly stable for a few years and then declined to just 29 bats in 2000 (fig. 3). This cave was located in a hayfield with a small tree growing at the edge of the sinkhole containing the cave entrance. This tree died in 1999 and increased sunlight allowed burdock (*Arctium minus*) to grow rampantly in the sinkhole, blocking the cave entrance. Removal of the burdock allowed an American hornbeam (*Carpinus caroliniana*) to grow large enough to once again shade the sinkhole. In 2009, this colony contained 430 bats.

Third, domestic cat predation on *C. t. virginianus* at the entrance of Sinnett Cave was a problem for several years. Just inside the cave entrance, the passage is < 1 m high, and the original round bar steel gate placed at the cave entrance (March 1981) caused bats to circle behind the gate, providing cats with increased opportunities to capture bats. In October 1998, the round bar gate was replaced with an angle iron gate constructed several m inside the cave where the cave ceiling is several m high. Once the bats passed through this gate, they no longer had an obstacle to negotiate in the low passage leading out of the cave, and mortality due to predation by cats has almost been eliminated at this site and the population is increasing (fig. 4).

Lastly, the maternity colony in Cave Mountain Cave has decreased in size over the last two and a half decades even though the cave has been protected with round bar, and later, angle iron gates. The reason for this decline is not known although there are two possible causes. First, sporadic observations over several years show that the bats begin returning to this colony as early as the third week in March. Therefore, the closure dates recommended by the USFWS[3] for summer *C. t. virginianus* colonies (April 1 through September 15) may not have begun early enough to prevent disturbance of this colony, especially if human traffic in the cave increased in late March as cavers try to get into the cave before it was closed for the summer. Secondly, as bat numbers in Cave Mountain

[3] Personal communication. 1987. Leonard Walker, Wildlife Biologist, U.S. Fish and Wildlife Service, Elkins, WV 26241.

Table 1—Number of *Corynorhinus townsendii virginianus* recorded at maternity colonies via annual, summer emergence counts in West Virginia, 1983 to 2009

Cave name	Year								
	1983	1984	1985	1986	1987	1988	1989	1990	1991
Cave Hollow/Arbogast	605	800	739	1,080	1,015	1,137	286	325	420
Cave Mountain	808	728	812	703	861	773	931	881	826
Cliff									
Hoffman School	755	755	771	739	780	930	753	711	777
Lambert		209[a]	230	277	96	58	49	65	116
Mill Run									
Mystic	254	250	209	239	267	283	274	287	253
Peacock	160	183	207	239	254	326	396	466	497
Schoolhouse	338	378	368	547	548	515	537	449	719
Sinnett/Thorn Mountain	153	216	238	338	426	454	560	538	560
Total	3,073	3,519	3,574	4,162	4,247	4,476	3,786	3,722	4,168

Cave name	Year								
	1992	1993	1994	1995	1996	1997	1998	1999	2000
Cave Hollow/Arbogast	423	454	491	559	513	454	538	620	618
Cave Mountain	805	762	796	742	768	736	637	568	529
Cliff	1,350[b]	1,292	1,350[b]	1,350[b]	1,243	1,004	1,179	1,250	1,250[c]
Hoffman School	906	942	857	849	980	970	828	850	890
Lambert	112	134	132	122	126	123	131	106	29
Mill Run		114	153	204	167	231	293	335	312
Mystic	338	357	319	367	377	397	406	488	485
Peacock	573	635	652	730	772	800	862	827	858
Schoolhouse	612	629	673	649	701	815	732	655	718
Sinnett/Thorn Mountain	466	168	304	418	344	279	187	183	245
Total	5,585	5,487	5,727	5,990	5,991	5,809	5,793	5,882	5,934

Cave name	Year								
	2001	2002	2003	2004	2005	2006	2007	2008	2009
Cave Hollow/Arbogast	614	596	691	664	648	698	756	728	850
Cave Mountain	529	622	532	512	510	564	432	424	357
Cliff	1,250[c]	1,002	933	1,027	976	910	880	880[c]	1,151
Hoffman School	910	902	931	1,050	928	1,175	1,029	1,077	1,208
Lambert	177	225	252	202	267	288	295	305	430
Mill Run	136	165	181	154	125	131	178	203	235
Mystic	465	479	510	552	536	576	569	598	618
Peacock	900	1,004	959	982	1,038	979	985	1,013	1,119
Schoolhouse	762	700	808	782	665	630	710	726	795
Sinnett/Thorn Mountain	167	202	148	313	297	361	430	419	482
Total	5,910	5,897	5,945	6,238	5,990	6,312	6,264	6,373	7,245

[a] Colony discovered in late summer 1984; first count conducted August 28, 1984.

[b] Estimate based on size of cluster observed in cave; not an emergence count.

[c] Count not conducted this year and colony size assumed to be the same as when last count was conducted.

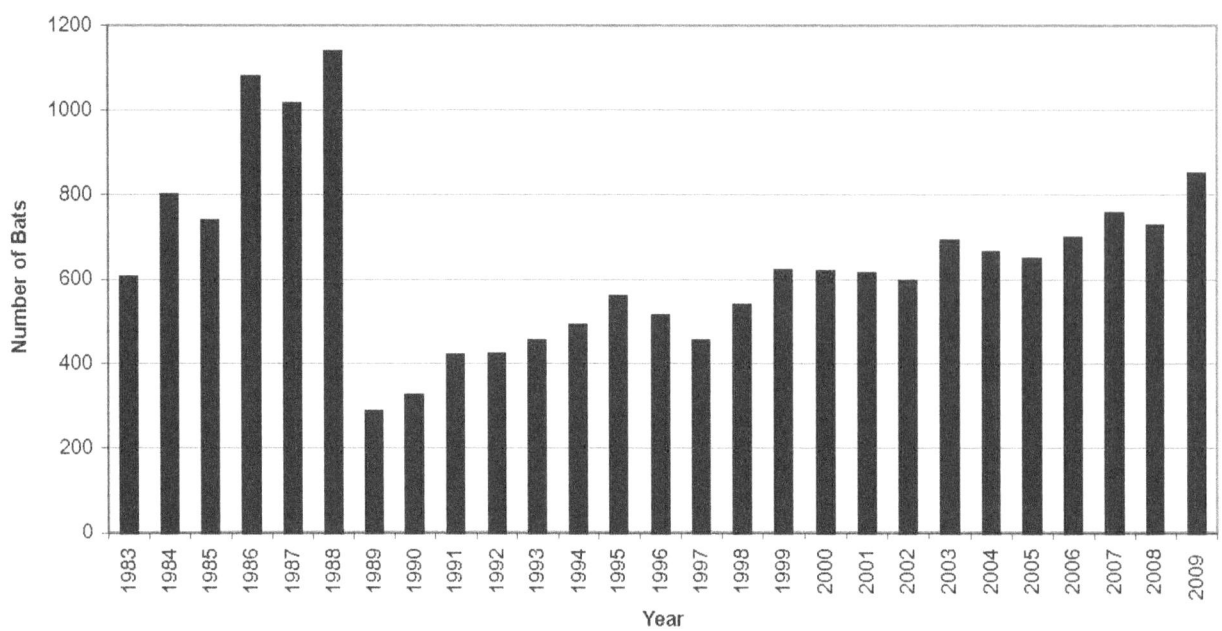

Figure 2—Number of *Corynorhinus townsendii virginianus* in the Cave Hollow/Arbogast Cave system maternity colony, Tucker County, WV, 1983 to 2009.

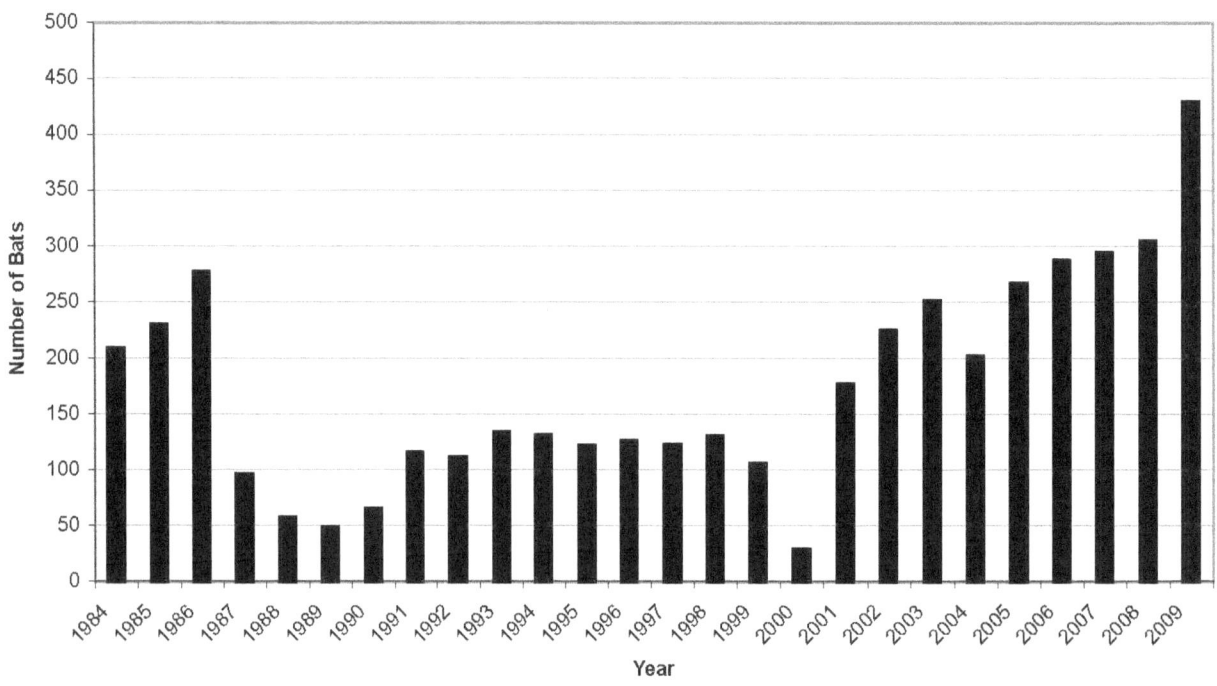

Figure 3—Number of *Corynorhinus townsendii virginianus* in the Lambert Cave maternity colony, Pendleton County, WV, 1984 to 2009.

Cave decreased, a new colony was discovered in Mill Run Cave 7.9 km away (*C. t. virginianus* were not observed in this cave in previous surveys), making it plausible that that some bats from Cave Mountain Cave founded this colony.

Bachelor colonies—*C. t. virginianus* bachelor colonies are largely unknown. Minor Rexrode Cave, Pendleton County,

was one of the "maternity" colony caves monitored in 1983 and USFWS and WVDNR biologists continued to monitor this site annually through 2001. However, biologists observing emergences at this cave noted that the bats did not seem to exhibit the same "urgency" to exit the cave in the evening and emergences often took longer than at the other sites. Harp trapping at the cave entrance in July 1999 resulted

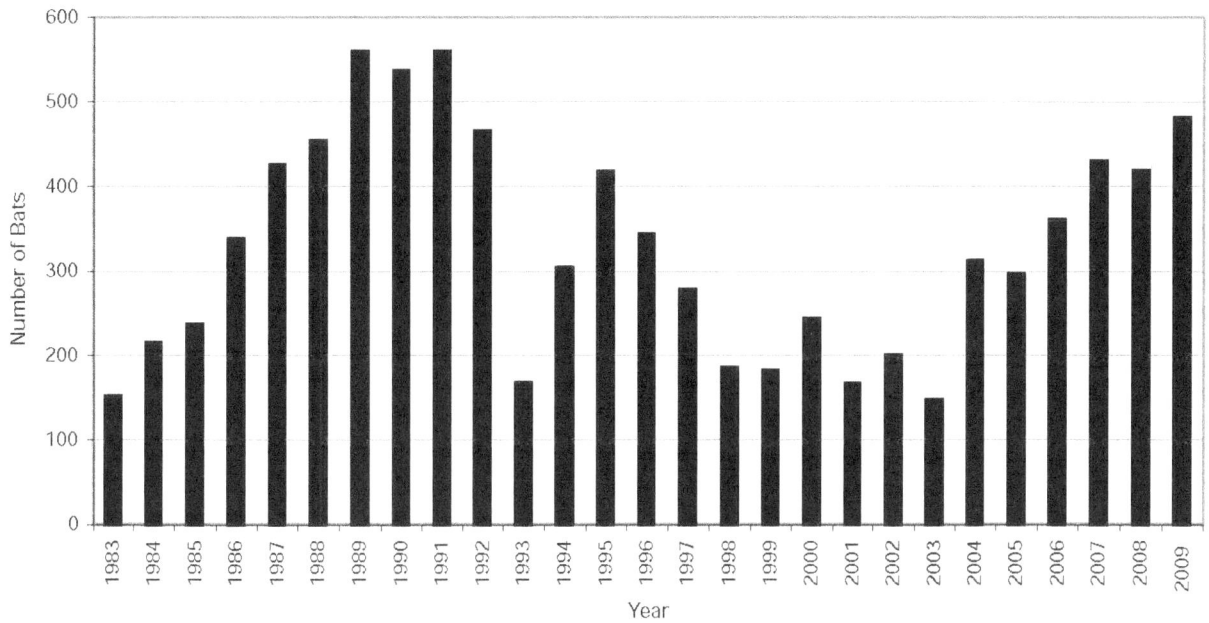

Figure 4—Number of *Corynorhinus townsendii virginianus* in the Sinnett/Thorn Mountain Cave system maternity colony, Pendleton County, WV, 1983 to 2009.

in the capture of 30 *C. t. virginianus*, of which 28 were males. Although only three *C. t. virginianus* were trapped at the cave on July 13, 2001, all were males. Adult male bats of four other species were also captured: *Eptesicus fuscus*, *M. lucifugus*, *M. septentrionalis*, and *P. subflavus*. Therefore, it appears Minor Rexrode Cave harbors a bachelor colony, although occasionally females, probably from one of the two maternity colonies located nearby in the same valley, use the cave. Bachelor colonies have also been documented in Hellhole, Pendleton County (U.S. Fish and Wildlife Service 1984) and by WVDNR biologists in Elkhorn Mountain Cave, Grant County (Stihler and others 1997).

During studies at Elkhorn Mountain Cave, Grant County, in late 1996 and early 1997, number of *C. t. virginianus* in the cave increased in the spring from 3 bats on April 4, 1997, to a maximum of 159 bats on August 29, 1996, and then declined in the fall to 12 bats on October 31, 1996 (fig. 5). As the number of bats increased toward the end of summer, the sex ratio shifted. Whereas only males were captured on June 30, 6.9 percent were females on July 2, 44.7 percent were females on September 11, and 16.0 percent were females on October 22. This finding contrasts with a study in Lee County, KY, which found that number of males in bachelor colonies declined in mid-August, coinciding with onset of mating (Lacki and others 1994). Bachelor colony sites may be important breeding locations in late summer and fall and may facilitate genetic mixing of bats from various summer and winter concentrations. This is evidenced by bats banded at Elkhorn Mountain Cave during summer and fall being

subsequently observed in four hibernacula up to 31.4 km from Elkhorn Mountain Cave.

Transitional caves—In addition to bachelor colony and maternity colony caves, there is a third category of cave used by *C. t. virginianus* in West Virginia. These are "transitional" caves used by significant numbers of *C. t. virginianus* (≤ 200+ bats) only in late summer and early fall as the bats move from summer colonies to their hibernacula. Three transitional caves have been identified and all are in Pendleton County: Blood Cave, Flute Cave, and Trout Cave.[4] None of these caves house significant numbers of *C. t. virginianus* during summer or winter.

Hibernacula

Most of the known *C. t. virginianus* hibernating in West Virginia are concentrated in a small number of caves with over 95 percent of the known hibernating *C. t. virginianus* in just three caves. The bats hibernate in densely packed clusters, typically in the same specific areas of the caves each winter. Hellhole contains the largest hibernating concentration of *C. t. virginianus* anywhere. In the listing petition (letter from Michael Harvey and John Hall to Lynn Greenwalt, U.S. Fish and Wildlife Service, October 15, 1976), Hall noted that in West Virginia *C. t. virginianus* are more dispersed in winter than in summer. This was largely because early surveys in Hellhole failed to locate

---

[4] West Virginia Department of Natural Resources, unpublished data.

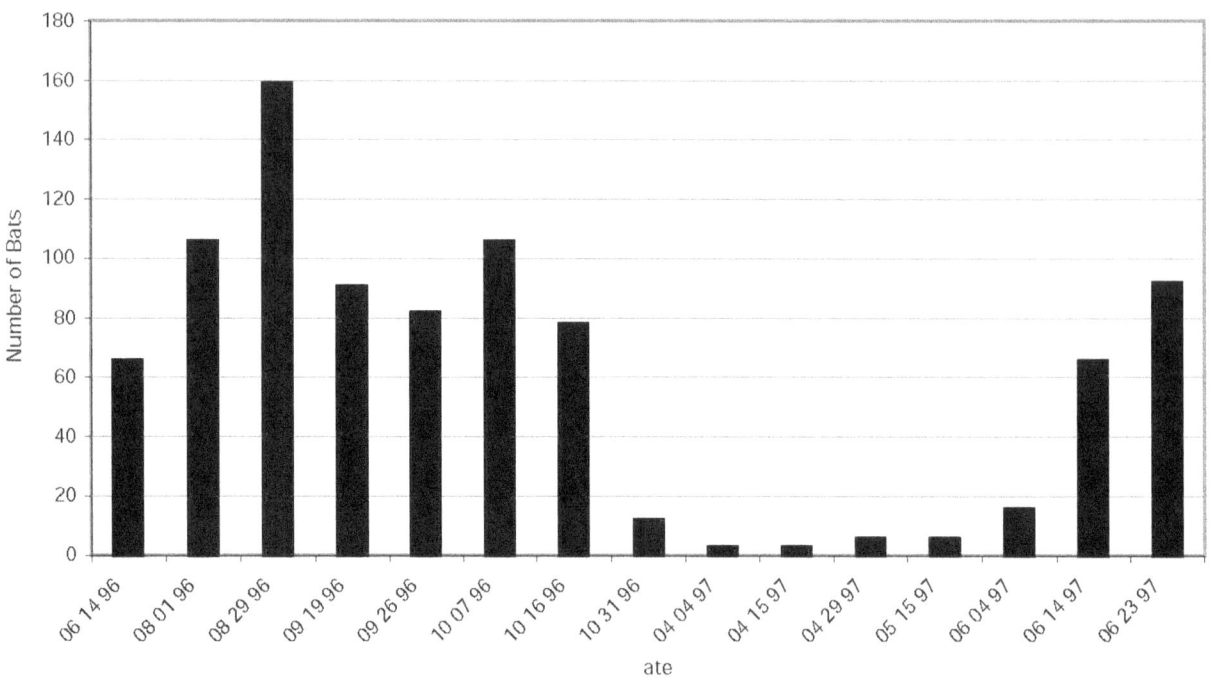

Figure 5—Number of *Corynorhinus townsendii virginianus* in the Elkhorn Mountain Cave bachelor colony, Grant County, WV, June 14, 1996 through June 23, 1997.

some areas of the cave which contained concentrations of hibernating *C. t. virginianus*. The first survey to include all areas where *C. t. virginianus* are now known to hibernate was conducted in 1986 when 2,914 *C. t. virginianus* were counted. A survey conducted in February 2010 documented 10,025 hibernating *C. t. virginianus* in Hellhole. However, the previous survey (February 2007) located only 5,006 *C. t. virginianus* in these areas. It seems possible that this large increase (100 percent in 3 years) may be a result of the bats shifting locations within the cave due to a reduction in human activity in the cave beginning in September 2007.[5]

In addition, 2 other caves (Sinnett and Schoolhouse) were visited in 2010 and, based on the 2010 data for these 3 caves and the 2009 survey data for 10 other *C. t. virginianus* hibernacula, number of *C. t. virginianus* known to hibernate in West Virginia caves was estimated at 12,059 individuals with 10,025 (83 percent) in Hellhole. Also, based on these data, three caves (Cave Hollow/Arbogast Cave system, Hellhole, and Schoolhouse Cave) contain 96 percent (11,559 individuals) of the known hibernating *C. t. virginianus* in West Virginia. This is an increase of 124 percent compared to the first complete count of these caves (1988 to 1989; 5,170 bats).

[5] Personal communication. 2010. Gordon Brace, Germany Valley Karst Survey, Falls Church, VA 22043.

WHITE-NOSE SYNDROME

White-nose syndrome (WNS), a condition that appears to be caused by the fungus *Geomyces destructans* (Gargas and others 2009), has resulted in the deaths of over a million bats in the Northeastern United States since it was first observed near Albany, NY, in 2006 (Blehert and others 2008). In January and February 2009, WNS was confirmed by the U.S. Geological Service National Wildlife Health Center (Madison, WI) in bats collected in Pendleton County, WV, and WNS was detected in four caves in that county (Cave Mountain Cave, Hamilton Cave, Trout Cave, and Cliff Cave). Cliff Cave is used by significant numbers of *C. t. virginianus* in both winter and summer; Cave Mountain Cave contains a maternity colony and a small number of bats in the winter, and the other two caves receive occasional use by this species. Although *C. t. virginianus* were present in three of the WNS-affected caves in 2009, none exhibited signs of WNS. In January 2010, WNS was confirmed by the Southeastern Cooperative Wildlife Disease Study (Athens, GA) in *M. lucifugus* from Hellhole. *P. subflavus* and *M. lucifugus* collected from Sinnett Cave in March 2010 also tested positive. In February and early March 2010, 12,059 hibernating *C. t. virginianus* were observed, including 10,025 in Hellhole and 199 in Sinnett Cave, and again, no *C. t. virginianus* exhibited visible signs of WNS. However, all other cave bat species within the current range of WNS have been affected with several species experiencing mortality levels in excess of 90 percent in affected hibernacula (Turner and Reeder 2009).

CONCLUSIONS

When *C. t. virginianus* was listed as federally endangered in 1979, populations of this bat using West Virginia cave roosts were declining, probably as a result of increased disturbance related to increased speleological use of these caves. Protection of cave roosts through cave closures and installation of fences and gates at cave entrances resulted in increases in numbers of bats at known maternity colonies of 77 percent. I believe changes in land cover were minimal over the study period and were not a factor in the observed population increase. For example, a comparison of land cover data from 1992 and 2009 [National Land Cover Dataset 1992 (Vogelmann 1998) and Landscape Fire and Resource Management Planning Tools Project (Ryan and others 2006)] show the changes in open and forest cover types in the three-county area where maternity colonies occur was < 1.6 percent during this 17-year period. *C. t. virginianus* readily adapts to gates, including angle iron gates, which are both secure and bat friendly. Several important *C. t. virginianus* caves in West Virginia are not currently gated with angle iron gates and, where feasible, these caves should be protected with angle iron gates when there are opportunities to do so. Future research should attempt to locate and protect additional caves and mines used by *C. t. virginianus*.

Monitoring of both maternity colonies and hibernacula confirmed increases in bat numbers after cave protection measures were implemented. In West Virginia, maternity colony data probably provide a better indication of population trends because of the difficulty of getting a complete survey of a large and complex hibernaculum such as Hellhole. Summer emergence counts before parturition provide good estimates of colony size even if the roost sites within the cave are not known.

While most efforts to date have focused on maternity colony and hibernation sites, importance of bachelor colonies and transitional caves should be further investigated. Although not the focus of this paper, status and conservation importance of the *C. t. virginianus* population in the New River Gorge National River area in Fayette County should be determined.

While the most serious threat to *C. t. virginianus* may be WNS, to date there is no evidence that WNS is affecting this species. Because *C. t. virginianus* often hibernate in the drier portions of caves [e.g., mean relative humidity in winter at the hibernation site in Schoolhouse Cave,

2009 to 2010 of 66 percent (West Virginia Department of Natural Resources data)], *G. destructans* may not grow as well as at sites where *M. lucifugus* and *P. subflavus* hibernate and where relative humidity is high and the bats are often covered with condensation. Although no visible *G. destructans* has been observed on hibernating *C. t. virginianus*, the fungus may still affect these bats without presenting the classic external fungal growth usually associated with WNS.

Because *C. t. virginianus* in the Pendleton County area of West Virginia and adjacent Virginia has a restricted range (an area approximately 48 km by 58 km in extent) and most of these bats are concentrated in a small number of caves, if WNS causes large-scale mortality events in *C. t. virginianus*, it is likely that most of the bats in this area will be impacted relatively quickly. *C. t. virginianus* in the New River Gorge National River (at the time of writing, approximately 97 km from WNS-affected sites) may not be impacted as soon. In 2009, with the largest concentration of *C. t. virginianus* in the world within the range of WNS, the USFWS, in consultation with State agencies and species experts, developed a captive propagation plan for *C. t. virginianus*. In November 2009, 40 *C. t. virginianus* from Pendleton County, WV, were transported to the Smithsonian Conservation Biology Institute near Front Royal, VA, where a protocol for the captive holding of these bats was developed with the hope of establishing a captive security population of *C. t. virginianus* isolated from WNS (Smithsonian Institution project proposal submitted to USFWS, September 2009).

Maternity colony counts conducted in June 2010 were the second highest on record and only 103 bats (1.4 percent) less than the 2009 total (7,245). In addition, counts conducted at 5 of the 10 maternity colonies in late July and early August 2010, after the young were volant, showed a 21 percent increase in number of bats over June 2010 numbers, suggesting the colonies were successful in producing young. Monitoring *C. t. virginianus* for impacts of WNS will continue to be a high priority.

ACKNOWLEDGMENTS

The author thanks the owners of *C. t. virginianus* caves for their cooperation and assistance in protecting important bats roosts; the USFWS for providing funding through section 6 grants for monitoring and protection of *C. t. virginianus* and their cave roosts; the U.S. Department of Agriculture Forest Service, Monongahela National Forest, for managing caves to benefit these bats and for providing WVDNR biologists access to these caves for monitoring *C. t. virginianus* populations; and the American Cave Conservation Association and numerous volunteers who have assisted in gating *C. t. virginianus* caves to reduce disturbance to these bats. The author also thanks those WVDNR employees who have dedicated many days and nights working on *C. t. virginianus* bat projects, especially Jack Wallace and Rick Doyle, and Tabitha Viner, a volunteer who has donated considerable vacation time to help monitor summer colonies of *C. t. virginianus* in West Virginia. Michael Dougherty (WVDNR) assisted with land cover data analyses. The Nature Conservancy's assistance with the WVDNR's acquisition and protection of an important *C. t. virginianus* cave was greatly appreciated.

LITERATURE CITED

Bagley, F.; Jacobs, J. 1985. Census technique for endangered big-eared bats proving successful. Endangered Species Technical Bulletin. 10(3): 5-7.

Barbour, R.W.; Davis, W.H. 1969. Bats of America. Lexington, KY: University Press of Kentucky. 286 p.

Blehert, D.S.; Hicks, A.C.; Behr, M. [and others]. 2008. Bat white-nose syndrome: an emerging fungal pathogen? Science Express. DOI: 10.1126/science.1163874.

Frum. W.G. 1947. Bats of West Virginia. Morgantown, WV: West Virginia University. 17 p. M.S. thesis.

Gargas, A.; Trest, M.T.; Christensen, M. [and others]. 2009. *Geomyces destructans* sp. nov. associated with bat white-nose syndrome. Mycotaxon. 108: 147-154.

Handley, C.O. 1959. A revision of the American bats of the genera *Euderma* and *Plecotus*. Proceedings of the U.S. National Museum. 110(3417): 95-246.

Kellogg, R. 1937. Annotated list of West Virginia mammals. Proceedings of the U.S. National Museum. 84(3022): 448-450.

Lacki, M.J.; Adam, M.D.; Shoemaker, L.G. 1994. Observations on seasonal cycle, population patterns and roost selection in summer colonies of *Plecotus townsendii virginianus* in Kentucky. American Midland Naturalist. 131(1): 34-42.

Piaggio, A.J.; Navo, K.W.; Stihler, C. 2009. Intraspecific comparison of population structure, genetic diversity, and dispersal among three subspecies of Townsend's big-eared bats, *Corynorhinus townsendii townsendii*, *C. t. pallescens*, and the endangered *C. t. virginianus*. Conservation Genetics. 10: 169-176.

Reese, A.M. 1934. The fauna of West Virginia caves. Proceedings of the West Virginia Academy of Science. 7: 39-53.

Ryan, K.C.; Lee, K.M.; Rollins, M.G. Z. [and others]. 2006. Landfire: Landscape Fire and Resource Management Planning Tools project. In: Andrews, P.L.; Butler, B.W., comps. Fuels management-how to measure success: conference proceedings. RMRS-P-41. Fort Collins, CO: U.S. Department of Agriculture Forest Service, Rocky Mountain Research Station: 193-200. [Data updated to 2009].

Stihler, C.W. 2011. Radiotelemetry studies of female Virginia big-eared bats (*Corynorhinus townsendii virginianus*) in Pendleton County, West Virginia. In: Loeb, S.C.; Lacki, M.J.; Miller, D.A., eds. Conservation and management of eastern big-eared bats: a symposium. Gen. Tech. Rep. SRS-145. Asheville, NC: U.S. Department of Agriculture Forest Service, Southern Research Station: 139-146.

Stihler, C.W.; Wallace, J.; Jones, A.; Mitchell, D. 1997. Endangered species Federal assistance performance report. Proj. E-1-14. Charleston, WV: West Virginia Division of Natural Resources. 57 p.

Turner, G.G.; Reeder, D.M. 2009. Update of white nose syndrome in bats, September 2009. Bat Research News. 50(3): 47-53.

U.S. Fish and Wildlife Service. 1984. A recovery plan for the Ozark big-eared bat and Virginia big-eared bat. Fort Snelling, MN: U.S. Fish and Wildlife Service. 119 p.

Varner, M.S. 2008. Spring emergence and fall swarm bat monitoring at New River Gorge National River Program. Report NPS/NER/NERI-1428-07B. Glen Jean, WV: U.S. Department of the Interior, National Park Service, New River National River.

Vogelmann, J.E.; Sohl, T.L.; Campbell, P.V.; Shaw, D.M. 1998. Regional land cover characterization using Landsat Thematic Mapper data and ancillary data sources. Environmental Monitoring and Assessment. 51: 415-428.

Wilson, L.W. 1946. Notes on bats from eastern West Virginia. Journal of Mammalogy. 29(1): 85-86.

Wilson, L.W. 1948. An introduction to the mammals of West Virginia. Charleston, WV: West Virginia Conservation Commission. 20 p.

PHYLOGENETIC AND POPULATION GENETIC ASSESSMENT OF RAFINESQUE'S BIG-EARED BAT *(CORYNORHINUS RAFINESQUII)*

Antoinette J. Piaggio, Research Biologist, U.S. Department of Agriculture, Wildlife Services, National Wildlife Research Center, 4101 LaPorte Avenue, Fort Collins, CO 80521

David A. Saugey, Wildlife Biologist, U.S. Department of Agriculture Forest Service, Ouachita National Forest, P.O. Box 189, Jessieville, AR 71949-0189

D. Blake Sasse, Nongame Mammal/Furbearer Program Leader, Arkansas Game and Fish Commission, 213A Highway 89 South, Mayflower, AR 72106

Abstract—Rafinesque's big-eared bat (*Corynorhinus rafinesquii*) is distributed across the Southeastern United States. Due to habitat loss and low population numbers, this species is a Federal species of concern and protected by every State within its range. Effective management of any species of concern is dependent on an unambiguous understanding of taxonomic relationships. However, for this species, there are discordant inferences about subspecific designations from previous studies. Further, there have been no assessments of population genetic status for this species. Such assessments could provide information on genetic diversity and population connectivity and increase our understanding of the need for management and conservation of this species. Therefore, our goals were to assess population level genetic diversity and connectivity among 5 colonies in Arkansas (139 individuals) and to infer the evolutionary relationships of these bats to *C. rafinesquii* collected across its distribution (additional 216 individuals). We used mitochondrial DNA control region sequences and 11 microsatellite loci to infer genetic relationships, estimate levels of genetic diversity, and examine population connectivity among 5 colonies in Arkansas. Although we identified two phylogenetically divergent mitochondrial DNA lineages, these correspond to neither current subspecific designation nor nonoverlapping geographical groups. Genetic diversity and population connectivity estimated from mitochondrial DNA was high in Arkansas populations probably due to occurrence of both evolutionary lineages within each colony. However, estimates from microsatellite DNA of genetic diversity, population connectivity, and effective population sizes in these populations were low. Further, our results suggested a weak signal of population bottleneck in Arkansas colonies and low genetic connectivity. Current conservation efforts should continue to focus on protection of roosts and improvement of habitat corridors to connect populations.

INTRODUCTION

Rafinesque's big-eared bat (*Corynorhinus rafinesquii*) is a medium-sized bat that ranges across a broad portion of the Southeastern United States (fig. 1; Bayless and others 2011). However, there has been concern about its status since the mid-20th century due to low population numbers and patchy distribution. Handley (1959) expressed concern for the status of this species based on lack of known large colonies and limited numbers of museum specimens. He concluded that populations had declined due to anthropogenic impacts in parts of their range. Jones and Suttkus (1975) published data from a 9-year study in Louisiana and concluded that these bats were rare likely due to severe population declines. They also concluded that reduction occurred because *C. rafinesquii* is sensitive to disturbance from humans at vulnerable maternity roost sites which were principally found in abandoned manmade structures. Based on concerns over status of this species, it was listed as vulnerable to extinction on the 2004 International Union for Conservation of Nature Red List, a Federal species at risk (U.S. Fish and Wildlife Service 1985), and a species of concern in every State, except Virginia, where they are considered endangered (Bayless and others 2011, Kentucky State Nature Preserves Commission 1996, Lance 1999).

In spite of conservation concerns, little is known about evolutionary relationships, genetic diversity, and gene flow among populations of *C. rafinesquii*. For any species of concern, it is important that evolutionary relationships, or taxonomy, of that species is understood. In a taxonomic revision of the genus *Corynorhinus* based on morphological characters, Handley (1959) designated two subspecies of *C. rafinesquii* assigning populations from the Southeastern United States (Alabama, Arkansas, Florida, Georgia, Louisiana, Mississippi, North Carolina, eastern Oklahoma, South Carolina, eastern Texas, and coastal Virginia) to *C. r. macrotis* and populations from East Central United States (northern Alabama, Arkansas, northern Georgia, Kentucky, southern Illinois, southern Indiana, northern Mississippi, eastern Missouri, western North Carolina, southern Ohio, eastern Oklahoma, western South Carolina, Tennessee, western Virginia, western West Virginia) to *C. r. rafinesquii*, with areas where the two subspecies overlapped (Handley 1959:152). More recently, Piaggio and Perkins (2005) tried to elucidate evolutionary relationships of *C. rafinesquii* using

Citation for proceedings: Loeb, Susan C.; Lacki, Michael J.; Miller, Darren A., eds. 2011. Conservation and management of eastern big-eared bats: a symposium. Gen. Tech. Rep. SRS-145. Asheville, NC: U.S. Department of Agriculture, Forest Service, Southern Research Station. 157 p.

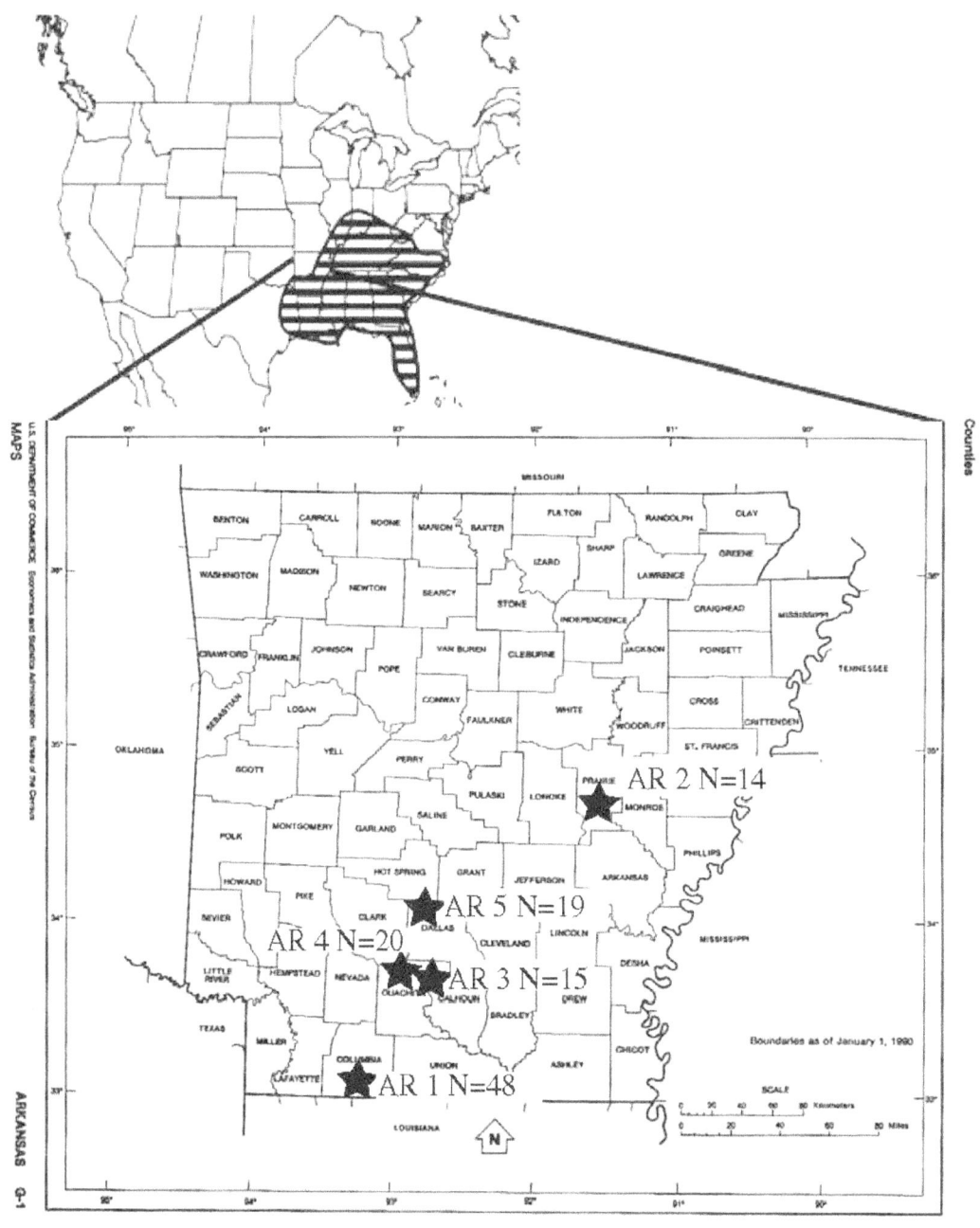

Figure 1—Distribution of *Corynorhinus rafinesquii* with Arkansas roosts sampled shown in detail (AR1, AR2, AR3, AR4, and AR5) and number of individuals sampled per colony noted. (Map from the University of Texas, Austin, TX, Perry Casteñeda Library map collection online http://www.lib.utexas.edu/maps/.)

limited sampling from portions of the species' range and both mitochondrial and nuclear DNA sequences. That study found that there was no correlation between the two designated subspecies of *C. rafinesquii*, from Handley (1959), and the molecular phylogeny. Piaggio and Perkins (2005) concluded that a more detailed study of *C. rafinesquii* including more samples representing a greater portion of their range was required to determine if any subspecific designation was warranted. To correctly determine conservation status of this species, it is critical that evolutionary relationships, and, thus,

taxonomy and geographical boundaries of taxonomic units, are understood. A molecular phylogenetic approach such as the one used in Piaggio and Perkins (2005) with additional samples from across the range of *C. rafinesquii* could provide such information.

Piaggio and Perkins (2005) found that there were two divergent evolutionary lineages of *C. rafinesquii*. However, both clades had samples from Arkansas and some samples in each clade were from the same colonies. After more than 10 years of study, there have been only five known continually active colonies of *C. rafinesquii* in Arkansas, all of which occupy abandoned humanmade structures (Saugey 2000). These colonies are found in a region of Arkansas that was historically dominated by bottomland hardwood forests which have been largely converted to agricultural uses and are one of the most endangered forest types in the United States (Abernathy and Turner 1987, The Nature Conservancy 1992, Turner and others 1981). It is assumed that mature, hollow trees in the bottomland hardwood forests represent historical roosting habitat for *C. rafinesquii* (Clark 1990, 1991). Therefore, it appears that these bats may use abandoned manmade structures because of loss of natural roosts. Because all of the known *C. rafinesquii* colonies in Arkansas were located in abandoned manmade structures, there was concern that these colonies were remnant populations and that they may have lost connectivity and suffered reduced genetic diversity due to the loss of contiguous bottomland habitat. Further, these colonies were considered threatened due to the ephemeral nature of their roosts.

Maintenance of genetic diversity within populations and connectivity among genetically diverse populations is crucial for sustaining the evolutionary potential of a species (England and others 2003). A loss of population connectivity as a result of reduced and/or fragmented habitat may increase susceptibility to a population bottleneck (Cornuet and Luikart 1996), which can allow genetic drift to affect a population resulting in low effective population size, loss of genetic diversity, and inbreeding. Such populations are likely more susceptible to disease, ecological catastrophes, and eventual extinction, thus, impacting evolutionary potential of that species (Altizer and others 2003, Lacy 1997). Analyses of maternally inherited mitochondrial DNA (mtDNA) and biparentally inherited autosomal microsatellites can be used to infer genetic relationships and to estimate various population parameters including genetic diversity, population connectivity, and effective population sizes (Avise 1995, Avise and Hamrick 1996, Haig 1998). If populations exhibit genetic evidence of population bottlenecks, reduced genetic diversity, and/or reduced effective population sizes, then targeted conservation efforts and management practices are needed.

Given the conservation status of *C. rafinesquii* and lack of data regarding genetic diversity for this species, we employed genetic markers, both mtDNA and microsatellites, to infer evolutionary relationships of *C. rafinesquii* with samples from across its range and to estimate genetic diversity, connectivity among populations, and effective population sizes among Arkansas colonies. We predicted that due to past habitat loss and subsequent disjunction and/or population reduction, we would detect population bottlenecks. If true, estimates of genetic diversity and population connectivity would be low and there might also be inbreeding and low effective population sizes. This, in turn, would guide recommendations for species' conservation from a genetic perspective.

MATERIALS AND METHODS

Study Area

We collected samples from across the Southeastern United States. The study area in Arkansas included widely spaced locations in Columbia, Dallas, and Ouachita Counties within the Tertiary Uplands of the southcentral Plains and Prairie County within the Grand Prairie of the Mississippi River Alluvial Plain, Arkansas (Arkansas Natural Heritage Commission 2003). The Tertiary Upland sites were dominated by commercial shortleaf and loblolly pine (*Pinus echinata* and *P. taeda*) plantations that largely replaced native oak-hickory-pine (*Quercus* spp.-*Carya* spp.) forests except in narrow streamside zones (Woods and others 2004). Forested tracts were interspersed with bayous and by pasture for grazing cattle. Most of the large bottomland hardwood timber had been harvested (Dahl 1990). The Grand Prairie was a loess-covered terrace that once contained an extensive tall grass prairie converted to cropland in the early 20th century (Holder 1970). Average precipitation was 127 cm, and average temperatures are highest in July (average 32 °C) and lowest in January (7 °C). Expansive areas of rice, soybeans, cotton, corn, and wheat were cultivated in the area (Woods and others 2004). Braided bayous were found throughout this area with bottomland hardwood forests occurring along drainages and floodplains, upland hardwood forests along hills and bluffs, and hardwood savannas along the edges of prairie terraces. Forested acres had been reduced by more than half through conversion to croplands and development (Shepherd 1984). The eastern border of the Grand Prairie was adjacent to the White River riparian area that contained some of the most extensive areas of remaining bottomland hardwood forests in Arkansas (Woods and others 2004).

Sample Collection

We collected tissue samples during 2000 to 2005 at five roosts in Arkansas (fig. 1). Sites AR1 (48 individuals), AR2 (14 individuals), and AR5 (33 individuals) were maternity roosts; AR3 (15 individuals) and AR4 (29 individuals) were hibernacula. However, the hibernacula used by individuals from AR1 and AR5 and the maternity roosts for individuals from AR3 and AR4 were known and adjacent to sites where samples were collected, e.g., abandoned house used as a maternity roost and adjacent well used as a hibernaculum. Therefore, we assumed that each of these sites represented a single and separate colony. Further, based on approximately 12 years of mark-recapture data representing 3,500 captures of bats at these sites, exchange of individuals was uncommon among sampled sites even when they were proximate (< 14 km) to one another. Therefore, we assumed that each sampled maternity roost or hibernation site was a single colony. We also sequenced DNA from 216 other individuals from other parts of the range of *C. rafinesquii* (Florida, Kentucky, Mississippi, North Carolina, Tennessee,

South Carolina, Louisiana, and Texas) and 5 other Arkansas individuals, and we included these in our phylogenetic analysis (table 1; fig. 1).

We captured individual *C. rafinesquii* in Arkansas colonies found in wells using a method employing an umbrella (England and Saugey 1999). When bats were found in abandoned buildings, we used hand nets for capture. Bats collected outside of Arkansas were captured using mist nets. We collected a 3-mm tissue biopsy from the right wing (Worthington Wilmer and Barratt 1996) before releasing bats at site of capture. Capture and sampling protocols were reviewed and approved by the University of Colorado, Boulder's Institutional Animal Care and Use Committee. We preserved samples in a 20-percent dimethyl sulfoxide and a 0.25M-ethylenediaminetetraacetic acid solution saturated with sodium chloride and optimized at pH 8.0 (Seutin and others

1991). We used half of each wing punch to extract genomic DNA using a DNeasy Blood & Tissue Kit (QIAGEN Inc., Valencia, CA) following the manufacturer's protocol.

DNA Amplification, Sequencing, and Genotyping

We amplified genomic DNA from each sample and the mtDNA control region was sequenced, following protocols described in Piaggio and Perkins (2005). We genotyped *C. rafinesquii* from Arkansas roosts (AR1, 48 individuals; AR2, 11 individuals; AR3, 15 individuals; AR4, 20 individuals; and AR5, 18 individuals) using 11 loci: EF15B, EF20C, EF21, EF14 (Vonhof and others 2002), NN8 (Petri and others 1997), PAUR 05 (Burland and others 1998), Cora_D12_D12, Cora_E07_E07, Cora_H07_C05, Cora_B07_H12, and Cora_E10_G03 (Piaggio

Table 1—Genetic samples of Rafinesque's big-eared bats (*Corynorhinus rafinesquii*) sequenced and analyzed with localities, ownership/donor, and GenBank accession numbers indicated

Taxon	Locality[a]	Donor/owner[b]	Pop[c]	Acc no[d]
C. mexicanus	Guanaceví, Durango, Mexico	CIIDIR CRD 3110 Celia López-González		AY713590
	Guanaceví, Durango, Mexico	CIIDIR CRD 3125 Celia López-González		AY713591
	Guanaceví, Durango, Mexico	CIIDIR CRD 3115 Celia López-González		AY713593
	Milpa Alta, Distrito Federal, Mexico	Rafael Avila-Flores		AY713785
C. rafinesquii	Arkansas, Columbia	USFS David Saugey	AR1	AY713635–AY713643 AY713666–AY713675 AY713684–AY713696 AY713717–AY713731
	Arkansas, Prairie	AGFC Blake Sasse	AR2	AY713652–AY713665
	Arkansas, Ouachita	USFS David Saugey	AR3	AY713900–AY713909 AY775995–AY775999
	Arkansas, Ouachita	USFS David Saugey	AR4	AY713910–AY713919 AY775976–AY775985 HQ239099–HQ239102 HQ239107–HQ239111
	Arkansas, Dallas	USFS David Saugey	AR5	AY713920–AY713929 AY775986–AY775994 HQ239095–HQ239098 HQ239112–HQ239121
	Florida, Osceola	Laura Finn Kelli Deichmueller		AY713789–AY713790
	Florida, Holmes	FFWCC Jeff Gore		AY713818
	Kentucky, Estill	KDFWR Traci Wethington		AY713877–AY713878 AY713881–AY713882
	Kentucky, Bath	Eric Britzke		AY713786–AY713788
	Louisiana, Union Parish	Chris Rice		HQ239178–HQ239194

continued

Table 1—Genetic samples of Rafinesque's big-eared bats (*Corynorhinus rafinesquii*) sequenced and analyzed with localities, ownership/donator, and GenBank accession numbers indicated (continued)

Taxon	Locality[a]	Donor/owner[b]	Pop[c]	Acc no[d]
C. rafinesquii (continued)	Mississippi, Perry	Austin Trousdale		AY713842–AY713854
	Mississippi, Wayne	Austin Trousdale		AY713855–AY713860
	Mississippi, Jones	Austin Trousdale		AY713861
	Mississippi, Noxubee	USFWS David Richardson		HQ239077–HQ239092
	North Carolina, Bladen	Mary Kay Clark		AY713595–AY713620
	South Carolina, Charleston	Heather Thomas		AY713698–AY713701 AY713751–AY713756 HQ239093–HQ239094 HQ239103–HQ239106
	South Carolina, Oconee	SCDNR Mary Bunch		AY713767
	South Carolina, Pickens	SCDNR Mary Brunch		AY713768
	South Carolina, Richland	SCDNR Mary Bunch		AY713792
	South Carolina, Dorchester	Piaggio		AY713791
	South Carolina, Orangeburg	Frances Bennett		AY713819–AY713820 AY713822
	South Carolina, Kershaw	Frances Bennett		AY713821
	South Carolina, Barnwell	Frances Bennett		AY713823
	South Carolina, Williamsburg	Frances Bennett		AY713824–AY713825 AY713827–AY713828
	South Carolina, Georgetown	Frances Bennett		AY713826
	South Carolina, Colleton	Frances Bennett		AY713829–AY713830
	Tennessee, Chester	Brian Carver		HQ239122–HQ239152
	Tennessee, Fentress	Mary Kay Clark		HQ239153–HQ239177
	Texas, Harrison	Leigh Stuemke/Chris Comer		HQ239208–HQ239209 HQ239213–HQ239215 HQ239218–HQ239220 HQ239223–HQ239225 HQ239228–HQ239230
	Texas, Liberty	Leigh Stuemke/Chris Comer		HQ239199 HQ239203–HQ239207 HQ239210–HQ239212 HQ239216–HQ239217 HQ23922–HQ239222 HQ239226–HQ239227 HQ239231–HQ239232
	Texas, Polk	Leigh Stuemke/Chris Comer		HQ239195–HQ239198 HQ239200–HQ239202

CIIDIR = Colección Regional Durango (Vertebrados), CIIDIR Durango, Instituto Politécnico Nacional, México; USFS = U.S. Forest Service, Ouachita National Forest; AGFC = Arkansas Game and Fish Commission; FFWCC = Florida Fish and Wildlife Conservation Commission; KDFWR = Kentucky Department of Fish and Wildlife Resources; USFWS = U.S. Fish and Wildlife Service, Noxubee National Wildlife Refuge; SCDNR = South Carolina Division of Natural Resources.

[a] State, county (or city, State, country).

[b] Person and/or organization that donated tissue and/or owns sample; museum catalog numbers provided when possible.

[c] Population belongs to; applicable only to Arkansas populations surveyed in detail in this study.

[d] GenBank accession number.

and others 2009a). We amplified products from these loci via polymerase chain reaction (PCR) with one primer end-labeled with TET, FAM, or HEX fluorescent label (Sigma-Genosys Co., USA). We amplified each microsatellite PCR for the primers designed from other bat species in a standard 25 µl reaction which contained optimized amounts of PCR water; 5X buffer C (Invitrogen by Life Technologies Corp., USA); 2.5 µl of dNTP (10 mM; Invitrogen by Life Technologies Corp., USA); 2.5 µl of each primer (1 pM/µl); Taq DNA polymerase (Promega Corp., USA); and 1 µl of genomic DNA. Amplification consisted of an initial denaturation at 94 °C for 2 minutes followed by 30 cycles of denaturing at 94 °C for 30 seconds, annealing at 56 °C (PAUR05 and EF15), 52 °C (EF21), or 46 °C (EF14, EF20C, and NN8) for 45 seconds, and extension at 72 °C for 45 seconds with a final extension period of 7 minutes at 72 °C. Amplification protocols for the *C. rafinesquii* primers are described in Piaggio and others (2009a).

We visualized genotypes from the primers designed from other bat species and some sequencing products on acrylamide gels on a MJ BaseStation 51™ sequencer (MJ Bioworks, Inc., Sauk City, WI). We scored microsatellite alleles with Cartographer 1.2.6 software (MJ Bioworks, Inc., Sauk City, WI) and confirmed these by manual examination. We visualized the *C. rafinesquii* specific microsatellites and remaining sequences on an AB 3130 (Applied Biosystems by Life Technologies Corp., Foster City, CA) automated genetic analyzer and scored with ABI GeneMapper® Software.

Sequence Analyses

We generated alignments of mtDNA control region sequences using Sequencher® 4.9 (Gene Codes Corp., Ann Arbor, MI) and checked by eye. We used *C. mexicanus* sequences generated from a previous study (Piaggio and Perkins 2005) as an outgroup for phylogenetic analyses because this is the sister taxon to *C. rafinesquii* (Hoofer and Van Den Bussche 2001, Piaggio and Perkins 2005). We completed maximum likelihood phylogenetic analyses using RAxML (Stamatakis 2006, Stamatakis and others 2008) available through Web-based Cyberinfrastructure for Phylogenetic Research (CIPRES) supercomputer [http://www.phylo.org/. (Date accessed: November 19, 2010)]. We implemented the estimation of the general time reversible substitution model with gamma distributed rate variation estimation using RAxML (Stamatakis and others 2005). We evaluated bootstrap analysis of nodal support with number of pseudoreplicates automatically generated by the program. We visualized the maximum likelihood tree output and edited for publication and a radial tree layout of this tree was generated in FigTree v.1.2.1 [http://tree.bio.ed.ac.uk/software/figtree/. (Date accessed: November 19, 2010)].

We quantified genetic diversity from DNA sequence data as number of individuals sequenced per population, number of unique haplotypes, haplotype diversity, nucleotide diversity (Nei 1987), parsimony informative sites, and average pairwise differences within Arkansas populations and other populations where there was adequate sample size for comparison (Union Parish, LA, $n = 17$; Noxubee County, MS, $n = 16$; Blanden County, NC, $n = 26$; Chester County, TN, $n = 31$; Fentress County, TN, $n = 25$; Liberty County, TX, $n = 17$). To evaluate how genetic diversity was distributed among Arkansas populations, we first estimated population differentiation using F_{ST} (Weir and Cockerham 1984) and ascertained significant substructure between populations with 5,000 randomization tests. We used sequential Bonferroni corrections to compute critical significance levels for these data (Rice 1989). We then evaluated the relationship between population differentiation (Slatkin's linear $F_{ST}/(1 - F_{ST})$; Slatkin 1993) and log-transformed geographic distances ($\log_{10}$km) to determine if there was isolation-by-distance (IBD). We also used this method to test for IBD across the range of the species by using the Arkansas populations and other populations from across the range where adequate sample size was collected (see above). We appraised nested levels of variation among colonies and within colonies using an analysis of molecular variance (AMOVA; Excoffier and others 1992) with 9,000 permutations. We performed these evaluations using Arlequin ver. 3.1 (Excoffier and others 2005) except for the calculation of the parsimony informative sites, which we evaluated with PAUP* 4.0b (Swofford 2002).

Microsatellite Analyses

We assessed microsatellite loci for null alleles using Micro-Checker (Van Oosterhout and others 2004). We also tested loci for significant departures from Hardy-Weinberg equilibrium (HWE) with 9,000 steps of a Markov chain and significant evidence of linkage disequilibria among loci using Arlequin ver. 3.1 (Excoffier and others 2005). We used sequential Bonferroni corrections to compute critical significance levels for multiple tests using these data (Rice 1989). We maintained genotype data in a spreadsheet, and then we used the software Convert (Glaubitz 2004) to transform this file into input files for other software packages used in further analyses.

We quantified intrapopulation genotypic variability as mean number of alleles (A), allelic richness (a), and number of private alleles (pa) per locus. We estimated the within-population inbreeding coefficient, F_{IS}, and tested for significant departure from zero with 1,000 randomizations. We performed these analyses with FSTAT 2.9.3 (Goudet 2001). We also estimated effective population size (N_e) for each population using the linkage disequilibrium model method for single sampling efforts implemented in the LDNE program (Waples and Do 2008). This program includes a bias correction from Waples (2006) for uneven sample sizes relative to N_e. We conducted estimates of N_e with parametric confidence intervals (CI) to include alleles with a frequency of ≥ 0.02.

We estimated population differentiation based on microsatellites for comparison to mtDNA estimates using traditional F_{ST} values (Weir and Cockerham 1984); we ascertained significance based on 9,000 randomizations with Monte Carlo simulations and Bonferroni corrections (Rice 1989). We further analyzed genetic structuring with an AMOVA using 9,000 permutations to determine significant deviations from random. We partitioned data in the same manner as the mtDNA AMOVA. We performed IBD tests as described for mtDNA. F_{ST} estimates, AMOVA evaluations, and IBD analyses were carried out using Arlequin ver. 3.1 (Excoffier and others 2005).

We used software Bottleneck (Cornuet and Luikart 1996) to examine evidence for a recent reduction in N_e as suggested by loss of rare allele classes. This program is a coalescent-based method for testing the hypothesis that a recent reduction in effective population size has occurred. We used 9,000 iterations to test the infinite alleles (IAM), stepwise mutation model (SMM), and two-phase model (TPM) with 70-percent SMM and 30-percent variance assuming drift-mutation equilibrium. We tested significance using a one-tailed Wilcoxon signed-rank test ($\alpha = 0.05$) performed in Bottleneck.

RESULTS

Phylogeny

Although *C. mexicanus* is the closest relative to *C. rafinesquii*, a large genetic divergence (> 15 percent; Piaggio and Perkins 2005) between these species was too great to provide any greater statistical reliability for ingroup relationships than midpoint rooting analyses. Therefore, we also generated trees using midpoint rooting. Trees

from both rooting strategies provided the same topology, so we omitted the outgroup to improve readability. We considered 1,064 base pairs from the control region. In the HVII region there was a C-repeat that varied in length among the samples. Often during the sequencing process, the polymerase failed in this repeat region, and determining number of repeats accurately was not possible. Therefore, we eliminated this repeat region across all samples for all analyses. Among the sequences, there were 810 constant sites, 68 variable sites that were parsimony uninformative, and 186 parsimony informative sites. Within the 360 *C. rafinesquii* sequences, there were 318 unique haplotypes. The maximum likelihood tree had 2 statistically supported lineages (clades A and B; figs. 2 and 3) after 1,000 bootstrap iterations. Average uncorrected sequence divergence between these lineages was 4.0 percent (fig. 2). Clade A contained individuals from across the species range, including individuals from each of the five Arkansas colonies (AR1 through AR5) and all other regions sampled (figs. 2 and 3). This clade had no significant bootstrap support (< 50 percent), and there was up to 2-percent sequence divergence within clade A. Clade B's members were only from each of the five known roosts in Arkansas (AR1 through AR5), Texas, and Louisiana. Clade B was well supported with significant bootstrap support

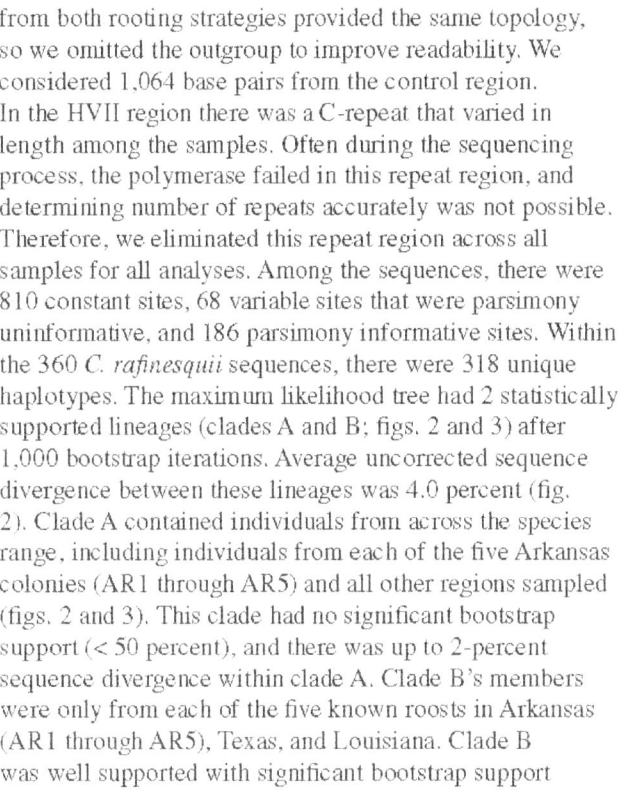

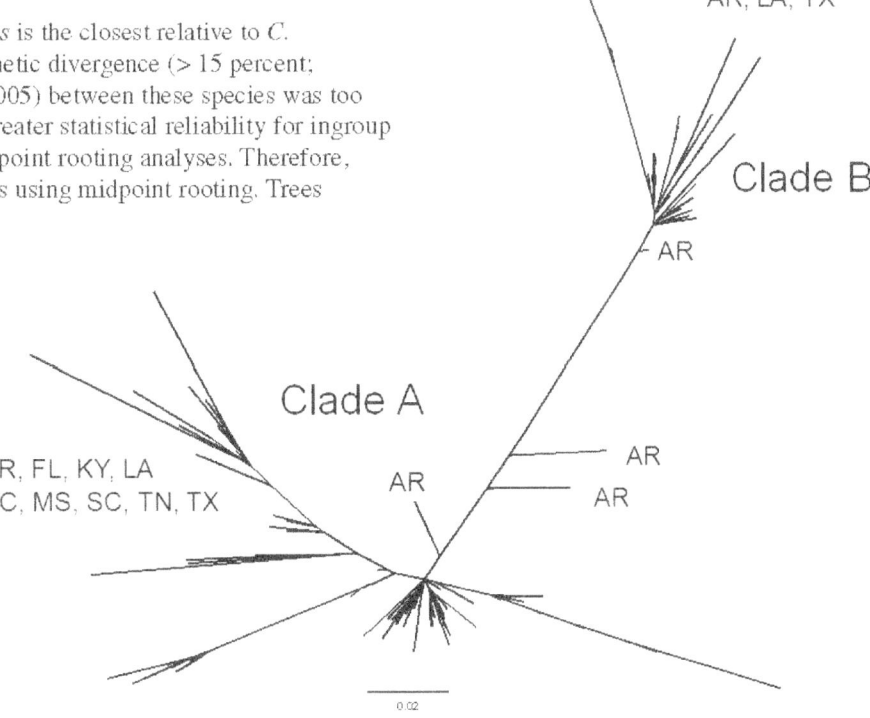

Figure 2—Radial tree layout of maximum likelihood tree inferred from *Corynorhinus rafinesquii* mitochondrial DNA control region. Model parameters of the GTR+G model parameters were estimated and enforced. Both midpoint-rooting and rooting with closest sister taxon strategies provided the same topology, so outgroup taxa were omitted to increase clarity. Samples from across *C. rafinesquii's* range are shown as States where they were collected.

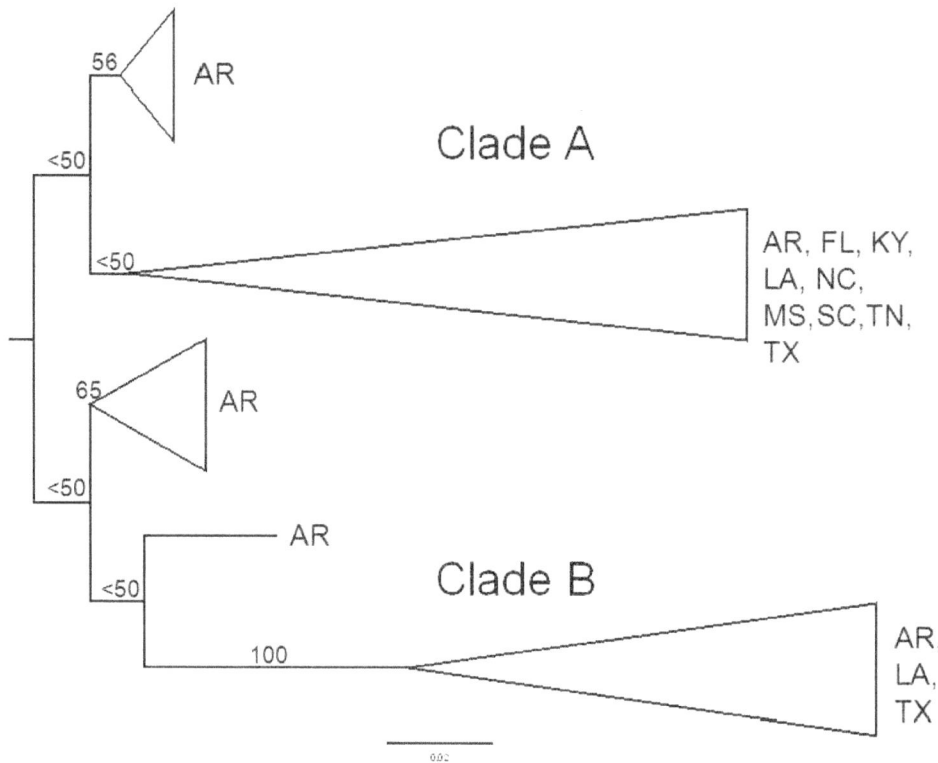

Figure 3—Maximum likelihood phylogram inferred from mitochondrial DNA control region. The GTR+G model parameters were estimated and enforced. Both midpoint-rooting and rooting with closest sister taxon strategies provided the same topology, so in presented trees outgroup taxa were omitted to improve readability. Support for nodes shown as ML bootstrap. Samples of *Corynorhinus rafinesquii* are shown as States where they were collected.

(100 percent), and it had < 1 percent sequence divergence. Lineages that were at least 4 percent divergent comprise the membership within Texas, Louisiana, and each of the five sampled Arkansas populations.

Mitochondrial DNA Sequence Diversity among Populations

The number of unique haplotypes found in each Arkansas colony ranged from 14 to 47, which for each colony is a high proportion of the total haplotypes (table 2). As a result, haplotype diversity was high, ranging from 0.99 to 1.00. Haplotype diversity was also high in other populations (0.87 to 0.99); Louisiana and Texas had the lowest (0.87 to 0.90). Nucleotide diversity was 0.005 to 0.027 within Arkansas colonies, and parsimony informative sites ranged from 45 to 61. The other populations had the same nucleotide diversity (0.005 to 0.024), but number of parsimony informative sites was lower (9 to 46). When examined more closely, Arkansas (except AR3 and AR5), Louisiana, and Texas, which are found in both clades, have at least twice as much nucleotide diversity and parsimony informative sites as North Carolina, Mississippi, and Tennessee populations which are only in clade A. Pairwise differences within only the Arkansas populations were higher (15.73 to 24.62) than the range of pairwise differences within the exclusively clade A populations (4.13 to 8.37). Pairwise differences among colonies in Arkansas were similar to within population differences but ranged lower (18.51 to 26.30) than between Arkansas and any other populations (96.79 to 115.07). Pairwise differences between Texas/Louisiana and North Carolina, Mississippi, and Tennessee populations were similar to within Arkansas (23.43 to 29.27) and lower among North Carolina, Mississippi, and Tennessee populations (6.55 to 19.18). The lowest pairwise differences were between Mississippi and Tennessee populations (6.55 to 7.64).

Pairwise F_{ST} estimates from mtDNA control region sequences ranged from 0.00 to 0.24, and 2 of 10 estimates revealed significant population structure (table 3). The correlation between pairwise genetic differentiation and geographical distance was not significant ($R = 0.15$, $P = 0.11$) among the Arkansas colonies. Across the species range, IBD was significant ($R = 2.5$, $P = 0.006$). The AMOVA suggested that 94 percent of genetic variation was within Arkansas colonies ($P = 0.001$), while the remaining genetic differentiation distributed among populations was significant, albeit low (6 percent; $P = 0.02$).

Table 2—Diversity statistics estimated from mitochondrial DNA control region sequences of five *Corynorhinus rafinesquii* colonies sampled in Arkansas and populations sampled from other locations within the overall range of this species

Pop	N	H	h	SE	π	SE	PI
AR1	48	47	0.999	0.005	0.023	0.001	61
AR2	14	14	1.000	0.027	0.027	0.001	51
AR3	15	14	0.991	0.028	0.005	0.003	45
AR4	29	28	0.998	0.010	0.024	0.012	52
AR5	33	32	0.998	0.008	0.010	0.008	54
LA	17	9	0.904	0.044	0.021	0.011	44
TX	17	7	0.868	0.050	0.024	0.013	46
NC	26	24	0.990	0.015	0.010	0.005	22
MS	16	14	0.983	0.028	0.004	0.003	9
TN (Chester)	31	28	0.994	0.010	0.005	0.003	23
TN (Fentress)	25	21	0.967	0.030	0.005	0.003	14

Pop = population belongs to; N = number of individuals sequenced is reported for each sampling area; H = diversity is measured within colonies or populations as the number of unique haplotypes; h = haplotype diversity; SE = standard error; π = nucleotide diversity; PI = parsimony informative sites; LA = Louisiana; TX = Texas; NC = North Carolina; MS = Mississippi; TN = Tennessee.

Microsatellite Genetic Diversity among Populations

Loci demonstrated linkage equilibria in all pairwise comparisons. There were six significant deviations from HWE after sequential Bonferroni corrections due to lower than expected heterozygosity (table 4). Null alleles can result in departures from HWE. Null alleles were possible in four of five colonies based on Micro-Checker analyses (Van Oosterhout and others 2004). Locus PAUR05 accounted for some of the null allele detections and departures from HWE in three colonies; therefore, we dropped this locus from further analyses. The remaining departures from HWE were found in one colony at locus EF15, in another at Cora_H07F_C05R, and another at locus NN8. We did not drop these loci because they were not out of equilibrium in most of the sampled colonies. Further, three of the departures from HWE and evidence of null alleles were from a single colony, AR3.

Genetic diversity, expressed as number of alleles per locus, ranged from 2 to 16 with the average across loci and colonies being 7.7 (table 5). Average a overall was 4.17, and pa were infrequent, ranging from 0 to 4 per locus and per colony. Average within population expected heterozygosity ranged

Table 3—Pairwise F_{ST} estimated from mitochondrial DNA control region sequences and microsatellite loci for each of the five *Corynorhinus rafinesquii* Arkansas colonies

	AR1	AR2	AR3	AR4	AR5
AR1		0.09	0.01	0.03	0.14[a]
AR2	0.11[a]		0.09	0.11	0.24[a]
AR3	0.001	0.15[a]		0.00	0.07
AR4	0.04[a]	0.26[a]	0.00		0.06
AR5	0.04[a]	0.13[a]	0.02	0.08[a]	

Pairwise F_{ST} estimated from mitochondrial DNA are above the diagonal, and estimates from microsatellite DNA are below the diagonal and in boldface type.

[a] $P \leq 0.05$ after Bonferroni corrections.

from 0.56 to 0.59. Inbreeding (F_{IS}) estimated for each colony ranged from 0.06 to 0.18 and was not significantly different from zero except in AR3 and AR4 ($P = 0.05$). Estimated N_e for each colony were low [AR1, 76 (CI 43-218); AR2, –17 (CI 19-∞); AR3, –81 (CI 56-∞); AR4, 19 (CI 11-39); AR5, 24 (CI 13-62)].

Results from the microsatellite DNA AMOVA were similar to the mtDNA AMOVA results; 96 percent of the overall genetic variation found within colonies ($P < 0.001$), while among-population variation was significant (4 percent; $P = 0.002$). The range of pairwise F_{ST} values estimated from microsatellite loci (table 3) was 0.00 to 0.24, comparable to the F_{ST} values estimated from mtDNA. However, a higher number of pairwise comparisons, 7 out of 10, were significantly differentiated. Pairwise linearized F_{ST} estimates from microsatellite DNA were not significantly correlated with log-transformed geographical distances ($R = 0.19$, $P = 0.06$). Therefore, there was no signal of IBD in Arkansas. Finally, there was significant heterozygosity excess detected by the Wilcoxon signed-rank test in two (AR1 and AR4) of the five Arkansas colonies under the IAM but not SMM or TPM in software Bottleneck.

DISCUSSION

Phylogeny

The mtDNA phylogeny (figs. 2 and 3) suggested there are two major divergent lineages within *C. rafinesquii* with an average of 4 percent sequence divergence between them. Our results are consistent with other data from control region, cytochrome *b*, and nuclear DNA sequence data (Lance 1999, Piaggio and Perkins 2005) that indicates a

Table 4—Expected heterozygosity and observed heterozygosity estimated for each microsatellite locus for each *Corynorhinus rafinesquii* Arkansas colony

Pop	AR1	AR2	AR3	AR4	AR5
EF15					
H_o	0.76	0.56	0.31	0.58	0.74
H_e	0.81	0.81	0.82[a]	0.73	0.78
EF21					
H_o	0.70	0.80	0.60	0.45	0.50
H_e	0.55	0.54	0.56	0.38	0.64
EF20					
H_o	0.31	0.63	0.25	0.35	0.37
H_e	0.32	0.73	0.24	0.34	0.32
NN8					
H_o	0.33	0.22	0.07	0.21	0.26
H_e	0.50	0.52	0.52[a]	0.48	0.51
EF14					
H_o	0.02	0.00	0.20	0.10	0.05
H_e	0.02	0.00	0.19	0.10	0.05
Cora_D12_D12					
H_o	0.67	0.44	0.73	0.45	0.28
H_e	0.64	0.58	0.62	0.61	0.34
Cora_E07_E07					
H_o	0.82	0.63	0.73	0.63	0.78
H_e	0.82	0.77	0.77	0.77	0.82
Cora_H07_C05					
H_o	0.36	0.25	0.27	0.37	0.50
H_e	0.58[a]	0.24	0.51	0.63	0.44
Cora_B07_H12					
H_o	0.83	1.00	0.73	0.90	0.89
H_e	0.89	0.88	0.78	0.91	0.88
Cora_E10_G03					
H_o	0.82	0.50	0.93	0.80	0.74
H_e	0.82	0.68	0.85	0.86	0.84

Pop = population belongs to; H_o = observed heterozygosity;

H_e = expected heterozygosity.

[a] Indicates significant departures from Hardy-Weinberg equilibrium (P < 0.05) after sequential Bonferroni corrections (Rice 1989).

lineage (clade B) that is restricted to Arkansas, Louisiana, and Texas, and another lineage (clade A) that is more cosmopolitan and occurs over the entire range of the species. Both clades co-occur in Arkansas, Louisiana, and Texas; and, specifically, both occur within each of the five sampled Arkansas colonies. We did not find these lineages to correlate to subspecies as proposed by Handley (1959). The mtDNA clade comprising only Arkansas, Texas, and Louisiana individuals (clade B) has the best statistical support, suggesting that these bats have been in this region for long enough to allow for this coalescence. Conversely, the mtDNA clade with members from across the range of *C. rafinesquii* (clade A) had no statistical support and shorter branches, suggesting this lineage dispersed more recently into the same region as clade B. Sequence pairwise differences within each Arkansas population were as high as among colonies. Other diversity measures (nucleotide diversity and parsimony informative sites) from Arkansas, Louisiana, and Texas were high when compared to populations that group entirely into clade A. This reflects the two divergent maternal lineages co-occurring within each colony in Arkansas and in regions of Texas and Louisiana. Because both lineages can be found in the same populations, this pattern shows evidence of some maternal structuring but cannot be considered to represent subspecies. Rather, this phylogeographic pattern could indicate that an isolation event or population bottleneck occurred in Arkansas resulting in the loss of clade A in Arkansas and, at a later time, there was another dispersal event or secondary contact (Marjoram and Donnelly 1994) where clade A was reintroduced. Phylogeographic patterns in other taxa suggest existence of a glacial refugium in the Interior Highlands, which includes Arkansas, Louisiana, and Texas, and the eastern highlands (see Mayden 1985, Zamudio and Savage 2003, Zeisset and Beebee 2008). Therefore, it is possible the phylogeographic pattern in *C. rafinesquii* reflects secondary contact between groups that occupied separate refugia, one in the Interior Highlands and the other possibly in the eastern highlands. Alternatively, presence of these divergent clades in the same Arkansas roosts and sampled areas of Texas and Louisiana could suggest multiple dispersal events from one or more source populations. Interestingly, the lowest mtDNA haplotype diversity was found in the Texas and Louisiana populations, but they shared the highest nucleotide diversity measures with Arkansas populations (except AR3 and AR5). Thus, this area harbors haplotypes that are more different from each other than haplotypes from the rest of the range. This may suggest that this area (Arkansas, Louisiana, and Texas) harbors older lineages than in the other sampled regions, and this is supported by the high bootstrap support of clade B (Hewitt 1996, 2000). Conversely, the short branch lengths and low nucleotide diversity coupled with high haplotype diversity within clade A suggest this lineage represents a recent expansion of this lineage which subsequently spread across the current range of *C. rafinesquii*.

Table 5—Diversity estimates and estimated effective population size from microsatellite loci genotyped for individuals from five *Corynorhinus rafinesquii* Arkansas colonies and inbreeding coefficients of each

Pop	F_{IS}	h	N_e	EF15			EF21			EF20			NN8			EF14		
				A	a	pa	A	a	pa	A	a	pa	A	a	pa	A	a	pa
AR1	0.06	0.51+/-0.28	76 (43, 218)	10	5.49	1	3	2.75	0	3	2.49	0	2	2.00	0	2	1.15	0
AR2	0.13	0.33+/-0.20	-17 (19, ∞)	6	5.69	0	3	2.70	0	4	3.88	1	2	2.00	0	1	1.00	0
AR3	0.18*	0.55+/-0.30	-81 (56, ∞)	7	6.10	0	4	3.57	1	3	2.42	0	2	2.00	0	2	1.86	0
AR4	0.17*	0.55+/-0.30	19 (11, 39)	6	4.74	0	3	2.68	0	3	2.32	0	2	2.00	0	2	1.58	0
AR5	0.10	0.53+/-0.29	24 (13, 62)	6	5.23	0	3	2.98	0	3	2.52	0	2	2.00	0	2	1.37	0
All	—	—	—	10	5.85	1	4	3.01	1	4	2.58	1	2		0	3	1.40	0

Pop	Cora_D12_D12			Cora_E07_E07			Cora_H07_C05			Cora_B07_H12			Cora_E10_G03		
	A	a	pa	A	a	pa	A	a	pa	A	a	pa	A	a	pa
AR1	3	2.97	0	9	5.85	1	5	3.19	1	16	8.03	0	11	6.02	2
AR2	3	3.00	0	5	4.75	1	3	2.75	0	7	7.00	0	6	5.50	0
AR3	4	3.43	1	7	5.38	0	5	3.39	0	12	7.30	0	7	6.01	0
AR4	3	2.96	0	6	5.02	0	4	3.22	0	13	8.47	1	10	6.68	1
AR5	3	2.56	0	7	5.47	0	4	2.77	1	13	7.73	0	11	7.11	1
All	4	3.00	1	10	5.69	2	7	3.19	2	18	8.42	1	15	6.60	4

Pop = population belongs to; F_{IS} = the inbreeding coefficient of each colony; diversity estimates are: h = gene diversity averaged across loci; N_e = effective population size; A = number of alleles; a = allelic richness; pa = private alleles; * $P = 0.05$.

Genetic Diversity within Populations

We predicted that due to habitat loss and subsequent disjunction and/or population reduction, we would detect population bottlenecks in Arkansas *C. rafinesquii* colonies. If true, estimates of genetic diversity and population connectivity would be low, and there might also be inbreeding and low effective population sizes. In fact, we found low genetic diversity across microsatellite loci. We also found significantly high pairwise F_{ST} estimates which indicate low colony connectivity in Arkansas. Further, our results showed that the microsatellite loci were out of short-term linkage equilibrium more than chance would suggest and, without evidence of significant linkage among the loci, revealed low effective population sizes within the last generation for each colony in Arkansas. This, paired with significantly high pairwise F_{ST} estimates from microsatellite data, is surprising over short distances for vagile, volant mammals. High microsatellite pairwise F_{ST} estimates and low N_e along with the detection of two loci very near fixation, with two (NN8) and three (EF14) alleles, can be taken as weak possible evidence of a population bottleneck in Arkansas colonies.

Our analyses detected population bottlenecks in two colonies. However, our data are at the lower limit for number of loci and per population sample size for robust bottleneck detection. Alternatively, it is possible that population bottlenecks have happened more recently than can be detected by these tests. Effective population sizes in AR2 and AR3 were negative, and the CI's included infinity, meaning these are either large populations or the estimate was meaningless. These two populations had the smallest sample sizes and, therefore, may not have allowed robust estimates. Nonsignificant F_{IS} estimates within each population (AR3 and AR4 were both $P = 0.05$, which may or may not be biologically relevant), and the AMOVAs, which suggested that most variation was attributed to within population differentiation, implies that any population bottleneck has not resulted in inbreeding. Violations of HWE and evidence of null alleles in AR3 may reflect low sample size and/or a Wahlund effect (the sampling of allelic differentiation of two subpopulations within a single sampled colony) due to our samples coming from a hibernaculum where it is possible that multiple unsampled populations may have congregated (Piaggio and others 2009b). However, this does not appear to be the case for AR4 which is also a hibernaculum.

Alternatively, the HWE violations in AR3, lowest mtDNA nucleotide diversity, and parsimony informative sites may be evidence of a recent population bottleneck which was not detected in our bottleneck analysis. Population bottlenecks in Arkansas colonies may also account for the lack of a significant signal of isolation by distance, which suggests there is something other than geography influencing differentiation. Alternatively and more likely, the influence of IBD could have been missed because of low power due to low number of populations sampled. Indeed, significant IBD was detected across the species range where higher sample sizes were obtained. So, either limited sampling in Arkansas accounts for the lack of IBD or there is another factor, i.e., barriers to gene flow, or factors affecting colonies in Arkansas differently than across the species range. In summary, gene flow was restricted among colonies of *C. rafinesquii* in Arkansas, and low effective population sizes suggest that genetic drift is the dominant force on allelic frequencies.

Our within-population diversity estimates from mtDNA and autosomal microsatellites are disparate for each colony in Arkansas. The mtDNA control region sequence diversity was high within colonies and equivalent to the estimated mtDNA control region diversity within populations of the widely distributed migratory bat (*Nyctalus noctula*) (Petit and Mayer 2000). Mitochondrial diversity within *C. rafinesquii* populations was similar or only slightly higher than mtDNA diversity within the sister taxon *C. townsendii* (Piaggio and others 2009b). Conversely, microsatellite genetic diversity within Arkansas colonies was low (Schlötterer and Pemberton 1994) in general. There are several potential explanations for the disparity in our estimates of genetic diversity between mtDNA and microsatellite loci. First, the mtDNA diversity may be large due to occurrence of two divergent lineages within each Arkansas colony. Second, half of the microsatellite markers we used were generated from other bat species (Vespertilionidae: *Eptesicus fuscus*, *Plecotus auritus*, and *N. noctula*) which may pose a problem due to ascertainment bias (Ellergren and others 1995, Webster and others 2002) and result in low estimates of genetic diversity. Third, these two markers are differentially inherited. Autosomal microsatellites are biparentally inherited; whereas, mtDNA is matrilineally inherited and has a smaller effective population size than nuclear DNA. Therefore, demographic processes will affect these markers differently. The different estimates of genetic diversity from mtDNA and microsatellites may then be evidence of very recent and rapid population bottlenecks in Arkansas. Indeed, although haplotype diversity is high in mtDNA, genetic diversity may have been lost (Kuro-o and others 2010). This may be supported by the high nucleotide diversity in some of the Arkansas colonies, which suggests that intermediate haplotypes have been lost. Although there may not be strong evidence of population bottlenecks, microsatellite results show clear population differentiation among most Arkansas colonies and low effective population sizes.

Implications for Conservation and Management

Based on results of the phylogenetic analysis, it is not appropriate to manage for two subspecies of *C. rafinesquii* as designated by Handley (1959). Rather, it is important to manage and conserve the lineages within *C. rafinesquii* that reflect the evolutionary history of this species. In particular, the lineage with the most limited range (clade B), found only in Arkansas, Louisiana, and Texas, harbors the greatest genetic diversity and includes haplotypes from both lineages.

Over the last 100 to 200 years, bottomland hardwood forests of Arkansas have been systematically cleared of timber, drained, and converted for agricultural use (Dahl 1990, Holder 1970, Woods and others 2004). Today < 10 percent of the original hardwood forests remain. If *C. rafinesquii* relied mostly on these forests for roosts (Clark 1990, 1991), then these bats have experienced habitat destruction and loss of preferred roosts. Further, *C. rafinesquii* in Arkansas now appear to largely occupy human-made structures which are ephemeral and may not provide the long-term habitat necessary to maintain stable populations. We predicted that if habitat loss has resulted in loss of connectivity and/or reduction of populations, then estimates of genetic diversity would be low within the Arkansas colonies. In fact, our estimates of diversity from microsatellite loci is comparable to populations of the federally endangered sister taxon *C. t. virginianus* whose populations are fragmented in four regional populations which are significantly differentiated from each other (Piaggio and others 2009b). This is especially noteworthy given the ongoing problem of loss of manmade structures in Arkansas. For example, AR4 is a hibernaculum in a well that was, until recently, adjacent to an abandoned house used by a maternity roost each summer. A routine check led to the discovery that the house had been demolished. Further, AR1 and AR5 were maternity roosts in abandoned houses, but these houses are now gone. All remaining known roosts of *C. rafinesquii* in Arkansas should be protected and efforts made to identify others and protect those as well.

Dispersal of individuals between populations is critical to maintain population connectivity and genetic diversity, and promoting this is crucial for management or conservation plans. Dispersal produces gene flow over geographic distances. Currently, it appears that dispersal among sampled Arkansas colonies is limited. Further efforts to locate populations of *C. rafinesquii* in remaining bottomland forests and management for forested corridors in bottomlands to provide natural roosts may be needed.

This may help establish connectivity among populations and increase genetic diversity. Without these efforts, colonies of *C. rafinesquii* in Arkansas may be susceptible to disease (Spielman and others 2004), ecological catastrophes, and extinction due to low genetic diversity and small effective population sizes. Finally, comparative studies of populations in other parts of the range are needed to assess whether they also exhibit reduced microsatellite genetic diversity, small effective population sizes, and low connectivity.

ACKNOWLEDGMENTS

We thank Paul Leberg, Mark Brigham, David Armstrong, Robert Guralnick, Susan Perkins, and anonymous reviewers for their comments. We are deeply indebted to Eric Routman for crucial and patient efforts to improve the manuscript. We extend sincere gratitude to institutions and individuals for tissue samples including the following: Celia López-González, Colección Regional Durango (Vertebrados), CIIDIR Durango, Instituto Politécnico Nacional; Jeff Gore, Florida Fish and Wildlife Conservation Commission; Traci Wethington, Kentucky Department of Fish and Wildlife Resources; Mary Bunch, South Carolina Department of Natural Resources; Dr. Richard Lance, U.S. Army; Robert Curry and David Richardson, U.S. Fish and Wildlife Service; Brian Carver, Freed-Hardeman University; Leigh Stuemke and Chris Comer, Stephen F. Austin State University; Christopher Rice; Frances Bennett; Eric Britzke; Mary Kay Clark; Kelli Deichmueller; Laura Finn; Rafael Avila-Flores; Heather Thomas; Austin Trousdale; and Maarten Vonhof. This study was partially supported by an American Museum of Natural History - Theodore Roosevelt Memorial Grant; an American Society of Mammalogists Grants-in-Aid; a University of Colorado Museum William H. Burt Grant; and the Department of Ecology and Evolutionary Biology, University of Colorado at Boulder.

LITERATURE CITED

Abernathy, Y.; Turner, R. 1987. U.S. forested wetlands: status and changes 1940-1980. BioScience. 37: 721-727.

Altizer, S.; Harvell, D.; Friedle, E. 2003. Rapid evolutionary dynamics and disease threats to biodiversity. Trends in Ecology and Evolution. 18: 589-596.

Arkansas Natural Heritage Commission. 2003. The Grand Prairie of Arkansas: past–present–future. Little Rock, AR: Arkansas Natural Heritage Commission; Conway, AR: U.S. Fish and Wildlife Service. 28 p.

Avise, J.C. 1995. Mitochondrial DNA polymorphism and a connection between genetics and demography of relevance to conservation. Conservation Biology. 9: 686-690.

Avise, J.C.; Hamrick, J.L. 1996. Conservation genetics: case histories from nature. New York: Chapman & Hall. 512 p.

Bayless, M.L.; Clark, M.K.; Stark, R.C. [and others]. 2011. Distribution and status of eastern big-eared bats (*Corynorhinus* spp.). In: Loeb, S.C.; Lacki, M.J.; Miller, D.A., eds. Conservation and management of eastern big-eared bats: a symposium. Gen. Tech. Rep. SRS-145. Asheville, NC: U.S. Department of Agriculture Forest Service, Southern Research Station: 13-25.

Burland, T.M.; Barratt, E.M.; Racey, P.A. 1998. Isolation and characterization of microsatellite loci in the brown long-eared bat, *Plecotus auritus*, and cross-species amplification within the family Vespertilionidae. Molecular Ecology. 7: 136-138.

Clark, M.K. 1990. Roosting ecology of the eastern big-eared bat, *Plecotus rafinesquii*, in North Carolina. Raleigh, NC: North Carolina State University. 112 p. M.S. thesis.

Clark, M.K. 1991. Foraging ecology of Rafinesque's big-eared bat, *Plecotus rafinesquii*, in North Carolina. Bat Research News. 32: 68.

Cornuet, J.M.; Luikart, G. 1996. Description and power analysis of two tests for detecting recent population bottlenecks from allele frequency data. Genetics. 144: 2001-2014.

Dahl, Thomas F. 1990. Wetlands losses in the United States 1780's to 1980's. Washington, DC: U.S. Department of the Interior, U.S. Fish and Wildlife Service. 21 p.

Ellegren, H.; Primmer, C.R.; Sheldon, B.C. 1995. Microsatellite "evolution": directionality or bias? Nature Genetics. 11: 360-362.

England, D.R.; Saugey, D.A. 1999. A safe and effective method to remove bats from abandoned water wells. Bat Research News. 40: 38-39.

England, P.R.; Osler, G.H.R.; Woodworth, L.M. [and others]. 2003. Effects of intense versus diffuse population bottlenecks on microsatellite genetic diversity and evolutionary potential. Conservation Genetics. 4: 595-604.

Excoffier, L.; Laval, G.; Schneider, S. 2005. Arlequin ver. 3.0: an integrated software package for population genetics data analysis. Evolutionary Bioinformatics Online. 1: 47-50.

Excoffier, L.; Smouse, P.E.; Quattro, J.M. 1992. Analysis of molecular variance inferred from metric distances among DNA haplotypes: application to human mitochondrial DNA restriction data. Genetics. 131: 479-491.

Glaubitz, J.C. 2004. CONVERT: a user-friendly program to reformat diploid genotypic data for commonly used population genetic software packages. Molecular Ecology Notes. 4: 309-310.

Goudet, J. 2001. FSTAT ver. 2.9.3, a program to estimate and test gene diversities and fixation indices (updated from Goudet

1995). Switzerland: University of Lausanne. http://www.unilch/izea/softwares/fstat.html. [Date accessed: May 12, 2011].

Haig, S.M. 1998. Molecular contributions to conservation. Ecology. 79: 413-425.

Handley, C.O., Jr. 1959. A revision of American bats of the genera *Euderma* and *Plecotus*. Proceedings of the United States National Museum. 110: 95-246.

Hewitt, G.M. 1996. Some genetic consequences of ice ages, and their role in divergence and speciation. Biological Journal of the Linnaean Society. 58: 247-276.

Hewitt, G.M. 2000. The genetic legacy of the Quaternary ice ages. Nature. 405: 907-913.

Holder, T.H. 1970. Disappearing wetlands of eastern Arkansas. Little Rock, AR: Arkansas Planning Commission. 72 p.

Hoofer, S.R.; van den Bussche, R.A. 2001. Phylogenetic relationships of plecotine bats and allies based on mitochondrial ribosomal sequences. Journal of Mammalogy. 82: 131-137.

Jones, C.; Suttkus, R.D. 1975. Notes on the natural history of *Plecotus rafinesquii*. Occas. Pap. of the Museum of Zoology. [Baton Rouge, LA]: Louisiana State University. 47: 1-14.

Kentucky State Nature Preserves Commission. 1996. Rare and extirpated plants and animals of Kentucky. Transactions of the Kentucky Academy of Sciences. 57: 69-91.

Kuro-o, M.; Yonekawa, H.; Saito, S. [and others]. 2010. Unexpectedly high genetic diversity of mtDNA control region through severe bottleneck in vulnerable albatross *Phoebastria albatrus*. Conservation Genetics. 11: 127-137.

Lacy, R.C. 1997. Importance of genetic variation to the viability of mammalian populations. Journal of Mammalogy. 78: 320-335.

Lance, R.F. 1999. Ecological and population genetic studies of forest-dwelling bats. Lafayette, LA: University of Southwestern Louisiana. 181 p. Ph.D. dissertation.

Marjoram, P.; Donnelly, P. 1994. Pairwise comparisons of mitochondrial DNA sequences in subdivided populations and implications for early human evolution. Genetics. 136: 673-683.

Mayden, R.L. 1985. Biogeography of the Ouachita highland fishes. Southwestern Naturalist. 30: 195-211.

Nei, M. 1987. Molecular evolutionary genetics. New York: Columbia University Press. 512 p.

Petit, E.; Mayer, F. 2000. A population genetic analysis of migration: the case of the noctule bat (*Nyctalus noctula*). Molecular Ecology. 9: 683-690.

Petri, B.; Pääbo, S.; Von Haeseler, A.; Tautz, D. 1997. Paternity assessment and population subdivision in a natural population of the larger mouse-eared bat (*Myotis myotis*). Molecular Ecology. 6: 235-242.

Piaggio, A.J.; Figueroa, J.A.; Perkins, S.L. 2009a. Development and characterization of 15 polymorphic microsatellite loci isolated from Rafinesque's big-eared bat, *Corynorhinus rafinesquii*. Molecular Ecology Resources. 9: 1191-1193.

Piaggio, A.J.; Navo, K.; Stihler, C. 2009b. Intraspecific comparison of population structure, genetic diversity, and dispersal among three subspecies of Townsend's big-eared bats, *Corynorhinus townsendii townsendii*, *C. t. pallescens*, and the endangered *C. t. virginianus*. Conservation Genetics. 10: 143-159.

Piaggio, A.J.; Perkins, S.L. 2005. Molecular phylogeny of North American long-eared bats (Vespertilionidae: *Corynorhinus*): inter- and intraspecific relationships inferred from mitochondrial and nuclear DNA sequences. Molecular Phylogenetics and Evolution. 37: 762-775.

Rice, W.R. 1989. Analyzing tables of statistical tests. Evolution. 43: 223-225.

Saugey, D.A. 2000. Radiotelemetry study of Rafinesque's big-eared bat (*Corynorhinus rafinesquii*) in southern Arkansas. Little Rock, AR: Arkansas Game and Fish Commission; final report. Nightwing Consulting. 97 p.

Schlötterer, C.; Pemberton, J. 1994. The use of microsatellites for genetic analysis of natural populations. In: Schierwater, B.; Streit, B.; Wagner, G.P.; DeSalle, R., eds. Molecular ecology and evolution: approaches and applications. Basel, Switzerland: Birkhäuser Verlag: 203-214.

Seutin, G.; White, B.N.; Boag, P.T. 1991. Preservation of avian blood and tissue samples for DNA analyses. Canadian Journal of Zoology. 69: 82-90.

Shepherd, B. 1984. Arkansas's natural heritage. Arkansas Natural Heritage Commission. Little Rock, AR: August House Publishers. 116 p.

Slatkin, M. 1993. Isolation by distance in equilibrium and non-equilibrium populations. Evolution. 47: 264-279.

Spielman, D.; Brook, B.W.; Briscoe, D.A.; Frankham, R. 2004. Does inbreeding and loss of genetic diversity decrease disease resistance? Conservation Genetics. 5: 439-448.

Stamatakis, A. 2006. RAxML-VI-HPC: maximum likelihood-based phylogenetic analyses with thousands of taxa and mixed models. Bioinformatics. 22: 2688-2690.

Stamatakis, A.; Hoover, P.; Rougemont, J. 2008. A fast bootstrapping algorithm for the RAxML Web-servers. Systematic Biology. 57: 758-771.

Stamatakis, A.; Ludwig, T.; Meier, H. 2005. Raxml-iii: a fast program for maximum likelihood-based inference of large phylogenetic trees. Bioinformatics. 21: 456-463.

Swofford, D.L. 2002. PAUP*: phylogenetic analysis using parsimony (*and other methods). Version 4.0. Sunderland, MA: Sinauer Associates, Inc. http://www.sinauer.com/detail.php?id=8060. [Date accessed: May 13, 2011].

The Nature Conservancy. 1992. The forested wetlands of the Mississippi River, an ecosystem in crisis. Baton Rouge, LA: The Nature Conservancy. 24 p.

Turner, R.E.; Forsythe, S.; Craig, N. 1981. Bottomland hardwood forest land resources of the Southeastern U.S. In: Clark, J.R.; Benforado, J., eds. Wetlands of bottomland hardwood forest. New York: Elsevier: 13-18.

U.S. Fish and Wildlife Service. 1985. Endangered and threatened wildlife and plants, animal candidate review for listing as endangered or threatened species. Federal Register. 50: 37,965.

Van Oosterhout, C.; Hutchinson, W.F.; Wills, D.P.M.; Shipley, P. 2004. Micro-Checker: software for identifying and correcting genotyping errors in microsatellite data. Molecular Ecology Notes. 4: 535.

Vonhof, M.J.; Davis, C.S.; Fenton, M.B.; Strobeck, C. 2002. Characterization of dinucleotide microsatellite loci in big brown bats (*Eptesicus fuscus*), and their use in other North American verspertilionid bats. Molecular Ecology Notes. 2: 167-170.

Waples, R.S. 2006. A bias correction for estimates of effective population size based on linkage disequilibrium at unlinked gene loci. Conservation Genetics. 7: 167-184.

Waples, R.S.; Do, C. 2008. LDNE: a program for estimating effective population size from data on linkage disequilibrium. Molecular Ecology Resources. 8: 753-756.

Webster, M.T.; Smith, N.G.C.; Ellegren, H. 2002. Microsatellite evolution inferred from human-chimpanzee genomic sequence alignments. Proceedings of the National Academy of Sciences. 99: 8748-8753.

Weir, B.S.; Cockerham, C.C. 1984. Estimating F-statistics for the analysis of population structure. Evolution. 38: 1358-1370.

Woods, A.J.; Foti, T.L.; Chapman, S.S. [and others]. 2004. Ecoregions of Arkansas (color poster with maps, descriptive text, summary tables, and photographs). Reston, VA: U.S. Geological Survey. http://www.epa.gov/wed/pages/ecoregions/ar_eco.htm. [Date accessed: November 11, 2010].

Worthington Wilmer, J.; Barratt, E. 1996. A non-lethal method of tissue sampling for genetic studies of chiropterans. Bat Research News. 37: 1-3.

Zamudio, K.R.; Savage, W.K. 2003. Historical isolation, range expansion, and secondary contact of two highly divergent mitochondrial lineages in spotted salamander (*Ambystoma maculatum*). Evolution. 57: 1631-1652.

Zeisset, I.; Beebee, T.J.C. 2008. Amphibian phylogeography: a model for understanding historical aspects of species distributions. Heredity. 101: 109-119.

CHARACTERISTICS OF ROOSTS USED BY RAFINESQUE'S BIG-EARED BAT (*CORYNORHINUS RAFINESQUII*) ON CAMP MACKALL, NORTH CAROLINA

Piper L. Roby, Biologist, Copperhead Consulting, Paint Lick, KY 40461

Mark W. Gumbert, Principal Biologist, Copperhead Consulting, Paint Lick, KY 40461

Price L. Sewell, Biologist, Copperhead Consulting, Paint Lick, KY 40461

Steven W. Brewer, Plant Ecologist and Statistician, Copperhead Consulting, Paint Lick, KY 40461

Abstract—Military bases are charged with stewardship of threatened and endangered species, and data collection on species of concern is important for management of these species on military land holdings. We studied roosting behavior of Rafinesque's big-eared bat (*Corynorhinus rafinesquii*) during a multiyear inventory on Camp Mackall and Fort Bragg, NC. From 2006 to 2009, *C. rafinesquii* were captured (*n* = 24), banded, and/or radio-tagged to gain information on roosting habits within and adjacent to bottomland hardwood forests. Twenty roosts were identified: 11 trees [9 tupelo (*Nyssa* spp.) and 2 bald cypress (*Taxodium distichum*)] and 9 anthropogenic structures. Bats used these roosts in similar proportions and switched roosts often (every 1.2 days). Diameter at breast height of roost trees ($\bar{x} = 83.0 \pm 6.7$ cm) used by *C. rafinesquii* was smaller than reported elsewhere for this species. In 2008, temperature data were collected in anthropogenic structures used as roosting sites. None of these roosts housed large numbers of bats, but the range of temperatures for two different roosts, each housing one pregnant female, was 24.5 to 46.0 °C for an attic roost on May 27, 2008, and 19.0 to 27.0 °C for a cistern roost on May 30, 2008. A female that roosted in the attic while pregnant then roosted in the basement of the same building the following September when she was postlactating. The significantly warmer attic temperatures may have allowed the female to avoid torpor, thereby contributing more metabolic resources to the developing fetus. Other temperature data collected suggest that bat use of other roosts was not affected by roost temperature. Choice of trees and anthropogenic structures used as roosting sites by *C. rafinesquii* was comparable to published studies of these bats in similar habitats, demonstrating the importance of these features to the persistence of local populations.

INTRODUCTION

The Sikes Act was amended in 1997 to direct military installations to create integrated natural resources management plans (Boice 2006). These plans must be reviewed at least every 5 years to ensure that military lands are managed to conserve and rehabilitate natural resources in their charge (Legacy Resource Management Program 2005). The 12 million ha managed by the U.S. Department of Defense houses three times more federally listed or imperiled species than all other Federal lands despite comprising only 3 percent of Federal land holdings (Stein and others 2008). Military land is relatively protected from urban encroachment and is presumably less inundated with potential agricultural pollutants, such as fertilizer and pesticides, than surrounding rural areas. This permits military lands to be a safe haven for species that might otherwise be negatively affected by human interactions. In some cases, military activity may even benefit some species. For example, Jentsch and others (2009) found that some pioneer plant species thrived after ground disturbance such as tank activity on a retired military base in Germany. Alternately, managing for some species can be beneficial to the military. Maintaining open stands in pine (*Pinus* spp.) forests for the red-cockaded woodpecker (*Picoides borealis*) created optimal training areas for troops by supplying open areas for maneuvers (Beaty and others 2003).

Fort Bragg was established as Camp Bragg in September 1918 in southcentral North Carolina among a large expanse of pine forests and sandy soil and was renamed Fort Bragg upon becoming a permanent post in September 1922 (Fort Bragg 2002). As the base expanded, forests were removed for development, timber, and agriculture, resulting in the reduction of a diverse ecosystem and the Federal listing of many endemic species (Britcher 2006). Two bat species with at least two levels of State status (Legacy Resource Management Program 2005) are known from Fort Bragg and Camp Mackall, NC: Rafinesque's big-eared bat (*Corynorhinus rafinesquii*) and southeastern myotis (*Myotis austroriparius*). These species are also designated as species of concern by the U.S. Fish and Wildlife Service (U.S. Fish and Wildlife Service 2010).

Loss of natural habitat has prompted the need for information on roosting and foraging requirements of *C. rafinesquii* so that land holdings can be managed appropriately for the species. Forests provide roost trees and foraging areas; however, anthropogenic structures could be significant roost structures, particularly where there is a lack of sufficient tree roosts, e.g., in younger aged forests. *C. rafinesquii* also exhibits frequent roost switching (Clark and others 1997, Gooding and Langford 2004, Lance and others 2001, Trousdale and others 2008); therefore, this species may benefit from greater roost diversity and

Citation for proceedings: Loeb, Susan C.; Lacki, Michael J.; Miller, Darren A., eds. 2011. Conservation and management of eastern big-eared bats: a symposium. Gen. Tech. Rep. SRS-145. Asheville, NC: U.S. Department of Agriculture, Forest Service, Southern Research Station. 157 p.

increased availability across the landscape. Variation in roost microclimate is required by these bats when roosting (Clark 1990, Hoffmeister and Goodpaster 1963, Hurst and Lacki 1999, Lewis 1995), and evidence suggests that the environment surrounding roosts, such as roads, water, and canopy cover (Clark 1990, Lance and others 2001), can be as important as the surrounding landscape in providing foraging opportunities (Menzel and others 2001).

Because no prior study of bats had been conducted on Camp Mackall and Fort Bragg, our objectives during this 6-year project were to: (1) document the presence of bat species on the base, (2) locate and characterize roosts used by *C. rafinesquii*, and (3) conduct an exploratory examination of temperature variation among roosts of this species. We expected to find a small population of *C. rafinesquii* at the site due to a limited amount of bottomland hardwood forest that contained relatively young trees with few roosting opportunities (Gooding and Langford 2004), and we predicted extensive use of anthropogenic structures by these bats.

STUDY AREA

The 65,084 ha of Camp Mackall and Fort Bragg (39°26´N, 123°48´W) are located within six counties in the sandhills ecoregion of the inner Coastal Plain physiographic region of North Carolina (Griffith and others 2002). The sandhills upland complex consists of mesic and wetland plant communities including pine/scrub oak sandhill and xeric sandhill scrub, coastal plain small stream swamp, and streamhead pocosin (Fort Bragg 2005). Woodlands on the base are composed primarily of loblolly pine (*P. taeda*) and shortleaf pine (*P. echinata*) in association with bald cypress (*Taxodium distichum*) and a mixture of hardwoods including, but not limited to, water tupelo (*Nyssa aquatica*), black tupelo (*N. sylvatica*), sweetgum (*Liquidambar styraciflua*), red maple (*Acer rubrum*), tuliptree (*Liriodendron tulipifera*), water oak (*Quercus nigra*), post oak (*Q. stellata*), blackjack oak (*Q. marilandica*), and turkey oak (*Q. laevis*).

Camp Mackall encompasses 3,211 ha of the total land holdings and lies 64.4 km west of the Fort Bragg cantonment in a rural region interspersed with small towns and villages. The area is surrounded by upland forest, agriculture, rural housing, and nonforested military training areas and airfields. Drowning Creek, a fourth-order blackwater stream, flows through Camp Mackall and is accompanied by bottomland hardwood forest in adjacent habitats. This forest type is important because although *C. rafinesquii* use several types of roosts, when the species is documented in trees, those trees are often located in bottomland hardwood forests (Carver and Ashley 2008, Gooding and Langford 2004, Lance and others 2001, Menzel and others 2003, Trousdale

and Beckett 2005). Bottomland hardwood forest in the riparian zone of Drowning Creek has an open understory and is comprised primarily of tupelo trees (*Nyssa* spp.) with scattered *T. distichum* and oaks. This habitat type accounts for 8.6 percent of all vegetation types on Camp Mackall as calculated using a Geographic Information System Fort Bragg vegetation layer for ArcView ver. 9.2/3 (Esri, Redlands, CA). Temperatures in this area ranged from 13 to 33 °C with an average of 22 °C during the study period when roost temperatures were collected in 2008.

METHODS

We deployed mist nets over creeks, water-filled road ruts, wildlife ponds, open bottomland forest, and dry road corridors in varying habitat types, e.g., bottomland hardwood forest, planted pine stands, and small sandy streams, twice a year from 2004 to 2009 in two of the following three seasons: spring (April, May, and June), summer (July and August), and fall (September and October). We deployed nets at sunset and typically left them in place for at least 5 hours after sunset. In most years, we netted 10 sites twice per year, but as many as 17 sites were netted in 2009. Each year we also visited a varying number of buildings, bridges, and other anthropogenic structures to search for bats. We conducted a total of 214 searches of structures (range: 13 to 102, mean: 35.7) from 2004 to 2009. From 2006 to 2009, no structure was searched during December, January, or February. We recorded data on captured bats including age (adult or juvenile), sex, body mass (g), and forearm length (mm). After a banding program was established at Camp Mackall and Fort Bragg in 2006, forearms of all *C. rafinesquii* caught ($n = 18$) were fitted with uniquely numbered aluminum alloy lipped identification bands (bat rings; Porzana Ltd., East Sussex, UK). We also fitted 11 *C. rafinesquii* with 0.48-g radio transmitters (model LB-2; Holohil Systems Ltd., Ontario, Canada) in May, June, or July depending on the year. We clipped a small amount of hair from between the scapulae, and a transmitter was applied using Skin Bond® adhesive (Smith & Nephew, Inc., Largo, FL). We held bats for 5 to 10 minutes after transmitter placement to ensure secure attachment prior to release at or near the point of capture.

Tracking commenced the day after bats were radiotagged to locate day roosts. We drove roads, on and off the base, while listening for signals using a receiver (model TRX-1000S) and a 3- or 5-element Yagi antenna (receiver and antenna; Wildlife Materials, Inc., Carbondale, IL). Once a roosting site was located, we attempted visual confirmation in roost trees with a basal opening and in anthropogenic structures used as roosts. When feasible, we estimated the height (m) at which the bats were roosting and the number of bats using the roost either visually or by conducting exit counts in the evening. We obtained locations of roosting sites using a handheld global positioning system (GPS) and recorded a description of the roost location. We took photographs and made graphical representations of roosting sites to aid in future identification. We attached uniquely numbered aluminum tree tags and high visibility flagging to tree roosts to aid in relocation. We recorded the species of tree, measured diameter at breast height (d.b.h.), estimated height of tree (m), noted condition of the tree (live, live-damaged, or snag), and the presence of vegetation layers surrounding the roost tree (canopy, subcanopy, and understory). These data were also taken on all trees within a plot surrounding the roost tree that were identified using a 10 basal area factor prism. Because this method is considered point sampling and not fixed-area sampling, the plots were not uniform in size. Rather, the "probability of a given tree being sampled is proportional to its size" (Avery and Burkhart 2002). Additionally, the plot radius factor is 2.75 feet, meaning "for each inch of dbh, a tree can be 2.75 feet from the point to still be included in the point's tally" (Avery and Burkhart 2002).

In 2008, we selected 4 anthropogenic structures (cistern, building 764, house, building 104) used as roosting sites by *C. rafinesquii* for collection of temperature data. For the cistern, building 764, and the house, we placed one iButton® (Maxim Integrated Products, Sunnyvale, CA) where bats had been observed roosting and another on the north side of a neighboring tree to collect ambient temperatures. The cistern was approximately 5.2 by 1.5 by 1.8 m in size and contained water 0.5 m deep year round. Building 764 was an aboveground concrete outbuilding approximately 4.5 by 4.5 by 3.0 m in size. The abandoned single-level, eight-room house overrun with vegetation, mostly wisteria (*Wisteria* sp.), was located off the military base. Because we discovered this roost on the last day of surveys in 2008, we placed the temperature data logger in a room adjacent to the one where bats were roosting to avoid disturbance. We placed temperature data loggers in three portions of building 104. This building roost was a large, old, three-story storage barn used for military training. Because bats had been observed roosting in all three portions of the building, we placed temperature data loggers in the attic, on the ground floor, and in the cinder block basement. We deployed iButtons® (programmed to record temperature every 2 hours) at the end of May, and we retrieved them on October 2, 2008. We checked structures periodically for bat use throughout the time that iButtons® were operating.

Landscape features such as distance to streams have been shown to be good predictors of roost selection by bats (Clark 1990, Kurta and others 2002, Watrous and others 2006). Therefore, we used Mann-Whitney U tests to examine differences between roost types in distance to significant landscape features, e.g., water, roads, firebreaks. Mann-Whitney U tests were also used to compare differences in number of roosts used between sexes and in tree size by genus. We used a Kruskal-Wallis test to compare temperature differences among three levels of roosts in building 104 and used Student's t-tests to examine differences between two different anthropogenic structure roosts and their associated ambient temperatures when bats were and were not present in the roosts. We chose to use nonparametric tests for most analyses due to low and unequal sample sizes. We conducted statistical analyses using XLSTAT (Addinsoft USA, New York, NY) and SYSTAT (Systat Software, Inc., Chicago, IL). ArcView ver. 9.3 (Esri, Redlands, CA) was used to measure distances from roosts to landscape features.

RESULTS

From 2004 to 2009 we made 840 bat observations, i.e., captures, recaptures, and visual observations, on Camp Mackall and Fort Bragg representing 10 species: 317 evening bats (*Nycticeius humeralis*, 37.7 percent); 234 red bats (*Lasiurus borealis*, 27.9 percent); 77 big brown bats (*Eptesicus fuscus*, 9.2 percent); 76 *C. rafinesquii* (first capture in 2006, 9.0 percent); 64 tri-color bats (*Perimyotis subflavus*, 7.6 percent); 54 Seminole bats (*L. seminolus*, 6.4 percent); 10 *Myotis austroriparius* (1.2 percent); 4 silver-haired bats (*Lasionycteris noctivagans*, 0.5 percent); 2 hoary bats (*Lasiurus cinereus*, 0.2 percent); and 2 Brazilian free-tailed bats (*Tadarida brasiliensis*, 0.2 percent). At Camp Mackall we captured 24 individual *C. rafinesquii* and made 76 observations of the species in trees and structures on and around the post. There were five captures in mist nets, but four of them were at a roost tree and three of the four were recaptures. Only one *C. rafinesquii* was caught in a mist net not placed near a roost. Of the 94 bats we banded, 18 were *C. rafinesquii* (4 adult males, 8 adult females, 4 juvenile males, and 2 juvenile females). We recaptured 39 percent of all banded *C. rafinesquii* (7 out of 18) with 58 percent of banded adults (7 out of 12) recaptured. We attached 11 transmitters to 9 individuals over 4 years (2 adult females were radio-tagged twice in 2 different years); bats A0798 and A0800 were lactating when radio-tagged on July 10, 2007, and pregnant when radio-tagged on May 29, 2008, and May 26, 2008, respectively. All remaining adult females fitted with radio transmitters were also reproductively active (one pregnant, two lactating, and one postlactating), but three adult males radio-tagged *C. rafinesquii* were nonreproductive.

We located 20 roosts used by *C. rafinesquii*, including 11 trees and 9 structures. Bats used an average of 3.0±0.3 (SE) roosts with a tracking duration between 3 and 7 days ($\bar{x} = 5$) depending on year of sampling. Males ($n = 3$) used 3.7±0.9 roosts (range: 2 to 5), and females ($n = 8$) used 2.8±0.3 roosts (range: 1 to 4), although the difference was not significant (Mann-Whitney U = 11.5, $P = 0.91$). We recorded 31 roost switches over 38 tracking days (1 bat tracked for 1 day) or 1 switch every 1.2 days. Bats moved an average of 2.5±2.9 km ($n = 18$, range: 0.06 to 8.73 km) between roosts. Distances moved by bats were either < 1 km ($n = 7$), 1 to 2 km ($n = 6$), or 6 to 9 km ($n = 5$). Females moved greater distances than males (Mann-Whitney U = 12, $P = 0.01$), and pregnant females moved farther than lactating females (Mann-Whitney U = 30, $P = 0.01$). The number of bats observed in a roost ranged from 1 to 11. For many of the tree roosts, visual observation of bats was not possible due to small or nonexistent basal openings or because bats roosted above a bend in the tree and could not be seen. Counts of bats were taken in all structures except one building located on private property where we were denied access. However, an exit count conducted at this structure yielded seven bats. We attempted exit counts of tree roosts on Camp Mackall, but successful exit counts could not be completed due to the dense canopy. The roost housing the greatest number of bats (11 adults) was a tree that we netted in 2008, where 3 of the 4 captured were previously banded. The next largest group of bats was located in 2009 and consisted of 10 bats (building 104: 5 adult females and 5 prevolant pups). Two of the five adults were recaptures from 2007. We banded the remaining eight bats, and one adult female was radio-tagged. Mean body mass of the adult females was 8.6 g, and mean body mass of young was 5.0 g, suggesting that females were carrying 58 percent of their body mass on average when transporting pups among roosts during flight. No bat was observed in the building the following day, and the radio-tagged adult female was subsequently located in a roost tree that was 1.4 km from building 104.

We successfully located radio-tagged bats 67 percent of the time. Bats used trees and buildings similarly (47 percent and 53 percent, respectively; Mann-Whitney U = 55.0, $P = 0.78$). Of the 11 tree roosts, 9 were *Nyssa* spp. (6 *N. aquatica*, 1 *N. biflora*, 1 *N. sylvatica*, 1 *Nyssa* sp.), and 2 were *T. distichum*. Mean d.b.h. for all trees was 83.0 ± 6.7 cm, but *T. distichum* used as roosts were larger in diameter than *Nyssa* spp. (Mann-Whitney U = 0, $P = 0.04$) (table 1). Of the 11 trees, 10 were live and possessed interior cavities, i.e., live-damaged. The one snag was a *Nyssa* spp. that contained an interior cavity. Of the nine anthropogenic structures, five were aboveground and four were underground. The aboveground roosts were abandoned buildings previously used for human lodging ($n = 2$) or animal shelters and storage of farm equipment ($n = 3$). Underground roosts were a cistern and a well that both contained water, a crawl space under a concrete slab that was previously the floor of a building, and a dry concrete culvert.

All roost trees were in bottomland hardwood forest, as opposed to anthropogenic structures which were located in upland habitats, i.e., developed and cleared upland pine forest/savanna. Of the four landscape feature distances we

Table 1—Characteristics of roost trees used by *Corynorhinus rafinesquii* and distances of roosts to selected landscape features on and around Camp Mackall, NC, 2006 to 2009

Roost characteristic	Mean ± SD	Minimum	Maximum
Nyssa sp. ($n = 9$)			
Diameter at breast height (cm)	75.1±5.1	56.5	104
Height of tree (m)	19.3±0.7	17	21
Taxodium distichum ($n = 2$)			
Diameter at breast height (cm)	119±2.8	116	121
Height of tree (m)	22.5±2.5	20	25
Diameter at breast height (cm)			
All other trees in plot ($n = 152$)	44.5±21.1	5.5	113
All other *Nyssa* spp. ($n = 61$)	43.7±18.5	19.0	96.0
All other *T. distichum* ($n = 6$)	63.6±35.2	16.5	112.5
All trees (m)			
Distance to capture site	938±199	60	1737
Distance to paved road	643±119	51	1210
Distance to firebreak	224±31.3	50	360
Distance to Drowning Creek	71.9±15.3	0	139
Structures (m)			
Distance to capture site	1530±742	0	5965
Distance to paved road	515±180	5	1420
Distance to firebreak	415±385	10	3495
Distance to Drowning Creek	1277±266	130	2960

SD = standard deviation.

measured, distance to capture site and distance to paved roads were not different between tree and anthropogenic structure roosts. However, tree roosts were closer than anthropogenic structures to firebreak roads (Mann-Whitney U = 87.0, $P = 0.003$) and Drowning Creek (Mann-Whitney U = 1.0, $P < 0.0001$).

Structures we selected for temperature monitoring housed at least one bat on at least one visit. The attic of building 104 possessed the highest maximum, the lowest minimum, and the highest daily mean temperatures among all structure roosts sampled (table 2); each of these statistics was outside

Table 2—Weekly maximum, minimum, and average temperatures of anthropogenic roosts of *Corynorhinus rafinesquii* from May 27 to October 1, 2008, on and around Camp Mackall, NC

Roosting site	Average weekly maximum ($n = 16$)	Average weekly minimum ($n = 16$)	Average for time period ($n = 1530$)
Building 764	34.4±2.5[b]	21.9±2.5[b]	27.1±4[b]
Cistern	32.4±2.7[b]	22.7±1.9[a]	27.0±3.6[b]
House	28.7±2.5[b]	19.3±2.4[b]	24.3±3.3[b]
Building 104 attic	51.2±3.9[a]	18.3±2.9[c]	29.9±9.5[a]
Building 104 ground	31.6±2.6[b]	19.3±2.6[b]	25.4±3.8[b]
Building 104 basement	27.5±1.5[b]	21.2±1.7[b]	24.2±2.3[b]

[a,b,c] Within columns, means without common letters are significantly different ($P < 0.05$).

the 95-percent confidence limits of temperature data for all structures combined. Temperatures in the attic of building 104 spanned the greatest range (16 to 57.5 °C) among the buildings sampled. The basement of building 104 had the lowest range in temperatures (16 to 29.5 °C) of the building roost sites, suggesting it was the most thermally stable roosting location among the structures measured. The different temperature regimes within building 104 may provide important roost choices for bats at different times of the year. The only other building for which we recorded

temperatures exceeding the 95-percent confidence limits was the cistern, which possessed the highest mean daily low temperatures recorded among the building roost sites.

Differences in temperatures among the three levels of building 104 were significant, and bat use varied with these temperature changes. During the day, the attic temperature was higher than the ground floor which in turn was higher than the basement temperature (fig. 1). An adult female (A0800) was observed using the attic of this roost while pregnant on May 27, 2008, where a maximum temperature of 46.0 °C and a minimum of 24.5 °C were recorded. On September 29, 2008, this individual, then postlactating, roosted in the basement of this building where the maximum temperature was only 23.0 °C and the minimum temperature was 20.5 °C. A comparison of all temperatures associated with the building in May showed a difference among levels ($K = 7.12$, df = 2, $P = 0.03$, $n = 9$) where the attic temperature was warmer than the basement (Bonferroni corrected significance level: 0.0167). In September, we observed a marginal difference among the temperatures in the three roosting areas of this building ($K = 6.18$, df = 2, $P = 0.05$, $n = 21$), where the attic temperature was warmer than the basement (Bonferroni corrected significance level: 0.0167). The pattern across sampling seasons was similar, with the attic warmer than the other levels of the roost structure (fig. 2). On October 1, 2008, we found no bat present, and there was no difference in temperatures ($K = 3.55$, df = 2, $P = 0.17$, $n = 21$).

Data for temperatures of two other structures (cistern and building 764) indicate that bats used these roosts without apparent association with roost temperatures. These two roosts

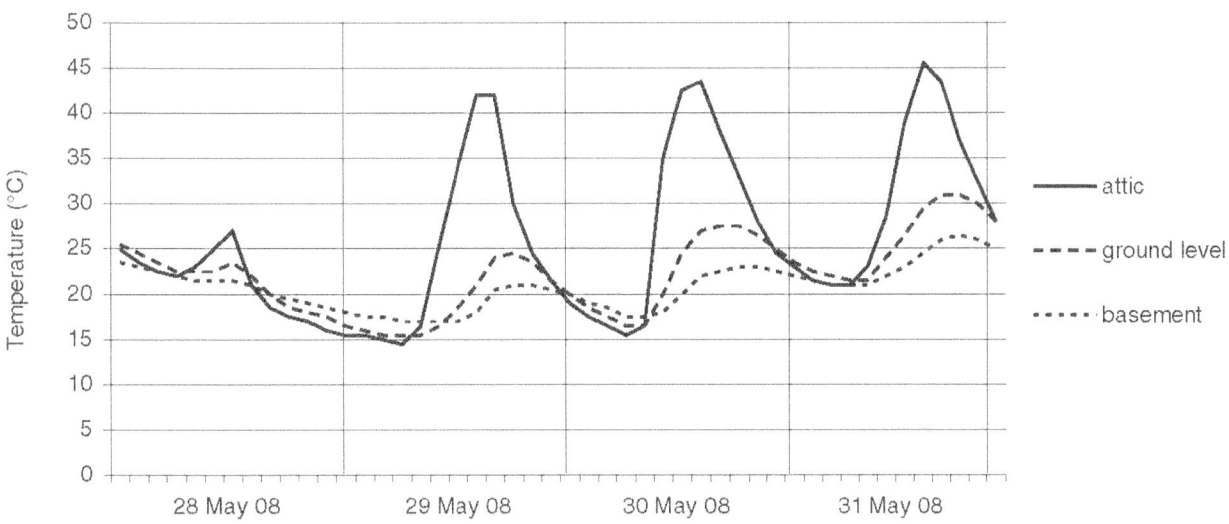

Figure 1—Temperatures in roost building 104 on 4 calendar days when bats were using the roost in May 2008 on Camp Mackall, NC. Each line represents temperature data collected with one iButton® per level.

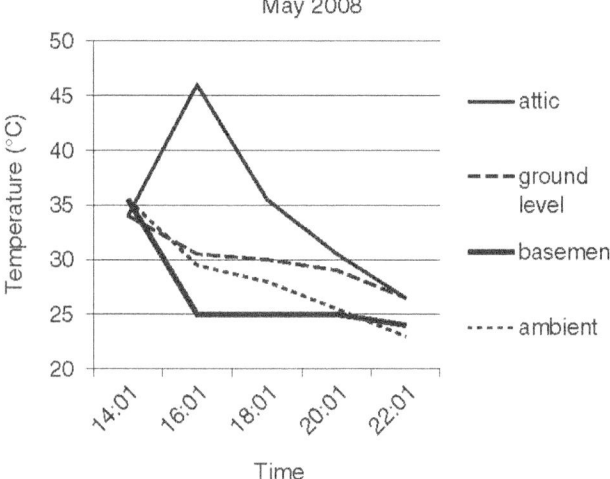

May 2008

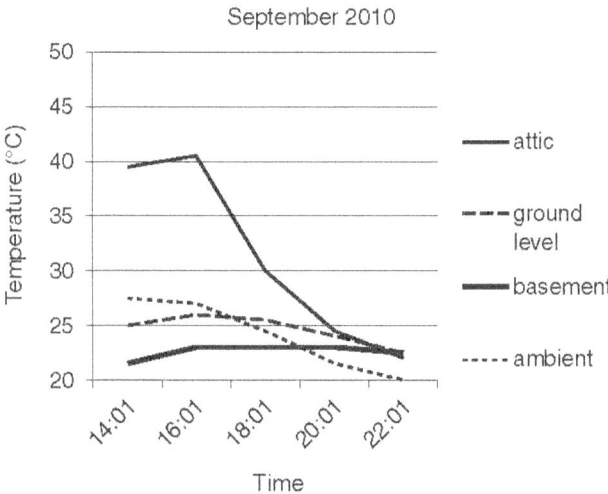

September 2010

Figure 2—Temperature profiles associated with building 104 on days when a female *Corynorhinus rafinesquii* was roosting inside on Camp Mackall, NC. iButton® was placed at noon on May 27, 2008, so first hour of the top graph represents acclimation to the environment.

were used by the same bat a few days apart and were checked on 2 days when no bats were present (table 3). On May 30, 2008, one male (A0701) and one pregnant female (A0798) *C. rafinesquii* (both radio-tagged) were found roosting in the cistern when the average roost temperature was lower than the average ambient temperature ($t = 3.2$, $P = 0.018$) and where maximum and minimum temperatures of 27 and 19 °C were recorded in the roost, respectively. The cistern was again cooler than ambient the next day ($t = 3.97$, $P = 0.007$) where maximum and minimum roost temperatures of 29 and 22 °C were recorded, but only the male was present (the female had moved to the barn). The male then moved to concrete building

764 on the third day where there was no difference between the building temperature and the outside air ($t = 0.72$, $P = 0.5$), and a maximum temperature of 32.0 °C and a minimum of 25.5 °C were recorded in the roost. The cistern was checked on 2 days during the summer, but no bat was observed on either day. There was no difference between the cistern and ambient temperatures on July 18, 2008 ($t = 0.34$, $P = 0.75$) or on July 22, 2008 ($t = 0.39$, $P = 0.71$).

DISCUSSION

During a 6-year study at Camp Mackall and Fort Bragg, we documented the presence of 10 bat species. We discovered a colony of *C. rafinesquii* only at Camp Mackall. Only a single *C. rafinesquii* was captured during extensive netting efforts within suitable habitat, with all other captures of this species made in or near roost sites. Monitoring population sizes of a highly mobile species that switches roosts often can be difficult (Clark 2000, Clark and others 1997, Gooding and Langford 2004, Lance and others 2001, Trousdale and others 2008). Relative to overall capture effort, however, our recapture rate was high, suggesting that the population of *C. rafinesquii* in the study area was small. The largest group we observed had 11 individuals; a small but not uncommon colony size across the range of the species (Barbour and Davis 1969, Jones and Suttkus 1975). The apparent local rarity of *C. rafinesquii* at Camp Mackall may be due to one or more factors including scarcity of food resources, higher rates of mortality, or limited roost availability. Future studies identifying availability of food resources and predation pressures would contribute to an understanding of the limits to the size of this population. We suggest that observations made in this study support the limited roost availability hypothesis. Several adult females were recaptured in multiple years, but no banded juvenile was identified after initial capture. Recapture of adults and not juveniles may indicate low survival rates or dispersal of juveniles out of the population. A study by Jones and Suttkus (1975) supports our conclusion of a small colony size at Camp Mackall by documenting recaptures of both adults and juveniles in larger colonies of *C. rafinesquii* in Louisiana and Mississippi.

Limited availability of natural roosts has been suggested as a reason for use of artificial roosts throughout the southern range of the species (Bennett and others 2008); however, it is likely that *C. rafinesquii* has used anthropogenic structures as long as structures have existed in the range of the species (Audubon 2003, Dalquest 1947, Handley 1959). Many buildings potentially used by bats were once scattered across Camp Mackall, as evidenced by the presence of numerous concrete foundations, but were removed after acquisition of the property by the military. In addition to the loss of anthropogenic roosts, many large trees were removed from the study area as part of the extensive timber harvests conducted

Table 3—Average daytime temperatures and SD (0800 to 2000 hours; *n* = 7 readings) of selected roosts of *Corynorhinus rafinesquii*, with and without bats present, on, and around Camp Mackall, NC, 2008

Roost	Date	Bat	Temperature (°C)		*P*-value
Cistern			Cistern	Ambient	
	May 30, 2008	F[a], M[b]	23.6±3.4	27.8±5.5	0.02
	May 31, 2008	M	25.7±3.1	30.2±4.9	0.01
	July 18, 2008	No bat	27.6±1.6	27.3±2.5	0.75
	July 22, 2008	No bat	31.2±3.2	32.1±6.1	0.71
Building 764			Building 764	Ambient	
	June 1, 2008	M	28.9±2.3	31.0±7.1	0.50

[a] F = pregnant female; [b] M = adult male.

in bottomland hardwood forests across the Southeastern United States (Tiner 1984). The forests on Camp Mackall were extensively logged up to the early 1980s.[1] The presence of large stumps throughout the area suggests that historical vegetation included large trees that likely provided more suitable roosts for *C. rafinesquii*. Roost trees used by this species at Camp Mackall were the largest trees measured. Trees in the current forest may just now be reaching sufficient size to develop cavities used as roosts by this species. Mean d.b.h. of roost trees were smaller than reported in some studies (129±7.3 cm, Carver and Ashley 2008; 120±3.5 cm, Gooding and Langford 2004) but similar to others (59 to 103 cm, Lance and others 2001; 81.9±25.4 cm, Rice 2009; 79.4 cm, Trousdale and Beckett 2005). The colony of *C. rafinesquii* at Camp Mackall may be either a recently established colony or a remnant population from a historically larger assemblage. Assuming the number and condition of anthropogenic structures remain the same and the forest continues to mature and additional roosts become available, a larger population of *C. rafinesquii* may be supported on Camp Mackall, especially if roost availability is the limiting factor to population size of this species in the area.

Anthropogenic structures may be important for maintaining populations of *C. rafinesquii* where natural roost sites are severely limited. The ratio of natural to anthropogenic roosts used by *C. rafinesquii* varies considerably across the range of

the species (Carver and Ashley 2008, Clark 1990, Clement and Castleberry 2008, Harvey and others 1999, Jones 1977, Lance and others 2001). The ratio of trees to structures used as roosts by *C. rafinesquii* in this study was 11 to 9, a ratio consistent with Trousdale and Beckett (2005) (14 trees to 11 structures) but unlike those of any other reports cited. Furthermore, an area on Fort Bragg (Overhills) containing > 20 abandoned buildings adjacent to a reservoir bordered by very young stands of *T. distichum* ($\bar{x}$ d.b.h. ca. 21 cm) never housed *C. rafinesquii* during searches from 2004 to 2009. These observations along with other studies (Clark 1990, Lance and others 2001, Trousdale and Beckett 2005) support the hypothesis that anthropogenic structures are functional as roosts of *C. rafinesquii* only in association with natural roosting habitat.

Radio-tagged *C. rafinesquii* were not located on 33 percent of transmitter days, i.e., one transmitter active for one day, but signals were often heard following a period of absence. Bats may have used underground structures in upland habitats on days when a radio signal was not detected (England and others 1990, Hoffmeister and Goodpaster 1963, Martin and others 2006). We found roosts for *C. rafinesquii* in four underground structures on the base. Cisterns and other underground structures that could be used by bats were widely scattered across the landscape and difficult to locate. The role that underground structures serve in the study area, as a component of the functionality of anthropogenic roost structures, is not fully understood and is a subject in need of further study.

Anthropogenic structures may offer similar temperature conditions to tree roosts (Rice 2009) but provide more space for maneuverability to escape predation (Clark 1990), greater roosting choices for thermoregulation within the same roost (Hoffmeister and Goodpaster 1963), and potential to switch thermal environments during day roosting without exposure to daytime predators. Regardless, temperature regimes of roost sites and the effect on roosting behavior of *C. rafinesquii* remain poorly understood. For example, two pregnant females during late May used two very different roosts with regards to temperature. Bat A0800 roosted in the hot attic of building 104 while bat A0798 used the much cooler cistern. The following day, bat A0798 moved to the barn where temperatures were probably more similar to building 104. We suggest this movement between thermally different roosts may have occurred to avoid prolonged torpor conditions. Similarly, *C. rafinesquii* may use the same roost throughout the year but use thermally different portions of the roost among seasons (Hoffmeister and Goodpaster 1963, Hurst and Lacki 1999). Bat A0800 that roosted in the hot attic of building 104 demonstrated this behavior by choosing the cooler basement within the building later in

---

[1] Personal communication. 2010. Steve Riley, retired Forester, Ft. Bragg, NC 28310.

the year after her pup was presumably volant. Pregnancy is energetically expensive (Racey 1973), so this bat may have chosen the warmer roosting conditions to passively rewarm prior to exiting the roost to feed at night (Winchell 1990). As with other species (Parkinson 2008), female *C. rafinesquii* may select warmer roosting conditions to avoid torpor when pregnant. Bats in torpor have a slower metabolic rate and, therefore, contribute fewer resources to a growing fetus under such conditions (Racey and Swift 1981). Later in the year, when the young are volant and the demands of reproduction have ceased, warmer roosts may be unnecessary or even counterproductive. Cooler roosts selected by bat A0800 later in the year may have provided an energy savings by permitting this bat to enter torpor during a period of lower temperatures when food availability was likely reduced.

Although roost quality depends in part on temperature regime, distances to landscape features used as flight corridors or feeding and drinking sites are also important (Clark 1990, Kurta and others 2002, Watrous and others 2006). Roost trees were located closer to Drowning Creek and firebreak roads than anthropogenic roost structures were to these features. This was due to buildings not being placed within the bottomland hardwood forest along Drowning Creek to avoid the potential of flooding. Nevertheless, proximity to permanent water has been suggested as an important habitat characteristic in selection of roosts by *C. rafinesquii* by enhancing access to food resources and drinking water (Clark 1990, Gooding and Langford 2004). Permanent water in the form of creeks or rivers can also provide flyways for these bats. Firebreak roads may provide flight corridors for commuting between roosts and foraging areas. Thus, roosting closer to these features should be advantageous to these bats. We suggest that use of anthropogenic structures by *C. rafinesquii* on Camp Mackall, situated farther from water and firebreak roads, may offset these distance constraints through advantages in maneuverability inside roosts and access to diverse temperature regimes.

We found distances that bats moved between roosts varied between sexes and reproductive condition classes. For example, males moved shorter distances between roosts than females. It is possible that males have fewer constraints and, thus, can use roosts that are less suitable for females. Roosts with lower temperatures may allow males to enter torpor and provide an energy savings advantage not available to reproductively active females that require warmer roosts for fetus development (Racey and Swift 1981). Thus, males may have more roosts available to them than females, and the need for longer movements is unnecessary. As documented in other species (Kurta and others 2002), lactating females moved shorter distances between roosts than pregnant females. Females with nonvolant young may move shorter distances due to the additional weight of the young. At least one female was documented transporting a pup exceeding 50 percent of her body mass > 1 km to another roost. This is consistent with a report by England and others (1990) who observed that female *C. rafinesquii* transport large juveniles (5 g) when disturbed or to seek more favorable roost temperatures.

Extensive habitat loss has placed bat populations at risk by reducing their population sizes to levels that will likely have difficulty resisting threats such as white-nose syndrome (*Geomyces destructans*) (Zimmerman 2009) and the rapidly growing use of wind turbines as an energy source (Baerwald and Barclay 2009, Cryan and Barclay 2009, Johnson and others 2003). A better understanding of habitat requirements is essential for creating and applying more effective protection strategies for remaining bat populations. Forests provide food and shelter to many bat species, but in light of extensive logging practices and urban development throughout the range of *C. rafinesquii* in the last century (Marks and Marks 2006), management and preservation of anthropogenic structures and construction of artificial roosts will likely play an important role in the protection of populations of this species in human-altered environments. For example, bat houses specifically designed for *C. rafinesquii* erected near existing roost trees are used more readily than ones placed farther from known tree roosts (Bayless 2008). We found that bats moved farther from tree roosts and Drowning Creek to roost in anthropogenic structures on Camp Mackall and suggest that placing artificial roosts in the vicinity of known tree roosts may be beneficial in providing additional roosting habitat. Structure roosts alone, without a suitable forest component, are not likely to provide long-term support for the population of *C. rafinesquii* on Camp Mackall as demonstrated by the uninhabited buildings and unsuitable trees at Overhills on Fort Bragg. Due to the limited availability of bottomland hardwood forest at Camp Mackall, we encourage land managers to consider sustaining large (d.b.h. > 85 cm) hollow trees of appropriate species, such as *T. distichum* and *Nyssa* spp. We believe such an approach can be integrated into the management practices currently in use and will provide suitable roosting habitat needed to maintain future populations of *C. rafinesquii* on Camp Mackall.

ACKNOWLEDGMENTS

We thank U.S. Department of Defense, Fort Bragg, for funding and support of this project. The Fort Bragg Endangered Species Branch, especially J. Britchard, J. Patten, and E. Evans, provided invaluable assistance and logistical support. This project would not have been possible without the dedication of the Copperhead Consulting field crew: C. Leftwich, J. Hawkins, J. Adams, E. Britzke, J. Hootman, D. Foster, G. Hurt, D. Pace, M. Gruen, and C.

Buell. We also acknowledge M. Lacki and two anonymous reviewers for their valuable comments and suggestions.

LITERATURE CITED

Audubon, J.J. 2003. The eccentric naturalist. In: Boewe, C., ed. Profiles of Rafinesque. Knoxville, TN: The University of Tennessee Press: 367-372.

Avery, T.E.; Burkhart, H.E. 2002. Forest measurements. 5th ed. New York: McGraw Hill. 456 p.

Baerwald, E.F.; Barclay, R.M.R. 2009. Geographic variation in activity and fatality of migratory bats at wind energy facilities. Journal of Mammalogy. 90: 1341-1349.

Barbour, R.W.; Davis, W.H. 1969. Bats of America. Lexington, KY: The University Press of Kentucky. 286 p.

Bayless, M. 2008. Rafinesque's big-eared bat use of artificial roosts [Abstract]. In: Rafinesque's big-eared bat working group 2d annual meeting: presentation abstracts. [Blacksburg, VA]: [Publisher unknown]. [Number of pages unknown].

Beaty, T.A.; Bivings, A.E.; Reid, T.G. [and others]. 2003. Success of the Army's 1996 red-cockaded woodpecker management guidelines. Federal Facilities Environmental Journal. 14(1): 43-53.

Bennett, F.M.; Loeb, S.C.; Bunch, M.S.; Bowerman, W.W. 2008. Use and selection of bridges as day roosts by Rafinesque's big-eared bats. American Midland Naturalist. 160: 386-399.

Boice, L.P. 2006. Defense and conservation: compatible missions. Endangered Species Bulletin. 31(2): 4-7.

Britcher, J.J. 2006. Woodpeckers find a home at Fort Bragg. Endangered Species Bulletin. 31(2): 28-30.

Carver, B.D.; Ashley, N. 2008. Roost tree use by sympatric Rafinesque's big-eared bats (*Corynorhinus rafinesquii*) and southeastern myotis (*Myotis austroriparius*). American Midland Naturalist. 160: 364-373.

Clark, M.K. 1990. Roosting ecology of the eastern big-eared bat, *Plecotus rafinesquii*, in North Carolina. Raleigh, NC: North Carolina State University. 111 p. M.S. thesis.

Clark, M.K. 2000. Observations on the life history of Rafinesque's big-eared bat (*Corynorhinus rafinesquii*) in the Carolinas, with emphasis on the use of bottomland hardwood forests [Abstract]. In: Abstracts for *Corynorhinus rafinesquii* workshop. [Guntersville, AL]: 5th annual meeting of the Southeastern Bat Diversity Network: 2.

Clark, M.K.; Hajnos, E.; Black, A. 1997. Radio-tracking of *Corynorhinus rafinesquii* and *Myotis austroriparius* in South Carolina. Bat Research News. 38(4): 136.

Clement, M.J.; Castleberry, S.B. 2008. Range, distribution and natural roosts of Rafinesque's big-eared bat in the Coastal Plain of Georgia [Abstract]. In: Abstracts of 38th annual North American symposium on bat research. [Scranton, PA]: North American Symposium on Bat Research: 13.

Cryan, P.M.; Barclay, R.M.R. 2009. Causes of bat fatalities at wind turbines: hypotheses and predictions. Journal of Mammalogy. 90: 1330-1340.

Dalquest, W.W. 1947. Notes of the natural history of the bat *Corynorhinus rafinesquii* in California. Journal of Mammalogy. 28: 17-30.

England, D.R.; Saugey, D.A.; McDaniel, V.R.; Speight, S.M. 1990. Observations on the life history of Rafinesque's big-eared bat, *Plecotus rafinesquii*, in southern Arkansas [Abstract]. Bat Research News. 30(4): 62-63.

Fort Bragg. 2002. Fort Bragg history: 1919-1939. http://www.bragg.army.mil/history/HistoryPage/History%20of%20Fort%20Bragg/Founding1919through1939.htm. [Date accessed: September 7, 2010].

Fort Bragg. 2005. Ft. Bragg vegetation layer for GIS. Fort Bragg, NC: North American Datum 1983, UTM zone 17 projection. http://spatialreference.org/ref/epsg/26917. [Date accessed: May 16, 2011].

Gooding, G.; Langford, J.R. 2004. Characteristics of tree roosts of Rafinesque's big-eared bat and southeastern bat in northeastern Louisiana. The Southwestern Naturalist. 49(1): 61-67.

Griffith, G.E.; Omernik, J.M.; Comstock, J.A. [and others]. 2002. Ecoregions of North Carolina and South Carolina. Reston, VA: U.S. Geological Survey. 1 :1,500,000; color poster with map, descriptive text, summary tables, and photographs.

Handley, C.O., Jr. 1959. A revision of American bats of the genera *Euderma* and *Plecotus*. No. 3417. In: Proceedings of the U.S. National Museum. Washington, DC: U.S. Government Printing Office: 95-246. Vol. 110, numbers 3416-3421.

Harvey, M.J.; Altenbach, J.S.; Best, T.L. 1999. Bats of the United States. Little Rock, AR: Arkansas Game and Fish Commission. 63 p.

Hoffmeister, D.F.; Goodpaster, W.W. 1963. Observations on a colony of big-eared bats, *Plecotus rafinesquii*. Transactions Illinois Academy of Science. 55: 87-89.

Hurst, T.E.; Lacki, M.J. 1999. Roost selection, population size and habitat use by a colony of Rafinesque's big-eared bats (*Corynorhinus rafinesquii*). American Midland Naturalist. 142: 363-371.

Jentsch, A.; Friedrich, S.; Steinlein, T. [and others]. 2009. Assessing conservation action for substitution of missing dynamics on former military training areas in Central Europe. Restoration Ecology. 17: 107-116.

Johnson, G.D.; Erickson, W.P.; Strickland, M.D. [and others]. 2003. Mortality of bats at a large-scale wind power development at Buffalo Ridge, Minnesota. American Midland Naturalist. 150: 332-342.

Jones, C. 1977. *Plecotus rafinesquii*. Mammalian Species. 69: 1-4.

Jones, C.; Suttkus, R.D. 1975. Notes on the natural history of *Plecotus rafinesquii*. Occas. Pap. of the Museum of Zoology, Louisiana State University. 47: 1-14.

Kurta, A.; Murray, S.; Miller, D.H. 2002. Roost selection and movements across the summer landscape. In: Kurta, A.; Kennedy, J., eds. The Indiana bat: biology and management of an endangered species. Austin, TX: Bat Conservation International: 118-129.

Lance, R.F.; Hardcastle, B.T.; Talley, A.; Leberg, P.L. 2001. Day-roost selection by Rafinesque's big-eared bats (*Corynorhinus rafinesquii*) in Louisiana forests. Journal of Mammalogy. 82: 166-172.

Legacy Resource Management Program. 2005. Resources for INRMP implementation—a handbook for the DoD Natural Resources Manager. https://www.denix.osd.mil. [Date accessed: January 2010].

Lewis, S.E. 1995. Roost fidelity of bats: a review. Journal of Mammalogy. 76: 481-496.

Marks, C.S.; Marks, G.E. 2006. Bats of Florida. Gainesville, FL: University Press of Florida. 176 p.

Martin, C.O.; Lance, R.F.; Sherman, A.R. [and others]. 2006. Bat use of elongated runway culverts at Meridian Naval Air Station, Mississippi [Abstract]. In: Sixteenth colloquium on conservation of mammals in the Southeastern United States and eleventh annual meeting of the Southeastern Bat Diversity Network. [Chattanooga, TN]: 16th Colloquium on Conservation of Mammals in the Southeastern US and 11th Annual Southeastern Bat Diversity Network: 13.

Menzel, M.A.; Menzel, J.M.; Ford, W.M. [and others]. 2001. Home range and habitat use of male Rafinesque's big-eared bats (*Corynorhinus rafinesquii*). American Midland Naturalist. 145: 402-408.

Menzel, M.A.; Menzel, J.M.; Kilgo, J.C. [and others]. 2003. Bats of the Savannah River Site and vicinity. Gen. Tech Rep. SRS-68. Asheville, NC: U.S. Department of Agriculture Forest Service, Southern Research Station. 69 p.

Parkinson, T. 2008. Thermal energetic of silver-haired bats (*Lasionycteris noctivagans*) and the implications for roost

selection: do bats like it hot? Winnipeg, Manitoba: The University of Winnipeg. 47 p. Honours thesis.

Racey, P.A. 1973. Environmental factors affecting the gestation in heterothermic bats. Journal of Reproduction and Fertility. 19 (Suppl.): 175-189.

Racey, P.A.; Swift, S.M. 1981. Variations in gestation length in a colony of pipistrelle bats (*Pipistrellus pipistrellus*) from year to year. Journal of Reproduction and Fertility. 61: 123-129.

Rice, C.L. 2009. Roosting ecology of *Corynorhinus rafinesquii* (Rafinesque's big-eared bat) and *Myotis austroriparius* (southeastern myotis) in tree cavities found in a northeastern Louisiana bottomland hardwood forest streambed. Monroe, LA: The University of Louisiana at Monroe. 117 p. M.S. thesis.

Stein, B.A.; Scott, C.; Benton, N. 2008. Federal lands and endangered species: the role of military and other Federal lands in sustaining biodiversity. BioScience. 58: 339-347.

Tiner, R.W., Jr. 1984. Wetlands of the United States: current status and recent trends. Washington, DC: U.S. Department of the Interior, Fish and Wildlife Service, National Wetland Inventory. 76 p.

Trousdale, A.W.; Beckett, D.C. 2005. Characteristics of tree roosts of Rafinesque's big-eared bat (*Corynorhinus rafinesquii*) in southeastern Mississippi. American Midland Naturalist. 154: 442-449.

Trousdale, A.W.; Beckett, D.C.; Hammond, S.L. 2008. Short-term roost fidelity of Rafinesque's big-eared bat (*Corynorhinus rafinesquii*) varies with habitat. Journal of Mammalogy. 89: 477-484.

U.S. Fish and Wildlife Service. 2008/2010. Endangered and threatened species in North Carolina. http://www.fws.gov/nc-es/es/countyfr.html. [Date accessed: September 7].

Watrous, K.; Donovan, T.; Mickey, R. [and others]. 2006. Predicting minimum habitat characteristics for the Indiana bat in the Champlain Valley. Journal of Wildlife Management. 70(5): 1228-1237.

Winchell, J.M. 1990. Time budgets and roosting ecology of an eastern pipistrelle bat (*Pipistrellus subflavus*) maternity colony. Boston: Boston University. 262 p. M.S. thesis.

Zimmerman, R. 2009. Biologists struggle to solve bat deaths. Science. 324: 2.

SEASONAL AND MULTIANNUAL ROOST USE BY RAFINESQUE'S BIG-EARED BATS IN THE COASTAL PLAIN OF SOUTH CAROLINA

Susan C. Loeb, Research Ecologist, U.S. Department of Agriculture Forest Service, Southern Research Station, Clemson, SC 29634

Stanley J. Zarnoch, Mathematical Statistician, U.S. Department of Agriculture Forest Service, Southern Research Station, Asheville, NC 28804

Abstract—Little is known about factors affecting year-round use of roosts by Rafinesque's big-eared bats (*Corynorhinus rafinesquii*) or the long-term fidelity of this species to anthropogenic or natural roosts. The objectives of this study were to test whether seasonal use of roosts by Rafinesque's big-eared bats varied with roost type and environmental conditions within and among seasons and to document multiannual use of natural and anthropogenic structures by this species. We inspected 4 bridges, 1 building, and 59 tree roosts possessing basal cavity openings; roosts were inspected at least once per week from May through October in every year from 2005 through 2008 and once a month from November through April in every year from 2005 through 2009. We found that use of anthropogenic roosts was significantly greater than the use of tree roosts in summer but that the use of structure types did not differ in other seasons. There was significant seasonal variation in use of anthropogenic and tree roosts. Anthropogenic roost use was higher in summer than in all other seasons. There was no significant difference in tree use among spring, summer, and fall, but use in winter was significantly lower in 2 years of the study. Overall use of anthropogenic and tree roosts was positively related to minimum temperature, but the relationship between use of roosts and minimum temperature varied among seasons. Bats showed multiannual fidelity (≥ 4 years) to all anthropogenic roosts and to some tree roosts, but fidelity of bats to anthropogenic roosts was greater and more consistent than to tree roosts. Our data indicate that Rafinesque's big-eared bats responded differently to environmental conditions among seasons; thus, a variety of structure types and characteristics are necessary for conservation of these bats. We suggest long-term protection of roost structures of all types is necessary for conservation of Rafinesque's big-eared bats in the southeast Coastal Plain.

INTRODUCTION

Day roosts are integral to the ecology and evolution of bats, and many aspects of roost use and selection have received attention over the past two decades (Barclay and Kurta 2007, Carter and Menzel 2007, Kunz and Lumsden 2003). Studies have concentrated on habitat factors affecting roost site selection (Kalcounis-Ruppell and others 2005, Lacki and Baker 2003), effects of microclimate and parasites on roost selection (Kerth and others 2001, Reckardt and Kerth 2007, Willis and Brigham 2005), and roost fidelity (Gumbert and others 2002, Kurta and Murray 2002, Trousdale and others 2008). However, most of these studies have been conducted during the summer, and, for most temperate and boreal bat species, little is known about use of tree roosts during other times of the year (although see Boyles and Robbins 2006, Hein and others 2005, Mormann and Robbins 2007).

Rafinesque's big-eared bats (*Corynorhinus rafinesquii*) that inhabit bottomland hardwood forests and their environs roost in large hollow trees and anthropogenic structures such as buildings, bridges, and wells (Bennett and others 2008; Carver and Ashley 2008; Gooding and Langford 2004; Lance and others 2001; Trousdale and Beckett 2004, 2005). Most studies have either examined use of anthropogenic structures or natural roosts, and few studies compare the use of anthropogenic and natural structures in a study area. Thus, it is unknown whether bats prefer one type of structure over the other or whether their preference varies seasonally.

Some studies have examined year-round roost use by Rafinesque's big-eared bats. In Louisiana and Mississippi, use of bridges as day roosts declines in winter (Ferrara and Leberg 2005b, Trousdale and Beckett 2004). Use of trees with basal openings or trees with basal and chimney openings also declines in winter in Louisiana, and bats appear to move to trees with chimney-only openings, particularly during periods of below freezing temperatures (Rice 2009). Trees with chimney-only openings have more stable temperatures, suggesting that thermal considerations may be important in selection of winter roost sites. Winter flooding may block the entrances to trees with basal openings, which may be another reason that the bats in winter select trees with chimney-only openings even though such trees provide less shelter from rain.

Multiannual roost use is another important aspect of roosting ecology. Long-term use of tree roosts appears to be related to roost type (cavity/crevice versus bark) and decomposition state of the tree. For example, bats that roost between the bark and bole of snags are less likely to reuse roosts in subsequent years than bats that roost in crevices or cavities in live-damaged trees (Barclay and Brigham 2001, Chung-MacCoubrey 2003, Lučan and others 2009, Willis and others

Citation for proceedings: Loeb, Susan C.; Lacki, Michael J.; Miller, Darren A., eds. 2011. Conservation and management of eastern big-eared bats: a symposium. Gen. Tech. Rep. SRS-145. Asheville, NC: U.S. Department of Agriculture, Forest Service, Southern Research Station. 157 p.

2003). Further, bats that roost in relatively permanent roosts such as caves or mines show greater fidelity to their roosts than bats that use relatively ephemeral roosts such as trees (Lewis 1995). While there are a few anecdotal accounts of multiannual use of anthropogenic roosts by Rafinesque's big-eared bats (Clark 1990, Jones and Sutkus 1975), there are no quantitative data on long-term fidelity to either anthropogenic or tree roosts.

The objectives of our study were to test whether seasonal use of roosts by Rafinesque's big-eared bats varied with roost type (anthropogenic versus tree) and environmental conditions, both within and among seasons, and to document multiannual use of natural and anthropogenic structures by this species. We hypothesized that use of anthropogenic roosts and tree roosts with basal or basal-plus chimney openings would be positively related to ambient temperature and rainfall on an annual basis but would vary with season. We also hypothesized that multiannual use of anthropogenic structures would be greater than multiannual use of natural roosts.

METHODS

Our study was conducted from May 2005 through April 2009 on the U.S. Department of Energy Savannah River Site (SRS) in Aiken and Barnwell Counties, SC. The SRS is a 78 000-ha National Environmental Research Park in the sandhills and Upper Coastal Plain physiographic regions. The site is primarily forested in mid- to late-successional pine (*Pinus* spp.), mixed pine-hardwood, and upland hardwood forests (Imm and McLeod 2005). However, approximately 20 percent of SRS is swamp and bottomland hardwood forest. SRS experienced extensive disturbance and land clearing from the mid-1800s to the early 1950s when the site became Federal property (White 2005). Chief disturbances to the swamp and along the major streams prior to and after 1950 were logging, damming, high flow rates, altered temperatures from reactor cooling waters, and changes in hydrology (Kolka and others 2005). Bottomland hardwood forests consisted primarily of blackgum (*Nyssa sylvatica*), laurel oak (*Quercus laurifolia*), water oak (*Q. nigra*), red maple (*Acer rubrum*), American holly (*Ilex opaca*), sweetbay (*Magnolia virginiana*), redbay (*Persea borbonia*), ironwood (*Carpinus caroliniana*), and sweetgum (*Liquidambar styraciflua*); whereas major tree species in the swamps were water tupelo (*N. aquatica*), baldcypress (*Taxodium distichum*), and red maple. Average low and high temperatures from 1893 to 2008 ranged from 2.7 and 14.4 °C in January to 21.0 and 33.2 °C in July (Southeast Regional Climate Center, http://www.sercc.com/cgi-bin/sercc/cliMAIN.pl?sc0074). Average annual rainfall for the area was 118.4 cm (Southeast Regional Climate Center, http://www.sercc.com/cgi-bin/sercc/cliMAIN.pl?sc0074) but was below average in every year of the study (2005 to 2006, 58.3 cm; 2006 to 2007, 101.3 cm; 2007 to 2008, 106.22 cm; 2008 to 2009, 96.9 cm).

We located roosts by inspecting trees with basal cavities in bottomland forests and the surrounding areas, bridges, and old buildings and by radiotelemetry. We found trees with basal cavities during systematic searches of areas that were likely to contain potential roosts, such as mature bottomland hardwood forests and cypress-tupelo swamps, and opportunistically while conducting radiotelemetry and habitat analyses. Mature bottomland hardwood forest and cypress-tupelo swamp forests were located from forest maps, and all accessible trees within an area were examined, using a light and mirror, for the presence of Rafinesque's big-eared bats. Bats that roosted under bridges were captured by hand or with hand nets. Bats in trees with basal openings were captured by placing a mist net over the cavity entrance and capturing the bats as they emerged at dusk. All captured Rafinesque's big-eared bats were weighed, sexed, and aged and examined for parasites and injuries. We placed an aluminum lipped band (Lambournes Sophos Ltd., West Midlands, Birmingham, England) and a colored plastic split ring band (A.C. Hughes, Ltd., Middlesex, England) on the forearms of each bat. Various band placement and color combinations allowed us to determine the identity of bats when observed in a roost if the bands were visible. Capture and handling procedures followed guidelines established by the American Society of Mammalogists (Gannon and others 2007) and were approved by the Clemson University Institutional Animal Care and Use Committee (protocol numbers 50057 and ARC2008-027).

To obtain additional roost locations, we attached radio transmitters (0.42 g; Holohil Systems Ltd, Ontario, Canada) to the dorsal surface of 49 bats with Skin Bond adhesive (Pfizer Hospital Products Group, Inc., Largo, FL). We held bats for ≥ 20 minutes before releasing them to ensure the transmitter was secure. On the following and subsequent days, we used three- or five-element Yagi antenna and receiver (Wildlife Materials, Inc., Murphysboro, IL) to track bats to day roosts. If the bat was tracked to a bridge or building, the bat's relative location within the structure was recorded. If the bat was tracked to a tree, the tree was flagged, marked with a numbered aluminum tag, and identified to location with a global positioning system device. We treated tree roosts identified during random or systematic searches in the same manner. We verified that trees discovered using telemetry were the actual roost by visual inspection of the cavity with a light and mirror or by observing emergence of the bat from the cavity at dusk.

After identifying roosts, we monitored them throughout the rest of the study with the exception of roosts with only an upper bole opening or those that could not be fully examined due to a bend in the tree or because the cavity entrance was too small. We examined each roost at least once a week from May through October and at least once a month from November through April, except in the winter of 2008 to 2009 when we examined roosts at least once a week. The number of examined roosts varied throughout the study because new roosts were continually added to the sample of roost trees, and six tree roosts broke or fell during the course of the study. Some roosts were periodically inaccessible due to high water. Trees that could not be examined regularly were not included in the analyses.

We defined seasons as spring (March and April), summer (May, June, July, and August), fall (September and October), and winter (November, December, January, and February) based on climatic conditions as well as the annual cycle of Rafinesque's big-eared bats. For example, females in this area form maternity colonies and are visibly pregnant in May, and colonies begin to break up at the end of August. Thus, May was considered a summer month and September a fall month. Further, because November temperatures, particularly minimum temperatures, were more similar to December, January, and February than to October, November was considered a winter month (fig. 1).

Temperature (°C), rainfall (mm), relative humidity (percent), and windspeed (m/second) were recorded hourly at a weather station maintained by other researchers on SRS (Coleman and others 2004). Daily maximum temperature (Tmax), minimum temperature (Tmin), average daily temperature (Tavg), minimum relative humidity (RHmin), average windspeed (WSavg), and total rainfall (Rainfall) were extracted for each day from mid-May 2005 through April 2009. Because Tmax, Tmin, and Tavg were highly correlated ($r > 0.70$), only Tmin was used in statistical models. We selected Tmin because we were particularly interested in the effects of low temperatures on winter roost use.

We used a split-split-plot approximation of a repeated measures model because both year and season were repeated in the model which presented a complex covariance structure. Under conditions of equal variances and equal pairwise correlations over time, the split-split plot is an optimal method of analysis (Littell and others 1998) and is valid under the Huynh-Feldt condition which is less stringent than equal variances and covariances. We used the PROC GLIMMIX procedure (Schabenberger 2005) in SAS (2003) to fit a generalized linear mixed model to the binary (absence = 0, presence = 1) data under the binomial distribution and logit link function, resulting in a logistic response model. A three-phased approach was used to analyze relationships between roost use (0, 1) and independent variables. In phase 1, we analyzed roost use using a split-split-plot design to test fixed effects of roost type (main plot), year (split plot), and season (split-split plot) and their two- and three-way interactions. In phase 2, we tested the effects of season and year separately for each roost type using a split-plot design because we found strong interactions in the phase 1 analysis between roost type and season ($P = 0.0239$) and year and season ($P = 0.0003$). In phase 3, we modeled the effects of environmental parameters on roost use for each roost

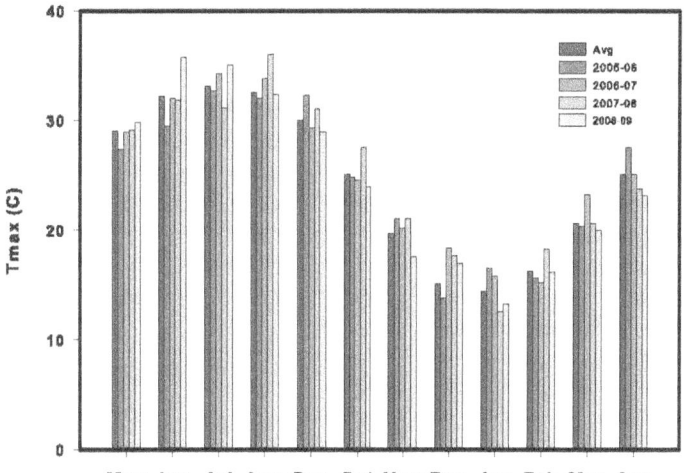

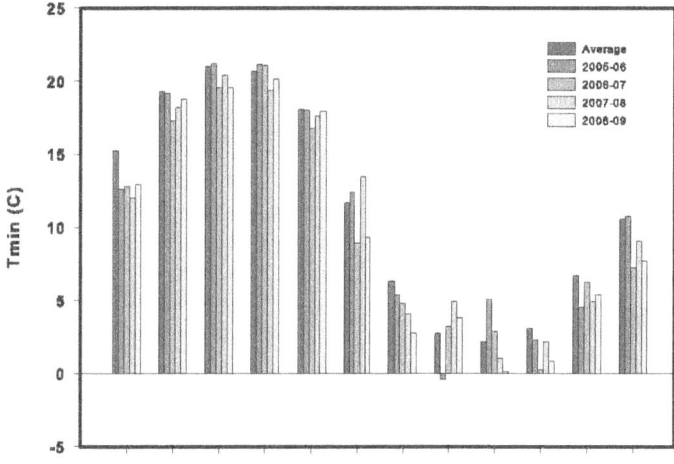

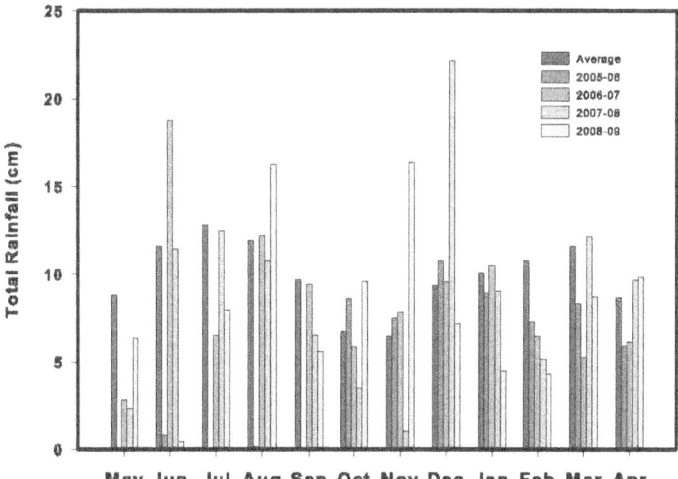

Figure 1—Long-term average (1893 to 2008) mean monthly maximum daily temperatures (Tmax), mean minimum daily temperatures (Tmin), and total rainfall (Rainfall) for the Savannah River Site, SC, and the mean maximum daily temperatures (Tmax), mean minimum daily temperatures (Tmin), and total rainfall (Rainfall) for each year of the study (2005 to 2009).

type by testing the effects of year, season, year*season, and the environmental covariates consisting of Tmin, RHmin, WSavg, Rainfall, and their interaction with season (that is, season*Tmin, season*RHmin, season*WSavg, and season*Rainfall). Homogeneity of the slope parameter over season for each of the four environmental covariates was tested by inspection of the covariate*season interactions and then reducing the full model by deleting the most nonsignificant covariate*season interaction. The reduced model was then refitted, the remaining covariate*season interactions inspected and deleted sequentially until all remaining covariate*season interactions were significant at the 0.05 level. Then this model was reduced sequentially by deleting the most nonsignificant covariate and then refitting and testing the remaining covariates until all remaining covariates were significant at the 0.05 level. For each of the final reduced models, significant covariate interactions with season indicated that the covariate slopes differed among the seasons. We used contrasts to determine which slopes were significantly different. The Bonferroni correction for each set of six pairwise comparisons among the seasonal slopes set the rejection level at $\alpha = 0.0083$ to ensure that the experimentwise error rate was maintained at 0.05 (Zarnoch 2009). All other tests were evaluated at $\alpha = 0.05$, and least square means ± 1 SE are presented.

RESULTS

Fifty-nine roost trees with basal cavities and five anthropogenic roosts were examined during the study.

Anthropogenic roosts were four girder-type bridges and one barn. Tree roosts were in tupelos (*N. aquatica* and *N. sylvatica*), oaks (*Q. laurifolia, Q. michauxii, Q. nigra,* and *Q. velutina*), American beech (*Fagus grandifolia*), sweetbay, sweetgum, river birch (*Betula nigra*), yellow-poplar (*Liriodendron tulipifera*), baldcypress, and sycamore (*Plantanus occidentalis*). There were a total of 5,152 roost inspections; the number of inspections per structure ranged from 2 to 195 for roost trees and 193 to 329 for anthropogenic roosts. The number of Rafinesque's big-eared bats found in a roost ranged from zero to 9 for trees and from zero to 15 for anthropogenic roosts.

Use of anthropogenic roosts was higher than tree roost use in every month except January 2008 and during most months in winter 2009 (fig. 2). Overall use of anthropogenic roosts was not significantly different from tree roost use based on the phase 1 analysis but there was a significant roost*season interaction ($F = 3.19$, $P = 0.0239$). Thus, we conducted pairwise comparisons between anthropogenic and tree roost use for each season. Anthropogenic roost use was higher than tree use in every season but the difference was only significant during summer (fig. 3).

Use of both roost types was lowest in winter, particularly November to January, but higher in other seasons (fig. 2). Roost use in winter 2006 to 2007, particularly anthropogenic roosts, did not decline as much as in other years during the winter. Although Tmax was greater in November, December, and January 2006 to 2007 than the long-term average, it was also greater than the long-term average in

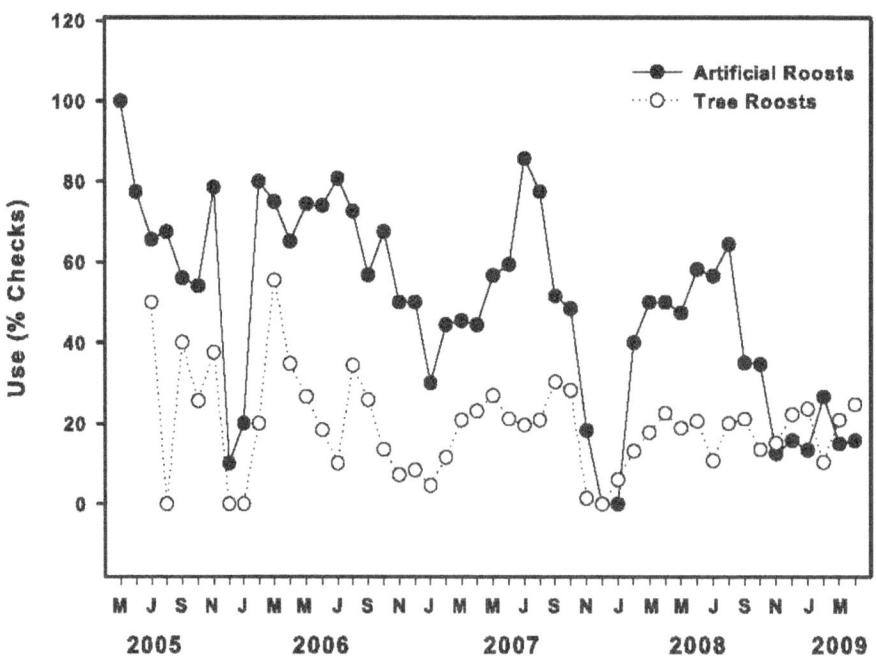

Figure 2—Percent of roost checks in which at least one Rafinesque's big-eared bat was observed in anthropogenic and tree roosts on the Savannah River Site, SC, May 2005 to April 2009.

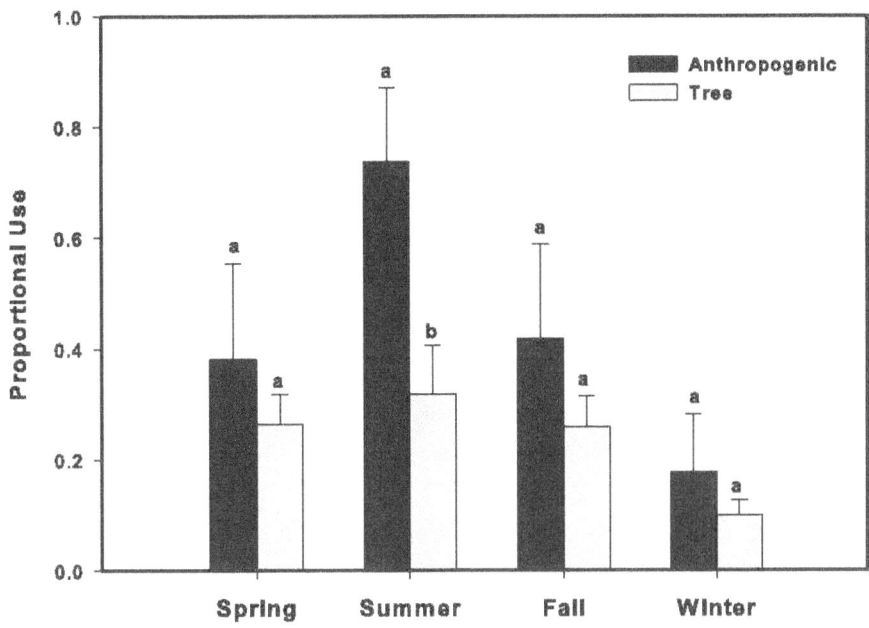

Figure 3—Mean use of anthropogenic and tree roosts by season by Rafinesque's big-eared bats on the Savannah River Site, SC, May 2005 to April 2009; means within a season with the same letter are not different (P > 0.05).

other years, and Tmin in 2006 to 2007 was similar to other years (fig. 1). The phase 2 analysis indicated that there was a significant interaction between year and season for both anthropogenic ($F = 2.51$, $P = 0.0192$) and tree roosts ($F = 2.02$, $P = 0.0368$). Thus, we examined seasonal use by year for each roost type. Use of anthropogenic structures was significantly greater in summer than in all other seasons in 2006 to 2007 and 2008 to 2009 and significantly greater in summer than in fall and winter in 2005 to 2006 and 2007 to 2008 (table 1). Tree roost use did not vary significantly among seasons in 2005 to 2006 and 2006 to 2007 but was significantly lower in winter than all other seasons in 2007

Table 1—Mean proportional use (± SE) of anthropogenic and tree roosts by season and year of Rafinesque's big-eared bats on the Savannah River Site, May 2005 to April 2009

Roost type	2005–06	2006–07	2007–08	2008–09
Anthropogenic roosts				
Spring	0.78±0.19[ab]	0.36±0.23[a]	0.47±0.28[ab]	0.07±0.07[a]
Summer	0.76±0.18[a]	0.76±0.17[b]	0.75±0.18[b]	0.67±0.22[b]
Fall	0.47±0.24[b]	0.53±0.25[a]	0.40±0.24[a]	0.28±0.21[a]
Winter	0.40±0.25[b]	0.27±0.20[a]	0.07±0.07[c]	0.11±0.10[a]
Tree roosts				
Spring	0.61±0.14[a]	0.26±0.09[a]	0.19±0.06[a]	0.11±0.03[ab]
Summer	0.58±0.33[a]	0.30±0.09[a]	0.27±0.06[a]	0.16±0.04[b]
Fall	0.43±0.16[a]	0.29±0.09[a]	0.21±0.05[a]	0.14±0.04[b]
Winter	0.35±0.16[a]	0.14±0.07[a]	0.02±0.0[b]	0.06±0.02[a]

[a,b,c] Proportions with the same letter within a year for a given roost type are not significantly different at the experimentwise error rate of 0.05 (Bonferroni correction, $P = 0.0083$).

Table 2—Results of phase 3 generalized linear mixed models testing the effects of environmental variables on use of anthropogenic and tree roosts by Rafinesque's big-eared bats on the Savannah River Site, SC, May 2005 through April 2009[a]

Models	Anthropogenic roosts				Tree roosts			
	Num. df[b]	Den. df[c]	F	P	Num. df[b]	Den. df[c]	F	P
Full model								
Year	3	12	2.90	0.0785	3	64	4.20	0.0089
Season	3	1199	0.13	0.9395	3	3660	3.48	0.0153
Year*Season	9	1199	2.27	0.0159	9	3660	1.52	0.1333
Tmin[d]	1	1199	20.27	< 0.0001	1	3660	4.95	0.0261
Rainfall	1	1199	0.39	0.5336	1	3660	0.60	0.4385
RHmin[e]	1	1199	12.13	0.0005	1	3660	0.23	0.6341
WSavg[f]	1	1199	2.05	0.1528	1	3660	0.21	0.6472
Tmin*Season	3	1199	4.19	0.0058	3	3660	5.57	0.0008
Rainfall*Season	3	1199	2.23	0.0828	3	3660	3.39	0.0172
RHmin*Season	3	1199	2.35	0.0712	3	3660	1.44	0.2302
WSavg*Season	3	1199	0.36	0.7808	3	3660	0.21	0.8915
Reduced model								
Year	3	12	2.67	0.0948	3	64	4.78	0.0045
Season	3	1210	3.76	0.0105	3	3738	9.09	< 0.0001
Year*Season	9	1210	2.24	0.0176	9	3738	1.71	0.0803
Tmin[d]	1	1210	16.73	< 0.0001	1	3738	5.19	0.0228
Tmin*Season	3	1210	3.71	0.0112	3	3738	5.69	0.0007
RHmin[e]	1	1210	13.70	0.0002				

[a] The full model and final reduced models are presented.

[b] Numerator degrees of freedom.

[c] Denominator degrees of freedom.

[d] Minimum temperature.

[e] Minimum relative humidity.

[f] Average windspeed.

to 2008 and significantly lower in winter than summer and fall in 2008 to 2009.

The phase 3 full model revealed use of anthropogenic roosts was significantly related to Tmin and RHmin (table 2). Anthropogenic roost use increased with increasing temperature and decreased with increasing RHmin. There was no effect of Rainfall or WSavg. However, examination of the reduced models revealed that the Tmin*season interaction was significant. The slope of use versus Tmin was significantly greater in winter than in fall ($P = 0.0018$) indicating that use was more sensitive to temperature in winter than in fall (fig. 4A). Overall, there was a significant and positive relationship between Tmin and use of tree roosts

(table 2), but the interaction between Tmin and season was also significant. Use of tree roosts was positively related to Tmin in fall and winter but negatively related to Tmin in summer (fig. 4B). The effect of Tmin was significantly different ($P \leq 0.0001$) between summer and fall with use decreasing with increasing Tmin in summer and increasing with temperature in fall and winter.

All five anthropogenic roosts were used in every year of study. Rafinesque's big-eared bats were present in anthropogenic roosts during 56.7 to 88.6 percent of roost checks. Of the nine trees found in year one, four were used in all years, two were used in 3 years, and three in 2 years. One of the trees used in 3 years fell in year three, and the

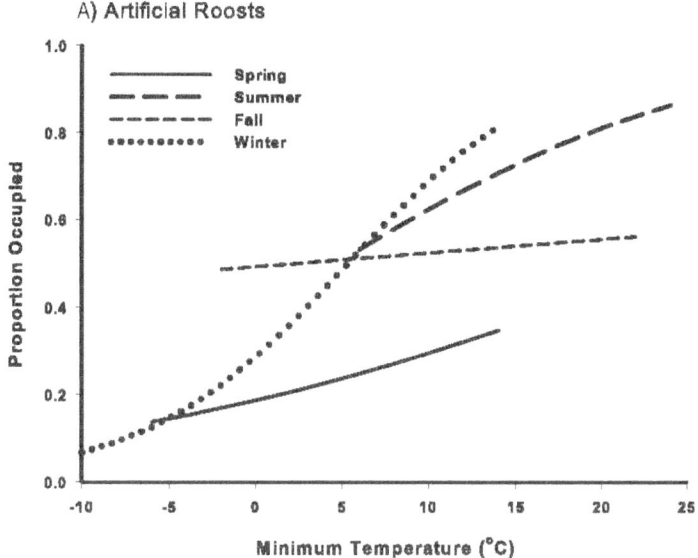

A) Artificial Roosts

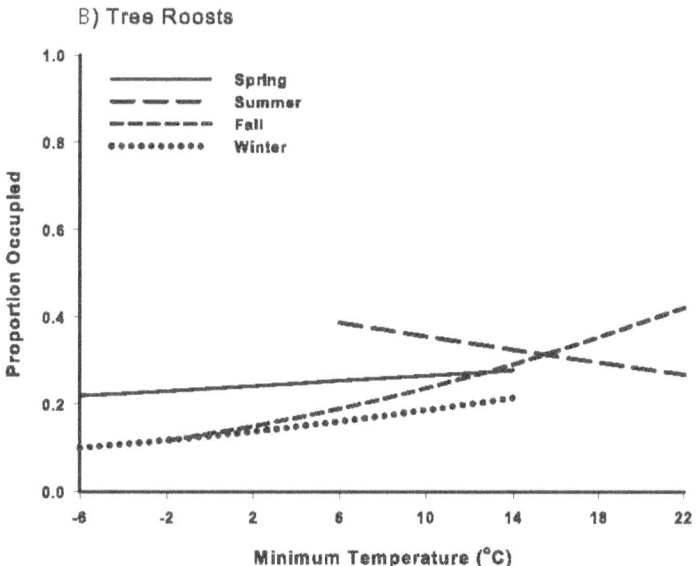

B) Tree Roosts

Figure 4—The relationship between the proportion of (A) anthropogenic roosts and (B) tree roosts occupied and minimum temperature (Tmin) for each season based on a typical year (year = 2) and typical minimum relative humidity (RHmin = 40.3 for anthropogenic roosts and RHmin = 38.1 for tree roosts) on the Savannah River Site, SC, May 2005 to April 2009. The curve segment length for each season is based on the range of minimum temperatures observed for each season and roost structure.

other was used in 2005 to 2006, 2006 to 2007, and 2008 to 2009. Of the nine trees found in year two, four were used for 3 years and five were used for 2 years; one of the trees used for 2 years fell during year four. Of the 24 trees found in year three, 15 were used in both years three and four, and 9 were only used in year three; 1 of these trees fell soon after it was discovered. The mean number of years trees were used was 3.1±0.31 for trees found in year one,

2.4±0.18 for trees found in year two, and 1.7±0.10 for trees found in year three. There was considerable variation in tree roost use across time. For trees checked ≥ 20 times, bats were present an average of 17.6 percent with a range of 1.0 to 89.2 percent.

Long-term use of roosts was accomplished by the same individual or group of individuals which was particularly evident for anthropogenic roosts. For example, orange 18 was captured and banded at bridge 603-01G in July 2003, prior to the initiation of this study, as a juvenile and was recaptured there in June 2005, July 2006, and August and October 2007. This bat was consistently observed roosting at this bridge throughout the 4-year study period and during periodic checks in summer 2009 after the study had concluded. Another example is green 22, an adult male, who was captured at bridge 603-02G in September 2004. He was observed at this bridge throughout the 4-year study period as well as summer 2009. This bat also used tree 358 during summer and fall 2006, summer and fall 2007, and winter and spring 2008 to 2009. Bridge 603-03G was used throughout the study period by a maternity colony. The bats were first observed using this bridge in September 2004, and anywhere from 1 to 15 individuals, including young, were observed at this bridge throughout the study, as well as in summer 2009. This colony also used two roost trees from summer 2007 through summer 2009. Conversely, some roosts used for 3 to 4 years were used by a sequence of different individuals. For example, tree 352 was used by orange 40, a juvenile male when banded, in fall 2005 and summer 2006; by green 28, an adult male, in summer and fall 2007; by pink 2, a juvenile male, in fall 2007; and by blue 3, an adult male, in summer 2008.

DISCUSSION

Decreased use of bridges and trees with basal cavities as day roosts by Rafinesque's big-eared bats in winter has been previously documented in Louisiana (Ferrara and Leberg 2005b, Rice 2009) and Mississippi (Trousdale and Beckett 2004). We also found decreased use of anthropogenic and tree roosts by Rafinesque's big-eared bats on the SRS in winter, but the seasonal patterns of use varied between types of roosts. Use of anthropogenic roosts peaked in summer but, in most years, there was no difference in use among fall, winter, and spring. In contrast, use of trees with basal cavities was similar during spring, summer, and fall but declined in winter, although the decline was only significant in the last 2 years of the study. Use of anthropogenic structures was also greater than use of tree roosts in summer but not in other seasons.

Differential use of anthropogenic and tree roosts may be due to differences in the microclimate of the various structures. On an annual basis, use of both anthropogenic and tree roosts was positively related to Tmin. However, we found that the relationship between roost use and Tmin varied among roost types and seasons. Use of anthropogenic roosts was more strongly influenced, i.e., a steeper slope, by Tmin in winter than in fall, and use of tree roosts was positively related to Tmin in spring, fall, and winter but negatively related to Tmin in summer. During summer, some tree roosts with basal cavities may be too warm and bats may need to search out other types of roosts such as bridges or other tree structures. Our finding that use of anthropogenic roosts was significantly greater than use of trees in summer but not significantly different during other seasons suggests that bats indeed moved from trees to anthropogenic roosts during the warmest months. In Colorado, big brown bats (*Eptesicus fuscus*) that roost in buildings are more likely to shift to new roosts or new areas within the same roost during unusually hot periods (Ellison and others 2007). Because anthropogenic roosts are larger, there may be a greater variety of microclimates within each structure where bats can move to select the best microclimate (e.g., Clark 1990, Jones and Suttkus 1975). Rafinesque's big-eared bats may also have moved to trees with chimney-only openings in summer. Rice (2009) found that cavity temperatures of roosts that have chimney-only entrances rise more slowly with increases in ambient temperature in summer and are more stable than those with basal cavities and basal-plus chimney openings.

While roost temperature may be an important factor governing differential use of anthropogenic and tree roosts during summer, other factors may also be important. Rafinesque's big-eared bats that use bridges as day roosts in Louisiana select the warmest areas of the bridges even when temperatures are quite high (Ferrara and Leberg 2005a). These areas are also the darkest portions of the bridges where bats are less likely to be detected by terrestrial predators. Although we did not measure light levels in trees and anthropogenic structures, it was often possible to spot bats under bridges and in the building without the aid of a light. It was never possible to see bats in trees without a light source. This suggests that bats were not using anthropogenic structures more often than trees due to light levels and that other features of anthropogenic structures may have reduced the risk of predation. For example, bats that used bridges often roosted in the middle of the bridge over water, putting them out of reach of snakes and raccoons, both of which were observed under bridges.

Although use of anthropogenic structures was not lower in winter than in fall and spring, there was a general trend for use to decline in winter as in tree roosts. We were not able to survey trees with chimney-only openings due to logistical constraints. However, Rice (2009) found that Rafinesque's big-eared bats in Louisiana often moved from trees with basal-only or basal-plus chimney openings to trees with chimney-only openings during winter. Therefore, it is likely that many of the bats that used anthropogenic roosts and trees with basal and basal-plus chimney openings during spring, summer, and fall moved to trees with chimney-only openings in winter. Lower use of roosts in winter may also be due to changes in clustering behavior. In summer, adult males usually roost by themselves, but during winter we have observed males roosting with large colonies as did Rice (2009) in Louisiana. Large aggregations of bats can increase the roost temperature by as much as 7 °C in summer (Willis and Brigham 2007). Thus, bats may form larger aggregations in winter for thermoregulatory reasons, resulting in fewer roosts being used.

There are few data on multiannual use of anthropogenic roosts by Rafinesque's big-eared bats and even fewer data on multiannual use of tree roosts. Based on large guano accumulations in building roosts in North Carolina, Clark (1990) concluded that Rafinesque's big-eared bats had used these roosts for many years. Jones and Sutkus (1975) reported on a big-eared bat colony that used a house roost over a 3-year period. Lewis (1995) predicted that bats will show greater fidelity to rare but stable roosts such as bridges and buildings than to more common and less stable roosts such as trees. Rafinesque's big-eared bats in Mississippi show greater short-term fidelity to anthropogenic roosts than to tree roosts (Trousdale and others 2008), and our data suggest that longer term fidelity to anthropogenic roosts was also greater and more consistent than to tree roosts. All five anthropogenic roosts were used in all 4 years of the study. We also checked these structures prior to and after the study, and all were used for at least 6 years. In contrast, only four of nine tree roosts that were examined throughout the study were used in all 4 years. However, most roost trees we found were used for at least 2 years and many for 3 years. In some cases, multiannual use was by one bat or group of bats, and in some cases it was by a succession of bats.

Multiannual use of crevice and cavity roosts has been found in several other bat species. For example, crevice roosts in ponderosa pine (*P. ponderosa*), alligator juniper (*Juniperus deppeana*), and pinyon (*P. edulis*) in New Mexico were reused by female long-eared myotis (*Myotis evotis*), fringed myotis (*M. thysanodes*), long-legged myotis (*M. volans*), and big brown bats during 75 percent of the summers they were monitored, 1 to 3 years postidentification (Chung-MacCoubrey 2003). In Canada, 6 of 11 big brown bat cavity roosts in live trembling aspen (*Populus tremuloides*) were used in the 2 years following their identification as roosts (Willis and others 2003). Willis and others (2003) also checked some trees that had been identified as roosts during a previous study and found that some of those trees were used 8 to 10 years after they were first identified as roosts. We only observed tree roosts for 4 years, and observations of these trees over longer periods of time will be necessary to fully understand long-term roost use by Rafinesque's big-eared bats. Nonetheless, our observations of multiannual use of anthropogenic and tree roosts suggest that long-term preservation of these roosts may be critical for long-term conservation of these bats, particularly in areas where roosts may be limiting. In addition, six tree roosts fell or broke during the 4 years of this study, suggesting the importance of recruiting new trees into the "roost tree population." We suggest that trees with small cavities also be conserved as many of these are likely to become suitable roost trees in future years.

CONCLUSIONS

Our data suggest that factors affecting use of roosts by Rafinesque's big-eared bats in bottomland hardwood forests may vary with roost type and season. Thus, conclusions based on data from anthropogenic roosts may not apply to tree roosts and vice versa. Our data also suggest that bats responded differently to environmental conditions among seasons and roost types. Because Rafinesque's big-eared bats in the Coastal Plain are typically found in an area throughout the year (this study, Rice 2009, Trousdale and Beckett 2004), studies of these bats should be conducted year round, when possible, to identify environmental and habitat factors affecting these populations. We encourage future studies of microclimate conditions within and between roost types to more fully understand roost selection by Rafinesque's big-eared bats on an annual basis. The long-term use of both anthropogenic and tree roosts by these bats emphasizes the importance of such structures to the ecology of Rafinesque's big-eared bats; when these are identified as used by these bats, we recommend that both types of structures be given long-term protection from disturbance and destruction.

ACKNOWLEDGMENTS

Funding was provided by the U.S. Department of Energy, Savannah River Operations Office through the U.S. Department of Agriculture Forest Service, Savannah River under Interagency Agreement DE-IA09-00SR22188. We thank John Blake and Kim Wright for logistical support; Eric Winters, Kelley Kryshtalowych, Lindsey Wight, Matt Goode, Caitlin McCaw, Adrienne Debiase, Jennifer Gulbransen, and Charles Dachelet for assistance in the field; and Laura Krysinsky and Camille Warbington for assistance with weather data. We thank M. Lacki, M. Kalcounis-Rueppell, and an anonymous reviewer for comments on earlier drafts.

LITERATURE CITED

Barclay, R.M.R.; Brigham, R.M. 2001. Year-to-year reuse of tree-roosts by California bats (*Myotis californicus*) in southern British Columbia. American Midland Naturalist. 146: 80-85.

Barclay, R.M.R.; Kurta, A. 2007. Ecology and behavior of bats roosting in tree cavities and under bark. In: Lacki, M.J.; Hayes, J.P.; Kurta, A., eds. Bats in forests: conservation and management. Baltimore, MD: Johns Hopkins University Press: 17-59.

Bennett, F.M.; Loeb, S.C.; Bunch, M.S.; Bowerman, W.W. 2008. Use and selection of bridges as day roosts by Rafinesque's big-eared bats. American Midland Naturalist. 160: 386-399.

Boyles, J.G.; Robbins, L.W. 2006. Characteristics of summer and winter roost trees used by evening bats (*Nycticeius humeralis*) in southwestern Missouri. American Midland Naturalist. 155: 210-220.

Carter, T.C.; Menzel, J.M. 2007. Behavior and day-roosting ecology of North American foliage-roosting bats. In: Lacki, M.J.; Hayes, J.P.; Kurta, A., eds. Bats in forests: conservation and management. Baltimore, MD: Johns Hopkins University Press: 61-81.

Carver, B.D.; Ashley, N. 2008. Roost tree use by sympatric Rafinesque's big-eared bats (*Corynorhinus rafinesquii*) and southeastern myotis (*Myotis austroriparius*). American Midland Naturalist. 160: 364-373.

Chung-MacCoubrey, A.L. 2003. Monitoring long-term reuse of trees by bats in pinyon-juniper woodlands of New Mexico. Wildlife Society Bulletin. 31: 73-79.

Clark, M.K. 1990. Roosting ecology of the eastern big-eared bat, *Plecotus rafinesquii*, in North Carolina. Raleigh, NC: North Carolina State University. 111 p. M.S. thesis.

Coleman, M.D.; Coyle, D.R.; Blake, J. [and others]. 2004. Production of short-rotation woody crops grown with a range of nutrient and water availability: establishment report and first-year responses. Gen. Tech. Rep. SRS-72. Asheville, NC: U.S. Department of Agriculture Forest Service, Southern Research Station. 21 p.

Ellison, L.E.; O'Shea, T.J.; Neubaum, D.J; Bowen, R.A. 2007. Factors influencing movement probabilities of big brown bats (*Eptesicus fuscus*) in buildings. Ecological Applications. 17: 620-627.

Ferrara, F.J.; Leberg, P.L. 2005a. Characteristics of positions selected by day-roosting bats under bridges in Louisiana. Journal of Mammalogy. 86: 729-735.

Ferrara, F.J.; Leberg, P.L. 2005b. Influence of investigator disturbance and temporal variation on surveys of bats roosting under bridges. Wildlife Society Bulletin. 33: 1113-1122.

Gannon, W.L.; Sikes, R.S.; Animal Care and Use Committee of the American Society of Mammalogists. 2007. Guidelines of the American Society of Mammalogists for the use of wild animals in research. Journal of Mammalogy. 88: 809-823.

Gooding, G.; Langford, J.R. 2004. Characteristics of tree roosts of Rafinesque's big-eared bat and southeastern bat in northeastern Louisiana. Southwestern Naturalist. 49: 61-67.

Gumbert, M.W.; O'Keefe, J.M.; MacGregor, J.R. 2002. Roost-site fidelity in Indiana bats in Kentucky. In: Kurta, A.; Kennedy, J., eds. The Indiana bat: biology and management of an endangered species. Austin, TX: Bat Conservation International: 143-152.

Hein, C.D.; Castleberry, S.B.; Miller, K.V. 2005. Winter roost-site selection by Seminole bats in the lower Coastal Plain of South Carolina. Southeastern Naturalist. 4: 473-478.

Imm, D.W.; McLeod, K.W. 2005. Plant communities. In: Kilgo, J.C.; Blake, J.I., eds. Ecology and management of a forested landscape: fifty years on the Savannah River Site. Washington, DC: Island Press: 106-161.

Jones, C.; Suttkus, R.D. 1975. Notes on the natural history of *Plecotus rafinesquii*. Occas. Pap. of the Museum of Zoology, Louisiana State University. 47: 1-14.

Kalcounis-Rueppell, M.C.; Psyllakis, J.M.; Brigham, R.M. 2005. Tree roost selection by bats: an empirical synthesis using meta-analysis. Wildlife Society Bulletin. 33: 1123-1132.

Kerth, G.; Weissman, K.; König, B. 2001. Day roost selection in female Bechstein's bats (*Myotis bechsteinii*): a field experiment to determine the influence of roost temperature. Oecologia. 126: 1-9.

Kolka, R.K.; Jones, C.G.; McGee, B.; Nelson, E.A. 2005. Water resources. In: Kilgo, J.C.; Blake, J.I., eds. Ecology and management of a forested landscape. Washington, DC: Island Press: 41-56.

Kunz, T.H.; Lumsden, L.F. 2003. Ecology of cavity and foliage roosting bats. In: Kunz, T.H.; Fenton, M.B., eds. Bat ecology. Chicago: The University of Chicago Press: 3-89.

Kurta, A.; Murray, S.W. 2002. Philopatry and migration of banded Indiana bats (*Myotis sodalis*) and effects of radio transmitters. Journal of Mammalogy. 83: 585-589.

Lacki, M.J.; Baker, M.D. 2003. A prospective power analysis and review of habitat characteristics used in studies of tree-roosting bats. Acta Chiropterologica. 5:199-208.

Lance, R.F.; Hardcastle, B.T.; Talley, A.; Leberg, P.L. 2001. Day-roost selection by Rafinesque's big-eared bats (*Corynorhinus rafinesquii*) in Louisiana forests. Journal of Mammalogy. 82: 166-172.

Lewis, S.E. 1995. Roost fidelity of bats: a review. Journal of Mammalogy. 76: 481-496.

Littell, R.C.; Henry, P.R.; Ammerman, C.B. 1998. Statistical analysis of repeated measures data using SAS procedures. Journal of Animal Science. 76: 1216-1231.

Lučan, R.K.; Hanák, V.; Horáček, I. 2009. Long-term re-use of tree roosts by European forest bats. Forest Ecology and Management. 258: 1301-1306.

Mormann, B.M.; Robbins, L.W. 2007. Winter roosting ecology of eastern red bats in southwest Missouri. Journal of Wildlife Management. 71: 213-217.

Reckardt, K.; Kerth, G. 2007. Roost selection and roost switching of female Bechstein's bats (*Myotis bechsteinii*) as a strategy of parasite avoidance. Oecologia. 154: 581-588.

Rice, C.L. 2009. Roosting ecology of *Corynorhinus rafinesquii* (Rafinesque's big-eared bat) and *Myotis austroriparius* (southeastern myotis) in tree cavities found in a northeastern Louisiana bottomland hardwood forest streambed. Monroe, LA: University of Louisiana, Monroe. 123 p. M.S. thesis.

SAS Institute Inc. 2003. SAS onlineDoc® 9.1.3. Cary, NC: SAS Institute Inc. http://support.sas.com/onlinedoc/913/docMainpage.jsp. [Date accessed: November 10, 2010].

Schabenberger, O. 2005. Introducing the GLIMMIX procedure for generalized mixed models. Pap. 196-30, SUGI 30 Proceedings. Cary, NC: SAS Institute. http://www2.sas.com/proceedings/sugi30/196-30.pdf. [Date accessed: November 10, 2010].

Trousdale, A.W.; Beckett, D.C. 2004. Seasonal use of bridges by Rafinesque's big-eared bat, *Corynorhinus rafinesquii*, in southern Mississippi. Southeastern Naturalist. 3: 103-112.

Trousdale, A.W.; Beckett, D.C. 2005. Characteristics of tree roosts of Rafinesque's big-eared bat (*Corynorhinus rafinesquii*) in southeastern Mississippi. American Midland Naturalist. 154: 442-449.

Trousdale, A.W.; Beckett, D.C.; Hammond, S.L. 2008. Short-term roost fidelity of Rafinesque's big-eared bat (*Corynorhinus rafinesquii*) varies with habitat. Journal of Mammalogy. 89: 477-484.

White, D.L. 2005. Land-use history. In: Kilgo, J.C.; Blake, J.I., eds. Ecology and management of a forested landscape. Washington, DC: Island Press: 2-12.

Willis, C.K.R.; Brigham, R.M. 2005. Physiological and ecological aspects of roost selection by reproductive female hoary bats (*Lasiurus cinereus*). Journal of Mammalogy. 86: 85-94.

Willis, C.K.R.; Brigham, R.M. 2007. Social thermoregulation exerts more influence than microclimate on forest roost preferences by a cavity-dwelling bat. Behavioral Ecology and Sociobiology. 62: 97-108.

Willis, C.K.R.; Kolar, K.A.; Karst, A.L. [and others]. 2003. Medium- and long-term reuse of trembling aspen cavities as roosts by big brown bats (*Eptesicus fuscus*). Acta Chiropterologica. 5: 85-90.

Zarnoch, S.J. 2009. Testing hypotheses for differences between linear regression lines. E-Res. Note SRS-17. Asheville, NC: U.S. Department of Agriculture Forest Service, Southern Research Station. 16 p.

WINTER ROOSTING BEHAVIOR OF RAFINESQUE'S BIG-EARED BAT IN SOUTHWESTERN ARKANSAS

D. Blake Sasse, Nongame Mammal Program Coordinator, Arkansas Game and Fish Commission, 213A Highway 89 South, Mayflower AR 72106

David A. Saugey, Wildlife Biologist, U.S. Forest Service, 8607 Hwy 7 North, Jessieville, AR 71949

Daniel R. England, Professor of Biology, Southern Arkansas University, Box 253, Waldo, AR 71770

Abstract—We studied roosting behavior of Rafinesque's big-eared bats (*Corynorhinus rafinesquii*) using water wells (*n* = 37 sites) in southwestern Arkansas from October through March, 1988 to 2009. Wells were lined with concrete, brick, or stone with a mean interior diameter of 74 cm (range: 51 to 78 cm). Most wells were used by < 20 bats, with colonies of > 40 bats observed in December, January, and February. Wells were used most often by females; however, as more bats moved to the wells in midwinter, sex ratios of bats in colonies tended toward a 50 to 50 ratio. Observed mass of Rafinesque's big-eared bats was 9.6 g for females and 9.1 g for males, with females significantly heavier than males (*P* < 0.001). Mass increased for both sexes from October to November, declined in December, January, and February, then increased again in March (*P* = 0.026). Rafinesque's big-eared bats were observed on 26 occasions to share wells with 1 to 12 southeastern bats (*Myotis austroriparius*) and were found roosting in a single well with 1 to 3 tri-colored bats (*Perimyotis subflavus*) 3 times. The number of wells available to Rafinesque's big-eared bats for roosting decreased during the 21 years of study, as did the maximum winter colony size at 7 of 15 wells (46.6 percent), indicating that the abundance and distribution of Rafinesque's big-eared bats in this region may be declining.

INTRODUCTION

Rafinesque's big-eared bat (*Corynorhinus rafinesquii*) has been documented from 42 of 75 Arkansas counties in the Mississippi River Alluvial Plain (commonly referred to as the Delta), the west Gulf Coastal Plain, and the Arkansas River Valley; the latter is a relatively narrow strip of land bordered to the south by the Ouachita Mountains and to the north by the Ozark Mountains (Fokidis and others 2005, Medlin and others 2006, Sasse and Saugey 2008). Historically these lowland areas were vegetated by bottomland hardwood forests where large hollow trees provided bat roosting sites that afforded protection from predators and provided stable internal environmental conditions. Changes in land use resulting in the draining of wetlands and the harvesting of potential roost trees have required Rafinesque's big-eared bats to switch to humanmade structures for maternity sites, where bats use larger open spaces such as attics and rooms for roosting (Clark 1990). Abandoned houses and outbuildings, however, have relatively short life spans, often deteriorating quickly after sustaining roof damage, and are not reliable as maternity sites from year to year. In Arkansas, abandoned humanmade structures are usually associated with hand-dug water wells which are lined with concrete tile, brick, or stonework resulting in stable, long-lived structures that are commonly used by bats for winter hibernation (Blair 1939, England and Saugey 1999, Lowery 1974, Saugey and others 1993, Tumlison and others 1992). We present data suggesting that water wells have allowed Rafinesque's big-eared bats to persist throughout their range in Arkansas, despite conversion of most of the surrounding forested habitat and loss of natural tree roosts. In this paper we review over 20 years of data on use of water wells as winter roosting sites by Rafinesque's big-eared bats in southwestern Arkansas and discuss the importance of these wells in sustaining populations of this species in this region.

METHODS

The study took place in Clark, Columbia, Lafayette, Nevada, Ouachita, and Sevier Counties in southwestern Arkansas, within the Tertiary Uplands of the southcentral Plains. Tertiary Upland sites are dominated by commercial shortleaf and loblolly pine plantations (*Pinus echinata* and *P. taeda*) that have replaced native oak-hickory-pine (*Quercus* spp.-*Carya* spp.) forests except in narrow streamside zones. Forested tracts are interspersed with bayous and pasture for grazing cattle. Most of the large bottomland hardwood timber has been harvested at least once, with the majority of these acres converted to other resource areas.

Because it was unclear how long wells would remain intact, we chose to survey for bats during the hibernation period when disturbance is normally to be avoided but when bats were most likely to be present for survey. Loss of structures used during the maternity period and a shortage of natural roosts such as large hollow trees suggested that local extirpation of populations in affected areas was possible, so we operated under the supposition that acquisition of winter natural history information was warranted because so little was known about Rafinesque's big-eared bats in Arkansas.

We located wells by searching old home sites, often identified by large, residual, hardwood shade trees in areas

Citation for proceedings: Loeb, Susan C.; Lacki, Michael J.; Miller, Darren A., eds. 2011. Conservation and management of eastern big-eared bats: a symposium. Gen. Tech. Rep. SRS-145. Asheville, NC: U.S. Department of Agriculture, Forest Service, Southern Research Station. 157 p.

revegetated with pine plantations. Thirty-seven wells were identified in six counties as used by Rafinesque's big-eared bats during winter months from 1988 to 2009. We were able to record interior dimensions and lining materials for only 15 of these wells, as these measurements were not taken until late in the study and access to some wells was either no longer permitted or the wells had been destroyed. Wells were surveyed for use by bats irregularly when personnel were available and when the low temperature during the previous evening was < 4.4 °C. Thus, the number of wells visited each season and the number of times each well was surveyed within a season varied considerably.

We recorded the total number of bats captured or visually counted at each visit. We captured bats from within wells using a device manufactured from a standard umbrella fitted with two control cords, two hardened edges, and from which the lock latch, normally used to maintain the umbrella in a rigid open position, was removed (fig. 1). The device was maneuvered underneath bats, and the hardened edges were used to gently lift bats off the wall of the well where they dropped into the umbrella (England and Saugey 1999). We recorded sex, age, body mass (g), reproductive condition, and left forearm length (mm) of each bat captured. We banded a subset of bats to assess fidelity to hibernation sites, movement patterns among sites, and association with maternity roosts. We released all bats back into the well once they had fully aroused and were capable of flight. Variation in body mass between the sexes and

among months of sampling was tested using a two-way analysis of variance.

We used roosts containing ≥ 10 Rafinesque's big-eared bats in calculating sex ratios of surveyed colonies. We estimated occupancy rates for all wells and for the 17 wells surveyed with a history of supporting ≥ 10 bats. We computed minimum winter colony size for 22 wells from 1990 to 1996, based on the number of individual bats captured and banded at each site during the winter, and compared these data using linear regression analysis to the maximum number of bats captured or observed during any single survey at these wells during winter sampling. Trends in maximum winter population counts from 1991 to 2009 at 15 wells with ≥ 4 years of data were analyzed using a Mann-Kendall nonparametric test. This nonparametric statistical method is based upon annual positive or negative changes in population size and is useful when assumptions required for analysis using regression techniques cannot be met. This test determines whether the population is increasing or decreasing and does not take into account the magnitude of change (Hollander and Wolfe 1973, Thompson and others 1998).

RESULTS

We located water wells on upland sites in hardwood or pine-hardwood stands and in the vicinity of small to midsized streams; wells were generally not adjacent to any large

Figure 1—Photograph of the sampling method used to extract bats from within water wells in southwestern Arkansas. (Photo by David A. Saugey)

Table 1—Monthly trends in occupancy rate, maximum bat counts, sex ratios, and mean body mass of Rafinesque's big-eared bats using water wells as roosting sites in southwestern Arkansas, 1988 to 2009

	October	November	December	January	February	March
Occupancy rate						
All wells						
Percent	94	100	94	97	92	86
N	31	40	88	78	65	73
Of colonies consisting of >10 bats at wells known to contain large colonies						
Percent	24	33	38	45	39	31
N	29	33	66	56	51	49
Maximum count						
n	50	38	89	88	103	65
N	31	50	128	92	76	73
Percent female in large colonies (>10 bats)						
Percent	67	54	50	45	70	60
SD	NA	13	14	11	19	33
N	1	7	16	15	12	10
Mass (g)						
Females						
Mean	9.25	10.63	10.32	9.28	8.91	8.96
SE	0.08	0.07	0.05	0.05	0.04	0.05
N	124	169	297	326	264	116
Males						
Mean	8.69	9.77	9.63	8.81	8.19	8.41
SE	0.09	0.08	0.05	0.06	0.06	0.09
N	90	130	278	289	126	48

N = sample size; SD = standard deviation; NA = not applicable; SE = standard error.

tracts of bottomland hardwood forest. We found wells that contained bats were lined with concrete, brick, or stone— surfaces that provided good roosting substrates. Twelve wells were constructed of round concrete segments with a mean internal diameter of 72 cm (range: 51 to 78 cm), 2 brick-lined wells were 77 and 83 cm in diameter, and 1 stone-lined well was 86 cm in diameter. The mean internal diameter of all wells we measured was 74 cm (SE = 2.1). A single well without lining was also used by Rafinesque's big-eared bats, but we were unable to measure the internal dimensions. Wells lined with ceramic tiles had very smooth surfaces and were not used by bats.

Observed mass of Rafinesque's big-eared bats was 9.6 g (SE = 0.03) for females (n = 1,296) and 9.1 g (SE = 0.03) for males (n = 961), with females heavier than males (F = 234, P < 0.001). Mass increased for both sexes from October to November; declined in December, January, and February; and increased again in March (F = 2.55, P = 0.026) (table 1). We found sex ratios of colonies of bats during winter surveys (n = 61) varied by size of colony and month of sampling, with males becoming a larger proportion of colonies as winter progressed, only to decline again with the approach of spring. We found large colonies with > 40 bats to have more equal sex ratios compared to smaller colonies; 10 of 12 (83 percent) of these large colonies were observed in the months of December or January. The maximum count of Rafinesque's big-eared bats at the majority (57 percent) of wells was < 20 bats, with 24 percent of wells supporting a maximum count of 21 to 39 bats, and only 19 percent of wells used by ≥ 40 bats.

The largest bat count ($n = 103$) we observed at any individual colony was on February 13, 2006, followed closely by maximum counts in December ($n = 89$) and January ($n = 88$). Wells with a history of use by Rafinesque's big-eared bats were occupied by at least one bat 86 to 100 percent of the time during winter months. However, wells with a history of supporting ≥ 10 bats were occupied by groups of ≥ 10 bats on only 24 to 45 percent of surveys, with the greatest likelihood of encountering larger colony sizes in January (table 1).

We found the total number of Rafinesque's big-eared bats known to use a well each winter, based on bat banding events, to be linearly associated with the maximum number of bats observed in the well on any one survey ($F = 564$; $P = < 0.001$; $R^2 = 0.90$) (fig. 2). Seven of fifteen (47 percent) wells we surveyed for at least 4 years had decreasing trends in maximum annual population counts; the remainder showed no trend. Of the seven wells surveyed for at least 10 years, three (43 percent) had decreasing trends in maximum population counts. The remainder showed no trend. Four (11 percent) wells used by Rafinesque's big-eared bats were destroyed during the survey period, and we suspected other wells were also destroyed, but landowner permission to access was not granted in recent survey years to determine their status. Abandoned buildings, also serving as maternity sites of Rafinesque's big-eared bats wintering in three of the wells studied, were destroyed late in the study possibly impacting the trends observed.

We observed Rafinesque's big-eared bats roosting in wells during the winter months with two other bat species. We found southeastern bats (*Myotis austroriparius*) roosting with Rafinesque's big-eared bats on 26 occasions. Sixteen of the occurrences of joint use by southeastern and Rafinesque's big-eared bats were observed in a single well where 1 to 12 southeastern bats were seen. Six southeastern bats were in another well that was occupied by the largest group ($n = 103$) of Rafinesque's big-eared bats observed during the study. Joint use was seen in nine other wells but only one or two southeastern bats were observed on these surveys. A single well was used by Rafinesque's big-eared bats and tri-colored bats (*Perimyotis subflavus*) on three occasions with one

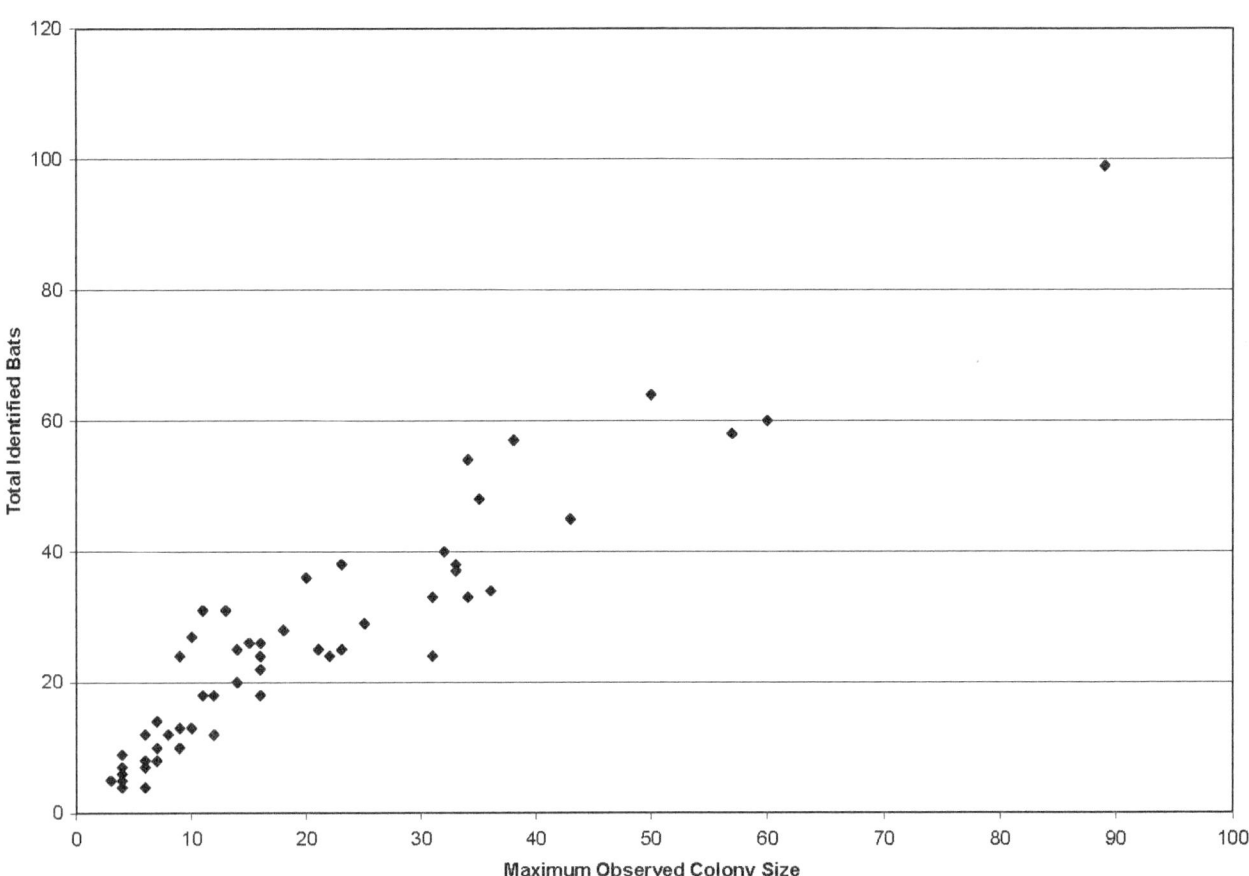

Figure 2—Relationship of winter maximum observed population counts of Rafinesque's big-eared bats to the minimum number of banded bats known to use water wells in southwestern Arkansas, 1990 to 1996.

bat observed on two occasions and three bats observed on another visit.

DISCUSSION

Because water wells are primarily associated with human dwellings, it is not surprising that wells in this study were found in upland areas where houses are more likely to be built rather than in flood plain forests typically associated with natural roosting sites of Rafinesque's big-eared bats. Rafinesque's big-eared bats are often found roosting in abandoned houses in upland sites during summer months (Clark 1990, Mirowsky and others 2004), and males in South Carolina have been found foraging primarily in young pine stands in areas separate from extensive bottomland hardwood forest (Menzel and others 2001).

Mean monthly body mass of male and female Rafinesque's big-eared bats was slightly higher than that observed in Mississippi, and lower than values reported for these bats in Louisiana, though the sample sizes in both studies were considerably smaller than in our study and did not reflect body condition of bats throughout the winter months (Jones and Suttkus 1975, Rice 2009). Nevertheless, our values are within the range expected in Arkansas and elsewhere throughout the distribution of the species (Jones 1977, Sealander and Heidt 1990).

Prior to our study the only extensive report on winter use of water wells by Rafinesque's big-eared bats was a cistern near Reelfoot Lake in western Tennessee (Hoffmeister and Goodpaster 1962). Though built of brick and stone, the inner face of the cistern was covered with cement, and bats were observed in it during the months of February, March, April, May, and September. Population counts ranged from 1 to 64 bats and, similar to our study, banding and population count data indicated significant movement among roosting sites during winter months (Hoffmeister and Goodpaster 1962). The interior dimensions of the Tennessee cistern were not reported, but a diagram indicates the inside diameter was probably much larger than wells in our study, though the entrance may have been of similar width (Hoffmeister and Goodpaster 1962). Other occurrences of this species in wells have been of individuals or small groups (Baker and Ward 1967, Blair 1939, Caire and others 1989, Steward and others 1986, Tumlison and others 1992). Stevenson (2008) examined the interior dimensions of Rafinesque's big-eared bat roost trees and found that they averaged only 40 cm in width, much less than the water wells used by Rafinesque's big-eared bats in our study.

The increase in colony size and trend towards more equal sex ratios in midwinter indicates that during the early and late winter, male Rafinesque's big-eared bats are more likely to use alternate roosting sites and do not move into wells until the coldest period of winter. We suggest that male Rafinesque's big-eared bats may be more tolerant of colder weather than females. Trousdale and Beckett (2004) often found solitary males roosting underneath bridges during the winter months in southern Mississippi. A colony of Rafinesque's big-eared bats that roosted underneath ammunition bunkers in Louisiana was primarily comprised of males during winter months, though the small numbers of bats observed in these structures suggests that this complex may not have been conducive to the formation of large winter colonies (Jones and Suttkus 1975).

The percentage of surveys where large colonies (> 10 bats) were observed in wells in our study (24 percent) was similar to the winter occupancy rates of tree cavities in Louisiana where only 18 percent of surveys found > 10 Rafinesque's big-eared bats from November through February (Rice 2009). In Mississippi, 6 of 14 (43 percent) trees used by Rafinesque's big-eared bats during the winter were used by > 5 bats (Stevenson 2008). The strong relationship between the total number of bats known to use a well throughout the winter, based on banding data, and the highest bat count observed in winter indicates that population trends at wells can be monitored using visual counts without the need to capture bats during the coldest winter months (December, January, and February) when populations of Rafinesque's big-eared bats in wells are usually highest. We hypothesize that water wells provide warm refugia during extreme cold weather, but data on internal and external temperatures associated with use of these wells by bats is needed to develop efficient long-term monitoring techniques.

Results of our surveys are consistent with data reported elsewhere that demonstrate Rafinesque's big-eared bats often cohabit roosting sites with southeastern bats and tri-colored bats in natural roosts, particularly live trees (Carver and Ashley 2008, Rice 2009, Stevenson 2008). This overlap in roosting preferences may confer an advantage in developing management strategies for roosting sites of these three species of bats in Southern U.S. forests.

The closure of old water wells will remain a management issue for Rafinesque's big-eared bats as many sites constitute pitfall dangers to humans and animals, particularly when the uppermost portion of the well casing is at or near ground level. This potential danger, along with concerns about potential impacts on water quality from using old wells as dump sites that could introduce pollution into the ground water, has resulted in the promulgation of State regulations requiring the closure of abandoned water wells as seen in our study. For Rafinesque's big-eared bats this is unfortunate because wells appear to constitute important winter habitat, especially in areas devoid of large cavity trees, caves, mines, or other suitable winter roosting sites. The loss of wells previously known to be roosting sites of Rafinesque's big-eared bats, coupled with the declining trend in maximum winter bat counts at remaining wells, indicates that this species may have difficulty maintaining population numbers across its distribution in Arkansas, at least outside of the remaining fragments of bottomland hardwood forest.

LITERATURE CITED

Baker, R.J.; Ward, C.W. 1967. Distribution of bats in southeastern Arkansas. Journal of Mammalogy. 48: 130-132.

Blair, W.F. 1939. Faunal relationships and geographic distribution of mammals in Oklahoma. American Midland Naturalist. 22: 85-133.

Caire, W.; Tyler, J.D.; Glass, B.P. [and others]. 1989. Mammals of Oklahoma. Norman, OK: University of Oklahoma Press. 567 p.

Carver, B.D.; Ashley, N. 2008. Roost tree use by sympatric Rafinesque's big-eared bats (*Corynorhinus rafinesquii*) and southeastern myotis (*Myotis austroriparius*). American Midland Naturalist. 160: 364-373.

Clark, M.A. 1990. Roosting ecology of the eastern big-eared bat, *Plecotus rafinesquii*, in North Carolina. Raleigh, NC: North Carolina State University. 112 p. M.S. thesis.

England, D.R.; Saugey, D.A. 1999. A safe and effective method to remove bats from abandoned water wells. Bat Research News. 40: 38-39.

Fokidis, H.B.; Brandebura, S.C.; Risch, T.S. 2005. Distribution of bats in bottomland hardwood forests of the Arkansas delta region. Journal of the Arkansas Academy of Science. 59: 51-56.

Hoffmeister, D.F.; Goodpaster, W.W. 1962. Observations on a colony of big-eared bats, *Plecotus rafinesquii*. Transactions of the Illinois State Academy of Science. 55: 87-89.

Hollander, M.; Wolfe, D.A. 1973. Nonparametric statistical methods. New York: John Wiley. 503 p.

Jones, C. 1977. *Plecotus rafinesquii*. Mammalian Species. 69: 1-4.

Jones, C.; Suttkus, R.D. 1975. Notes on the natural history of *Plecotus rafinesquii*. Occas. Pap. of the Museum of Zoology, Louisiana State University. 47: 1-13.

Lowery, G.H., Jr. 1974. The mammals of Louisiana and its adjacent waters. Baton Rouge, LA: Louisiana State University Press. 565 p.

Medlin, R.E., Jr.; Brandebura, S.C.; Fokidis, H.B.; Risch, T.S. 2006. Distribution of Arkansas's bottomland bats. Journal of the Arkansas Academy of Science. 60: 189-191.

Menzel, M.A.; Menzel, J.M.; Ford, W.M. [and others]. 2001. Home range and habitat use of male Rafinesque's big-eared bats (*Corynorhinus rafinesquii*). American Midland Naturalist. 145: 402-408.

Mirowsky, K.; Horner, P.A.; Maxey, R.W.; Smith, S.A. 2004. Distributional records and roosts of southeastern myotis and Rafinesque's big-eared bat in eastern Texas. Southwestern Naturalist. 49: 294-298.

Rice, C.L. 2009. Roosting ecology of *Corynorhinus rafinesquii* (Rafinesque's big-eared bat) and *Myotis austroriparius* (southeastern myotis) in tree cavities found in a northeastern Louisiana bottomland hardwood forest streambed. Monroe, LA: University of Louisiana at Monroe. 117 p. M.S. thesis.

Sasse, D.B.; Saugey, D.A. 2008. Rabies prevalence among and new distribution records of Arkansas bats. Journal of the Arkansas Academy of Science. 62: 159-160.

Saugey, D.A.; England, D.R.; Chandler-Mozisek, L.R. [and others]. 1993. Arkansas range extensions of the eastern small-footed bat, and northern long-eared bat and additional county records for the silver-haired bat, hoary bat, southeastern bat, and Rafinesque's big-eared bat. Proceedings of the Arkansas Academy of Science. 47: 102-106.

Sealander, J.A.; Heidt, G.A. 1990. Arkansas mammals: their natural history, classification, and distribution. Fayetteville, AR: University of Arkansas Press. 308 p.

Stevenson, C.L. 2008. Availability and seasonal use of diurnal roosts by Rafinesque's big-eared bat and southeastern myotis in bottomland hardwoods of Mississippi. Starkville, MS: Mississippi State University. 109 p. M.S. thesis.

Steward, T.W.; McDaniel, V.R.; England, D.R. 1986. Additional records of distribution and hosts for the bat bug, *Cimex pilosellus*, in Arkansas. Proceedings of the Arkansas Academy of Science. 40: 95-96.

Thompson, W.L.; White, G.C.; Gowan, C. 1998. Monitoring vertebrate populations. San Diego: Academic Press. 365 p.

Trousdale, A.W.; Beckett, D.C. 2004. Seasonal use of bridges by Rafinesque's big-eared bat, *Corynorhinus rafinesquii*, in Mississippi. Southeastern Naturalist. 3: 103-112.

Tumlison, R.; Karnes, M.; Clark, M. 1992. New records of vertebrates in southwestern Arkansas. Proceedings of the Arkansas Academy of Science. 46: 109-111.

FORAGING AND ROOSTING ECOLOGY OF RAFINESQUE'S BIG-EARED BAT AT THE NORTHERN EDGE OF THE RANGE

Joseph S. Johnson, Research Associate, University of Kentucky, Department of Forestry, Lexington, KY 40546

Michael J. Lacki, Professor, University of Kentucky, Department of Forestry, Lexington, KY 40546

Abstract—Limited data exist on foraging and roosting habits of Rafinesque's big-eared bat (*Corynorhinus rafinesquii*) at the northern edge of the species' range, where habitat use may differ from that reported for southern portions of the distribution. To provide land managers with regional data on habitat use of Rafinesque's big-eared bat, we radio-tagged 15 adult bats to document diurnal and nocturnal habitat use in western Kentucky during June and July 2009. We tracked 12 females (7 lactating, 5 postlactating) and 2 males to 35 day roosts, including 29 baldcypress (*Taxodium distichum*), 4 water tupelo (*Nyssa aquatica*), 1 sweetgum (*Liquidambar styraciflua*), and 1 concrete bridge. Roost trees consisted of a basal entrance to the roost cavity ($n = 2$, 5.9 percent), a basal and top entrance ($n = 15$, 44.1 percent), a top entrance ($n = 14$, 41.2 percent), and entrances located in the mid-section of the bole ($n = 3$, 8.8 percent). Males switched roosts every 1.3 ± 0.04 days, lactating females every 2.2 ± 0.3 days, and postlactating females every 2.7 ± 0.7 days. Home range estimates did not differ between lactating (178.5 ± 103.4 ha, $n = 6$) and postlactating females (231.7 ± 66.7 ha, $n = 6$; $P = 0.17$). Second-order habitat use by females ($n = 11$) was nonrandom ($P < 0.001$), with home ranges closest to forested and herbaceous wetlands and upland deciduous forests and farthest from agriculture and open fields. Third-order habitat use for females ($n = 11$) did not differ from random ($P = 0.47$). Our data indicate importance of a variety of roost types, wetlands, and upland forests to Rafinesque's big-eared bat in western Kentucky.

INTRODUCTION

Studies examining foraging and roosting habits of North American bat species have increased in the past two decades in response to technological advancements in miniature radio transmitters and ultrasonic bat detectors (Barclay and Kurta 2007, Lacki and others 2007). While much has been learned of the diet, nocturnal habitat use, and day-roosting habits of North American bats, research suggests that these behaviors can vary geographically within species (Lacki and others 2010), highlighting the need for regional studies examining requirements and preference for each species. Rafinesque's big-eared bat (*Corynorhinus rafinesquii*) is considered vulnerable throughout its range (NatureServe 2010) and has been the focus of several studies aimed at identifying habitat features important to day roosting. However, most of this research has investigated day roosting in the southern portion of the range (Bennett and others 2008; Clark 1990; Clark and others 1998; Cochran 1999; Gooding and Langford 2004; Lance and others 2001; Mirowsky and others 2004; Rice 2009; Stevenson 2008; Trousdale and Beckett 2004, 2005; Trousdale and others 2008) with few studies (Carver and Ashley 2008, Hurst and Lacki 1999) conducted near the northern edge of the range.

While day-roosting habitat of Rafinesque's big-eared bat has received attention, only three studies have collected data on home range or nocturnal habitat use (Clark and others 1998, Hurst and Lacki 1999, Menzel and others 2001), and no study has examined diurnal and nocturnal habitat use concurrently. Further, the only published data on nocturnal habits of the species were collected in upland forests (Hurst and Lacki 1999, Menzel and others 2001) where habitat types differ from those available in bottomland hardwood forests. Nocturnal habitat use by bats is driven by prey availability and structure and composition of habitats (Hayes and Loeb 2007, Lacki and others 2007). Thus, even though dietary studies have shown Rafinesque's big-eared bat to be a moth specialist (Hurst and Lacki 1997, Lacki and LaDeur 2001, Lacki and others 2007), it is not known whether habitat structure or moth availability imparts a larger influence on nocturnal habitat use in this species. The goal of our study was to examine foraging and roosting habits of adult female and male Rafinesque's big-eared bats in a landscape dominated by bottomland hardwood forests in western Kentucky.

MATERIALS AND METHODS

Study Area

Our study took place on Ballard and Boatwright Wildlife Management Areas (WMAs) in Ballard County, KY (37.091°N, 89.091°W). The management areas were part of the Ohio River flood plain and contain more than 8 000 ha of seasonally flooded forests, lakes, and agricultural land. The WMAs consist of several disconnected land parcels distributed across the western edge of Ballard County. Dominant tree species include baldcypress, water tupelo,

Citation for proceedings: Loeb, Susan C.; Lacki, Michael J.; Miller, Darren A., eds. 2011. Conservation and management of eastern big-eared bats: a symposium. Gen. Tech. Rep. SRS-145. Asheville, NC: U.S. Department of Agriculture, Forest Service, Southern Research Station. 157 p.

oak species (*Quercus* spp.), and hickories (*Carya* spp.). Topography is predominantly flat and ranges from 280 to 350 m asl. Mean monthly rainfall in the area is 8.5 to 13.4 cm between April and September (National Oceanic and Atmospheric Administration 2002). Mean monthly temperatures measured with HOBO data loggers (model U23-002, Onset Computer Corp., Pocasset, MA) were 22.6 to 27.8 °C between June and September 2009.

Capture and Radio-tagging

We employed capture, handling, and radiotelemetry techniques consistent with the American Society of Mammalogists' guidelines (Gannon and others 2007) and approved by the University of Kentucky, Institutional Animal Care and Use Committee (IACUC no. A3336-01). We captured bats at 12 locations across 19 nights of sampling in 38-mm diameter polyester mist nets (Avinet, Inc., Dryden, NY) placed over forest roads, lake edges, in an old campground, and outside entrances to known Rafinesque's big-eared bat roost trees. Nets ranged in size from 2.6 to 7.8 m high and 2.6 to 18 m wide. We recorded age, sex, reproductive condition, body mass, and right forearm length for all bats. We aged bats as adult or juvenile by examining ephiphyseal-diaphyseal fusions (calcification) of long bones in the wing (Anthony 1988). We classified females as nonreproductive, pregnant, or lactating based on the presence of a fetus or teat condition (Racey 1988) and classified males as nonreproductive or scrotal based on swelling of the epididymides (Krutzsch 2000, Racey 1988). We fitted adult males and reproductive adult females with 0.42-g (model LB-2N or LB-2NT; Holohil Systems Ltd., Carp, Ontario, Canada) radio transmitters attached between the shoulder blades using surgical adhesive (Torbot Group, Inc., Cranston, RI). Radio-tagged bats were visually monitored after release to ensure their flight capabilities had not been noticeably affected, and briefly monitored with telemetry equipment to ensure that bats continued to fly after passing out of sight.

Day Roosting

We tracked radio-tagged bats to their day roosts each day using TRX-1000S telemetry receivers (Wildlife Materials, Inc., Murphysboro, IL) and three-element Yagi antennas (Advanced Telemetry Systems, Inc., Isanti, MN). We recorded day-roost locations using a Garmin 60CSx handheld Global Positioning System (Garmin International, Inc., Olathe, KS) and recorded a chronological account of each bat's day-roost locations. We examined roost switching using two methods: dividing number of roost days observed for individual bats by the number of times that bat switched roosts, i.e., length of continuous residency; and calculating roost diversity (H') for each individual (Trousdale and others 2008). Length of

continuous residency (days), roost diversity (H'), distances traveled between consecutive roosts, and distances between roosts and capture sites for lactating and postlactating females were compared using Wilcoxon tests (SAS Institute 2001), with all tests based on a significance level of 0.05. Males were not included in the analysis due to low sample size ($n = 2$), but mean values are reported.

We measured habitat characteristics of the roost tree and forested stands for each day-roost tree following Baker and Lacki (2006). Habitat characteristics of roost trees included tree species, diameter at breast height (d.b.h.) or above any basal swell, roost tree height, number of cavities, maximum cavity height inside the tree, minimum cavity height inside the tree, height of entrance to the main cavity, entrance dimension (length, width, and height), presence of basal cavity entrances, presence of a "top" cavity entrance (broken tree tops, hollow knots, or other cavities), presence of entrances along the tree bole (broken tree tops, hollow knots, or woodpecker cavities), dimensions of basal entrances, and whether or not the roost tree was alive or dead. Stand-level habitat characteristics included canopy height, canopy cover (percent), and distance to the nearest cavity tree. Distances were measured with meter tapes or laser rangefinders (Opti-Logic Corp., Tullahoma, TN) for distances > 25 m; heights were measured with a laser hypsometer (Opti-Logic Corp., Tullahoma, TN); diameters were measured with a d.b.h. tape (Forestry Suppliers, Inc., Jackson, MS), and canopy cover was visually estimated. Because many roost trees were in standing water, trees were measured in August when water level was near the summer minimum. Roost trees were categorized into roost types based on the location of entrances to the main cavity following Rice (2009), with the addition of a fourth roost type. Roost trees were classified as type I if possessing only a basal entrance to the main cavity, type II if possessing basal and top entrances, type III if possessing a top but not a basal entrance, and type IV if possessing only bole entrances to the main cavity. Habitat values for day roosts used by lactating and postlactating females were compared using Wilcoxon tests (SAS Institute 2001). Habitat values were also compared among the four roost types using Kruskal-Wallis tests; all tests were based on a significance level of 0.05. Day roosts used by males were not included in analysis due to low sample size of radio-tagged males ($n = 2$), but mean values are reported.

We counted the number of bats inhabiting each roost through emergence counts, visual inspection of trees with large basal openings, or by taking digital photographs of tree cavities when possible. Emergence counts were conducted from 15 minutes prior to sunset to ca. 1 hour after sunset with the assistance of night-vision goggles (ATN Corp., San Francisco, CA). We compared estimates of roosting bats among roost tree types based on the maximum count for each roost known to be used by reproductive females using Kruskal-Wallis tests, with tests based on a significance level of 0.05.

Home Range and Nocturnal Habitat Use

Nocturnal locations of radio-tagged bats were triangulated during the first 5 hours of the evening to generate home range estimates and analyze habitat use. Two field personnel communicating with hand-held radios took simultaneous bearings on radio-tagged bats at 2-minute intervals, following an individual bat for no more than five consecutive bearings (10 minutes) to reduce autocorrelation among locations (Swihart and Slade 1985). Because some bats foraged in the vicinity of their roost for the first hour after emergence and then flew several km to a different foraging area, we distributed tracking efforts for each bat as evenly as possible across the 5-hour period to ensure representation of all activity areas used during the tracking period. Because the study area was predominately flat, radio signals from transmitters were never detected from distances > 1 km from the signal source during daytime tracking efforts. As a result, personnel tracking bats at night could not establish permanent telemetry stations from which bearings could be taken on several bats throughout the night (Johnson and others 2007). Instead, personnel tracked bats from vehicles, moving to locations where a selected bat was known to forage to take bearings before shifting locations to track a new bat. We ensured that each bat could be located throughout the tracking period by following bats to various foraging areas as the night progressed. A dense network of roads in the study area facilitated this approach and allowed personnel to select temporary tracking stations situated close to the signal source, eliminating the need for a third person to ground truth estimated locations (Johnson and others 2007).

Bearings were triangulated in Locate III (Nams 2006) and imported into ArcView ver. 3.2 (Esri Corporation 1999). Triangulated locations were reviewed, and locations triangulated > 1 km away from either observer's location were discarded because daytime tracking efforts found this to be the maximum effective transmitter range in the local topography. Remaining locations were used to calculate 95-percent home ranges using the fixed kernel method (Seaman and Powell 1996, Seaman and others 1999), using least square cross-validation (Worton 1989) and the Animal Movement extension (Hooge and Eichenlaub 1997). Day-roost locations were used in home range calculations, with a roost used as a single location regardless of the number of days a bat occupied the roost. We determined the minimum number of nocturnal locations necessary to obtain stable home range estimates (Aebischer and others 1993) by calculating estimates for bats in five-location increments. We graphed the change in home range estimates and determined when the graph reached an asymptote or oscillated about the mean. The mean number of locations needed to stabilize home range estimates was used as the minimum number of locations required to include a home range estimate for further analysis. We compared 95-percent home range estimates for lactating and postlactating females using a Wilcoxon test (SAS Institute 2001) and a significance level of 0.05. Male home range was not analyzed due to low sample size ($n = 1$).

Nocturnal habitat use was analyzed at the second- and third-order levels defined by Johnson (1980) using the Euclidean distance method (Conner and Plowman 2001, Conner and others 2003). In this approach, second-order habitat use refers to placement of home ranges on the landscape, while third-order use refers to use of habitats within home ranges. We chose the Euclidean distance method because it inherently considers telemetry error in its calculations, takes patch size and shape into account, has a lower type I error rate, and does not require a defined study area for third-order analysis (Bingham and Brennan 2004, Conner and others 2003). For second-order analysis, we defined the study area by creating a minimum convex polygon surrounding all bat locations using the Animal Movement extension (Hooge and Eichenlaub 1997) and then buffering this polygon by the greatest distance any bat was observed traveling in a single night (4334 m). We selected five habitats for analysis based on the 2001 National Land Cover Database (NLCD, available at http://kygeonet.ky.gov, see Homer and others 2004): (1) forested and herbaceous wetlands (23.6 percent of study area), (2) upland deciduous forests (14.5 percent), (3) agricultural and open fields (45.9 percent), (4) edges of fields and upland forested areas, and (5) edges of lakes and forested wetlands. Lakes composed 12.9 percent of the study area; thus, we considered this habitat to be lake edge because habitat structure, including edges, has been shown to influence habitat use in big-eared bats, and because big-eared bats are less likely to forage over open water (Lacki and Dodd 2011). Developed areas were not included in the analysis because they composed a small portion of the study area (3.1 percent) and, thus, were likely to be found avoided in the analysis simply because these habitats were scarce on the landscape. We verified the NLCD by comparing habitat polygons to 2008 aerial photographs (http://kygeonet.ky.gov) and by driving and walking the study area. Only nocturnal locations of bats with the minimum number of locations to generate home range estimates were used for analysis. Due to low sample size of bats, we combined lactating and postlactating females for analysis. For second- and third-order analyses, mean distances of random and bat locations to available habitats were compared using a multiple analysis of variance to determine if use differed from random (SAS Institute 2001). Where habitat use was nonrandom, habitats were ranked from closest to farthest from bat locations using t-tests (SAS Institute 2001), with tests based on a significance level of 0.05 (Conner and Plowman 2001, Conner and others 2003).

RESULTS

We captured 23 adult (20 females, 2 males, and 1 of unknown sex) and 5 juvenile (4 females and 1 male) Rafinesque's big-eared bats between June 9 and July 10, 2009. We captured 61 percent (n = 17) over road corridors and in a forest gap created by an abandoned campground. The remaining 11 bats were captured emerging from 2 known roost trees. Females were already lactating at the time the first Rafinesque's big-eared bat was captured; the first volant juvenile was captured on July 1. We radio-tagged 13 adult females (8 lactating and 5 postlactating) and 2 adult male bats (1 with the epididymides beginning to swell and a second with no sign of swelling). Radio transmitters increased wing loading of radio-tagged bats by a maximum 4.9 percent [$\bar{x}$ = 4.4±0.1 (SE) percent] of body mass.

We successfully tracked 14 of 15 radio-tagged bats on 147 of 151 (97.4 percent) potential roost days before radio transmitters were shed ($\bar{x}$ = 10.8 ± 0.8 days). One lactating female was not relocated during the day despite radio signals being detected during evening foraging bouts. No difference was found in length of continuous residency (P = 0.75), roost diversity (P = 0.52), distances traveled between consecutive roosts (P = 0.19), and distances between roosts and capture sites (P = 0.52) for lactating and postlactating females (table 1).

Radio-tagged bats were tracked to 34 day-roost trees, consisting of tree cavities in 29 baldcypress, 4 water tupelo, and 1 sweetgum. One concrete bridge was regularly used by a radio-tagged male. Roost trees were located in flooded forests and along lake edges, with 30 of 34 tree roosts (88.2 percent) standing in 0.2 to 1.1 m of water at the time of discovery. Basal entrances often consisted of irregular cracks and fissures in the tree bole, and accurate measurements of basal openings could not be acquired on a consistent basis. Additionally, 15 (83.3 percent) of the roost trees with basal entrances were partially submerged in

water, further preventing accurate measurement of entrance dimensions. Twelve day roosts were used by more than one radio-tagged bat; three of which were used by both lactating and postlactating females and two by males and lactating females. No habitat characteristic differed among trees used by lactating and postlactating females (table 2). The majority of roost trees were type II (44.1 percent) and type III (41.2 percent) trees (table 3). Type II trees were shorter in height (KW = 8.3 df = 3, P = 0.04) than type I trees, reflecting that many type II trees had top entrances because of broken tree boles (minimum tree height was 4.7 m).

Roosting bats were counted during emergence on 21 roost days and by taking digital photographs on 77 roost days. While males were tracked to 2-day roosts known to be used by reproductive females, the maximum number of bats counted emerging from a roost while a male was known to be present was two. Roost counts ranged from 1 to 96, with colonies of ≥ 20 bats counted at all 4 roost types (table 4). No difference in maximum roost count was detected among roost types.

The minimum number required for home range estimates to stabilize was 26.3±2.1 locations. This minimum was collected for 11 females and 1 male bat ($\bar{x}$ = 42.1±2.8 locations) tracked during 3.3±0.30 nights. No difference was detected in home range estimates between lactating (178.5 ± 103.4 ha, range = 23.1 to 689) and postlactating (231.7±60.7 ha, range = 83.5 to 454) females (P = 0.17). The only male home range estimated was 8.1 ha. Second-order habitat use by females was nonrandom (Wilk's lambda = 0.003, F = 365, P < 0.001). Home ranges were closer to forested and herbaceous wetlands (t = 42.5, P < 0.001), upland deciduous forests (t = 19.3, P < 0.001), and edges of lakes and forested wetlands (t = 13.5, P < 0.0001) than expected, and farther from edges of fields and upland forests (t = 2.33, P = 0.04) and agriculture and open fields (t = 2.68, P = 0.02) than expected. Home ranges were composed of 52.7 percent

Table 1—Summary of roost-switching behaviors of Rafinesque's big-eared bats during June and July 2009, Ballard County, KY[a]

Roost-switching behaviors	Lactating females	Postlactating females	Males
Number of radio-tagged bats	7	5	2
Number of days tracked	11.3±1.3 (7–18)	9.6±1.0 (7–13)	12.0±3.0 (9–15)
Length of residency (days)	2.2±0.3 (1–6)	2.7±0.7 (1–8)	1.3±0.04 (1–8)
Roost diversity (H′)	0.62±0.09 (0.41–1.0)	0.53±0.10 (0.22–0.75)	0.91±0.09 (0.82–1.0)
Distance to next roost (m)	321±214 (15.1–3389)	655±178 (16.3–1107)	457±334 (69.0–1473)
Distance from capture site (m)	490±201 (60.4–3342)	570±167 (62.1–1139)	297±169 (65.2–1417)

[a] Data are presented as mean ± SE and range.

Table 2—Mean ± SE of habitat characteristics of day roosts of Rafinesque's big-eared bats during June and July 2009, Ballard County, KY

Habitat characteristics	Lactating female	Postlactating female	Male
Number of roost trees	24	10	5
Diameter (cm)	150.5±7.65	135.4±11.8	150.6±14.8
Tree height (m)	17.5±1.2	17.9±2.1	20.5±3.3
Tree height – canopy height (m)[a]	0.04±1.0	−0.9±2.3	−0.2±0.4
Canopy cover (percent)	27.7±5.4	26.5±8.8	20.0±9.1
Type I trees (percent of total)	0.0	10.0	20.0
Type II trees (percent of total)	41.7	60.0	40.0
Type III trees (percent of total)	45.8	20.0	40.0
Type IV trees (percent of total)	12.5	10.0	0.0
Alive (percent of total)	83.3	60.0	100.0
Cavity height (m)[b]	13.5±2.0	10.7±1.6	13.1±4.6
Number of cavity entrances	4.9±0.77	7.0±1.9	10.2±4.7
Distance to nearest cavity tree (m)	33.0±8.9	61.0±28.9	20.8±8.9

[a] Measure of the difference between the tree height and the height of the surrounding canopy.

[b] Cavity heights could not be measured for type III and type IV roosts, reducing sample sizes to 10 for lactating females, 8 for postlactating females, and 3 for males.

Table 3—Mean ± SE of habitat characteristics of day roosts of Rafinesque's big-eared bats by roost type during June and July 2009, Ballard County, KY

Habitat characteristics	Type I	Type II	Type III	Type IV
Number of roost trees	2	15	14	3
Diameter (cm)	98.2±9.6	137.9±7.2	155.5±11.5	159.3±10.6
Tree height (m)	29.7±2.5	16.1±1.5	17.7±1.3	22.9±3.3
Tree height – canopy height (m)	0.0±0.0	−2.9±1.7	1.5±1.2	4.4±3.4
Canopy cover (percent)	37.5±12.5	27.3±7.3	32.9±7.5	13.3±6.0
Alive (percent of total)	50.0	66.7	100	100
Cavity height (m)[a]	8.1±2.5	13.0±1.6	—	—
Number of cavity entrances	1.0±0.0	7.4±1.7	5.0±1.3	6.0±1.7
Distance to nearest cavity tree (m)	20.2±7.2	49.1±19.7	29.0±12.9	65.2±37.6

[a] Cavity heights could not be measured for type III and type IV roosts.

Table 4—Summary of roost counts at day roosts of Rafinesque's big-eared bats by roost type during June and July 2009, Ballard County, KY

Summary of roost counts	Type I	Type II	Type III	Type IV
Number of roosts counted	2	12	9	2
Total number of nights counted	37[a]	43	9	3
Mean number of bats	5.5	23.5	5.9	27.7
Maximum number of bats	25	96	20	33

[a] One male roost was counted 31 times, with a maximum count of 1 individual.

herbaceous and forested wetlands, 22.0 percent upland deciduous forests, 15.7 percent agriculture and open fields, 8.0 percent lakes, and 1.6 percent developed areas. Third-order habitat use by females did not differ from random (Wilk's lambda = 0.54, F = 1.0, P = 0.47).

DISCUSSION

Use of large tree hollows as day roosts by Rafinesque's big-eared bats in bottomland hardwood forests is well documented (Carver and Ashley 2008, Clark 1990, Gooding and Langford 2004, Lance and others 2001, Mirowsky and others 2004, Rice 2009, Stevenson 2008, Trousdale and Beckett 2005). Rafinesque's big-eared bats primarily day roosted in hollow baldcypress trees (85.3 percent of all tree roosts), similar to results from eastcentral Mississippi (Stevenson 2008) where baldcypress was among the most common tree species used despite constituting 4 percent of available cavity trees. In northeastern Louisiana, Rice (2009) found Rafinesque's big-eared bats roosting in only two baldcypress trees, but this represented 66.7 percent of available cypress trees. Other studies of Rafinesque's big-eared bats have reported roost trees consisting primarily of a single species, usually water tupelo (Carver and Ashley 2008, Gooding and Langford 2004, Rice 2009). Studies from eastcentral Mississippi (Stevenson 2008), southern Mississippi (Trousdale and Beckett 2005), and westcentral Louisiana (Lance and others 2001), however, found use of a wide variety of tree species as day roosts, including baldcypress, water tupelo, black tupelo (*N. sylvatica*), magnolia species (*Magnolia* spp.), sweetgum, oak species, American sycamore (*Platanus occidentalis*), and hickories.

While most studies have not compared roosts to random trees, the smallest mean diameter of roost trees of Rafinesque's big-eared bats reported is 79.4 cm (Trousdale and Beckett 2005) and is often > 100 cm (Carver and Ashley 2008, Gooding and Langford 2004, Rice 2009). Large diameter cavity trees may benefit Rafinesque's big-eared bats by providing large amounts of space for roosting bats, allowing for larger potential colony sizes, or may exhibit more favorable microclimates. Rice (2009) found that diameter and inside cavity height were positively correlated, with cavity height influencing the number of days roost trees were used. While we did not compare roost trees to random trees, the large overall mean diameter (146.5 cm) of roost trees located in this study supports previous research demonstrating the importance of large diameter trees. We did not measure cavity height for type III and type IV roost trees. Regardless, mean cavity height for type I and II roosts was greater than heights reported elsewhere, likely because our sample of day roosts consisted of a larger number of completely hollow cypress trees than were present in other studies (Rice 2009, Stevenson 2008). Additional work comparing used and unused trees is needed to determine if cavity height is significant in roost tree selection by Rafinesque's big-eared bats in western Kentucky.

Although we found limited tree species diversity in day roosts used by Rafinesque's big-eared bats, day roosts were diverse in terms of roost type. This is in agreement with two recent studies (Rice 2009, Trousdale and Beckett 2005) that had a larger focus on radiotelemetry than previous studies (Clark 1990, Gooding and Langford 2004, Mirowsky and others 2004). Rice (2009) documented a decrease in use of type I and II roosts from summer to winter and that these roost types had less stable microclimates during the summer and winter than type III roosts. Rice (2009) visually confirmed use of type III roosts during the summer through emergence counts and during winter using radiotelemetry, but variation in seasonal use of type III roosts was not quantified. Regardless, type III roosts were used exclusively by radio-tagged bats during an exceptionally cold period. Trousdale and Beckett (2005) also found use of 3 roost types during the summer months, locating 12 type IV roosts (85.7 percent), 1 type I roost (7.1 percent), and 1 (7.1 percent) tree with a basal and bole entrance (most similar to a type II roost). Not all telemetry studies have tracked Rafinesque's big-eared bats to a diversity of roost types. Carver and Ashley (2008) reported 96 percent (n = 24) of day roosts were type I trees; Lance and others (2001) reported 100 percent (n = 4) type I trees, and Stevenson (2008) reported only roosts with basal cavities (type I or II, n = 49).

Our data were limited to two summer months within 1 year, and it is uncertain whether or not seasonal variation in use of roost types exists or how these data compare to day roosting behavior of adult females during the remainder of the year. Additionally, the number of day roosts we located was limited, especially among type I and IV trees, while variability in habitat characteristics of trees within each roost type was often substantial. For example, type II trees ranged from 4.7 to 25.3 m in height, including trees with snapped tops above the surrounding canopy and old trees in advanced stages of deterioration. Thus, more research is needed to locate and characterize day-roost trees. Regardless, findings of Rice (2009) suggest that thermal properties of cavities differ among roost types and vary seasonally within roost types. Intuitively, thermal properties of cavities are likely influenced by the number and location of cavity entrances and that a diversity of roost types aids Rafinesque's big-eared bats in enduring variable environmental conditions throughout the year. Regardless, we recommend that future work examine not only seasonal variation in cavity temperatures among roost types but also focus on thermoregulatory strategies among sexes and reproductive classes of bats using these roost types.

Our observations of roost switching in Rafinesque's big-eared bats are similar to other findings from bottomland hardwood forests. In northeastern Louisiana, Rice (2009) found that radio-tagged females switched roosts every 2.8 days from September through November, similar to our results for lactating and postlactating females. In South Carolina, Lucas (2009) observed a lactating female and two juvenile males switching roosts every 1.3 days, while we observed lactating females switching every 2.2 days. Both Rice (2009) and Lucas (2009) reported males switching roosts less frequently, but our sample size for males was too small to compare to females. Trousdale and others (2008) reported switching every 2.6±2.0 days (pooling data from all bats), and Stevenson (2008) reported that 10 males and 4 females (ages and reproductive condition not reported) switched roosts an average of 3 times (range = 1 to 9) during tracking sessions. We observed a range and mean of distances traveled between sequential roosts similar to those reported by Trousdale and others (2008) ($\bar{x}$ = 573 ± 640 m, range = 120 to 4000) during the summer. Distances reported by Rice (2009) were somewhat smaller than our results, ranging from 0 to 778 m ($\bar{x}$ = 177) for males and 0 to 1726 m ($\bar{x}$ = 291) for females.

Our data represent the first published account of home range size and habitat use of Rafinesque's big-eared bats in bottomland hardwood forests. While we did not detect differences in the size of home ranges between lactating and postlactating females, our sample sizes were small, and we observed large variation in home range size. This variation indicates a larger sample size is necessary to accurately characterize home range sizes and to test for differences among sexes and reproductive classes; thus, our inability to detect differences should be treated with caution. Further, because no other data on home range sizes of Rafinesque's big-eared bats have been collected in bottomland hardwood forests, comparison with home range estimates from other

forested systems (Hurst and Lacki 1999, Menzel and others 2001) is of limited value.

We found that establishment of home ranges by reproductive female Rafinesque's big-eared bats was nonrandom and that they were located closest to forested and emergent wetlands and farthest from agriculture and open fields. These results are at least partly driven by the importance of forested wetlands for day roosting; Ballard and Boatwright WMAs provided these bats with an "island" of conserved bottomland hardwood forest in a largely agricultural landscape. Because home ranges consisted primarily of wetlands and upland deciduous forests, with agriculture and open fields comprising a small percent of home ranges, our results confirm that bats spent more time foraging in forested habitats than in agricultural habitats. Hurst and Lacki (1999) found these bats preferred to forage in oak and oak-hickory stands over other forested stands. Hurst and Lacki (1999) noted that more than half of noctuid moths in the genus *Catocala*, important prey items of Rafinesque's big-eared bats (Hurst and Lacki 1997), feed on oaks and hickories in their larval stages, suggesting a partial explanation for the selection of oak and oak-hickory stands for foraging by Rafinesque's big-eared bats. Additional studies of moth families commonly eaten by big-eared bats have found that the preferred prey species are more positively associated with riparian or upland forests than open habitats and forest edges (Burford and others 1999, Dodd and others 2008). Regardless, numerous studies have demonstrated the use of habitats with edges or vertical structure for foraging by *Corynorhinus* bats (reviewed in Lacki and Dodd 2011), including Rafinesque's big-eared bats (Hurst and Lacki 1999), suggesting some interplay between habitat use by a gleaning species of bat and predator avoidance by moths (Lacki and Dodd 2011). We suggest that Rafinesque's big-eared bats in western Kentucky concentrated their foraging efforts in and adjacent to wetland and upland deciduous forests in response to localized abundance of preferred moth prey in these habitats. Insect sampling and dietary analysis are needed to confirm this prediction and determine the potential role of other factors, such as structural benefits of foraging habitat, in nocturnal habitat use.

Our data highlight the importance of bottomland hardwood forests for foraging and roosting in Rafinesque's big-eared bats. While larger sample sizes for various sexes and reproductive classes and research earlier and later in the growing season are still needed, our data indicate that use of type III and IV day roosts during the summer is potentially underestimated in studies using cavity search methods and shows that open habitats, while used, are of lesser importance compared to upland and forested wetlands as foraging habitats. We recommend studies examine roost microclimates and thermoregulation throughout the year to elucidate the advantages, if any, of various roost types. We also encourage simultaneously examining diurnal and nocturnal behaviors of Rafinesque's big-eared bats to link use with availability and to make more sound recommendations on how to protect and enhance habitat for this species.

ACKNOWLEDGMENTS

Funding for this project was provided by the Kentucky Division of Fish and Wildlife Resources (KDFWR) and the University of Kentucky, College of Agriculture. We thank G. Langlois and D. Fraser for their hard work in the field. We also thank B. Slack, J. MacGregor, D. Baxley, and R. Colvis of the KDFWR for their help, without which this project would not have been possible. Protocols for handling and tracking bats were approved by the University of Kentucky, Institutional Animal Care and Use Committee (IACUC no. A3336-01). This investigation is connected with a project of the Kentucky Agricultural Experiment Station (KAES no. 10-09-044) and is published with the approval of the director.

LITERATURE CITED

Aebischer, N.J.; Robertson, P.A.; Kenward, R.E. 1993. Compositional analysis of habitat use from animal radio-tracking data. Ecology. 74: 1313-1325.

Anthony, E.L.P. 1988. Age determination in bats. In: Kunz, T.H., ed. Ecological and behavioral methods for the study of bats. Washington, DC: Smithsonian Institution Press: 47-58.

Baker, M.D.; Lacki, M.J. 2006. Day-roosting habitat of female long-legged myotis in ponderosa pine forests. Journal of Wildlife Management. 70: 207-215.

Barclay, R.M.R.; Kurta, A. 2007. Ecology and behavior of bats roosting in tree cavities and under bark. In: Lacki, M.J.; Hayes, J.P.; Kurta, A., eds. Bats in forests: conservation and management. Baltimore, MD: The Johns Hopkins University Press: 17-59.

Bennett, F.M.; Loeb, S.C.; Bunch, M.S.; Bowerman, W.W. 2008. Use and selection of bridges as day roosts by Rafinesque's big-eared bats. American Midland Naturalist. 160: 386-399.

Bingham, R.L.; Brennan, L.A. 2004. Comparison of type I error rates for statistical analyses of resource selection. Journal of Wildlife Management. 68: 206-212.

Burford, L.S.; Lacki, M.J.; Covell, C.V., Jr. 1999. Occurrence of moths among habitats in a mixed mesophytic forest: implications for management of forest bats. Forest Science. 45: 323-332.

Carver, B.D.; Ashley, N. 2008. Roost tree use by sympatric Rafinesque's big-eared bats (*Corynorhinus rafinesquii*) and

southeastern myotis (*Myotis austroriparius*). American Midland Naturalist. 160: 364-373.

Clark, M.K. 1990. Roosting ecology of the eastern big-eared bat, *Plecotus rafinesquii*, in North Carolina. Raleigh, NC: North Carolina State University. 121 p. M.S. thesis.

Clark, M.K.; Black, A.; Kiser, M. 1998. Roosting and foraging activities of *Corynorhinus rafinesquii* and *Myotis austroriparius* within the Francis Beidler Forest, South Carolina. Raleigh, NC: North Carolina Museum of Natural Sciences; draft report C7745.11. [Number of pages unknown.]

Cochran, S.M. 1999. Roosting and habitat use by Rafinesque's big-eared bat and other species in a bottomland hardwood forest ecosystem. Jonesboro, AR: Arkansas State University. 109 p. M.S. thesis.

Conner, L.M.; Plowman, B.W. 2001. Using Euclidean distances to assess nonrandom habitat use. In: Millspaugh, J.; Marzluff, J., eds. Radio telemetry and animal populations. San Diego: Academic Press: 275-290.

Conner, L.M.; Smith, M.D.; Burger, L.W. 2003. A comparison of distance-based and classification-based analyses of habitat use. Ecology. 84: 526-531.

Dodd, L.E.; Lacki, M.J.; Rieske, L.K. 2008. Variation in moth occurrence and implications for foraging habitat of Ozark big-eared bats. Forest Ecology and Management. 255: 3866-3872.

Esri Corporation. 1999. ArcView GIS. Version 3.2. Redlands, CA: Environmental Systems Research Institute, Inc.

Gannon, W.L.; Sikes, R.S.; Animal Care and Use Committee of the America Society of Mammalogists. 2007. Guidelines of the American Society of Mammalogists for the use of wild mammals in research. Journal of Mammalogy. 88: 809-823.

Gooding, G.; Langford, J.R. 2004. Characteristics of tree roosts of Rafinesque's big-eared bat and southeastern bat in northeastern Louisiana. Southwestern Naturalist. 49: 61-67.

Hayes, J.P.; Loeb, S.C. 2007. The influence of forest management on bats in North America. In: Lacki, M.J.; Hayes, J.P.; Kurta, A., eds. Bats in forests: conservation and management. Baltimore, MD: The Johns Hopkins University Press: 207-236.

Homer, C.; Huang, C.; Yang, L. [and others]. 2004. Development of a 2001 national land-cover database for the United States. Photogrammetric Engineering and Remote Sensing. 70: 829-840.

Hooge, P.N.; Eichenlaub, B. 1997. Animal Movement extension to ArcView. Version. 1.1. Anchorage, AK: U.S. Geological Survey, Alaska Science Center - Biological Science Office.

Hurst, T.E.; Lacki, M.J. 1997. Food habits of Rafinesque's big-eared bat in southeastern Kentucky. Journal of Mammalogy. 78: 525-528.

Hurst, T.E.; Lacki, M.J. 1999. Roost selection, population size and habitat use by a colony of Rafinesque's big-eared bats (*Corynorhinus rafinesquii*). American Midland Naturalist. 142: 363-371.

Johnson, D.H. 1980. The comparison of usage and availability measurements for evaluating resource preference. Ecology. 61: 65-71.

Johnson, J.S.; Lacki, M.J.; Baker, M.D. 2007. Foraging ecology of long-legged myotis (*Myotis volans*) in north-central Idaho. Journal of Mammalogy. 88: 1261-1270.

Krutzsch, P.H. 2000. Anatomy, physiology and cyclicity of the male reproductive tract. In: Crichton, E.G.; Krutzsch, P.H., eds. Reproductive biology of bats. London, United Kingdom: Academic Press: 91-137.

Lacki, M.J.; Amelon, S.K.; Baker, M.D. 2007. Foraging ecology of bats in forests. In: Lacki, M.J.; Hayes, J.P.; Kurta, A., eds. Bats in forests: conservation and management. Baltimore, MD: The Johns Hopkins University Press: 83-128.

Lacki, M.J.; Baker, M.D.; Johnson, J.S. 2010. Geographic variation in roost-site selection of long-legged myotis in the Pacific Northwest. Journal of Wildlife Management. 74: 1218-1228.

Lacki, M.J.; Dodd, L.E. 2011. Diet and foraging behavior of *Corynorhinus* in Eastern North America. In: Loeb, S.C.; Lacki, M.J.; Miller, D.A., eds. Conservation and management of eastern big-eared bats: a symposium. Gen. Tech. Rep. SRS-145. Asheville, NC: U.S. Department of Agriculture Forest Service, Southern Research Station: 39-52.

Lacki, M.J.; LaDeur, K.M. 2001. Seasonal use of lepidopteran prey by Rafinesque's big-eared bats (*Corynorhinus rafinesquii*). American Midland Naturalist. 145: 213-217.

Lance, R.F.; Hardcastle, B.T.; Talley, A.; Leberg, P.L. 2001. Day-roost selection by Rafinesque's big-eared bats (*Corynorhinus rafinesquii*) in Louisiana forests. Journal of Mammalogy. 82: 166-172.

Lucas, S.L. 2009. Roost selection by Rafinesque's big-eared bats (*Corynorhinus rafinesquii*) in Congaree National Park—a multiscale approach. Clemson, SC: Clemson University. 58 p. M.S. thesis.

Menzel, M.A.; Menzel, J.M.; Ford, W.M. [and others]. 2001. Home range and habitat use of male Rafinesque's big-eared bats (*Corynorhinus rafinesquii*). American Midland Naturalist. 145: 402-408.

Mirowsky, K.; Horner, P.A.; Maxey, R.W.; Smith, S.A. 2004. Distributional records and roosts of southeastern myotis and Rafinesque's big-eared bat in eastern Texas. Southwestern Naturalist. 49: 294-298.

Nams, V.O. 2006. Locate III user's guide. Tatamagouche, Nova Scotia, Canada: Pacer Computer Software.

National Oceanic and Atmospheric Administration. 2002. Monthly station normals of temperature, precipitation, and heating and cooling degree days 1971–2000: Kentucky. Asheville, NC. 25 p.

NatureServe. 2010. NatureServe explorer: an online encyclopedia of life [Web application]. Version 7.1. Arlington, VA: NatureServe. http://www.natureserve.org/explorer. [Date accessed: May 19, 2011].

Racey, P.A. 1988. Reproductive assessment in bats. In: Kunz, T.H., ed. Ecological and behavioral methods for the study of bats. Washington, DC: Smithsonian Institution Press: 31-45.

Rice, C.L. 2009. Roosting ecology of *Corynorhinus rafinesquii* (Rafinesque's big-eared bat) and *Myotis austroriparius* (southeastern myotis) in tree cavities found in a northeastern Louisiana bottomland hardwood forest streambed. Monroe, LA: University of Louisiana at Monroe. 137 p. M.S. thesis.

SAS Institute. 2001. SAS. Version 8. Cary, NC.

Seaman, D.E.; Millspaugh, J.J.; Kernohan, B.J. [and others]. 1999. Effects of sample size on kernel home range estimates. Journal of Wildlife Management. 63: 739-747.

Seaman, D.E.; Powell, R.A. 1996. An evaluation of the accuracy of kernel density estimators for home range analysis. Ecology. 77: 2075-2085.

Stevenson, C.L. 2008. Availability and seasonal use of diurnal roosts by Rafinesque's big-eared bat and southeastern myotis in bottomland hardwoods of Mississippi. Mississippi State, MS: Mississippi State University. 123 p. M.S. thesis.

Swihart, R.K.; Slade, N.A. 1985. Testing for independence of observations in animal movements. Ecology. 66: 1176-1184.

Trousdale, A.W.; Beckett, D.C. 2004. Seasonal use of bridges by Rafinesque's big-eared bat, *Corynorhinus rafinesquii*, in southern Mississippi. Southeastern Naturalist. 3: 103-112.

Trousdale, A.W.; Beckett, D.C. 2005. Characteristics of tree roosts of Rafinesque's big-eared bat (*Corynorhinus rafinesquii*) in southeastern Mississippi. American Midland Naturalist. 154: 442-449.

Trousdale, A.W.; Beckett, D.C.; Hammond, S.L. 2008. Short-term roost fidelity of Rafinesque's big-eared bat (*Corynorhinus rafinesquii*) varies with habitat. Journal of Mammalogy. 89: 477-484.

Worton, B.J. 1989. Kernel methods for estimating the utility distribution in home-range studies. Ecology. 70: 164-168.

RADIOTELEMETRY STUDIES OF FEMALE VIRGINIA BIG-EARED BATS (*CORYNORHINUS TOWNSENDII VIRGINIANUS*) IN PENDLETON COUNTY, WEST VIRGINIA

Craig W. Stihler, Wildlife Biologist, West Virginia Division of Natural Resources, Elkins, WV 26241

Abstract—Virginia big-eared bats (*Corynorhinus townsendii virginianus*) have benefited from the protection of important cave roosts, but understanding habitat use outside of caves will allow land managers to manage foraging habitats as well. Thus, I conducted a radiotelemetry study at Cave Mountain Cave, a maternity colony cave in Pendleton County, WV, between 1991 and 1998. Forty-five female *C. t. virginianus* were radio-tagged and tracked during four 2-week sessions from mid-May through late August. To minimize disturbance, only one session was conducted in any year. Bats were tracked from the time they left the roost in the evening until they returned to day roost in the cave the next morning. Bats traveled up to 11.3 km from the cave to forage and used a variety of habitats including deciduous forest, mixed deciduous/coniferous forest, old fields, hayfields, and corn fields. Foraging areas contained significantly more open habitat and had a greater habitat interspersion index (interspersion of open and forest habitats) than random plots. The bats often night roosted near foraging areas; most night roosts were buildings, but one State highway bridge was used during all four tracking sessions. To date, most conservation measures for this bat have focused on cave protection, but land managers can provide noncave habitats by maintaining a mosaic of forested and open habitats around cave roosts and retaining structures that provide night roosts.

INTRODUCTION

The Virginia big-eared bat (*Corynorhinus townsendii virginianus*) was one of two subspecies of *C. townsendii* listed as federally endangered in 1979 (U.S. Fish and Wildlife Service 1979). The listing package noted that increased disturbance of cave roosts from speleological recreation was resulting in population declines. In the early 1980s, most important *C. t. virginianus* caves in West Virginia were closed to recreational human traffic, either seasonally or year round, to reduce disturbance to maternity colonies and hibernating concentrations. Many of these caves were protected with fences or gates to control human entry. These management activities resulted in an increase in *C. t. virginianus* numbers in these caves (Stihler 2011).

In the late 1980s, biologists in Virginia and West Virginia began to determine the habitat needs of *C. t. virginianus* outside of their cave roosts. Of particular concern at the time was the continuing spread of the exotic gypsy moth (*Lymantria dispar*) into the range of *C. t. virginianus* in West Virginia and the potential impacts of both forest defoliation and gypsy moth control measures on the food base of *C. t. virginianus* which consists largely of moths (Dalton and others 1986, Lacki and Dodd 2011). Light-tagging studies were conducted cooperatively between these States to obtain information on foraging habitats and behaviors, but most of the bats were lost from sight shortly after release. In 1991, I initiated a radiotelemetry study in West Virginia to obtain better information on habitats used by *C. t. virginianus* during the summer and distances the bats traveled to forage from the cave roosts.

STUDY AREA AND METHODS

The study was located in the Ridge and Valley Province near the town of Upper Tract, Pendleton County, WV (fig. 1). The study area was centered on Cave Mountain Cave on Cave Mountain and included the area within an 11.3-km radius

Figure 1—Location of the *Corynorhinus townsendii virginianus* radiotelemetry study area centered on Cave Mountain Cave, Pendleton County, WV.

Citation for proceedings: Loeb, Susan C.; Lacki, Michael J.; Miller, Darren A., eds. 2011. Conservation and management of eastern big-eared bats: a symposium. Gen. Tech. Rep. SRS-145. Asheville, NC: U.S. Department of Agriculture, Forest Service, Southern Research Station. 157 p.

of the cave entrances, the greatest distance we tracked a bat from the cave. This area is east of, and in the rain shadow of, the Allegheny Front, the Eastern Continental Divide. The area around the cave is rugged and contains steep slopes and numerous rock outcrops. The study area was mostly second- or third-growth forests (82 percent forested) and was largely undeveloped (table 1). Forests in the study area were dominated by oaks (*Quercus* spp.), sometimes mixed with or dominated by pines (*Pinus* spp.) on ridge tops and dry slopes. Cove hardwood forests occurred in the ravines. The South Branch of the Potomac River and North Fork of the South Branch of the Potomac River ran through the study area; the flood plains of the rivers contained concentrations of agricultural lands, i.e., hayfields, row crops, and pasture. Cave Mountain Cave is within the Monongahela National Forest, and much of the study area was located within The Nature Conservancy's designated Smoke Hole Canyon-North Fork Mountain Bioreserve.

Cave Mountain Cave housed a maternity colony of > 600 *C. t. virginianus* during the summer and a small number of hibernating *C .t. virginianus* in the winter. The cave was gated and closed to human entry during the maternity period (April 1 to September 15). This cave has multiple entrances located in a limestone cliff approximately 128 m above the South Branch of the Potomac River.

Bats were tracked during four 14-night tracking sessions; to minimize disturbance to the colony, only one session was carried out in any year. The four sessions corresponded roughly to four life stages (table 2): (1) after the bats arrived at the maternity site, but before parturition; (2) early lactation; (3) late lactation; and (4) after young became volant and left the cave in the evening. Ten to fourteen bats were tracked each session; however, no more than eight bats

Table 1—Land cover type composition of the *Corynorhinus townsendii virginianus* radiotelemetry study area (401 ha) centered on Cave Mountain Cave, Pendleton County, WV

Land cover type	Study area
	percent
Deciduous forest	73.07
Mixed coniferous/deciduous forest	9.04
Agricultural/open	17.03
Urban	0.40
Open water	0.45
Wetlands	< 0.01
Total	100.00

Table 2—*Corynorhinus townsendii virginianus* radiotelemetry sessions conducted at Cave Mountain Cave, Pendleton County, WV, and number of bats tagged each session, 1991 to 1998

Session	Year	Dates	Total number of bats tagged
1	1991	May 13–June 1	10
2	1994	June 25–July 9	14
3	1992	July 11–July 25	10
4	1998	August 9–August 22	11

were tracked at any time. Because only a small amount of adhesive was used in an attempt to minimize weight and to allow the transmitters to fall off the bats after a relatively short time, some of the transmitters remained on the bats only a few days. Transmitter loss in August seemed to be related to hair loss associated with molting. When this occurred, additional bats were captured during a second trapping effort and tracked for the remainder of the session.

Bats were trapped at one of the cave entrances using one or more harp traps (0.91 m by 0.91 m); during the trapping effort, the other entrances to the cave were blocked with tarps. Only female *C. t. virginianus* were radio-tagged. After trimming the fur in the area where the transmitter was to be attached, each transmitter (Holohil Systems Ltd., Carp, Ontario, Canada) was affixed to the bat between the scapulae using Skin-Bond surgical adhesive (Smith & Nephew United, Inc., Largo, FL). The smallest transmitters available when each tracking session took place were used (0.51 to 0.65 g). Transmitter weight represented 5.25±0.55 percent of body mass.

Bats were tracked each night from the time they emerged from the cave in the evening until they returned to the cave in the morning. If a bat was not observed returning to the cave, tracking was terminated when it was light enough that the bat was no longer likely to return to the cave. Bats were located using Wildlife Materials, Inc. (Murphysboro, IL) model TRX-2000S or Advanced Telemetry Systems, Inc. (Isanti, MN) model R4000 receivers and three-element directional Yagi antennae and vehicle-mounted omnidirectional antennae. Citizens' Band radios and low-band State radios were used by observers to communicate with each other, but because of the rugged terrain, communication was sometimes difficult. Four to ten observers collected data each night. At emergence, at least one observer was positioned to monitor bats exiting the cave and alert other observers when each bat had emerged. Other observers were stationed on high points throughout the study area and tracked each bat as it traveled to a foraging area. Readings were taken by multiple observers every other minute on the even-numbered minutes. If more than one bat was being tracked, locations were recorded on odd-numbered minutes for one bat and on even-numbered minutes for the other bat. Once a bat was tracked to a foraging area, observers coordinated their observations to best delineate the area where that particular bat was foraging. Night roosts were also recorded; when a bat appeared to night roost, i.e., steady signal suggesting the bat was not flying, the roost was confirmed by quietly approaching the roost to determine the bat's location.

For each reading taken, the observer recorded the observer's location, time (watches synchronized beforehand), receiver used, transmitter frequency, azimuth (uncorrected for declination), whether or not the signal was variable, and whether or not an attenuator was used when taking the reading. Signal strength and receiver gain setting were also recorded. Although these last two items were subjective, observers attempted to standardize these ratings among each other. Observers also noted when a reading was attempted but no signal was detected.

Because the study area was rugged and contained numerous steep slopes and outcroppings, signal bounce was a problem that could lead to misinterpretation of the data. To minimize this error, locations for each minute were plotted, and the data were reviewed to determine if the plotted locations "made sense." For example, if two readings suggested the bat was near a third observer, but that observer could not pick up a signal from the bat, the data point was discarded. Or, if the readings positioned the bat much closer to observer one than observer two, but observer one's signal was much weaker, the data were again suspect and discarded. After the "clean" data for an individual bat were plotted, areas of high use were delineated for each bat. Areas of high use were defined as areas where a bat spent > 30 minutes actively flying. I assumed that the high-use areas were foraging areas because the bats were active in relatively small areas for extended periods of time. In addition, the signals received from the bats' transmitters while in these areas varied greatly in intensity suggesting the bats were flying erratically or in loops, as expected of foraging insectivorous bats.

Telemetry points and high-use areas were plotted on U.S. Geological Survey 7.5-minute topographic maps. High-use areas for each bat were digitized using ArcMap (Environmental Systems Resource Institute 2009). Habitat use was analyzed using the National Land Cover Dataset 2001 (NLCD01, http://www.epa.gov/mrlc/nlcd-2001.html). Although this dataset was created after the telemetry project was completed, land use in this area changed little during and shortly after the study, and it is representative of the land cover type distribution during the project period. For the analyses, land cover types were combined into two broad

categories: forest (mainly deciduous forest) and open (mainly field, pasture, and row crops) (fig. 2). NLCD01 classes—developed open space, shrub/scrub, grassland/herbaceous, pasture/hay, cultivated crops, and emergent herbaceous wetlands—were reclassified as open habitat. Deciduous forest, evergreen forest, mixed forest, and woody wetlands classes were reclassified as forest habitat. All remaining classes (open water, developed low, medium, high intensity, and barren) were reclassified to "no data."

To examine the interspersion of open and forested habitats across the landscape and in high-use areas, an interspersion index was created using the ESRI Spatial Analyst focal variety tool (Environmental Systems Resource Institute 2009). An index of interspersion was assigned to each NLCD01 30-m pixel in the forest/open cover type dataset. A 5-pixel diameter circle was created centered on each pixel, and, if the circle contained only one cover type, that pixel was assigned a value of one; if it contained two cover types, i.e., both open and forest, it was assigned a value of two. These data were then combined to create an interspersion map for the study area.

To provide a measure of habitat availability in the study areas as a whole, a set of 5,000 random points was established within the study area, and 500-m radius circular plots were created centered on each random point. For each high-use area and random plot the proportion of open habitat and mean interspersion index were calculated using ESRI Spatial

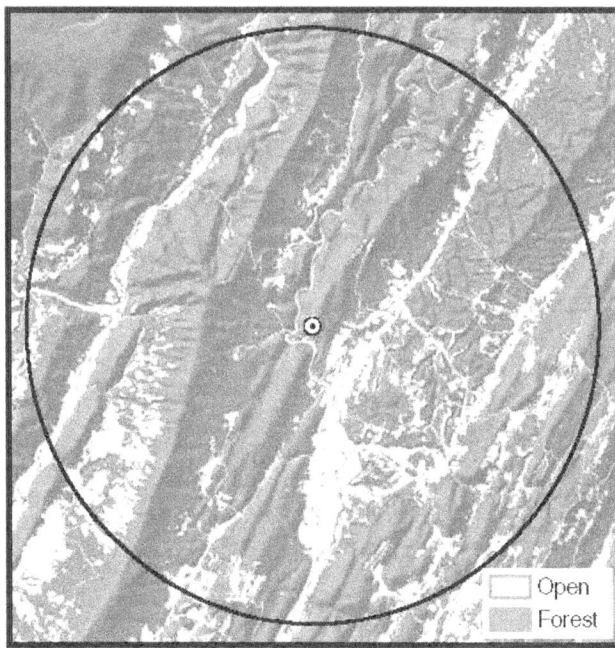

Figure 2—Map of the Pendleton County, WV, *Corynorhinus townsendii virginianus* radiotelemetry study area showing land cover types grouped into two broad categories: open (light gray) and forested (dark gray).

Analyst. These data were analyzed using the nonparametric Kruskal-Wallis chi-square test. To examine distance to foraging areas, the distance from the centroid of each high-use area was measured using ESRI Spatial Analyst, and the mean distances during each session were compared using Tukey's Honestly Significant Difference test. Statistical tests were run using R (R Development Core Team 2010).

RESULTS

Distances Traveled from Cave

The greatest distances bats traveled from the cave were 11.3 km in session 1, 10.8 km in session 2, 6.5 km in session 3, and 7.4 km in session 4 (fig. 3). Thus, maximum distances traveled were greatest early in spring, before parturition, and least in mid- to late July, during late lactation. A similar seasonal pattern was observed for the mean distances to high-use area centroids. The mean distances to the centroids of high-use areas were: session 1, 6.5 km; session 2, 4.1 km; session 3, 3.5 km; and session 4, 6.0 km. Mean distance was significantly less ($P < 0.1$) in session 3 (late lactation) than in session 1 (prelactation) or session 4 (postlactation). There was no significant difference between early and late lactation.

As expected, most of the foraging habitat used by the bats was considerably closer to the cave than the greatest

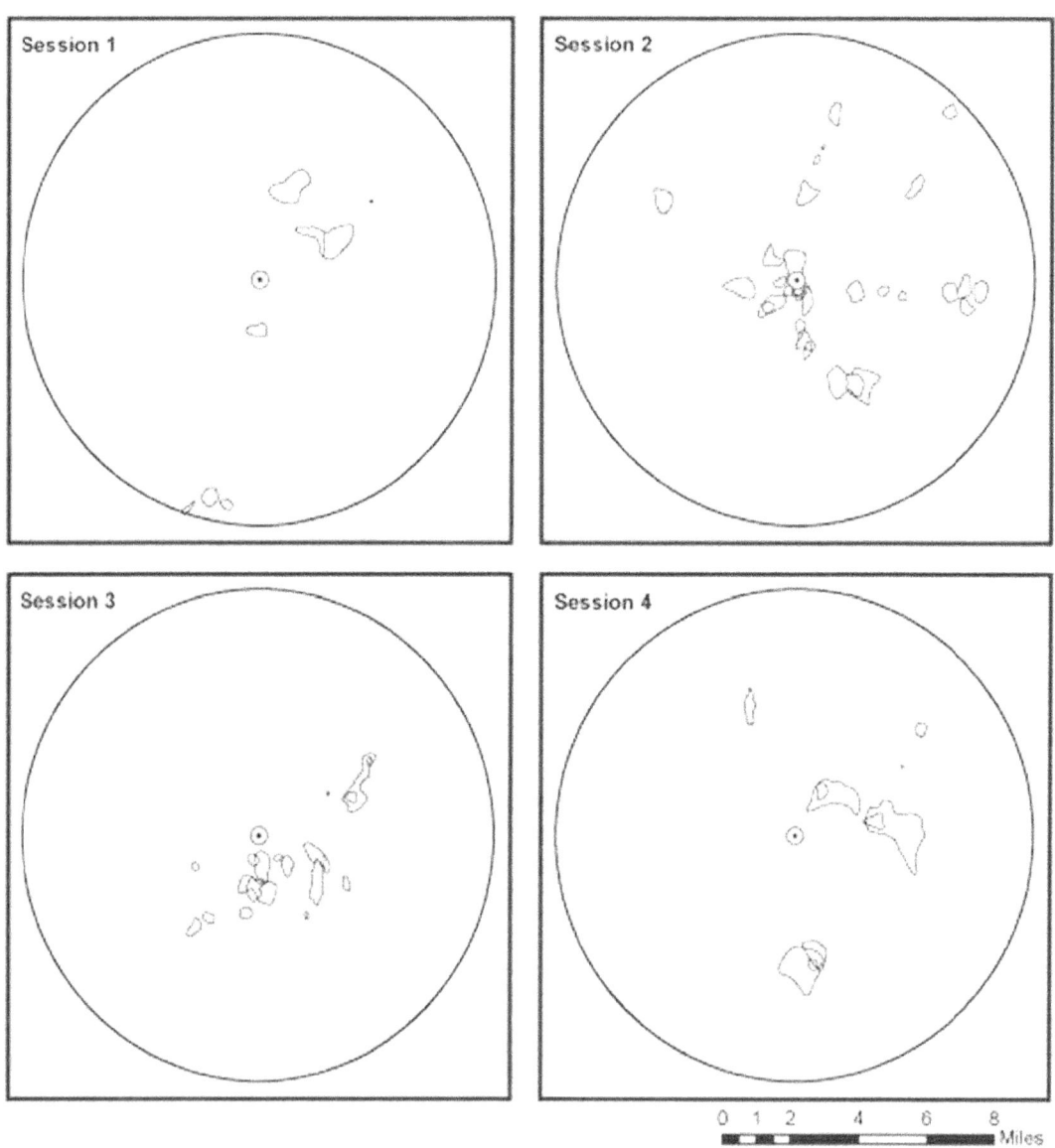

Figure 3—Map of high-use (foraging) areas used by female *Corynorhinus townsendii virginianus* from the Cave Mountain Cave maternity colony, Pendleton County, WV, during four radio tracking sessions: session 1, May 13 to June 1, session 2, June 25 to July 9; session 3, July 11 to July 25; and session 4, August 9 to August 22.

distances traveled. Although the bats traveled up to 11.3 km from the cave, 59.5 percent of the foraging habitat occurred within 5 km of the cave, and 80.5 percent of the foraging habitat occurred within 6 km of the cave (fig. 4).

Habitat Use

The high-use areas for all bats during each radio tracking session are shown in figure 3. The amount of open habitat in the high-use areas was significantly greater (Kruskal-Wallis $\chi^2 = 23.838$, $P < 0.001$) than in the random plots (fig. 5). On average, high-use areas contained 35.02±0.35 percent open habitat compared to 16.85±0.20 percent open habitat in the random plots. There were no significant seasonal differences in the amount of open habitat in the high-use areas (Kruskal-Wallis $\chi^2 = 3.11$, $P = 0.375$). Although not statistically significant, the amount of open habitat in the foraging areas was greatest (54.0 percent) during session 4. Percent open habitat observed in other sessions was 28.9 percent in session 1, 30.3 percent in session 2, and 33.2 percent in session 3. High-use areas also had a significantly greater amount of habitat interspersion than the random plots (Kruskal-Wallis $\chi^2 = 24.349$, $P < 0.001$) (fig. 6). High-use areas had a mean interspersion value of 1.65±0.32, while the random plots had a mean value of 1.46±0.32. There were no significant seasonal differences in the amount of habitat interspersion in the high-use areas (Kruskal-Wallis $\chi^2 = 1.607$, $P = 0.658$).

Although the cover-type data lumped many habitat types into broad categories, foraging areas were visited during the study to provide greater detail on the habitat types used by the bats. Most of the open habitats were either hayfields or old fields. Grazed lands were rarely used by the bats, although

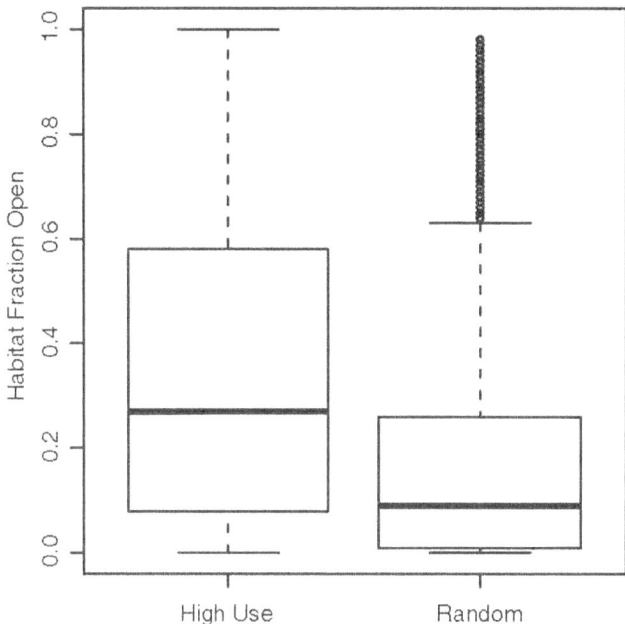

Figure 5—Box plot comparing proportion of habitat classified as open in *Corynorhinus townsendii virginianus* high-use areas in Pendleton County, WV, and random plots within the study area. Dark bar indicates median value.

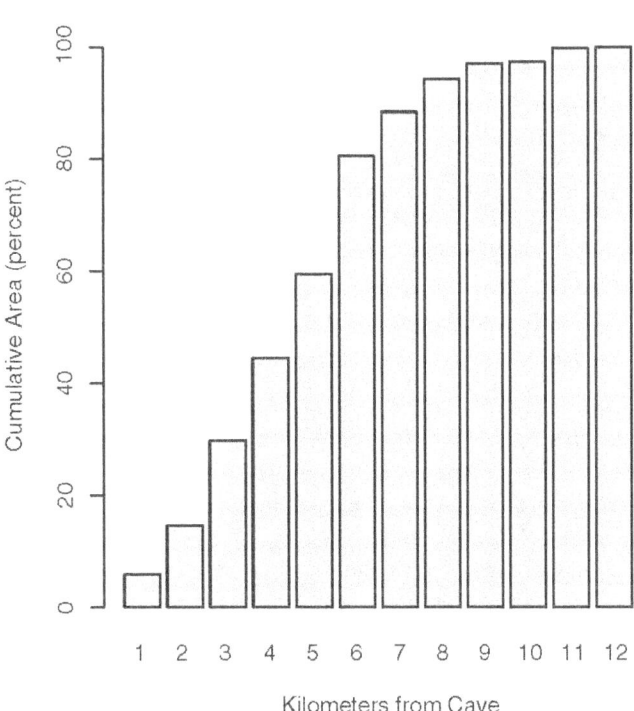

Figure 4—Cumulative percent of *Corynorhinus townsendii virginianus* foraging habitat contained in consecutive 1-km wide rings centered on the entrance of Cave Mountain Cave, Pendleton County, WV.

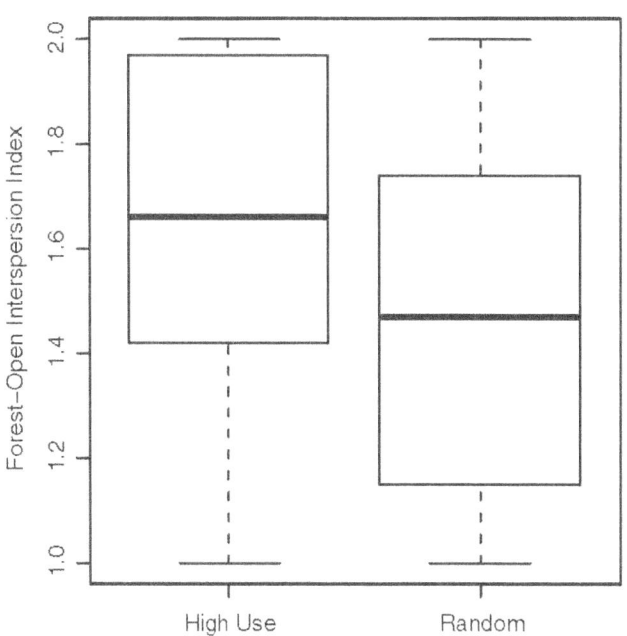

Figure 6—Box plot comparing interspersion indices of *Corynorhinus townsendii virginianus* high-use areas in Pendleton County, WV, and random plots within the study area. Dark bar indicates median value.

two bats during tracking session 2 foraged in a lightly grazed pasture with numerous thistles, scattered trees, and riparian vegetation along a small stream flowing through the pasture.

There was little overlap of high-use areas among seasons. Overlap in foraging areas ranged from < 1.0 percent between session 3 and session 4 to 5.6 percent between session 2 and session 3, i.e., early and late lactation.

Night Roosts

Bats often used night roosts near the foraging areas during sessions 1, 3, and 4. Most of the night roosts were anthropogenic structures including barns, a chicken coop, various outbuildings, the porch of an abandoned house, and a concrete bridge (three-span continuous steel beam bridge with a composite concrete deck). This bridge was used as a night roost during all four tracking sessions, and multiple bats were observed roosting under the bridge at one time. In addition, after one bat appeared to be night roosting on a forested hillside, the site was visited the next day, and a large rock outcrop was found at the site. During session 2 (early lactation) the bats returned to the cave up to three times during the night and rarely used night roosts. Bats rarely returned to the cave during the night during the other sessions.

Other Observations

One bat tracked during session 1 switched cave roosts and moved to a maternity colony in Schoolhouse Cave located on the west side of North Fork Mountain approximately 9.2 km from Cave Mountain Cave. Each evening this bat crossed the mountain to forage on the east side of North Fork Mountain. On two occasions during session 3 and one occasion during session 2, a bat did not return to the cave roost before morning; in all three cases, the bat returned to the cave early the following evening.

DISCUSSION

C. t. virginianus at the Cave Mountain Cave study site foraged in areas with a mixture of forested and open habitats but selected areas that contained a significantly larger proportion of open habitat than found in random plots. Data from light-tagging studies of *C. t. virginianus* in Virginia and West Virginia (Stihler and others 1996)[1] also documented the use of both open (hay, alfalfa, and corn fields) and forested habitats. In contrast, radio-tagged male and female *C. t. virginianus* on the Daniel Boone National Forest (DBNF) in Kentucky "foraged along cliffs and in forest habitat

within hollows enclosed by cliffs" (Adam and others 1994). Although clearings were uncommon in the Kentucky study area, no radio-tagged bats were tracked to openings that were available. However, using echolocation call monitoring to examine habitat use on the DBNF, Burford and Lacki (1995) documented significantly greater *C. t. virginianus* activity (passes per minute) in old field habitats than in forest or cliff top habitats.

Female *C. t. ingen*s in Oklahoma use open habitat in proportion to its availability in early lactation, late lactation, and fall (August through October) but avoid it during midlactation (Clark and others 1993, Wethington and others 1996). Open habitat made up 29.7 percent of the available habitat in Oklahoma. However, at the West Virginia site, where open habitat made up 17.0 percent of the available habitat, areas with greater percentage of open habitats were selected as foraging sites throughout the summer. During the present study, *C. t. virginianus* foraged in corn fields in August (session 4), a habitat not used in earlier tracking sessions. High use of corn fields in August is probably the reason the proportion of open habitat was highest during session 4. Use of corn fields could be related to the second generation peak flights of corn earworm (*Helicoverpa zea*), European corn borer (*Ostrinia nubilalis*), or fall armyworm (*Spodoptera frugiperda*).[2]

Other than corn fields during session 4, most of the open areas used by *C. t. virginianus* were hayfields or old fields. Similar results were found during light-tagging studies in West Virginia where no *C. t. virginianus* foraged in a grazed pasture located approximately 400 m from the cave roost, even though both hayfields and forest in the same general area were used (Stihler and others 1996). Although insect abundance at these sites was not measured, it seems likely that insect abundance was low in the grazed areas because vegetative structure was low (mostly short grass). The only pasture used by the bats did have some vegetative structure in an abundance of thistles and riparian vegetation along a small stream. Only one bat appeared to forage over water, but this bat may have been foraging around young sycamore (*Plantanus occidentalis*) trees growing on the banks of and on a small island in the South Branch. In addition, the bats never appeared to go to the river to drink after emerging from the cave in the evening.

Foraging areas used by *C. t. virginianus* exhibited a higher degree of habitat interspersion than random plots, suggesting that forest edges may be important. Indeed, *C. t. ingens* in Oklahoma use edges more than expected based on their availability (Clark and others 1993). However, neither the

[1] Dalton, V.M.; Brack, V.W., Jr.; Williams, C. 1989. Foraging ecology of the Virginia big-eared bat: performance report. Richmond, VA: Virginia Department of Game and Inland Fisheries. Unpublished report. 14 p.

[2] Personal communication. 2010. Sherri Hutchinson and Laura Miller, West Virginia Department of Agriculture, Plant Industries Division, 1900 Kanawha Blvd., East, Charleston, WV 25305.

telemetry data nor the light-tagging studies conducted in West Virginia support this assumption. On several occasions multiple observers tracked bats foraging in an open field from positions along the edges, and bats never seemed to be foraging along the field edge. Similar observations were made for bats foraging in small woodlots. These results are further corroborated by observations during light-tagging studies in Pendleton County (Stihler and others 1996). Bats foraged low over hayfields and in and above the forest canopy, and when foraging around trees, bats appeared to follow the surface contours of the tree canopies. While this could include edge habitat, especially when the bats foraged around a single tree or small group of trees, the bats generally foraged in the woods away from the forest/field edge. The selection of areas with high habitat interspersion may be related to the availability of a variety of food items throughout the night in areas offering a mix of foraging habitats (Lacki and Dodd 2011). For example, one bat tracked all night for 7 nights between May 23 and June 1 foraged in hayfields early in the evening, night roosted for approximately 55 minutes, and then foraged in wooded habitats for the remainder of the night. The bat never foraged along the forest edge but was always either in the field or in the woods. This suggests that the mix of habitats and associated feeding opportunities were the driving force in selecting foraging areas with high interspersion, not the availability of edge.

The greatest distance traveled from the maternity cave (11.3 km) and the greatest mean distance to all high-use areas (6.5 km) occurred in the spring (session 1) before the females had given birth; during lactation the greatest distance bats traveled was 10.8 km, but the mean distances to foraging areas were 4.1 km in early lactation and 3.5 km in late lactation. Following lactation, the bats again increased the distances they traveled with a maximum distance of 7.4 km and a mean distance to high-use areas of 6.0 km. These data suggest that female *C. t. virginianus* forage closer to the roost during lactation when they also return to the cave during the night to nurse their pups. Distances observed during the present study are considerably greater than those observed at other study sites. At a maternity roost in Kentucky, the greatest distance a *C. t. virginianus* was tracked from the maternity roost was 3.65 km which was recorded in August (Adam and others 1994). The greatest distance to a foraging area recorded for *C. t. ingens* in Oklahoma was 7.0 km and occurred during the late lactation; during early lactation the greatest distance observed was 2.0 km (Clark and others 1993). In August, the greatest distance to a foraging area recorded for *C. t. ingens* in Oklahoma was 5.5 km (Wethington and others 1996). These differences may be due to the larger number of big-eared bats in the West Virginia study area and the need for these bats to disperse over a larger area to reduce interspecific competition for food and/or foraging

areas. The total population of *C. t. ingens* in Oklahoma maternity colonies was approximately 650 bats (U.S. Fish and Wildlife Service 1995), while the colony in Cave Mountain Cave numbered between 637 and 826 bats during the study period, and the 6 maternity colonies within the study area contained a total of more than 2,000 bats.

As observed in *C. t. ingens* (Clark and others 1993), the females returned to the roost up to three times a night during early lactation, and the number of returns decreased as lactation progressed. Before parturition and after the young became volant, most bats left the cave in the evening and did not return until morning. The number of feeding bouts per night probably did not change over the summer, but between bouts the bats night roosted closer to their foraging areas and away from the cave outside of the lactation period. Most of the night roosts used were buildings. The use of buildings as night roosts was also observed in *C. t. virginianus* in Virginia (see footnote 1).

CONCLUSIONS

In the largely forested landscape around a maternity colony cave in West Virginia, female *C. t. virginianus* used foraging areas that contained more open habitat and had a greater interspersion of open and forested habitats than was expected based on availability. Land managers may be able to improve or maintain foraging habitats for *C. t. virginianus* by creating or maintaining open fields in the vicinity of summer roosts. Because open habitats are often the areas most suitable for future development, these habitats may be lost to development. Further, open habitats may return to forests without active management, e.g., burning, mowing, and herbicides. The creation of a mosaic of open and forested habitat types may provide foraging bats a more diverse prey base where they can switch foraging habitats from night to night or throughout the night depending on prey availability. During this study, female bats traveled up to 11.3 km from the cave to forage. However, 80.5 percent of the foraging habitat used during the four tracking sessions occurred within 6.0 km of the cave. Efforts to maintain or create foraging habitat would be most effective when done within 6.0 km of the maternity colony roost. Although most foraging activity occurred in forests, old fields, and hayfields, corn fields were used in August, and agricultural use of pesticides could pose a risk to foraging bats and their pups.

Because *C. t. virginianus* usually night roosted near their foraging areas in uninhabited structures such as barns and abandoned houses, maintenance or creation of suitable roost structures near foraging habitats should benefit them. Bridges may also provide important night roosts, and bridge designs, such as the steel beam/concrete deck bridge used during all four sessions, could be employed to provide additional roosting opportunities within the forage areas of maternity colonies, although more research is needed to determine the best design for creating night roosts.

ACKNOWLEDGMENTS

The author expresses his appreciation to the Monongahela National Forest for granting access to Cave Mountain Cave and for partial funding for this project, the U.S. Fish and Wildlife Service for providing additional funding, and the numerous people who contributed to the West Virginia Nongame Wildlife Fund which also funded much of this work. This project would not have been possible without the access provided by numerous landowners within the project area and the hard work and dedication of several West Virginia Department of Natural Resources (WVDNR) employees, especially Jack Wallace, Donna Mitchell, Bill Roody, and Jeff Hajenga, who spent many long nights tracking bats and long days contacting landowners. The assistance of numerous volunteers contributed to the success of this effort. The assistance of WVDNR technical support staff with the analysis of the data, especially Michael Dougherty and Jeremy Rowan, was greatly appreciated. The author also expresses his gratitude to Dave Dalton, Ginny Dalton, The Nature Conservancy, Steve Kimble, and Thorn Spring Park for their assistance and support.

LITERATURE CITED

Adam, M.D.; Lacki, M.J.; Barnes, T.G. 1994. Foraging areas and habitat use of the Virginia big-eared bat in Kentucky. Journal of Wildlife Management. 53(3): 462-469.

Burford, L.S.; Lacki, M.J. 1995. Habitat use by *Corynorhinus townsendii virginianus* in the Daniel Boone National Forest. The American Midland Naturalist. 134: 340-345.

Clark, B.S.; Leslie, D.M., Jr.; Carter, T.S. 1993. Foraging activity of adult female Ozark big-eared bats (*Plecotus townsendii ingens*) in summer. Journal of Mammalogy. 74(2): 422-427.

Dalton, V.M.; Brack, V.W., Jr.; McTeer, P.M. 1986. Food habits of the big-eared bat, *Plecotus townsendii virginianus*, in Virginia. Virginia Journal of Science. 37(4): 248-254.

Environmental Systems Resource Institute. 2009. ArcMap. Version 9.3.1. Redlands, CA.

Lacki, M.J.; Dodd, L.E. 2011. Diet and foraging behavior of *Corynorhinus* in Eastern North America. In: Loeb, S.C.; Lacki, M.J.; Miller, D.A., eds. Conservation and management of eastern big-eared bats: a symposium. Gen. Tech. Rep. SRS-145. Asheville, NC: U.S. Department of Agriculture Forest Service, Southern Research Station: 39-52.

R Development Core Team. 2010. R: a language and environment for statistical computing. Vienna, Austria: R Foundation for Statistical Computing. [ISBN 3-900051-07-0].

Stihler, C.W. 2011. Status of the Virginia big-eared bat (*Corynorhinus townsendii virginianus*) in West Virginia: twenty-seven years of monitoring cave roosts. In: Loeb, S.C.; Lacki, M.J.; Miller, D.A., eds. Conservation and management of eastern big-eared bats: a symposium. Gen. Tech. Rep. SRS-145. Asheville, NC: U.S. Department of Agriculture Forest Service, Southern Research Station: 75-84.

Stihler, C.W.; Dalton, V.M.; Wallace, J.L.; Brack, V., Jr. 1996. Radio telemetry and light-tagging studies of *Corynorhinus townsendii virginianus*: preliminary results [Abstract]. Bat Research News. 37(4): 152.

U.S. Fish and Wildlife Service. 1979. Endangered and threatened wildlife and plants: listing of Virginia and Ozark big-eared bats as endangered species, and critical habitat determination. 50 CFR Part 17. Federal Register. 44(232): 69,206-69,208.

U.S. Fish and Wildlife Service. 1995. Ozark big-eared bat (*Plecotus townsendii ingens* (Handley)) revised recovery plan. Tulsa, OK. 51 p.

Wethington, T.A.; Leslie, D.M., Jr.; Gregory, M.S. 1996. Prehibernation habitat use and foraging activity by endangered Ozark big-eared bats (*Plecotus townsendii ingens*). The American Midland Naturalist. 135(2): 218-230.

COMPARISON OF SURVEY METHODS FOR RAFINESQUE'S BIG-EARED BATS

Matthew J. Clement, Ph.D. candidate, University of Georgia, D.B. Warnell School of Forestry
and Natural Resources, Athens, GA 30602

Steven B. Castleberry, Professor, University of Georgia, D.B. Warnell School of Forestry
and Natural Resources, Athens, GA 30602

Abstract—Rafinesque's big-eared bat (*Corynorhinus rafinesquii*) is designated a species of concern by the U.S. Fish and Wildlife Service and therefore has been a focus of recent research. Relative to other North American bats, the species is reported to be difficult to survey using mist nets and bat detectors. However, it is unclear if low detection is due to difficulties in detecting Rafinesque's big-eared bat or low bat abundance. We employed mist nets and bat detectors and visually surveyed potential roosts at sites with known Rafinesque's big-eared bat populations to determine if detection rates were low even when bats were abundant and estimated the hourly cost per detection of each technique. We mist netted for 39 nights and captured 51 Rafinesque's big-eared bats, yielding a capture rate of 0.99 bats per hour. Captures were higher in summer (1.10 captures per hour) than during winter (0.75 captures per hour), and during summer captures per hour were higher in sloughs (1.53) than on roads (0.54). We acoustically surveyed bat activity on 85 nights and detected 54 Rafinesque's big-eared bat passes, yielding a detection rate of 0.07 bat passes per hour. Detections per hour were higher in sloughs (0.60) than along roads (0.04). We visually surveyed 1,606 potential roost sites and made 178 roost observations, yielding an observation rate of 0.28 per hour. Although mist nets had the highest hourly capture rate, roost searches were the most cost-effective method, costing $50.49 per detection, followed by mist nets and bat detectors. In addition to costs, project goals must also be considered when selecting survey methods.

INTRODUCTION

Rafinesque's big-eared bat (*Corynorhinus rafinesquii*) is a small, insectivorous bat found in the Southeastern United States (Jones 1977) and is considered uncommon throughout its range (Harvey and others 1999). While it is found under bridges and in abandoned buildings (Bennett and others 2008, Menzel and others 2001), its natural roosts are primarily caves in karst regions (Barbour and Davis 1969) and hollow trees in bottomland forests in the Coastal Plain (Carver and Ashley 2008, Gooding and Langford 2004). Rafinesque's big-eared bat is of particular interest because bottomland forests have been reduced dramatically in size since the precolonial period (Fredrickson 1997).

Rafinesque's big-eared bat has been designated a species of concern by the U.S. Fish and Wildlife Service and State wildlife agencies and, therefore, has been the target of recent research efforts (e.g., Bennett and others 2008, Carver and Ashley 2008, Medlin and Risch 2008, Piaggio and others 2009). Unfortunately, there is evidence that Rafinesque's big-eared bat is unusually difficult to survey using standard techniques. Several investigators have reported that Rafinesque's big-eared bats are difficult to capture in mist nets (Hurst and Lacki 1999, Lance and Garrett 1997, Mirowsky and others 2004, Trousdale and Beckett 2002, Trousdale and others 2008). This has been attributed to their low wing loading and low aspect ratio (Jones and Suttkus 1971) which allow them to be extremely maneuverable in flight (Norberg 1990). However, a study in Arkansas reported

relatively high capture rates for Rafinesque's big-eared bats (Medlin and Risch 2008). Several studies have dealt with the reported difficulty by netting at known roosts (Carver and Ashley 2008, Lance and others 2001, Trousdale and Beckett 2005) or conducting visual surveys of potential roosts (Bennett and others 2008, Gooding and Langford 2004).

A second challenge to studying Rafinesque's big-eared bats is that they are "whispering bats" that echolocate at low intensity (Griffin 1958). This fact has limited the use of ultrasonic detectors for Rafinesque's big-eared bat surveys. Several acoustic surveys of bat communities within the range of Rafinesque's big-eared bats have reported that they are virtually undetectable using bat detectors (Ford and others 2006, Loeb and O'Keefe 2006, Menzel and others 2005, Murray and others 1999). O'Farrell and Gannon (1999) were able to acoustically detect only one Townsend's big-eared bat (*C. townsendii*), a congener, at 57 recording sites. In contrast, Burford and Lacki (1995) reported acoustically detecting Virginia big-eared bats (*C. t. virginianus*) in every habitat sampled.

We compared the effectiveness of mist nets, bat detectors, and visual surveys of potential roosts in detecting Rafinesque's big-eared bats in bottomland forests in the Coastal Plain of Georgia. Specifically, we investigated (1) the hourly rates of detection for each method in areas where Rafinesque's big-eared bats were known to be abundant, and (2) the cost per detection for each method in areas where Rafinesque's big-eared bats were known to be abundant.

Citation for proceedings: Loeb, Susan C.; Lacki, Michael J.; Miller, Darren A., eds. 2011. Conservation and management of eastern big-eared bats: a symposium. Gen. Tech. Rep. SRS-145. Asheville, NC: U.S. Department of Agriculture, Forest Service, Southern Research Station. 157 p.

STUDY AREA

We conducted our study at eight sites in the Coastal Plain physiographic region of Georgia, USA, that were known to contain Rafinesque's big-eared bats. All study sites were State managed (owned or leased by the State) and located within a major river flood plain with baldcypress (*Taxodium distichum*)-gum (*Nyssa* spp.) swamps and bottomland hardwoods as major habitat components. We conducted field work in Beaverdam Wildlife Management Area (WMA), Chickasawhatchee WMA, Clayhole Swamp WMA, Little Satilla WMA, Moody Forest Natural Area, Ocmulgee WMA, Riverbend WMA, and Tuckahoe WMA. Habitat composition varied across study sites but generally consisted of large areas of loblolly pine (*Pinus taeda*) with smaller areas of slash pine (*P. elliottii*), shortleaf pine (*P. echinata*), and hardwoods on upland sites and baldcypress-gum swamps and bottomland hardwoods in areas bordering each river. At most sites, upland forests were almost entirely < 80 years old, while bottomland forests were often older.

METHODS

Mist Netting

We captured bats in mist nets (Avinet, Inc., Dryden, NY) during the summers (mid-May to mid-August) of 2007 and 2008 on all eight field sites and during the winter (February and March) of 2010 at Riverbend WMA only. We placed one to three single-high nets in potential flyways such as roads and over water sources such as sloughs and puddles (Kunz and others 2009). All winter netting was conducted over roads due to very deep water in sloughs. Netting sites were selected on an ad hoc basis with the goal of maximizing captures of Rafinesque's big-eared bat. We selected one to five (mean = 3.2) netting locations at each field site. We tried to separate netting locations in space to avoid conditioning bats to netting locations (Kunz and Brock 1975). As a separate technique, we targeted bats exiting known roosts because Rafinesque's big-eared bats frequently have been reported to be more difficult to capture in mist nets than other bats (Hurst and Lacki 1999, Lance and Garrett 1997, Mirowsky and others 2004, Trousdale and Beckett 2002, Trousdale and others 2008). When we targeted a known roost, we placed a mist net approximately 0.5 m from a basal opening of the roost tree. Because this research was part of a larger study, we generally constrained mist netting to 1 to 2 hours per night. We often closed the nets as soon as we captured bats to avoid capturing more bats than needed for a concurrent radiotelemetry study. We measured mist-net success rate for each technique (flyways and water sources or targeting known roosts) by calculating bat captures per hour (CPH).

Acoustic Survey

We performed acoustic surveys during the summer of 2007 at Moody Forest Natural Area, Ocmulgee WMA, and Tuckahoe WMA. Each bat detector (AR125, Binary Acoustic Technology, Tucson, AZ) was housed in a piece of PVC pipe, mounted on a tripod, positioned 1.5 m above the ground and aimed downward at a 45-degree angle at a sheet of plexiglass. Calls were recorded on a laptop computer (model NX570X, Gateway, Inc., Irvine, CA) connected to each detector. The AR125 uses a direct digital conversion technology so that recordings are wideband, full spectrum, and realtime, in contrast to frequency division or time division detectors (Parsons and others 2000). Detectors were turned on before sunset and retrieved after sunrise. We use the term "call" to describe an individual pulse of echolocation and the term "bat pass" to describe a sequence of one or more calls separated by less than one second (Hayes 1997).

We recorded bat calls at sites along roads at both upland and bottomland sites within each field site. Recording sites were not the same as mist-net sites. We identified potential recording locations using ArcMap, ver. 9.2 (Esri, Redlands, CA) and 30- by 30-m resolution 44-class land cover type data obtained from the University of Georgia, Natural Resources Spatial Analysis Laboratory. We located all unpaved roads in the Georgia Department of Transportation's Road Characteristics inventory on each field site. We then randomly selected an equal number of roadside recording points that were either in (1) stands of baldcypress-gum swamp and/or bottomland hardwoods and > 90 m from a different stand type or (2) stands of loblolly-shortleaf pine, loblolly-slash pine, and/or longleaf pine and > 90 m from a different stand type. Recording sites were ≥ 250 m apart. We selected 14 pairs of roadside locations (1 bottomland and 1 upland pine) and recorded each pair simultaneously with a bat detector at each location. Each pair was surveyed on 3 nights over 2 months. We selected six additional recording sites in baldcypress-gum swamp and/or bottomland hardwoods and > 90 m from a different stand type, but in sloughs instead of beside roads. Each of these sites was surveyed on 1 night in late July or early August.

We recorded voucher calls outside six known Rafinesque's big-eared bat roosts during evening emergence to aid in identifying calls of Rafinesque's big-eared bat. Emergence calls are not an ideal source of voucher calls because calls emitted during emergence may differ from calls emitted during commuting or foraging (Berger-Tal and others 2007). However, given the low intensity of Rafinesque's big-eared bat echolocation, we judged that recording during emergence was the only feasible way to obtain numerous voucher calls (O'Farrell and Gannon 1999). Therefore, we treated emergence calls as representative of their repertoire. We analyzed all calls with SCAN'R (Binary Acoustic

Technology, Tucson, AZ) with the following settings: pop filter on, fit restriction high, trigger level 20 dB, minimum frequency cutoff 15 kHz, peak power 13 dB, minimum duration 1 millisecond. The first two settings restrict the number of fragmented and partial calls which cannot be used to identify bats. The remaining settings are permissive and intended to maximize the number of calls, given they meet the fit restriction. Most calls recorded during emergence had the short duration, high frequency, and downward sweep typical of vespertilionid echolocation, but nine calls in three

bat passes were very long with modulated frequencies. We suspect these were social calls and excluded them from the call library. We quantified the variation in voucher calls of Rafinesque's big-eared bats for the following acoustic parameters: maximum frequency, minimum frequency, dominant frequency, bandwidth, and curvature. We assessed the comprehensiveness of our library by examining the cumulative variation in the measured parameters (Duffy and others 2000). We randomly sorted the reference calls in our library 20 times and tracked the change in the range of

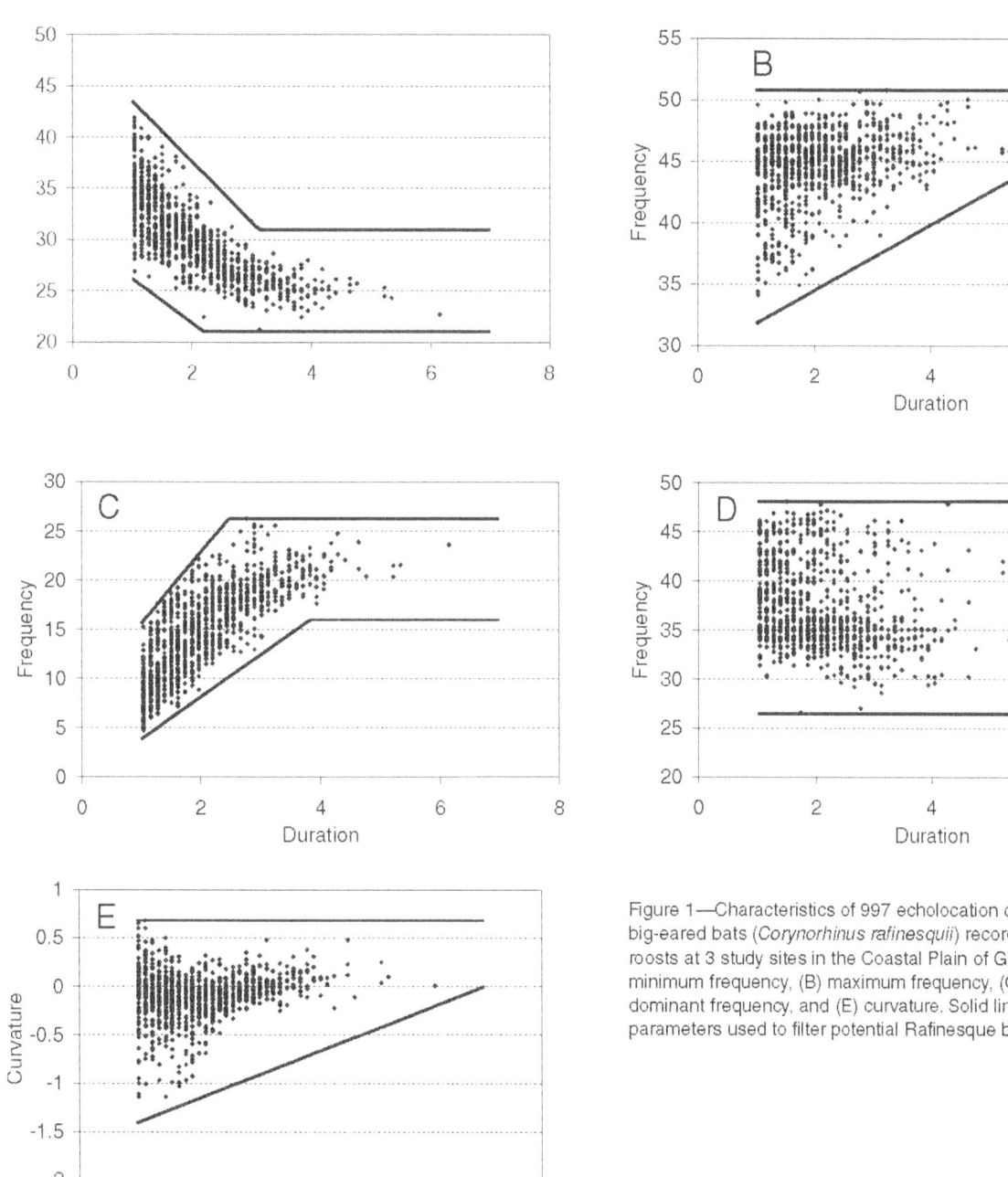

Figure 1—Characteristics of 997 echolocation calls of Rafinesque's big-eared bats (*Corynorhinus rafinesquii*) recorded as bats exited roosts at 3 study sites in the Coastal Plain of Georgia, 2007; (A) minimum frequency, (B) maximum frequency, (C) bandwidth, (D) dominant frequency, and (E) curvature. Solid lines indicate the call parameters used to filter potential Rafinesque big-eared bat calls.

values as call number increased. We assumed an asymptote indicated a comprehensive library.

In analyzing calls from unknown bats, we used the same SCAN'R settings and used the parameters from our library to create a simple quantitative filter that selected only those calls that fell within the variation found in the voucher calls (fig. 1). We then reviewed the entire bat pass containing the selected calls and eliminated those that were part of a sequence of calls dissimilar to our voucher calls. We divided the remaining calls into "probable Rafinesque's big-eared bat" if the call sequence had ≥ 4 calls or if a second harmonic was visible and "possible Rafinesque's big-eared bat" otherwise. We measured bat detector success by calculating bat pass detections per detector per hour (DPH).

We captured few bats of other species and, therefore, did not obtain original voucher calls for any other species. However, without information on call characteristics of other species, we cannot distinguish between their calls and Rafinesque's big-eared bat calls. Sympatric species include the tri-colored bat (*Perimyotis subflavus*), evening bat (*Nycticeius humeralis*), southeastern myotis (*Myotis austroriparius*), Brazilian free-tailed bat (*Tadarida brasiliensis*), big brown bat (*Eptesicus fuscus*), eastern red bat (*Lasiurus borealis*), Seminole bat (*L. seminolus*), hoary bat (*L. cinereus*), and possibly the silver-haired bat (*Lasionycteris noctivagans*; Menzel and others 2000). Based on our experience, species with echolocation calls that might overlap the frequency range of Rafinesque's big-eared bat were the evening bat, big brown bat, hoary bat, and silver-haired bat. We used information from the published literature (Betts 1998, Murray and others 2001, O'Farrell and others 2000, Surlykke and Moss 2000) on bat echolocation calls to distinguish Rafinesque's big-eared bat passes from these four bat species.

Roost Searches

We conducted visual surveys of hollow trees with basal cavity openings in forested wetlands at all eight field sites during the summers of 2007 and 2008. We used the U.S. Fish and Wildlife Service's National Wetland Inventory to identify forested wetlands that were either seasonally flooded or semipermanently flooded (Cowardin and others 1979). Seasonally flooded wetlands have surface water early in the growing season, while semipermanently flooded wetlands have surface water during the entire growing season. Because wetland areas generally were linear, we created 500-m long by 30-m wide transects along the approximate center of all wetland areas using ArcMap, ver. 9.2. We randomly selected transects to survey at each site. We conducted roost searches by searching for trees with basal hollows within 15 m of the center of the transect during daylight hours. When we located a hollow tree, we visually inspected the cavity for bats using a spotlight and mirror. We searched each transect three times during the same summer field season. If bats were present

in a tree during a survey, this counted as one observation, regardless of the number of bats present. If a tree was observed to be occupied during multiple surveys this counted as multiple observations. In repeat surveys all trees were rechecked, regardless of their previous occupancy status. The three surveys were not independent because we searched the same trees each time, and trees that were occupied during the first survey were often occupied in later surveys. While this type of pseudoreplication would increase type I error in many statistical tests, it does not affect the calculation of an average. We measured roost search success by calculating bat roost observations per hour (OPH).

Cost Efficiency

We compared the relative cost of mist-net surveys and acoustic surveys on our field sites by calculating the hourly cost of each method and dividing by detections per hour to get cost per detection. We divided survey costs into fixed costs, such as equipment purchases, and variable costs, such as field labor and analysis labor. The hourly price of a fixed cost declines with increasing survey hours, while hourly price of a variable cost is relatively constant as number of survey hours changes. We calculated cost estimates with and without equipment costs for use when equipment is available and does not need to be purchased. For bat detector surveys, necessary equipment included a bat detector, computer, weather protection unit, tripod, marine battery, power inverter, and call analysis software. Field labor included travel time and equipment setup and takedown time for one worker. Analysis labor included separating bat calls from insect noise, extracting parameter values, manually screening calls for errors, an initial scan to identify potential calls, and a second scan to identify probable calls. We assumed that a call library had already been constructed. If not, additional field work and analysis would be required. For mist-net surveys, equipment included four sets of poles and eight nets of various lengths, stakes, and bat bags. Field labor included transportation, equipment setup and takedown, and time spent monitoring nets for two workers. No analysis labor was required. For roost searches, equipment included five 1-million candle watt spotlights and two mirrors. Field labor included transportation, setting up transects, labeling trees, and searching for bats. No analysis labor was required. Field labor was paid $7.00 per hour, and analysis labor was paid $22.36 per hour, standard rates for a forestry worker I and a PhD student at the Warnell School of Forestry and Natural Resources at the University of Georgia.

RESULTS

Mist Netting

Combining all sites and seasons but excluding nights when we targeted known roosts, we used mist nets on 39 nights for 51.6 hours. We captured a total of 61 bats, for a rate of 1.18 CPH. Our most commonly captured species was Rafinesque's big-eared bat, with 51 captures, for a rate of 0.99 CPH. We also captured five southeastern myotis (0.10 CPH), four eastern red bats (0.08 CPH), and one big brown bat (0.02 CPH). We captured bats of any species on 22 nights (56 percent) and Rafinesque's big-eared bat on 18 nights (46 percent). Netting in sloughs appeared to be more productive than netting along roads. During the summer, we captured 9 Rafinesque's big-eared bats (0.54 CPH) along roads during 16.7 hours over 14 nights and 30 bats (1.53 CPH) in sloughs during 19.6 hours over 17 nights. During the winter, all netting was along roads at Riverbend WMA, and we captured 12 Rafinesque's big-eared bats (0.75 CPH) during 16.1 hours of netting over 9 nights. During the summer, we recorded 1.50 CPH at Riverbend WMA and 1.10 CPH at all eight sites combined. We targeted 23 Rafinesque's big-eared bat roosts with nets set 0.5 m from the roost for a total of 16.6 hours. We captured 36 (2.17 CPH) Rafinesque's big-eared bats at 18 of the 23 roosts (78 percent).

Acoustic Survey

Using SCAN'R, we identified 997 calls in 130 bat passes that we recorded outside known Rafinesque's big-eared bat roosts, which we used as our reference library. Minimum and maximum values of call parameters varied with call duration, which we incorporated into the filter used to identify potential Rafinesque's big-eared bat calls (fig. 1). The cumulative variation of all call parameters rose dramatically for the first 100 calls and then increased

gradually (fig. 2), indicating our library was nearly comprehensive.

We discarded 5 nights of recording due to equipment malfunction, leaving us with 85 recording nights. In total, we recorded 13,551 bat passes or 17.71 DPH. Our quantitative filter based on call parameters identified 458 unique bat passes that contained potential Rafinesque's big-eared bat calls. Our assessment of the entire call sequences eliminated 385 bat passes from further consideration. Eliminated calls were either part of a feeding buzz of a different bat species or a fragmented call and bore no resemblance to a typical Rafinesque's big-eared bat call (fig. 3). We divided the retained bat passes into 54 "probable" and 19 "possible" Rafinesque's big-eared bat passes. Considering only probable calls, DPH was 0.07. Once again, we had higher success in sloughs with 0.60 DPH in sloughs and 0.04 DPH along roads. We recorded a probable bat pass at 16 of 34 recording sites (47 percent) and on 19 of 85 nights (22 percent).

Roost Searches

We searched 97 seasonally flooded or semipermanently flooded transects containing 1,606 hollow trees 3 times each. The roost searches took approximately 640 hours and yielded 215 observations of roosting bats for a rate of 0.34 roost OPH. Rafinesque's big-eared bat was the most commonly observed species with 178 observations of 109 unique roosts (0.28 OPH).

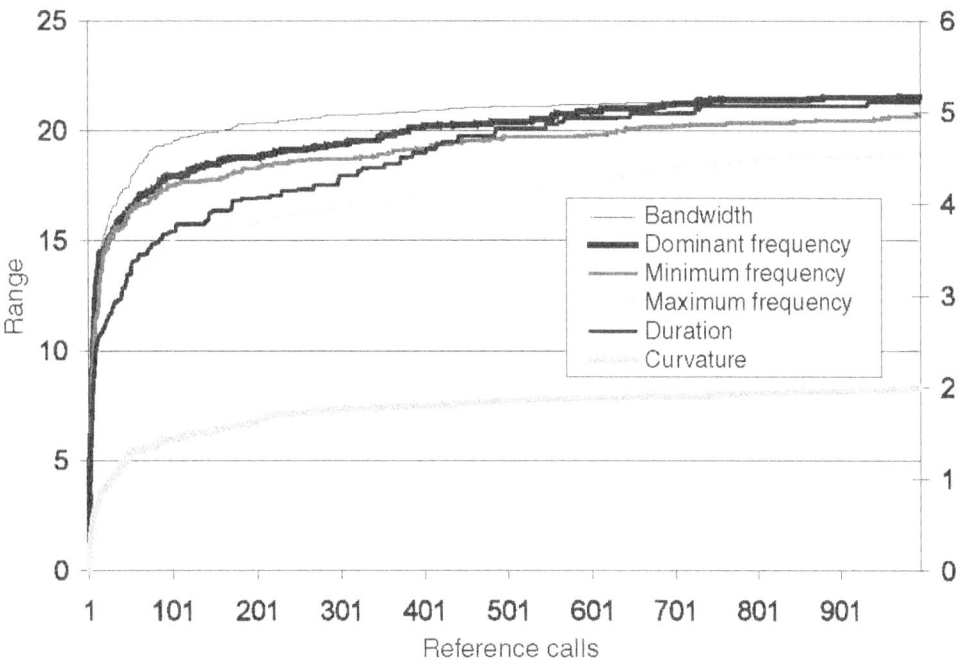

Figure 2—Variation in call parameters of Rafinesque's big-eared bats (*Corynorhinus rafinesquii*) as a function of number of reference calls recorded as bats exited roosts at three study sites in the Coastal Plain of Georgia, 2007. Values for duration and curvature are shown on right axis.

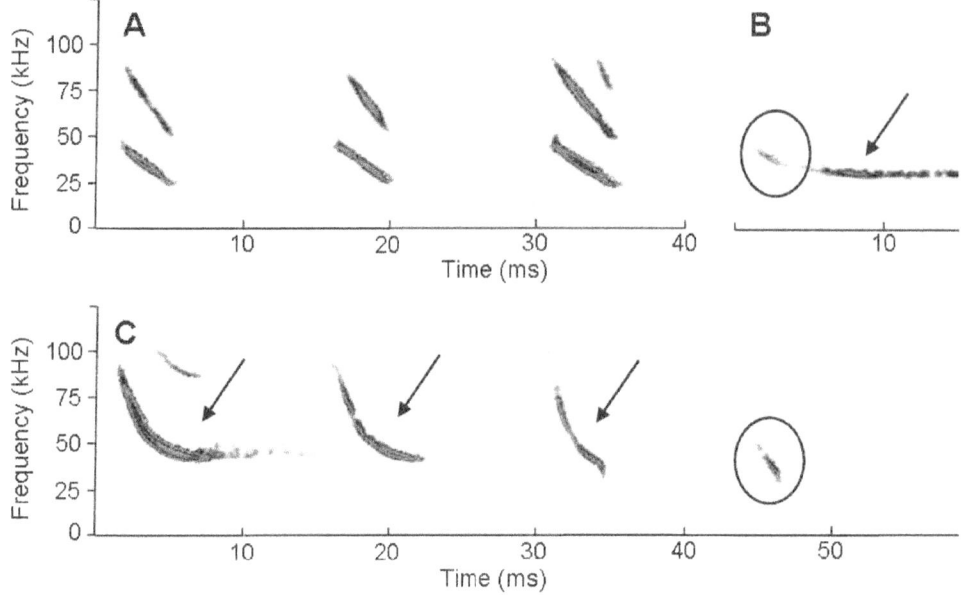

Figure 3—Examples of bat calls recorded at three study sites in the Coastal Plain of Georgia, 2007. Silent periods between calls have been reduced to better present call details. (A) Typical Rafinesque's big-eared bat (*Corynorhinus rafinesquii*) bat pass; (B) fragmented call that a quantitative filter identified as a potential Rafinesque's big-eared bat call (circle), but was discarded based on additional portions of the same call (arrow); (C) feeding buzz call that a quantitative filter identified as a potential Rafinesque's big-eared bat call (circle), but was discarded due to dissimilarity of preceding calls (arrows).

Cost Efficiency

Following our protocols, bat detector surveys had the lowest hourly labor cost of any method, followed by roost searches and mist netting (table 1). However, the capture rate with mist nets was so much higher than the other methods that it had the lowest labor cost per capture, with roost searches being almost twice as expensive and bat detector surveys being more than three times as expensive. Roost searches had by far the lowest hourly equipment costs of any method, followed by bat detectors and mist nets. Because of the low equipment costs, roost searches had the lowest total cost per observation, followed closely by mist netting, with bat detectors being over three times as expensive.

Table 1—Labor cost and total cost per detection of Rafinesque's big-eared bat (*Corynorhinus rafinesquii*) using three different survey techniques

Costs	Bat detector	Mist net	Roost search
Variable costs			
Field labor per night	$8.75	$36.01	$70.00
Analysis labor per night	$48.45	$0.00	$0.00
Hours per night	9.0	1.3	5.0
Hourly cost	$6.36	$27.28	$14.00
Fixed costs			
Equipment	$2,197	$1,514	$110
Nights	45	39	162
Hours per night	9.0	1.3	5.0
Hourly cost	$5.42	$29.86	$0.14
Hourly detection rate	0.07	0.99	0.28
Labor cost per detection	$90.79	$27.59	$50.00
Total cost per detection	$168.29	$57.78	$50.49

Cost efficiency was affected by the survey protocol. When mist netting in sloughs, CPH increased to 1.53. If we had maintained this higher capture rate for the entire study, the total cost per detection would have dropped to $37.35 which would be more cost effective than roost searches. During our limited acoustic surveys of sloughs, DPH was 0.60. If we had maintained this higher detection rate for the entire study, the total cost per detection would have been the lowest overall at $15.11 per detection.

DISCUSSION

Overall, we found that roost searches were the most cost-effective technique considering labor and equipment costs, but mist netting had the highest capture rate and was most cost effective if we considered only labor costs. In addition to the cost differences, each survey technique measured a different component of bat ecology. Roost searches recorded day roost observations; mist-net surveys recorded captures of commuting and foraging bats; and bat detector surveys recorded bat echolocation activity. While we identified the most cost-effective methods when following our protocols, different protocols could affect calculations. For example, mist netting for more hours could reduce the hourly labor cost because the fixed labor cost of erecting and collapsing nets would become a smaller portion of labor costs. However, mist netting for more hours could also lower CPH because bat captures are usually highest early in the evening (Kunz and Brock 1975). Other protocol changes could also affect cost estimates.

Although we identified cost-effective methods for conducting Rafinesque's big-eared bat surveys, project goals must be considered in selecting a survey method. Roost searches locate bat roosts as well as large numbers of bats. The 109 unique roosts found with this technique held approximately 409 total bats based on counts of visible bats. However, roosts found with this technique are limited to those with basal hollows, which might not be representative of all roosts. Using mist nets to survey bats eliminates uncertainty about species identification and allows collection of additional data, such as sex, age, and reproductive condition. Additionally, if bats are required for radio tracking, mist netting would be a more efficient survey method. Locating roosts by radio tracking bats captured in mist nets would eliminate the bias towards trees with basal hollows but would incur additional labor and equipment costs. Despite the costs and difficulty of assembling a call library, there are advantages to using bat detectors. Mist nets typically are ineffective in open areas (Kunz and others 2009), and it may be more practical to randomly assign survey points with detectors than with mist nets. Bat detectors can be left unattended at night, allowing workers to collect data day and night with analysis completed at a later date. Detectors can

more easily survey multiple sites simultaneously, allowing for better statistical control of temporal variation in data (Hayes 1997). Ultimately, it is necessary to consider the research question, field conditions, and available resources to select a survey method, but our analysis can be useful for informing the decision-making process.

In contrast to previously published reports (Hurst and Lacki 1999, Lance and Garrett 1997, Mirowsky and others 2004, Trousdale and Beckett 2002, Trousdale and others 2008), we found that Rafinesque's big-eared bats were not prohibitively difficult to capture in mist nets in areas where they were known to roost. Comparison with some readily available studies from other sites in the southeastern Coastal Plain (Miller 2003, Trousdale and Beckett 2002, Vindigni and others 2009) or with some highly cited studies from other regions (Johnson and others 2004, Kunz 1973, Kunz and Brock 1975, Kurta and Teramino 1992, Zielinski and Gellman 1999) indicates that our Rafinesque's big-eared bat CPH of 0.99 was higher than nearly all reported CPH. In those studies, only 3 of 46 species' CPH were higher than 0.99. While it is difficult to compare CPH across different studies due to confounding factors including abundance of bats, habitat structures that concentrate bat activity, duration of netting, season, and placement of mist nets (Mallory and others 2004), the high CPH in this study is not consistent with the claim that Rafinesque's big-eared bats are unusually difficult to capture in mist nets. Another recent study also demonstrated the feasibility of mist netting Rafinesque's big-eared bats by capturing 67 bats (0.19 CPH) during 72 nights of mist netting (Medlin and Risch 2008). In contrast to our result that sloughs were the most productive area, Medlin and Risch (2008) captured more bats over land corridors than over water corridors and recommended surveying over land, not water. Given the disagreement in results, future projects should consider mist netting at a variety of sites. The lack of capture success in previous studies could be due to a factor other than an inherent difficulty in capturing Rafinesque's big-eared bats, such as small populations or a lack of habitat structures that concentrate activity (Mallory and others 2004). We cannot definitively state which factors were responsible for our relatively high CPH, but we can conclude that when our techniques were applied to several sites known to harbor Rafinesque's big-eared bat roosts, we were able, on average, to capture a bat with 1 hour of mist netting.

Rafinesque's big-eared bats are reported to be exceptionally difficult to detect with bat detectors (Ford and others 2006, Loeb and O'Keefe 2006, Menzel and others 2005, Murray and others 1999). Only one study has reported high success in detecting a congener, Virginia big-eared bat, with bat detectors (Burford and Lacki 1995). However, calls in that study were identified by listening to tape recordings made with a heterodyne detector, so they may have been recording other species as well. While more time and expense was required to detect Rafinesque's big-eared bats, we found that acoustic surveys have potential as a technique in areas with sufficient numbers of bats. We detected Rafinesque's big-eared bats at 47 percent of recording sites, including upland pine sites where no bats were detected by the other two methods. Comparison with some readily available studies from other sites in the southeastern Coastal Plain (Menzel and others 2002, Vindigni and others 2009) or with some frequently cited studies from other regions (Gannon and others 2003, Gehrt and Chelsvig 2004, Hayes 1997, Humes and others 1999) indicates that our Rafinesque's big-eared bat DPH of 0.07 was not the lowest reported DPH. In those studies, 9 of 33 species' DPH were lower than 0.07. It is difficult to compare DPH across studies due to differences in placement of detectors (Weller and Zabel 2002), technology employed (Johnson and others 2002), suite of species on a field site (Duffy and others 2000), forest structure (Patriquin and others 2003), season (Hayes 1997), and the definition of bat passes (Gannon and others 2003). Despite the caveats, our results suggest that Rafinesque's big-eared bats are difficult but not impossible to survey with bat detectors.

We are confident that we identified bat passes correctly, although such self-assessment may be inaccurate (Betts 1998). Our literature review suggested that the 54 probable Rafinesque's big-eared bat passes were unlikely to have come from other bat species. Although minimum frequencies were similar in some cases, the echolocation calls differed in other characteristics. Big brown bats have a minimum call frequency near 25 kHz, but call duration is over 10 milliseconds (Surlykke and Moss 2000), longer than any of our probable Rafinesque's big-eared bat calls. Although big brown bat call duration falls to < 5 milliseconds during feeding buzzes, frequency also falls below 20 kHz and interpulse interval falls to 10 milliseconds (Surlykke and Moss 2000), neither of which was consistent with our probable Rafinesque's big-eared bat calls. Typical hoary bat calls are both longer duration and have a lower characteristic frequency than the voucher Rafinesque's big-eared bat calls, but their repertoire includes some shorter and higher calls that could overlap with Rafinesque's big-eared bats (O'Farrell and others 2000). However, if these calls were fragments or part of a feeding buzz, then our inspection of the entire call sequence should have identified them as hoary bat calls (fig. 3). With a mean minimum frequency of 27 kHz, silver-haired bat calls overlap with Rafinesque's big-eared bats, but mean call duration is longer, and this species is known for a pronounced bend in its call which would distinguish it from Rafinesque's big-eared bats (Betts 1998). With an average around 37 kHz, evening bat echolocation minimum frequency is only consistent with Rafinesque's big-eared bat calls with a duration < 2 milliseconds (fig. 1). However, evening bat calls have an average duration of 5 milliseconds and a maximum frequency over 50 kHz

(Murray and others 2001) which is not consistent with Rafinesque's big-eared bat calls. Therefore, all species with a minimum call frequency similar to that for Rafinesque's big-eared bats generally differ in another characteristic, such as duration, curvature, or maximum frequency.

Because our library did not include any other bat species we cannot provide estimates of error rates. To calculate DPH, we assumed that we had no identification error, but this may not be true. For any future projects that attempt more extensive acoustic surveys, we would recommend using a call library that includes sympatric bat species so that error rates can be estimated.

Our mist-net and bat detector results gave radically different impressions of the bat community in bottomland forests in Georgia. Nearly 84 percent of bats captured when netting away from known roosts, but only 0.4 percent of our acoustic detections, were probable Rafinesque's big-eared bats. Researchers have long recognized that both mist netting and acoustic surveys yield biased estimates of bat communities, with some species being more capture resistant (Thomas and West 1989). Several studies investigating these biases also found that whispering bats were a larger percentage of captures when mist netting than when recording, although differences were not as dramatic as in the current study (Duffy and others 2000, Loeb and O'Keefe 2006, O'Farrell and Gannon 1999). We concur with previous conclusions that mist nets and bat detectors are each biased against certain species and recommend using both methods in combination as well as careful interpretation of results (Murray and others 1999, O'Farrell and Gannon 1999).

Compared to other surveys in Coastal Plain bottomlands (Medlin and Risch 2008, Trousdale and Beckett 2002, Vindigni and others 2009), Rafinesque's big-eared bats were an unusually large component of captures. This may be due to the community of bats present, the goals of the study, or the availability of sites for mist netting. The fact that roost searches yielded few southeastern myotis roosts may explain the relative rarity of that species among mist-net captures relative to other studies (e.g., Medlin and Risch 2008). Additionally, our goal was to survey for Rafinesque's big-eared bats, so we focused netting in sloughs supporting large diameter trees, while some studies targeted other rare species in addition to Rafinesque's big-eared bats (e.g., Trousdale and Beckett 2002). Other study sites had landscape features, such as heliponds, that were lacking on our sites, which could affect trapping success (Vindigni and others 2009). Given the results of our acoustic surveys, it is obvious that many other bats share bottomland habitats with Rafinesque's big-eared bats. However, some factor in their ecology or our protocol prevented us from capturing them, whether it was related to foraging habits, commuting paths, or ability to avoid mist nets.

Our finding that call parameter variation increased dramatically through 100 calls implies that some previous studies may have suffered from inadequate call libraries. O'Farrell and others (2000) found that hoary bat call variation and an inadequate call library led to erroneous conclusions. Calls recorded during our field surveys fell within the range of reference calls but tended to be flatter and have less downward curvature and in a few cases were longer than any reference calls. This trend in our recordings indicated that calls of emerging bats were biased, with shorter and steeper calls. Although the bias was undesirable, we do not believe it impaired our ability to identify Rafinesque's big-eared bat calls because they still fell within the range of reference calls, apart from duration in a small number of cases.

We were able to catch Rafinesque's big-eared bats almost as frequently over sloughs (59 percent of nights) as when we netted at known roosts (78 percent of nights). Traditional mist netting may have rivaled netting at known roosts because more bats use certain sloughs than a single roost or because bats are more vigilant as they exit their roosts. Higher vigilance during emergence may be due to the threat of predators at that time (Fenton and others 1994). While the best mist-netting technique depends on local conditions and the research question, we found that mist netting in sloughs was an effective strategy in our study area and may be the best course if researchers do not want to disturb bats at their roosts.

ACKNOWLEDGMENTS

We thank J. Adams and C. Carpenter for field assistance. The Nature Conservancy provided access to Moody Forest Natural Area and onsite housing. The Georgia Department of Natural Resources provided access and housing at all other sites. Funding was provided by the Georgia Department of Natural Resources, Wildlife Resources Division and the Daniel B. Warnell School of Forestry and Natural Resources at the University of Georgia.

LITERATURE CITED

Barbour, R.W.; Davis, W.H. 1969. Bats of America. Lexington, KY: University Press of Kentucky. 286 p.

Bennett, F.M.; Loeb, S.C.; Bunch, M.S.; Bowerman, W.W. 2008. Use and selection of bridges as day roosts by Rafinesque's big-eared bats. American Midland Naturalist. 160(2): 386-399.

Berger-Tal, O.; Berger-Tal, R.; Korine, C. [and others]. 2008. Echolocation calls produced by Kuhl's pipistrelles in different flight situations. Journal of Zoology. 274(1): 59-64.

Betts, B.J. 1998. Effects of interindividual variation in echolocation calls on identification of big brown and silver-haired bats. Journal of Wildlife Management. 62(3): 1003-1010.

Burford, L.S.; Lacki, M.J. 1995. Habitat use by *Corynorhinus townsendii virginianus* in the Daniel Boone National Forest. American Midland Naturalist. 134(2): 340-345.

Carver, B.D.; Ashley, N. 2008. Roost tree use by sympatric Rafinesque's big-eared bats (*Corynorhinus rafinesquii*) and southeastern myotis (*Myotis austroriparius*). American Midland Naturalist. 160(2): 364-373.

Cowardin, L.M.; Carter, V.; Golet, F.C.; LaRoe, E.T. 1979. Classification of wetlands and deepwater habitats of the United States. FWS/OBS-79/31. Washington, DC: U.S. Department of the Interior. 131 p.

Duffy, A.M.; Lumsden, L.F.; Caddle, C.R. [and others]. 2000. The efficacy of anabat ultrasonic detectors and harp traps for surveying microchiropterans in south-eastern Australia. Acta Chiropterologica. 2(2): 127-144.

Fenton, M.B.; Rautenbach, I.L.; Smith, S.E. [and others]. 1994. Raptors and bats - threats and opportunities. Animal Behaviour. 48(1): 9-18.

Ford, W.M.; Menzel, J.M.; Menzel, M.A. [and others]. 2006. Presence and absence of bats across habitat scales in the upper Coastal Plain of South Carolina. Journal of Wildlife Management. 70(5): 1200-1209.

Fredrickson, L.H. 1997. Managing forested wetlands. In: Boyce, M.S.; Haney, A., ed. Ecosystem management: applications for sustainable forest and wildlife resources. New Haven, CT: Yale University: 147-177.

Gannon, W.L.; Sherwin, R.E.; Haymond, S. 2003. On the importance of articulating assumptions when conducting acoustic studies of habitat use by bats. Wildlife Society Bulletin. 31(1): 45-61.

Gehrt, S.D.; Chelsvig, J.E. 2004. Species-specific patterns of bat activity in an urban landscape. Ecological Applications. 14(2): 625-635.

Gooding, G.; Langford, J.R. 2004. Characteristics of tree roosts of Rafinesque's big-eared bat and southeastern bat in northeastern Louisiana. Southwestern Naturalist. 49(1): 61-67.

Griffin, D.R. 1958. Listening in the dark: the acoustic orientation of bats and men. New Haven, CT: Yale University Press. 413 p.

Harvey, M.J.; Altenbach, J.S.; Best, T.L. 1999. Bats of the United States. Little Rock, AR: Arkansas Game and Fish Commission. 63 p.

Hayes, J.P. 1997. Temporal variation in activity of bats and the design of echolocation-monitoring studies. Journal of Mammalogy. 78(2): 514-524.

Humes, M.L.; Hayes, J.P.; Collopy, M.W. 1999. Bat activity in thinned, unthinned, and old-growth forests in western Oregon. Journal of Wildlife Management. 63(2): 553-561.

Hurst, T.E.; Lacki, M.J. 1999. Roost selection, population size and habitat use by a colony of Rafinesque's big-eared bats (*Corynorhinus rafinesquii*). American Midland Naturalist. 142(2): 363-371.

Johnson, G.D.; Perlik, M.K.; Erickson, W.I.P.; Strickland, J.D. 2004. Bat activity, composition, and collision mortality at a large wind plant in Minnesota. Wildlife Society Bulletin. 32(4): 1278-1288.

Johnson, J.B.; Menzel, M.A.; Edwards, J.W.; Ford, W.M. 2002. A comparison of 2 acoustical bat survey techniques. Wildlife Society Bulletin. 30(3): 931-936.

Jones, C. 1977. *Plecotus rafinesquii*. Mammalian Species. 69: 1-4.

Jones, C.; Suttkus, R.D. 1971. Wing loading in *Plecotus rafinesquii*. Journal of Mammalogy. 52(2): 458-460.

Kunz, T.H. 1973. Resource utilization: temporal and spatial components of bat activity in central Iowa. Journal of Mammalogy. 54(1): 14-32.

Kunz, T.H.; Brock, C.E. 1975. Comparison of mist nets and ultrasonic detectors for monitoring flight activity of bats. Journal of Mammalogy. 56(4): 907-911.

Kunz, T.H.; Hodgkison, R.; Weise, C.D. 2009. Methods of capturing and handling bats. In: Kunz, T.H.; Parsons, S., eds. Ecological and behavioral methods for the study of bats. 2d ed. Baltimore, MD: The Johns Hopkins University Press: 3-35.

Kurta, A.; Teramino, J.A. 1992. Bat community structure in an urban park. Ecography. 15(3): 257-261.

Lance, R.F.; Garrett, R.W. 1997. Bat fauna of central Louisiana forests. Texas Journal of Science (Suppl.). 49(3): 181-189.

Lance, R.F.; Hardcastle, B.T.; Talley, A.; Leberg, P.L. 2001. Day-roost selection by Rafinesque's big-eared bats (*Corynorhinus rafinesquii*) in Louisiana forests. Journal of Mammalogy. 82(1): 166-172.

Loeb, S.C.; O'Keefe, J.M. 2006. Habitat use by forest bats in South Carolina in relation to local, stand, and landscape characteristics. Journal of Wildlife Management. 70(5): 1210-1218.

Mallory, E.P.; Brokaw, N.; Hess, S.C. 2004. Coping with mist-net capture-rate bias: canopy height and several extrinsic factors. Studies in Avian Biology. 29: 151-160.

Medlin, R.E., Jr.; Risch, T.S. 2008. Habitat associations of bottomland bats, with focus on Rafinesque's big-eared bat and southeastern myotis. American Midland Naturalist. 160(2): 400-412.

Menzel, J.M.; Menzel, M.A., Jr.; Kilgo, J.C. [and others]. 2005. Effect of habitat and foraging height on bat activity in the Coastal Plain of South Carolina. Journal of Wildlife Management. 69: 235-245.

Menzel, M.A.; Carter, T.C.; Menzel, J.M. [and others]. 2002. Effects of group selection silviculture in bottomland hardwoods on the spatial activity patterns of bats. Forest Ecology and Management. 162(2-3): 209-218.

Menzel, M.A.; Chapman, B.R.; Ford, W.M. [and others]. 2000. A review of the distribution and roosting ecology of the bats in Georgia. Georgia Journal of Science 58: 143-178.

Menzel, M.A.; Menzel, J.M.; Ford, W.M. [and others]. 2001. Home range and habitat use of male Rafinesque's big-eared bats (*Corynorhinus rafinesquii*). American Midland Naturalist. 145(2): 402-408.

Miller, D.A. 2003. Species diversity, reproduction, and sex ratios of bats in managed pine forest landscapes of Mississippi. Southeastern Naturalist. 2(1): 59-72.

Mirowsky, K.M.; Horner, P.A.; Maxey, R.W.; Smith, S.A. 2004. Distributional records and roosts of southeastern myotis and Rafinesque's big-eared bat in eastern Texas. Southwestern Naturalist. 49(2): 294-298.

Murray, K.L.; Britzke, E.R.; Hadley, B.M.; Robbins, L.W. 1999. Surveying bat communities: a comparison between mist nets and the Anabat II bat detector system. Acta Chiropterologica. 1(1): 105-112.

Murray, K.L.; Britzke, E.R.; Robbins, L.W. 2001. Variation in search-phase calls of bats. Journal of Mammalogy. 82(3): 728-737.

Norberg, U.M. 1990. Vertebrate flight: mechanics, physiology, morphology, ecology, and evolution. New York: Springer Verlag. 291 p.

O'Farrell, M.J.; Corben, C.; Gannon, W.L. 2000. Geographic variation in the echolocation calls of the hoary bat (*Lasiurus cinereus*). Acta Chiropterologica. 2(2): 185-195.

O'Farrell, M.J.; Gannon, W.L. 1999. A comparison of acoustic versus capture techniques for the inventory of bats. Journal of Mammalogy. 80(1): 24-30.

Parsons, S.; Boonman, A.M.; Obrist, M.K. 2000. Advantages and disadvantages of techniques for transforming and analyzing chiropteran echolocation calls. Journal of Mammalogy. 81(4): 927-938.

Patriquin, K.J.; Hogberg, L.K.; Chruszcz, B.J.; Barclay, R.M.R. 2003. The influence of habitat structure on the ability to detect ultrasound using bat detectors. Wildlife Society Bulletin. 31(2): 475-481.

Piaggio, A.J.; Figueroa, J.A.; Perkins, S.L. 2009. Development and characterization of 15 polymorphic microsatellite loci isolated from Rafinesque's big-eared bat, *Corynorhinus rafinesquii*. Molecular Ecology Resources. 9(1): 1191-1193.

Surlykke, A.; Moss, C.F. 2000. Echolocation behavior of big brown bats, *Eptesicus fuscus*, in the field and the laboratory. Journal of the Acoustical Society of America. 108(5): 2419-2429.

Thomas, D.W.; West, S.D. 1989. Sampling methods for bats. In: Carey, A.B.; Ruggiero, L.F., eds. Wildlife-habitat relationships: sampling procedures for Pacific Northwest vertebrates. Gen. Tech. Rep. PNW-GTR-243. Portland, OR: U.S. Department of Agriculture Forest Service, Pacific Northwest Research Station. 20 p.

Trousdale, A.W.; Beckett, D.C. 2002. Bats (Mammalia: Chiroptera) recorded from mist-net and bridge surveys in southern Mississippi. Journal of the Mississippi Academy of Sciences. 47(4): 183-188.

Trousdale, A.W.; Beckett, D.C. 2005. Characteristics of tree roosts of Rafinesque's big-eared bat (*Corynorhinus rafinesquii*) in southeastern Mississippi. American Midland Naturalist. 154(2): 442-449.

Trousdale, A.W.; Beckett, D.C.; Hammond, S.L. 2008. Short-term roost fidelity of Rafinesque's big-eared bat (*Corynorhinus rafinesquii*) varies with habitat. Journal of Mammalogy. 89(2): 477-484.

Vindigni, M.A.; Morris, A.D.; Miller, D.A.; Kalcounis-Rueppell, M.C. 2009. Use of modified water sources by bats in a managed pine landscape. Forest Ecology and Management. 258(9): 2056-2061.

Weller, T.J.; Zabel, C.J. 2002. Variation in bat detections due to detector orientation in a forest. Wildlife Society Bulletin. 30(3): 922-930.

Zielinski, W.J.; Gellman, S.T. 1999. Bat use of remnant old-growth redwood stands. Conservation Biology. 13(1): 160-167.

www.ingramcontent.com/pod-product-compliance
Lightning Source LLC
Chambersburg PA
CBHW081212280526
45787CB00006B/2391